Film
Review
1985-6

Film Review
1985-6

INCLUDING VIDEO RELEASES

F. Maurice Speed

COLUMBUS BOOKS
LONDON

Copyright © 1985 F. Maurice Speed
First published in Great Britain in 1985 by Columbus Books
Devonshire House, 29 Elmfield Road, Bromley, Kent BR1 1LT

Designed by Fred Price

British Library Cataloguing in Publication Data
Film review. ——1985–6.
1. Moving-pictures——Periodicals
791.43′05 PN1993

ISBN 0–86287–230–8
ISBN 0–86287–231–6 pb

Printed and bound by R.J. Acford
Chichester, Sussex

Contents

Introduction

F. MAURICE SPEED

One of the most important statements of this cinematic year, at least to my mind, was that made at the beginning of 1985 by Jeanine Basinger, Professor of Film at the American Wesleyan University of Connecticut, who also happens to be a trustee of the American Film Institute. 'Filmmakers need to realize that making it long is not necessarily making it better,' said Professor Basinger. 'When we go out to a movie it's not simply to spend time. We're only getting our money's worth if we are being entertained. They ought to think about it: *a film should be good, not long.*' The italics are mine, for those words should be inscribed over the portals of every film studio and written at the beginning of every film script.

This is something which I have been repeating again and again (sometimes to the irritation of the moviemakers, as witness the letters of complaint I have received from time to time) in my film columns for more than 40 years. So many movies are too long for their own good; boring films could have been made mildly entertaining, at least, by more ruthless use of the editor's scissors. Bad films could have been made bearable and good ones could have come very near to being outstanding if only the director, producer, editor or whoever would have had the courage to snip anything from 10 to 20 minutes out of their dearly beloved! It does not take a professional critic to see how many movies have been spoilt in terms of entertainment value by the self-indulgence of their makers.

I stick resolutely to my oft-repeated claim that any film which runs over the 90-minute mark – or, to stretch a point, say 105 at the most – must be a really fine effort if it is to hold the audience's attention for so long. It has got to be a great movie to hold that attention for 2 hours and a veritable celluloid masterpiece to send you home warmly appreciative after 3 hours in a cinema seat. Of course, it *can* and it *has* been done, and more than once. I must have seen *Gone with the Wind* more than six times now in its various presentations and yet its 3 hours and 40 minutes have never seemed to me to be one minute too long and it has always been with some reluctance that I have finally staggered out of the cinema into the sunshine – or, more likely, in London the rain or snow.

Professor Basinger was right on target in another remark she made about movie length. In her view, comedies suffer the most from being overlength and from padding, which she suggested was why we have a dearth of good comedies. 'In the old days,' she continued, 'audiences couldn't keep up with the film. They'd go ahead of you. The movie had more laughs than you had. Today, if there's a laugh every 20 minutes we feel we've seen a good comedy.'

Respected British, now New York-based, film historian William K. Everson (who on past occasions has contributed a number of brilliant features to this annual) never hesitates to speak (or write) his mind and he is on record as saying: 'I'd like to take a pair of scissors and whittle away at so many movies I've seen in the past few years. Films are also getting very shapeless, with no beginnings, middle or end – in that order. They all start with a teaser, since they will end up on TV. Then they try to maintain the pace and that kills the film, or they cannot maintain that pace, which equally kills the film. The film goes into a kind of spiral.' Everson looks back with a nostalgic feeling for the 'short, sweet and marvellous' films of yesteryear, screen classics like 1932's *One Way Passage* (69 minutes) and *The Most Dangerous Game* (63 minutes). 'Every time they remake the latter they stretch it by about another 10 minutes,' complains Everson.

Writing about such matters in *Variety*, Ralph Tyler has said that it is almost a rule of thumb that remakes are longer than the originals and he has quoted 15 Oscar-nominated movies which fall into that category, all but two of which have had some 30 minutes more running times than the originals. The two 'outsiders' he pointed were *It Happened One Night* (which shrank some 41 minutes when it was remade as a musical) and *Double Indemnity* (which shed just over 30 minutes when remade for TV).

As Tyler so rightly pointed out, nobody really knows how long a feature film *should* be. The Academy of Motion Picture Arts and Sciences define a feature film as being over 30 minutes long – but Alfred Hitchcock is on record as saying that the length of a film should be directly related to the endurance of the human bladder.

That much feared *New York Times* film critic Bosley Crowther (and I am still quoting Mr Tyler) roared in 1944, 'Mankind is not shaped to sit through a two-hour movie', and he repeated that statement again and again down the years. But even he could not stem the celluloid tide and today two hours is the normal length of a feature film; the modest little movie of today exceeds in length the epic movies of the past. As in so many areas the exception has, with time, become the rule.

It is not only because I think that artistically the long film is at fault that I am so critical of it, but also because I feel that overlong films have contributed, at least in some small way, to the flow of audiences away from the cinemas. Like watering the milk or otherwise weakening anything liquid,

7

On the Other Side of the Camera Alfred Hitchcock (with hands in pocket, centre) on the set of Universal's *Rope*, an experimental film he made in 1948 using long, uncut sequences. James Stewart (standing right) was the star. *Rope* was recently re-issued.

or solid, the result is likely to be less appetizing than it might have been. The film audience should never be allowed to feel bored while watching a movie, for therein lies disaster. Writers, directors and producers should realize that however close to their heart certain sequences, gimmicks or the desire for individual style may be, the story is the heart of any movie and that story must be told in as straightforward a manner as possible: told without frills, without excursions, without indulgences if the film is to keep its audiences happy and amused and asking for more. People must come out of the cinemas warm with the glow of recalled pleasure, not depressed or bored or anxious to get home to the telly to be cheered up by *Coronation Street*.

I am giving the final word on this subject to Paul Roth, a past president of NATO and current chief of a major chain of American cinemas. Earlier this year he said: 'In physics for every action there is a reaction. In the entertainment world for every action there's an overreaction.' And you can say that again, and again, and again.

Turning now to another of my most persistent criticisms: the needless and prolific use of four-letter words and other foul language in modern movies. Thankfully, though still far too common, this blemish is becoming apparently less obligatory than it seemed to be for a while in the near past. It appears likely that like every other cinematic 'wave' it will

work itself through and out, and a balance will finally be restored. I think it may be significant that in America there has recently been quite a strong reaction against this kind of 'humour' and it seems that comics whose livelihoods have depended on this type of humour are now finding it increasingly difficult to get bookings to the top-flight places of entertainment, such as Vegas, Atlantic City and Reno. It appears that there have been a number of audience 'walk-outs' during this kind of act and it is pretty certain that this will not be overlooked by the moviemakers. Nowadays everyone in the film business is acutely aware of the need to keep cinemagoers coming back for more and a real effort is being made to keep the cinema seats filled.

Leading the fight to get people back into the cinema was the British film industry, which in March 1985 began its 'British Film Year' with the slogan 'Cinemas – the Best Place to See a Film'. The 'Year's' programme of activities included a promise by the major circuits to spend £1 million a month on bringing their cinemas up to date, both technically and in terms of comfort for their patrons. This should do a lot to stop the trickle of complaints, too often seen in the press, about dirty cinemas, uncomfortable seating and below-standard projection.

The British film industry needed this kind of boost. For while admissions actually went up in 1983, increasing to around 70 million (against the previous year's all-time low of 64 million) the latest figures I have seen for 1985 so far suggest there may be a reversal of that hopeful trend; indeed *Variety* has already computed from the figures for the first three months of the year that the final total for 1985 might

On the Other Side of the Camera David Lean on the set of *A Passage to India* (Thorn-EMI), the adaptation of the E.M. Forster novel which marked Lean's return to direction after some 15 years, his last film being *Ryan's Daughter* made in 1970.

well fall as low as 40 million. But one has to accept all these figures with considerable caution.

A less than cheerful statistic was that Britain was losing one screen every week during 1984 and the first part of 1985. But this has not prevented the very commercially minded American Multi Cinemas company from announcing recently that it is about to expand its activities in Britain and hopes to have 50 cinemas (representing a total of 300 screens) operating before long. It made a significant start to this programme by opening a 10-screen cinema complex in Milton Keynes.

In America the moviegoing position is a lot rosier than elsewhere, with ticket sales rising by 17 per cent during 1984. After a slide starting in 1980 the German cinemas clawed back almost a 100 million admissions in 1983, but the yet-to-be-finalized figures for 1984 are not likely to be as cheering. In France the attendance 'explosion' of recent years – some called it a 'miracle' – appears sadly to be over with a decrease in ticket sales by some 4.7 per cent for 1984 (following that marvellous peak figure in excess of 200 million admissions in 1982); the decline has continued during at least the earlier part of 1985. (In spite of this fall, 280 new cinemas opened in France during 1983.)

Writing about explosions inevitably reminds me of the activities worldwide of the Cannon Group (which includes companies on both the production and projection sides of the film business), which is expanding at a remarkable rate. With 136 screens already operating in Britain, during 1985 the Group purchased the Dutch City Cinema Circuit, which added to the Yuschinski chain of cinemas it has already acquired gives it 49 screens and makes it the largest exhibition set-up in that country. The Group then moved into Italian exhibition, taking over the Italian Gaumont's 53 cinemas (for which it paid some 15 million dollars). It then began to take an interest in spreading into South Africa.

The same kind of optimism about the future of cinemagoing prevails in the United States, where during the year 705 new screens were added to that country's previous hefty total of 18,884 happily and gainfully operating at the beginning of the year (rising from the 12,650 total operating in 1962). Nearly every week one reads in *Variety* about new cinemas that are planned or those that have opened. Another country where the cinema is expanding is India. Here 518 new cinemas (well, screens) went into operation for the first time during the 1983–4 period. And, just for the record, in November 1984 the 'most expensive and technically advanced cinema in the world' was opened in Tokyo. (Also, just for the record, in 1985 in Burbank, home of some of America's major production companies, like Warner Bros., the first new cinema to be built there was opened. It was a 10-screen complex and was quite an event.)

Towards the end of 1984 the major American film companies had so many completed movies on their hands that they had to postpone the release of some of their scheduled 1984 releases to well into 1985. During 1984, according to the annual survey[1] carried out by *Variety*, a total of 411 features were released in the States, against the previous year's total of 365, and the 330 films offered during 1982. This meant that 8 new feature films were on offer to exhibitors every week of the year, without taking account of the dozens of re-issues being offered, the hundreds of revivals being unspooled in the so-called 'art houses', the goodly number of dubbed and undubbed foreign language features floating around, plus the normal trickle of pornographic pictures. These all add up to a daunting total for the year of nearly 1,000 movies seeking bookings into the cinemas.

I have not seen any comparable figures for Britain but certainly, going on the flood of press shows of new films practically every week of the year (often at the rate of three a day), there must be far more new films on offer than in the

---

[1]*Variety* in a feature published in May (1985) revealed the somewhat astonishing fact that when film production statistics are compiled and published the so-called 'secret' features are not taken into consideration, even though these amounted to a staggering total of 170 films in 1984!

These so-called 'secret' movies are apparently made without any advance notice and production publicity, mostly on 16mm stock and with small or positively minute budgets. They are often halted by financial troubles for varying periods (some, once stopped, never get going again) and very few, if and when finished, become successful 'sleepers' as they are termed in the trade. Another reason put forward for this secrecy is that producers are often worried that some other richer set-up will steal their ideas and bring the movie to the market before them, or even that a TV producer will do the same thing.

To add weight to the feature *Variety* added a long list of such 'secret' productions completed but so far unveiled.

past, ironically at a time when there are fewer patrons to see them.

The cost of making movies continues to rise inexorably – at well beyond the inflation rate. In the United States the average rise was in the neighbourhood of 21 per cent above the 1984 cost, and a rise of 50 per cent above the 1980 figure. (The average budget for a feature film has been: 1981, $11,300 million; 1982, $11,800 million; 1983, $11,900 million; 1984, $14,400 million.)

Jack Valenti, President of the Motion Picture Association of America, said in 1985 that 8 out of every 10 movies made in the United States never recover their cost from the home market and 6 out of that 10 never recover their production money, even with worldwide distribution. (It is interesting to note that the moviemakers apparently get about 39 per cent of the box-office takings while the exhibitors get only around 11 per cent.)

As a consequence, it is no wonder that some producers are shooting their productions on 16mm stock and then blowing them up to the normal 35mm film size, thus saving themselves 50 per cent of the cost of film. But while this method is becoming increasingly popular (films made this way include *The Draughtsman's Contract*, *Angelo, My Love* and *My Dinner with André*) there *are* drawbacks (such as the transference from one size to another entailing the loss of

On the Other Side of the Camera John Schlesinger – unconsciously giving the Victory sign – at work on the Hemdale-Rank release *The Falcon and the Snowman*. He co-produced as well as directed this thriller which was based on a true-life story. It turned out to be a considerable success.

something like a third of the picture on each frame) which makes it unlikely that the scheme will be adopted for major first feature films.

The British film has continued to keep up a very high standard during [2]1984 and at least the major part of 1985. One has only to look through the year's releases to confirm this; films like *The Killing Fields*, *The Company of Wolves*, *A Passage to India*, *The Bounty*, *The Hit, 1984, A Private Function* and *The Shooting Party* – to name just a few – all added to the prestige and popularity of the British movie. Although more insular movies like *Cal, Comfort and Joy, Another Country* and *Secret Places*, among many others, are unlikely to be widely released overseas they are a credit to the industry.

The British studios enjoyed a very busy and successful time with the Floors Full notices being up at most of them for most of the year. It appears that some 40 features were completed during 1984 and that is a formidable total.

The most eagerly awaited announcement of the British Film Year was the Government's plans for the future funding of the industry. This came in the form of a White Paper at the beginning of July which included the expected decision to terminate the Eady Fund and the National Film

[2]There follows a list of the most successful, wholly British-financed films in terms of box-office takings up to the end of October, 1984: *Educating Rita, The Company of Wolves, Another Country, The Dresser, Comfort and Joy, Bloodbath at the House of Death, The Hit, Bullshot* and *Cal*. The twelve top-grossing movies from any source up to the end of that year: *Indiana Jones and the Temple of Doom, Never Say Never Again*, the re-issue of Disney's *The Jungle Book, Police Academy, Sudden Impact, Terms of Endearment, Educating Rita, Trading Places, Greystoke, Jaws 3D, Footloose* and *Splash*.

Finance Corporation and replace them with a £10 million Fund for low- and medium- budget productions over a period of five years. The suggested package brought little joy and quite a bit of adverse comment from Britain's moviemakers, who seemed to find the paper both 'confused' and 'confusing'.

One interesting proposal by the government was a levy of about 10 per cent on blank audio and video recording tape, and the money raised to be divided between record companies, moviemakers, artistes and anyone else with a copyright title. In return it was suggested that the current law against home taping should be repealed.

During the next few months the arguments set off by the White Paper are going to continue and before the final plan is settled there are obviously some changes to be made.

Now for a round-up of other matters which have made news during this cinematic year. For instance, in March Australian Press Baron Rupert Murdoch (owner of *The Sun* and *The Times* newspapers in Britain, as well as other newspapers worldwide) announced agreement with TCF Holdings (the 20th Century-Fox parent company) about his purchase of 50 per cent of the share capital of the film company for $250 million. This followed his failure in 1984 to take over Warner Bros.

The summer of 1984 saw a strike by members of the Directors' Guild of America averted at the last moment by new terms offered them by their bosses, the bone of contention being the size of directors' 'cut' which they should get from the income from video cassette versions of their movies. (The final agreement came with the offer of upping this share from 1.2 to 1.5 per cent of the producers' gross figure – though this is simplifying a somewhat complicated final agreement.)

In March 1985 the members of the Writers' Guild of America walked out when negotiations for a new deal for scenarists collapsed. Here again the unhappiness was over video cassette income. But this strike was shortlived and after twelve days the walkers-out became walkers-in when they were offered the same sort of terms as those which had prevented the directors' strike.

In contrast, on about the same date that the American writers called off their strike, their British counterparts, the Writers' Guild of Great Britain, emerged after two years of strikeless argument with their bosses the British Film and TV Producers' Association and the Independent Programme Producers' Association, having made their first-ever comprehensive agreement concerning cinema films, made-for-TV movies and TV series and serials. In the future, if you are ever lucky enough to get a job scripting a feature film your reward will be a minimum of £20,000 – and at least £12,000 for a TV movie.

In late July, Lee Electric (which already owned a three-stage studio elsewhere in London) announced they had purchased Shepperton Studios for more than £3½ million. Shepperton had been busy during the year with several films – including *The Company of Wolves* and *A Passage to India* – being completed there.

Returning to the 16mm film for a moment, this may be given a real fillip in the future by the unveiling by American Multi-Cinema of a new stereophonic system which they promised would have a revolutionary impact on the exhibition side of 16mm movies.

On the Other Side of the Camera Oscar-winning actor Robert Duvall wrote, directed and produced *Angelo, My Love.*

On the Other Side of the Camera Actor-turned-director Leonard Nimoy, famous for playing the man with the big ears, Spock, in the television and feature film series *Star Trek* (Paramount). He made his debut behind the camera with the third feature film, *Star Trek III: The Search for Spock.*

All knowledgeable film fans will know about the hand-and-footprints of famous film stars recorded in concrete or whatever in the forecourt of Grauman's Chinese Theatre in Hollywood and will welcome the initiative of the British film industry in launching a similar permanent record in Lon-

On the Other Side of the Camera Writer-director Bob Fosse rehearses his stars, Eric Roberts and Caroll Baker for a scene in the Ladd Co/Warner release *Star 80*. Former child actor and vaudeville star, later dancer and choreographer and stage director, Fosse won an Oscar for his second film directing assignment, *Cabaret*, in 1972.

don's Leicester Square as a part of the British Film Year festivities in the spring of 1985. The promise is that this 'star pavement' will eventually encircle the Square (sic), which contains four of London's top showpiece cinemas: the Odeon, the Leicester Square Theatre, the Empire (with the adjoining Ritz, or Empire 2) and the Warner. Monday 6 May saw the ceremonial start of the project with Charlton Heston, Omar Sharif, Anna Neagle, John Mills and Alan Bates making their impressions.

In the film business one should never give up hope. In the spring of 1985 Dylan Thomas's *The Doctor and the Devils* went into production at Shepperton Studios 30 years after the Welsh poet delivered the script to the Rank Organization for early production. For all those years the movie has been hovering on the edge of production and now at last it is actually being made under Freddie Francis's guiding hand with Fox handling the distribution.

France went one better than that by staging the world premiere of a movie that was made more than 60 years ago but never released! *L'Hirondelle et la Mésange (The Swallow and the Titmouse)* was made in 1920 by a famous Belgian

stage director, André Antoine, who, it appears, did a lot of pioneering work in the cinema. Cinémathèque Française gave Henri Colpi (editor of *Hiroshima Mon Amour* and many other historic French films) six hours of assorted celluloid plus Antoine's original script and he eventually came up with an hour-and-a-quarter movie.

Some time in 1985 we may expect to see another old movie for the first time. This is Erich von Stroheim's unfinished *Queen Kelly*, which originally went into production in 1928. Only recently has some 22 minutes of the film, shot in German East Africa (as it was then), been discovered.

Also taking advantage of this revived interest in as yet unseen old masterpieces is Maud, daughter of the famous French silent comic Max Linder, who has been gathering her father's films from various sources. With her documentary about him, *The Man in the Silk Hat*, she hopes to re-introduce his work to moviegoers and establish him in his rightful place as the comic to whom Chaplin admitted he owed a great debt.

Another overlooked comic work received recognition this year: although it did not appear to make a great impression on British moviegoers, Richard Loncraine's *The Missionary* walked off with the Grand Prize at the Charousse Humour Film Festival.

In Paris in February 1985 *Emmanuelle* chalked up a record by ending a run at the Parafrance Champs-Elysées theatre which had lasted uninterrupted for 11 years! Now,

On the Other Side of the Camera Euzhan Palcy who both wrote and directed the highly acclaimed Martinique production *Rue Cases Nègres – Black Shack Alley*. Made in 1983 and released in Britain by Artificial Eye the following year, the film won a Silver Lion at the Venice Festival and a much-prized César from the French Film Academy.

after more than 3¼ million admissions there, it moves on to the Montmartre Paramount cinema to continue its run!

Another little bit of celluloid history was made in the summer of 1985 with the screen acting debut of Tyrone Power Junior (aged 23) in Fox's sci-fi feature *Cocoon*.

A new system for converting old black-and-white features into colour is due to be seen this year (1985) with the re-issue of the video cassette version of *Yankee Doodle Dandy*. Although it is admitted that the results so far are not good enough for cinema presentation, it is hoped that this situation will change.

Untenanted since 1979 (when *Excalibur* was made there), Ireland's Ardmore Studios were sold in the summer of 1984 to a Pakistani shipping magnate, Mahmud Sipra, who is also a film director and has most recently been helming a big spectacular, *The Khyber Horse*, filmed on location in Pakistan.

The production of Universal/Mirage's *Out of Africa* was held up when the African extras went on strike, objecting to being expected to wear just a pair of shorts ('indecent dress') – though they did offer, it seems, to waive that objection if the producers paid them extra!

Contrary to previous stories that we should see no more Bergman films in our cinemas, we *shall* be seeing his *After the Rehearsal*, though only on his condition that it is publicized as a 'TV' rather than a 'cinema' film!

And film critics and other writers on films will have to be careful what they say in future, after German writer Rolf Giesen has been taken to court over something he wrote in his book *Movies Nobody Cares For*. Most of those involved took his book about German celluloid 'turkeys' good-naturedly but there were exceptions, one of whom is taking legal action against the writer. So I shall, after all, have to leave to your imagination that list of the year's twelve film turkeys with which I had planned to finish this year's comments! Now, taking my tongue out of my cheek, let me wish all readers a very happy and rewarding cinematic year.

Play It Again, Sam – Hollywood Sequels and Remakes

ALAN WARNER

We know that John L. Sullivan (Joel McCrea's movie-directing character in Preston Sturges' biting satire on Hollywood called *Sullivan's Travels*) never got to make *Ants in Your Pants of 1941* as a successor to *Ants in Your Pants of 1939*, but such sequels were as common then as they are today. In those days, successions of *Gold Diggers*, *Big Broadcasts* and *Broadway Melody* pictures were prominent on the major studios' production schedules. When Hollywood discovered a winning formula, it was not about to let it go and this inclination to produce sequels is as evident as ever today. Nevertheless it is not always possible to involve the same production team the second time

Howard Hawks' 1946 film of Raymond Chandler's *The Big Sleep* was set in a very moist Los Angeles. For his 1977 remake, Michael Winner transferred the action to an English seaside town with Robert Mitchum stepping into Humphrey Bogart's shoes as Philip Marlowe. Mitchum had also played the 'private dick' two years earlier in Dick Richards' remake of *Murder My Sweet* (originally made with Dick Powell in 1944) titled *Farewell My Lovely*.

around. *Airplane!*, for instance, set the box-offices alight in 1980, thanks to that innovative comedic madness created by the three writer-directors Jim Abrahams, David and Jerry Zucker; and when they declined Paramount's request for a successor, the studio gave the project to someone else and the result (*Airplane II: the Sequel*) was far from satisfying. Similarly, the unexpected business that Jack Haley Jr's original *That's Entertainment!* brought MGM in 1974 prompted the Culver City production chiefs to press forward with plans for *That's Entertainment, Part II*, but the nimble fingers of maestro Haley were not in charge and, though the sequel drew on dramatic and comedy, as well as musical, footage from the diamond-studded archives, the overall compilation paled by even the most unbiased comparison.

But to be fair, sequels have often been very worthwhile and equally successful as the original film. The *Star Wars* series proves this beyond all doubt and the *Indiana Jones* stories are also building momentum as they progress. As a random earlier example, I would recommend the consistently entertaining *The Return of Frank James* from 1940 (it succeeded 1939's *Jesse James*) with Henry Fonda, under Fritz Lang's direction, as Jesse's brother avenging the former's murder.

Series of related subjects involving pivotal heroes in revolving situations often fare much better, though the recent *Superman* series abruptly lost much ground and credibility. By sheer contrast, the James Bond series have proved to be spectacular in their staying power, though no one could have foreseen 007's cinematic longevity when *Doctor No* went into production in 1962. Bond, like Sherlock Holmes, Charlie Chan, the Thin Man, Philo Vance and a plethora of other detectives, was a literal character (in this case, a government spy) whom movie producers recruited and who's persona, certainly in Bond's case, was extended to fit the sexually-explicit image that such heroes now exude. Bond went through that other difficult change to which figures in such series often fall victim, namely switching actors in midstream! In Bond's case, Sean Connery had become a household name in five successive Bond features when the producers garnered much publicity searching for a replacement to star in *On Her Majesty's Secret Service* in 1969; their choice, George Lazenby, proved less successful than everyone had hoped, and luckily Connery returned for a final foray with the original producers, who then wisely chose Roger Moore (already known to TV viewers as another fictional hero, *The Saint*). He ably assumed the Bond mantle for *Live and Let Die* in 1973.

Keeping entire ensembles together for ongoing movie series has often proved a nightmare for producers, one which television producers have also been forced to face over the years. As an example, the Andy Hardy team was consistent for the most part although Lionel Barrymore was Judge Hardy in their very first adventure. Trouble arises when plot complications do not allow for automatic extensions, as Warner Bros. discovered when the success of *Four Daughters* in 1938 created demand for a sequel. John Garfield's character 'Mickey Borden' had been killed off, so the leading players, namely Claude Rains, May Robson, Gale

May McAvoy and Al Jolson in *The Jazz Singer*, the first talking motion picture made back in 1927. Warner Bros. remade it in 1952 with Danny Thomas and Peggy Lee. In 1980 it was reworked again, this time as rock singer Neil Diamond's first movie. Lucie Arnaz took the female lead in this latter version with Laurence Olivier playing the Cantor for whom Diamond sings *Kol Nidri*.

Page, the Lane Sisters and Garfield, were assigned new characters and the studio virtually started over again from scratch. *Daughters Courageous* finally emerged as a semi-remake, followed closely by two straightforward sequels, *Four Wives* and *Four Mothers*! Many years later, *Four Daughters* was totally remade as the 1954 musical *Young at Heart* with Frank Sinatra and Doris Day.

Traditional horror characters such as Dracula and Frankenstein are constantly revived in motion pictures and have also been the subject of first-class lampoons, as in *Love at First Bite* (1979) and *Young Frankenstein* five years earlier. Certain comic-strip heroes have switched both formats and media as in

the case of the cloaked good-guy known as Batman, whose popularity in cinema serials of 1943 and 1949 was rekindled in a hit 1966 television series which in turn spawned a full-length feature film and, eventually, a small-screen weekly cartoon show. What Batman did not achieve was movie parenthood, for one regular route which scriptwriters take to extend lives of popular characters is literally to create offshoots; Frankenstein, King Kong, Lassie, Robin Hood, Dracula, Sinbad and Monte Cristo all had 'Sons' who were crafted for central roles in pictures, not to mention the Daughters and Brides who emerged in Houses and under Curses waging Evils, Horror and Revenge in whatever else the cinemas could entice us with!

What is clear when you begin to examine movie sequels is that their actual titles are less creative today than in the 1940s and 1950s. For instance, *The Fly* was naturally followed-up with *Return of the Fly* (1959), *The Invisible Man* in 1933 was succeeded by *The Invisible Man Returns* (1939) and eventually *The Invisible Man's Revenge* (1944). Even *Village of the Damned* in 1960 was emulated by *Children of the Damned* in 1964. Compare those with such creative sequel titles as *Friday the 13th Part 2* (1981), *Friday the 13th, Part III* (1982) and then *Friday the 13th: The Final Chapter* in 1984, which did not prove to be the fatal blow, as *Friday the 13th: A New Beginning* emerged in 1985. Also remember the sequels to *Jaws*, *The Omen* and *The Godfather*.

One old trick of providing an authentic streak to a sequel is to include a flashback to the original footage; this method was effectively used in *Demetrius and the Gladiators* (1954) which the advertising proclaimed 'begins where *The Robe* left off'! It in fact opened with shots of Richard Burton and Jean Simmons from *The Robe*, whereas only Victor Mature appeared in both films.

Looking at some of today's movies, it is obvious that so-called sequels are often little more than thinly-disguised retreads of the original storylines. Legitimate remakes have long been one of the cinema's most intriguing formulas and proved an endless source of inspiration. Take, for instance, a 1938 film called *Three Blind Mice*, in which three sisters (played by Loretta Young, Marjorie Weaver and Pauline Moore) travelled from Kansas to California in search of rich husbands; in 1941, it was remade as *Moon over Miami* with two sisters (Betty Grable and Carole Landis) going off to Florida to find loaded gentlemen, while in 1947 it was June Haver, Vivian Blaine and Vera-Ellen who were *Three Little Girls in Blue* on the same man-seeking mission, this time in Atlantic City. Ironically, the same studio (20th Century-Fox) later produced *How to Marry a Millionaire* which, while not strictly based on the *Three Blind Mice* concept, looked startlingly similar, as Betty Grable, Marilyn Monroe and Lauren Bacall took up residence in a Manhattan apartment with nothing more than the opposite sex on their minds! Then there was the 1939 wisecracking comedy *The Women*, sold by MGM's publicity department with such adlines as: '135 Women with nothing on their minds but MEN!', and starring Norma Shearer, Joan Crawford and Rosalind Russell. It was reworked as a glossy Technicolor musical called *The Opposite Sex* in 1956 with June Allyson, Dolores Gray and Joan Collins and played like a lead balloon! Its bite had disappeared and, though the settings were for the most part unchanged, it was hard to believe that the same Clare Booth Luce play was its inspiration.

In a 1942 movie called *Ball of Fire*, Charles Brackett and Billy Wilder created a zany group of professors who gather together to compile an encyclopedia and are sidetracked by the arrival in their midst of a striptease dancer called Sugarpuss O'Shea. Barbara Stanwyck starred as the latter with the whimsical professors led by Gary Cooper, Oscar Homolka, Henry Travers, S.Z. 'Cuddles' Sakall and nasal-toned Richard Haydn. Gene Krupa and his orchestra were featured accompanying the vocalizing Sugarpuss in a sequence which proved unwittingly prophetic for, six years later, Goldwyn remade *Ball of Fire* as *A Song is Born*, setting it in the midst of the dance band music era and showcasing the orchestras of Tommy Dorsey, Charlie Barnet, Lionel Hampton, Benny Goodman and Louis Armstrong. Danny Kaye replaced the Gary Cooper character and Virginia Mayo was the showgirl, renamed Honey Swanson.

Other intriguing cross-fertilizations retaining basic plotlines but radically altering settings include 1949's *House of Strangers* (Edward G. Robinson as the patriarch of a New York-Italian banking family) which became 1954's *Broken Lance* (Spencer Tracy as a cattle baron); 1953's *Pickup on South Street* (Richard Widmark as a pickpocketing gangster on a New York subway) became 1967's *The Cape Town Affair* (James Brolin with light fingers on a South African bus); and 1936's *The Petrified Forest* (Leslie Howard as the weary poet wandering across the Arizona desert and encountering a group of gangsters) was transformed into 1945's *Escape in the Desert* (Philip Dorn as the Dutch airman travelling across the States and coming upon some escaped Nazi prisoners). I've always thought the second version of *Destry Rides Again* was an oddball, yet when one discounts the rousing and fun-filled 1939 original, the 1954 treatment adds up to a reliable little western. Certainly Audie Murphy could not begin to walk in James Stewart's shoes and Mari Blanchard was no Marlene Dietrich, but quite naturally, comparisons remain.

The other major surgery that Hollywood has favoured over the years is the musicalization of successful stories. Most notably, 1946's *Anna and the King of Siam* (Rex Harrison and Irene Dunne) was turned by Rogers and Hammerstein into 1956's *The King and I* (Yul Brynner and Deborah Kerr); 1940's *The Philadelphia Story* (Cary Grant, Katharine Hepburn, James Stewart) gained a Cole Porter score and became 1956's *High Society* (Bing Crosby, Grace Kelly, Frank Sinatra), and 1928's *Rain* (Gloria Swanson), also made as 1932's *Rain* (Joan Crawford), was turned into a part-musical in 3-D in 1953 under the title *Miss Sadie Thompson* with Rita Hayworth (dubbed by Jo Ann Greer) singing the Oscar-nominated 'Blue Pacific Blues'. There was also the bittersweet *Goodbye Mr Chips* in 1939 (Robert Donat and Greer Garson) which, via a Leslie Bricusse score, became the insipid *Goodbye Mr Chips* of 1969 (Peter O'Toole and Petula Clark). Though not official remakes, 1955's *I Am a Camera* (Julie Harris) shared the same basic storyline as the *Cabaret* musical, filmed in 1972 with Liza Minnelli, and there are strong similarities between *Intermezzo/Escape to Happiness* (Hollywood's 1939 remake of Ingrid Bergman's sixth Swedish film and that same actress's American debut) and *Honeysuckle Rose*, the 1980 picture that teamed Willie Nelson with Dyan Cannon and Amy Irving.

Unofficial remakes are not as uncommon as one might think, and another good case is *Soldiers Three*, a 1951 MGM release based on Rudyard Kipling stories about the British Army in India during the 1890s; starring Stewart Granger, Walter Pidgeon and David Niven, it was virtually *Gunga Din* (RKO 1939) minus the central character and was produced by Pandro S. Berman, RKO's old production chief!

From time to time, remakes have outshone their forerunners, as in the case of *His Girl Friday*, Howard Hawks' 1940 reworking of Lewis Milestone's 1931 *The Front Page*, the title under which the third version was

James Stewart and Katharine Hepburn in the 1940 comedy *The Philadelphia Story*, which was remade as the 1956 musical *High Society* with (inset from left to right) Bing Crosby, Grace Kelly and Frank Sinatra. Most of the wry wit from the former disappeared in the musical version: Miss Kelly's approach to the Tracy Lord character was worlds apart from Miss Hepburn's, Crosby marched heavily in Cary Grant's lightweight footsteps and Frank Sinatra had what James Stewart didn't have . . . a Cole Porter ballad with which to serenade the heroine!

also released in 1974. *His Girl Friday* fairly bristled with fast-paced quips from beginning to end, a feat carried off by Cary Grant sparring with the sassy Rosalind Russell, whose character of the female newspaper reporter 'Hildy Johnson' was originally written as a male role, portrayed by Pat O'Brien in 1931 and by Jack Lemmon in 1974. It is, however, generally agreed that the majority of remakes have not matched their predecessors and recent examples, such as the 1981 version of *The Postman Always Rings Twice* and 1982's *Cat People*, have added fuel to this argument.

What fascinates the trivia buff is not just the parallels in dialogue and setting, but other production elements common to the various versions. Music often provides a link with a previous interpretation of an identical story, as for the 1952 MGM remake of *The Prisoner of Zenda*, which used the Alfred Newman score written for the 1937 Selznick version. Also, in the 1982 TV-movie retread of *The Letter*, Laurence Rosenthal's score included portions of Max Steiner's music written for the 1940 Warner Bros. theatrical treatment of the W. Somerset Maugham story.

One must also make special mention here of a select group of performers who have appeared in both original versions and remakes of key movies. Clark Gable really leads this field unchallenged having starred memorably in 1932's *Red Dust* and returned in the same role twenty-two years later in *Mogambo*. Jungle fever certainly ran high in that first version with Jean Harlow and Mary Astor vying for Gable's attention. In *Mogambo*, the temperature was cooler with Ava Gardner substituting for Harlow and Grace Kelly in the Mary Astor role. Incidentally, *Mogambo* was the second retread of *Red Dust*, after *Congo Maisie* in 1940.

In 1984, we saw Jane Greer in *Against All Odds*, the brave but overall unsatisfying remake of the 1947 film noir classic *Out of the Past*, which was originally shown in England under the title of its source book, *Build My Gallows High*. First time out, the attractive, sleek, blonde Miss Greer played the gangster's moll for whom private eye Robert Mitchum falls; in *Against All Odds*, Rachel Ward plays the Greer role with Jeff Bridges portraying Mitchum's character, while Jane Greer appears as the girl's mother.

Surprisingly, one of the great screen adventures that I mentioned earlier, namely *Gunga Din*, has not been remade for television, whereas many of the consistently popular films have been recrafted for the home audience, among which were: *The Hunchback of Notre-Dame* (TV movie: 1982) with Anthony Hopkins; *Camille* (TV movie: 1984) starring Greta Scacchi in Garbo's famed role; *The Scarlet Pimpernel* (TV movie: 1982) with Anthony Andrews as the foppish Sir Percy Blakeney, a role for which Leslie Howard was justifiably celebrated in 1935; and *The Corn is Green* (TV movie: 1979) which found George Cukor directing Katharine Hepburn in the schoolteacher role portrayed so vividly in 1945 by Bette Davis. Actually, television has long been a breeding ground for reworkings

Robert Taylor and Greta Garbo starred in *Camille* (1937), one of the many novels which have been reworked for the small screen. The 1984 TV movie version toplined Greta Scacchi and Colin Firth.

of previous big-screen hits. In the 1950s and 1960s, some of the major studios first got their feet wet in TV production with small-format remakes. Fox had a series of 'Pocket Editions' which, when looking back through earlier *Film Review* annuals, you will discover were released at first in UK cinemas. I particularly recall a shortened version of *Laura* with Dana Wynter, but I never saw *Crack Up*, which brought Bette Davis and Gary Merrill together in a new version of their *Phone Call from a Stranger* feature. Warners' comparable series got a brief airing on BBCTV at the time, with *Girl on the Subway* starring James Garner, Natalie Wood and Charlie Ruggles, based on 1950's *Pretty Baby* feature that had starred Dennis Morgan, Betsy Drake and Edmund Gwenn.

The transition from property to property is not always so smooth; however, a story by James H. Street called 'Letter to the Editor' was adapted as a 1937 screenplay called *Nothing Sacred* by Ben Hecht with Budd Schulberg, Ring Lardner Jr and Dorothy Parker (though only Hecht received screen credit). The Selznick screwball comedy had Carole Lombard wrongly diagnosed as dying of radium poisoning with reporter Fredric March seizing the opportunity to explode the story in the New York press, so much so that Lombard fakes her terminal illness in order to become a celebrity martyr! A huge success, *Nothing Sacred* was later adapted as a Broadway musical called *Hazel Flagg* and, when the storyline was used as the Dean Martin-Jerry Lewis screen comedy *Living It Up* in 1954, the sources had become so interwoven that it was clearly not a direct remake of the original movie. For the record, the 'Hazel Flagg' character was re-written for Lewis.

Certainly from a critical standpoint, remakes appear to be unsafe bets and even considering mere box-office success, audience-pleasers like 1980's *The Blue Lagoon* (originally a 1949 British hit) and 1978's *Heaven Can Wait* (treading the footsteps left by 1941's

Here Comes Mr. Jordan) are outnumbered by such leaden failures as the 1979 reworking of John Ford's 1937 classic, *The Hurricane* (the remake was such a dismal failure that it has been retitled *Forbidden Paradise* for limited television runs), May Britt floundering in Marlene Dietrich's shadow when Fox decided to remake *The Blue Angel* in 1960, the tragically inadequate attempt to update Bette Davis' 1939 milestone *Dark Victory* as *Stolen Hours* with Susan Hayward in 1963, the vain attempts by David Niven and June Allyson to breathe life into the 1957 remake of the 1936 classic comedy of manners *My Man Godfrey*, an exercise already attempted by Miss Allyson with Jack Lemmon in 1956 when Columbia tried a new version of the Clark Gable-Claudette Colbert 1934 *tour de force It Happened One Night*, as well as 20th Century-Fox's Cinemascope retread of their 1939 hit *The Rains Came* which emerged as *The Rains of Ranchipur* in 1955.

On the other hand, 1941's luminous Sam Spade detective yarn, *The Maltese Falcon* (with Humphrey Bogart, Mary Astor, Sydney Greenstreet and Peter Lorre), had been made twice before, once under the same title in 1931 (with Ricardo Cortez and Bebe Daniels) and five years later as *Satan Met a Lady* (with Warren William as the sleuth and Bette Davis as his blonde client). Furthermore, George Stevens' masterful *A Place in the Sun* (1951) was adapted from a 20-year-old picture called *An American Tragedy*, William Wyler's epic success *Ben-Hur* had been previously filmed by Cecil B. DeMille in 1925 with Ramon Novarro in the role assumed by Charlton Heston in 1959, and the Charles Boyer-Irene Dunne tearjerker *Love Affair* (1939) provided the base for the Cary Grant-Deborah Kerr hit of 1957, *An Affair to Remember*. An interesting aside: when Fox purchased the remake rights to *Love Affair*, they commissioned Harry Warren, Harold Adamson and Leo McCarey to write a title song, but only when the composition was completed did the studio realize that they could

not retain the original title; which is why, to this day, the official name of the song is 'An Affair to Remember (Our Love Affair)'.

Understandably, the great classic adventure stories will continue to be updated; the likes of Robin Hood, Beau Geste, Scaramouche and endless groupings of Musketeers will no doubt be recast *ad infinitum*, yet it remains questionable whether the 1935 telling of *Mutiny on the Bounty* will ever be totally eclipsed. At least, when the original *Mutiny* is shown on home screens, its original title card is intact, for often earlier versions are given television titles so as to separate them from the remakes; for example, the 1934 Charles Laughton-Norma Shearer version of *The Barretts of Wimpole Street* is programmed in the States now as *Forbidden Alliance*, the 1936 *Anything Goes* becomes *Tops is the Limit* (the BBC showed it as such a few years back), and the original 1942 *Mississippi Gambler* is now screened as *Danger on the River* so as not to conflict with the 1953 remake which starred Tyrone Power.

In whichever direction the movie industry of the future finds itself, you can be sure that familiarity will continue to breed contentment, with various heroes and heroines of yesteryear finding new lives in reconstructed formulas. Remember that when Esther Blodgett was initially transformed in *A Star is Born* (with Janet Gaynor in 1937), she became a mere movie actress, while in 1954 Judy Garland portrayed her as a band singer turned musical star, and, by 1976, she was Esther Hoffman (played by Barbra Streisand), a nightclub singer in the world of rock 'n' roll! So keep a sharp eye and ear on what you're watching (you won't always be told what is going on . . . for example, don't look for any reference in the credits in 1981's *Rich and Famous* to 1943's *Old Acquaintance*, which was based on the same play), for more often than you might think ghosts of the past are hovering off-camera! Or, as Dooley Wilson might suggest (in the words of Herman Hupfeld) . . . 'You must remember this'.

TV Feature Films of the Year

You may have noticed that both the BBC and ITV are showing fewer made-for-TV feature films than in the past, some weeks not showing a single such movie. This is due in part to a change in the attitude and the policy of major American film production companies. Towards the end of 1984 it became apparent that Paramount, 20th Century-Fox, Universal and MGM/UA were more or less ceasing to make such movies (and mini-series), while Warner and Columbia had cut their TV feature output right down.

This change of policy has more or less been forced on the film companies for financial reasons. While the normal TV feature film can expect to bring only $300,000 return (with a mini-series expectation of about a million dollars) a successful television series can bring the makers well over the million and, indeed, in some cases double that figure in the domestic market alone, with sales abroad representing so much cream and sugar. The situation was put in a nutshell by Rich Frank (what a name to conjure with in film circles!), who is the President of Paramount's TV wing. He said, 'We can't make money out of TV movies.' And if they cannot make money out of them, then obviously they are not going to make them.

The major details that follow relate to feature films of the made for, and shown on, TV by both the BBC and ITV during the period 1 July 1984 to 31 July 1985. Dates in brackets denote year of production.

Airwolf (1983). Feature film introduction to a series in which a hush-hush helicopter is stolen and taken to Libya, giving the CIA the task of getting it back. Featuring Jan Michael-Vincent, Ernest Borgnine, Alex Cord, David Hemmings and Belinda Bauer. Dir. and Screenplay: D.P. Bellisario. ITV, 12 October 1984.

Along Came a Spider (1969). Somewhat convoluted tale about a woman who, convinced her husband has been murdered, sets out with an ingenious if unlikely plan to kill the killer. But Suzanne Pleshette as the lady in question papers over the cracks with her sizzling performance. Also featuring Ed Nelson, Andrew Prine and Brooke Bundy. Dir: Lee H. Katzin. Screenplay: Barry Oringer. ITV, 1 July 1984.

Angel (1982). Top-class Irish film actually made for TV but first shown in the cinema – see 'Releases of the Year' section in the 1983–4 *Film Review*. Channel 4, 15 November 1984.

Arthur's Hallowed Ground (1983). Top-flight cameraman Freddie Young doing a good job with his fine first fling at direction in a nostalgic, very English story about cricket. A lovely performance by veteran music hall star Jimmy Jewell as the dedicated pitch-tender. Featuring Jean Boht and David Swift. Dir: Freddie Young. Screenplay: Peter Gibbs. Channel 4, 30 August 1984.

Attica: the Story of a Prison Riot (1980). The story of the large-scale, and finally deadly, confrontation between jailed and gaolers which adopts a propaganda tone as it suggests something is very wrong with the US penal system. Featuring Henry Darrow, Charles Durning, Joel Fabiani and George Grizzard. Dir: Marvin J. Chomsky. Screenplay: James Henderson; based on the book by Tom Wicker. ITV, 15 June 1985.

Banacek: Detour to Nowhere (1972). Private Eye Banacek – alias George Peppard – sniffs out the perpetrators of an initially successful, heist of more than a million pounds of gold from an armoured truck in a hold-up that results in the death of two of the vehicle's crew. Featuring Christine Belford, Don Dubbins and Murray Matheson. Dir: John Smight. Screenplay: Anthony Wilson. ITV, 8 August 1984.

Banyon (1971). Well-made pilot feature for a series which never really took off and only had a short life. Robert Forster as the Los Angeles private eye of the title who becomes framed for the murder of a waitress and to save his own skin has to find the real killer. And such is the movie's mood it all works out as good, clean (well, nearly) fun. Featuring Darren McGavin, José Ferrer, Anjanette Comer and Hermione Gingold. Dir: Robert Day. Screenplay: Ed Adamson. BBC1 24 August 1984.

Beauty and the Beast (1976). Prosaic remake of Jean Cocteau's poetic screen version of the old fairy tale that was made for the small screen but turned up on the big one in London two years later. George C. Scott as a bulbous Beast and Trish van Devere as Beauty. And it is English-made. Featuring Virginia McKenna and Bernard Lee. Dir: Fielder Cook. Screenplay: Sherman Yellen. BBC1, 8 September 1984.

Berlin Tunnel 21 (1981). Impressively well made thriller, based on fact, about an attempted escape from East to West Berlin *under* that infamous Wall. Made on location and all the more convincing for that. Featuring Richard Thomas, Horst Buchholz, Ute Christensen, Kenneth Griffith and José Ferrer. Dir: Richard Michaels. Screenplay: John Gay; based on the book by Donald Linguist. BBC1, 15 February 1985.

Beyond Sorrow, Beyond Pain (1983). Remarkable, thought-provoking documentary from Sweden about a Swedish girl who, horrified when the doctors more or less wash their hands of her American boyfriend who has been crippled, mentally and physically, after a car crash, takes on the job of rehabilitating him and achieves marvellous results. Written and directed by the girl herself, Agneta Elers-Jarleman. BBC2, 9 February 1985.

The Birth of the Beatles (1979). The story of the rise, and rise, *and* rise of the group from Hamburg success to worldwide triumph. Stephen McKenna as John, Rod Culbertson as Paul, John Altman as George and Ray Ashcroft as Ringo. Also featuring Ryan Michael, David Wilkinson, Brian Jameson (as Brian Epstein) and Wendy Morgan. Dir: Richard Marquand. Screenplay: John Kurland and Jacob Eskendar. Beatles numbers performed by Rain. BBC1, 26 January 1985.

The Boy who Drank Too Much (1980). The 'Boy' is an outstanding ice hockey player whose high school adversary is the bottle. Luckily he has a very good friend whose patience is exemplary. The actual ice hockey sequences are among the best ever screened. Featuring Scott Baio, Don Murray, Lance Kerwin, Ed Lauter, Marieclare Costello and Stephen Davies. Dir: Jerrold Freeman. Screenplay: Edward de Blasio; based on the story by Shep Greene. Channel 4, 30 April 1985.

The Brotherhood of the Bell (1970). Glenn Ford as a member of a secret society who in return for big favours to its members eventually seeks payment in return. When Mr Ford's bill comes along the cost is too high for him to meet. Also featuring Rosemary Forsyth, Dean Jagger, Maurice Evans, Will Geer, Bill Smithers and William

Conrad. Dir: Paul Wendkos, Screenplay: David Karp. BBC1, 5 January 1985

The Cable Car Murder (1971). An excellent pilot feature to a series that never was, about a San Francisco black inspector (Robert Hooks) and his Irish sergeant side-kick (Jeremy Slate) investigating the killing of a local tycoon's son whose body is found in a cable car. So good one wonders why the series never got off the planning board. Also featuring Robert Wagner, Carol Lynley and José Ferrer. Dir: Jerry Thorpe. Screenplay: Herman Miller. BBC1, 22 January 1985.

Can You Hear the Laughter? (1979). Biopic about Freddie Prinze, a comedian virtually unknown in Britain but a popular TV comic in the US (where he starred in the *Chico* series) who found sudden fame too much to take and died from drugs and the like at the age of 22! Featuring Ira Augustain, Ken Sylk and Kevin Hooks. Dir: Burt Brinckerhoff. Screenplay: Dalene Young. BBC1, 28 June 1985.

Chautauqua Girl (1983). Understandably voted the best Canadian TV programme of its year; a warm, winning and quite wonderful recreation of life in a small Canadian farming town in the 1920s; where the charming girl of the title ensures that in spite of all adversity, the town shall be host to a travelling circus. Featuring Janet Laine-Green, Terrence Kelly and Jackie Burroughs. Dir: Rob Iscove. Screenplay: Jeannine Locke. Channel 4, 22 May 1985.

The Children of An Lac (1980). Ina Balin re-acting her real-life role as one of the American women who fought against all restraints and cut through miles of red tape in order to evacuate hundreds of Vietnamese children from Saigon before it fell to the Viet Cong in 1975: a film that is moving, exciting and well made. Featuring Shirley Jones. Channel 4, 20 November 1984.

Children of Divorce (1980). Seen through the eyes of the children involved; a story of three divorces and the bad, and lasting, effect they have on the youngsters. Well made with a passionate plea at its heart. Featuring Barbara Feldon, Lance Kerwin, Stacey Nelkin and Billy Dee Williams. Dir.

and Screenplay: Joanna Lee. BBC2, 2 August 1984.

China Rose (1983). Against nicely photographed, fascinating Hong Kong backgrounds, the thriller story of a man (George C. Scott) trying to trace his son, missing in China, and finding romance with unlikely but pretty interpreter Ali MacGraw. Also featuring Michael Biehn and Dennis Lill. Dir: Robert Day. Screenplay: David Epstein. BBC1, 30 September 1984.

Choice of Heart (1983). Far above average TV real-life feature-drama about Jean Donovan, a man-mad student who turned to Catholicism, became a missionary in South America and was one of three Sisters murdered in El Salvador in 1980. Well scripted, nicely acted and directed with more than usual sensitivity. Featuring Melissa Gilbert, Pamela Bellwood, Helen Hunt, Martin Sheen and Mike Farrell. Dir: Joseph Sargent. Screenplay: John Pielmeier. Channel 4, 18 June 1985.

A Christmas without Snow (1979). Delightful little Christmassy TV feature about a young divorced teacher (Michael Learned) from the big town who finds new interests in a small town to which she moves, especially when she joins the local choir preparing for its annual production of Handel's *Messiah*. Also featuring John Houseman and James Cromwell. Dir. and Screenplay: John Korty. Channel 4, 18 December 1984.

A Circle of Children (1977). Deservedly highly thought of American TV feature film about the relationship between two women; one, the regular teacher (Rachel Roberts) at a school for disturbed youngsters with emotional problems, the other (Jane Alexander), a rich but not happy lady who turns to volunteer work at the school to bring an interest into her life. Also featuring David Ogden Stiers, Nan Martin and Matthew Laborteaux. Dir: Don Taylor. Screenplay: Steven Gethers. ITV, 18 March 1985.

Cool Million: Mask of Marcella (1972). Feature film pilot to a subsequent series featuring the same characters: James Farentino as the private eye paid a six-figure sum to solve the mystery of the missing heiress and finding after 13 years the trail has got pretty cold! Also featuring Barbara Bouchet, John Vernon, Christine Belford, Jackie Coogan, Lila Kedrova and Patrick O'Neal. Dir: Gene Levitt. Screenplay: Larry Cohen. ITV, 1 August 1984.

The Country Girls (1983). Charming, visually stunning story of two Irish girls from their severe convent school and life in the big city until they decide to emigrate, all shown with a lovely sense of humour. Made for TV but shown in the cinemas in the spring of 1984. Featuring Maeve Germaine, Jill Doyle and Sam Neill. Dir: Desmond Davis. Screenplay: Edna O'Brien; based on her own novel. Channel 4, 20 June 1985.

The Court Martial of George Armstrong Custer (1977). General Custer may be long dead after that Little Big Horn fiasco but the moviemakers will not let him lie down for long; here they imagine he survived to face a court martial for ignoring orders. And the supposition makes for a gripping and very good teleplay. Featuring James Olson, Blythe Danner, Brian Keith and Ken Howard. Screenplay: Joan Gay; based on the D.C. Jones novel. BBC2, 26 July 1984.

Coward of the County (1981). Kenny Rogers as a lad with a problem. Having promised his dad he will never take up arms, the events of Pearl Harbour put him in a dilemma – will he or won't he enlist? Also featuring Fredric Lehene, Larho Woodruff and Marieclare Costello. Dir: Dick Lowry. Screenplay: Clyde Ware and Jim Byrnes. Channel 4, 3 July 1984.

Crime Club: The Last Key (1975). A publicity seeker confesses to a murder. But did he really do it? That is the mystery the highly exclusive Crime Club set out to solve. Featuring Scott Thomas, Eugene Roche and Robert Lansing. Dir: Jeannot Szwarc. Screenplay: G.R. Kearney. ITV, 16 August 1984.

A Cry in the Wilderness (1973). George Kennedy, fearing madness after being bitten by a rabid skunk, chains himself up – just in case – to protect his family and then finds that they are all threatened by floods. Also featuring Joanna Pettet and Lee H. Montgom-

ery. Dir: Gordon Hessler. Screenplay: Stephen and Elinor Sknarp. ITV, 8 July 1984.

Damien: The Leper Priest (1980). True story of a priest who worked in a leper colony and selflessly fought for an improvement in living conditions. Set in Hawaii a century ago, it is rather horrific at times. Featuring Ken Howard, Mike Farrell, Wilfrid Hyde White and David Ogden Stiers. Dir. and Screenplay: Steven Gethers. Channel 4, 4 June 1985.

The Dangerous Days of Iowa Jones (1966). Roamin' cowpuncher Robert Horton (who hoped this might found a series – but it did not) is deputized by the dying sheriff to take a couple of lawbreakers to the nearest lawman, an assignment which brings him plenty of assorted dangers – and a dame, Diane Baker. Also featuring Sal Mineo, Nehemiah Persoff, Gary Merrill and Royal Dano. Dir: Alex March. Screenplay: Frank Fenton and Robert Thompson. BBC2, 22 May 1985.

Dark Mirror (1984). In 1946 they made a Hollywood film with this title and of which this TV feature is more or less a remake. It is a thriller about twin sisters, one good and the other less so, both played here by Jane Seymour. So alike are they that nobody really knows which is which: useful when one of them becomes implicated in the murder of a lawyer stabbed to death in his own home. A good story, competently handled and very well played. Also featuring Vincent Gardenia, Stephen Collins and Hank Brandt. Dir: Richard Lang. Screenplay: Corey Blechman, based on Nunnally Johnson's 1946 script. BBC1, 13 February 1985.

Dark Night of the Scarecrow (1981). What a pity to see the talented Charles Durning in this kind of minor horror shocker, playing the leader of a vigilante group killed off by the title killer. Also featuring Claude Earl Jones, Tonya Crowe and Larry Drake. Dir: Frank de Felitta. Screenplay: J.D. Feigelson. Channel 4, 21 May 1985.

Daughter of the Mind (1969). Guilt-ridden Professor Ray Milland, feeling that he is guilty of his daughter's death in a car smash when he was driving, begins to imagine her ghost is haunting

him whereas in fact? Not fair to divulge! Also featuring Don Murray, Gene Tierney, Barbara Dana and John Carradine. Dir: Walter Grauman. Screenplay: Luther Davis. ITV, 7 August 1984.

Deadly Harvest (1972). Adaptation of a best-selling Geoffrey Household thriller about a Russian defector, living peacefully in California as a vintner, suddenly finding his past catching up with him and his life is threatened. And if the CIA appear involved they do not exactly look to be on his side! Featuring Richard Boone, Patty Duke and Michael Constantine. Dir: Michael O'Herlihy. Screenplay: Daniel Ullman; based on Household's *Watcher in the Shadows*. BBC1, 17 July 1984.

Deadly Harvest (1972). Clint Walker as a North American farmer defending his produce, farm and family from hungry and ruthless food-seeking armed gangs when freak weather causes famine. One of those films which start well but rather tail off. Also featuring Nehemiah Persoff, Gary Davies, Dawn Greenhalgh and Kim Cattrall. Dir: Timothy Bond. Screenplay: Martin Lager. BBC1, 19 January 1985.

Death Among Friends (1975). Normal sort of whodunnit except that in this case the investigating detective is female, a certain Mrs (Lieutenant) 'R' – a nice performance by Kate Reid – who is set the task of working out which of the guests of a wealthy estate owner strangled his – or her – host on the tennis court. Also featuring John Anderson, A. Martinez, Martin Balsam, Jack Cassidy, Paul Henreid and Denver Pyle. Dir: Paul Wendkos. Screenplay: Ralph Ross. ITV, 19 August 1984.

Death Car on the Freeway (1979). Or, mayhem on the roads of Los Angeles, where TV reporter Shelley Hack investigates – at her peril – the motor car murders of several nice old ladies. To bring things to a head the young snooper deliberately drives herself into a confrontation with the killer. Also featuring George Hamilton, Peter Graves, Barbara Rush, Dinah Shore and Frank Gorshin. Dir: Hal Needham. Screenplay: William Wood. ITV, 27 August 1984.

A Death in Canaan (1978). Tense and enthralling in parts, limp and listless in others, this is British director Tony Richardson's American TV movie debut: based on an actual murder trial in 1973 of a 18 year-old lad accused of killing his mother; a trial which went on to make American legal history. Featuring Paul Clemens, Tom Atkins, Brian Dennehy and Conchita Ferrell. Dir: Tony Richardson. Screenplay: Robert W. Christiansen and Rick Rosenberg; based on the book by Joan Barthel. BBC1, 22 June 1985.

The Disappearance of Aimée (1976). Faye Dunaway pulling out all the stops as the famous 1930s evangelist Aimée McPherson; here brought to court by the Los Angeles DA on a charge of faking her own kidnapping. Also featuring Bette Davis, James Sloyan and James Woods. Dir: Anthony Harvey. Screenplay: John McGreevey. Channel 4, 6 November 1984.

Don't Steal My Baby (1977). (American title: *Black Market Baby*.) Melodramatic treatment of the serious subject of the baby adoption racket, with nice girl Linda Purl dragged into it unwillingly by smooth-talking classmate Desi Arnaz Jr who is in cahoots with a crooked lawyer. Also featuring Jessica Walter and Tom Bosley. Dir: Robert Day. Screenplay: Andrew Peter Marin; based on the book *A Nice Italian Girl* by Elizabeth Christman. BBC1, 23 January 1985.

Egon Schiele (1979). The story of the Viennese painter of that name whose works and life were pretty sensational: he was put on trial both for his obscene paintings and the debauching of his young models! Featuring Felix Mitterer, Jeanette Hirschberger and Karoline Zeisler. Dir. and Screenplay (latter with W.D. Fischer): John Goldschmidt. BBC1, 17 May 1985.

The Elevator (1974). Familiar thriller about a group of assorted – naturally all-star! – characters, including a couple of killers, trapped in a lift, and their subsequent differing reactions to the heightening tension. Featuring James Farentino, Don Stroud, Roddy McDowall, Craig Stevens, Teresa Wright, Myrna Loy and Carol Lynley. Dir: Jerry Jameson. No Screenplay credit listed. ITV, 15 July 1984.

Ellery Queen : Too Many Suspects (1975). Jim Hutton (son) and David Wayne (cop father) between them solve the problem of who killed Miss Gray, a fashion designer who leaves them an odd sort of clue to go on. This feature TV film was an excellent start to the successful 'Queen' series that followed. Also featuring Ray Milland, Kim Hunter and Gail Strickland. Dir: David Greene. Screenplay: Richard Levinson and William Link. ITV, 7 August 1984.

Errol Flynn: My Wicked, Wicked Ways (1985). A generally amusing biopic about the famous film swashbuckler whose lifestyle – wine, women and drugs in a big way – lends itself to this sort of fairly superficial treatment. But while it misses out on the darkest side of Flynn's character it does enough to suggest the man behind the movie mask: all based on Flynn's bestseller about himself. Featuring Duncan Regehr, Barbara Hershey, Darren McGavin, Lee Purcell, Barrie Ingham, George Coe and Pamela Mason. ITV, 8 June 1985.

Escape (1980). Timothy Bottoms playing real-life character Dwight Worker who, found to be carrying cocaine, was sent to a terrible jail in Mexico City (without trial) and there planned with an American girl visitor to be the first to escape from the place since Pancho Villa succeeded in so doing in 1913. All nicely handled. Also featuring Kay Lenz and Colleen Dewhurst. Dir: Robert Lewis. Screenplay: Michael Zager; based on the book by Dwight and Barbara Worker. BBC1, 15 October 1984.

Escape to Mindanao (1968). Highly incredible but well made and ultimately gripping POW 'escape' movie, with Americans George Maharis and Nehemiah Persoff breaking out of their Japanese prison camp in the Philippines with a stolen secret that will aid their free compatriots . . . if they can get as far as safety. Also featuring James Shigeta and Willi Koopman. Dir: Don McDougall. Screenplay: Harold Livingstone; based on the story by Orville Hampton. BBC2, 13 December 1984.

Express to Terror (1979). (American title: *Supertrain*). Melodrama about a new nuclear-powered train and its debut run between New York and Los Angeles, with an assassin on board whose job it is to see one of the passengers does not reach the end of the line alive. Featuring Steve Lawrence, Don Meredith, Char Fontane, George Hamilton, Stella Stevens, Keenan Wynn and Robert Alda. Dir: Dan Curtis. Screenplay: Earl W. Wallave. ITV, 12 January 1985.

The Eyes of Charles Sand (1972). From the pen of Henry Farrell who wrote *Whatever Happened to Baby Jane*, this is an odd little story about a man with powers to look into the future who is drawn into a case of murder most foul. Featuring Peter Haskell, Barbara Rush, Bradford Dillman and Joan Bennett. Dir: Reza S. Badiyi. Screenplay: Henry Farrell and Stanford Whitmore. BBC1, 6 February 1985.

The Fall Guy (1981). Lee Majors as the Hollywood stunt expert who fills in between jobs with a few bounty hunter assignments, tracking down and bringing bail jumpers to justice for a fee (a routine unique to American legal procedure). Also featuring Douglas Barr, Heather Thomas, Janet Leigh, Eddie Albert, James Coburn and Farrah Fawcett. Dir: Russ Mayberry. No screenplay credit listed. ITV, 10 August 1984.

FDR: The Last Year (1980). Jason Robards giving a splendid performance as the US President in a Canadian-made TV biopic. Also some good work by players in real-life roles, including Wensley Pithey (as Churchill), Kim Hunter, Sylvia Sidney and Eileen Heckart. Dir: Anthony Page. Screenplay: Stanley Greenberg; based on the book by Jim Bishop. Channel 4, 23 October 1984.

Fear on Trial (1975). TV film about the McCarthy attack on stage and film players by means of a blacklist which did harm to those who resisted the 1950–60 enquiry into their political sympathies. It won an Emmy for its script and several nominations for members of the cast, which include George C. Scott, William Devane, David Susskind and Dorothy Tristan. Dir: Lamont Johnson. Screenplay: David Rintels; based on the autobiography of John Henry Faulk. Channel 4, 25 June 1985.

Fer-de-Lance (1974). TV disaster thriller which was previously shown in the cinemas with the title of *Death Dive*, a more reasonable title (and in fact actually shown on ITV with that title on 18 January 1983). This tells the story of a crippled submarine on the ocean bed with a family of deadly snakes loose on board. Featuring David Janssen, Hope Lange, Ivan Dixon, Robert Ito and Charles Knox Robinson. Dir: Russ Mayberry. Screenplay: Leslie Stevens. ITV, 18 February 1985.

Flash Gordon – The Greatest Adventure of All (1981). TV feature cartoon about the famous comic-strip character. Dir: Owen Wetzler. Screenplay: S.A. Peeples. ITV, 5 April 1985.

Flight to Holocaust (1976). Sons of famous stars, Patrick Wayne and Christopher Mitchum, along with female partner Fawne Harriman, as a sort of Trouble Shooters Inc. trio facing up to the problem of the rescue of the survivors of a plane that has crashed into the 20th floor of a Los Angeles skyscraper. Also featuring Rory Calhoun, Lloyd Nolan, Desi Arnaz Jr and Sid Caesar. Dir: Bernard J. Kowalski. Screenplay: Robert Heverly. ITV, 5 January 1985.

Forever (1978). More Californian teenager teething troubles; youthful romantic ideas undermined by the intrusion of hard reality. The youngsters, and the film are all very pleasant. Featuring Stephanie Zimbalist, Dean Butler and Beth Raines. Dir: John Korty. Screenplay: Kisuna Jacobsen. BBC2, 30 August 1984.

Friendly Fire (1979). About the disturbed parents of a young soldier officially 'killed by artillery fire from friendly sources' who determinedly set out to find exactly what those words mean. A basically true story of the Vietnam war, it brought the producers an award. There have been too many Vietnam movies, both small and large, but few have been as good as this one. Featuring Carol Burnett, Ned Beatty, Sam Waterston and Timothy Hutton. Dir: David Greene. Screenplay: Fay Kanin; based on the book by C.D.B. Bryan. BBC1, 14 August 1984.

F. Scott Fitzgerald and 'The Last of the Belles' (1974). Biopic about the famed author which manages to squeeze in as a bonus one of his short stories. Richard Chamberlain stars as the writer. Also featuring Blythe Danner and Susan Sarandon. Dir: George Schaefer. Screenplay: James Costigan. Channel 4, 13 November 1984.

Ghost Dancing (1983). Not seen on the large screen for quite a while, Dorothy McGuire is the splendid star of this small-screen feature, playing a poor farming widow who is literally driven to take explosive action when her water supply is taken away to supply the needs of the nearby town. Also featuring Bruce Davison and Bill Erwin. Dir: David Greene. Screenplay: Phil Penningroth. Channel 4, 4 September 1984.

A Girl in the Park (1979). Pilot feature for yet another TV series which was still-born; based on G.K. Chesterton's 'Father Brown' stories but with the backgrounds transposed to the United States. When an actress (Kay Lenz) is terrorized she is unable to get the cops interested and it is left to the logical Father Brown (Barnard Hughes) to work it all out satisfactorily for her. Dir: John Moxey. Screenplay: Don Mankiewicz and Gordon Cotler. BBC1, 31 August 1984.

Girls of the Road (1979). Annie Potts and Kim Darby as two glamorous lorry drivers trying to prevent Harry Dean Stanton from re-possessing their iron steeds because of payment problems (a foretaste of *Repo Man* to come) in an at least lively and interesting (Billy Carter, President Jimmy's brother, makes his screen debut) feature. Dir: Robert Greenwald. Screenplay: Robie Robinson. ITV, 1 April 1985.

Giro City (1982). Made-for-TV film shown in the cinema (Gate) in October 1982 (reviewed in the 1983–4 *Film Review*). Grittily realistic, left-leaning story about TV investigative journalism and its frustrations from the Establishment. Glenda Jackson at her least glamorous and most sincere. Also featuring Jon Finch and Kenneth Colley. Dir. and Screenplay: Karl Francis. Channel 4, 27 June 1985.

Gnomes (1980). Small-screen feature cartoon – deserving of the large-screen exposure it has not had – about a centenarian gnome who has the idea he has not yet matured enough to embark on the wedded state, and the blonde gnomess who tries to persuade him otherwise. Dir: Jack Zander. Screenplay: Sam Moore and Maurice Rapt. Channel 4, 26 December 1984.

Good Against Evil (1977). Thriller straight from the Hammer Horror era written by one of the most dependable of its scripters, Jimmy Sangster. The Evil here is provided by the nasty coven of witches (male and female) who hatch up some pretty unpleasant plans for poor little heroine Elyssa Davalos. Also featuring Richard Lynch, Dan O'Herlihy and Dick Rambo. Dir: Paul Wendkos. Screenplay: J. Sangster. ITV, 15 February 1985.

Great Expectations (1981). Very tolerable cartoon treatment of the Dickens classic. ITV, 31 December 1984.

Happily Ever After (1978). According to the *TV Times*, Suzanne Somers won star spot in this romantic story about a young singer who finds the competitive world of Vegas showbiz hard to take, through her attracting *50 million* viewers to the American version of our own *Man about the House* series! Also featuring Bruce Boxleitner, Eric Braeden, John Rubenstein and Bill Lucking. Dir: Robert Scheerer. Screenplay: G.M. White. ITV, 10 June 1985.

Hardhat & Legs (1980). The chequered romance of a divorcée, with ex-hubbie and children custody problems, and the tough building employee who is trying to dodge the nasty intentions of a crooked bookie's gorillas. The nicely smooth script lifts the film above average. Featuring Kevin Dobson and Sharon Glass. Dir: Lee Philips. Screenplay: Garson Kanin and Ruth Gordon. ITV, 2 August 1984.

Harpy (1971). Rather odd little piece about a modern mountain man who rears and trains birds of prey, and the little Indian boy companion who thwarts the man's ex-wife's plans to abort the boss's romance with his pretty secretary. Fascinating atmosphere and backgrounds. Featuring Hugh O'Brian, Elizabeth Ashley and Tom Nardini. Dir: G.S. Sindell. Screenplay: William Wood. BBC1, 1 July 1984.

Heat of Anger (1972). Some good old stars – Susan Hayward, James Stacy, Lee J. Cobb – involved in a murder mystery which starts with a fight between a father and his daughter's wooer which takes place on the top of an uncompleted skyscraper. Dir: Don Taylor. Screenplay: Fay Kanin. ITV, 9 August 1984.

Hitchhike (1974). A woman motorist picks up a man asking for a lift and soon finds she has a killer on her hands. Featuring Cloris Leachman, Cameron Mitchell and Sherry Jackson. Dir: Gordon Hessler. Screenplay: Yale M. Udoff. ITV, 9 December 1984.

Hollow Image (1979). Another angle to the colour problem: this time a black girl finds herself in a quandary when after struggling from Harlem ghetto to fashion stardom she goes back home to come up against the old problems of race and place. Featuring Saundra Sharp, Robert Hooks and Dick Anthony Williams. Dir: Marvin J. Chomsky. Screenplay: Lee Huskins. Channel 4, 21 August 1984.

Home for the Holidays (1972). Beware that cosy title – the film in fact is a horror piece about a family under threat from a ruthless killer. Featuring Walter Brennan, Sally Field, Julie Harris, Eleanor Parker and Jessica Walter. Dir: John Llewellyn Moxey. Screenplay: Joseph Stefano. ITV, 25 December 1984.

Horror at 37,000 Feet (1972). Even more than usually incredible story about some old stones with evil powers that bring about a terrifying aerial experience for the passengers who share a trip with them. All nicely tense and made with a certain panache. Featuring Buddy Ebsen, Chuck Connors, Tammy Grimes, Jane Merrow, France Nuyen and William Shatner. Dir: David Lowell Rich. Screenplay: Ron Austin and Jim Buchanan. BBC1, 12 September 1984.

The House (1984). Intriguing fantasy premise: England is in Europe, between Latvia and Russia, and has declared war on the former. England is winning until the Russian Bear enters the fray. Featuring Stephen Rea, Dudley Sutton, Diana Armstrong, Alun Armstrong, Nigel Hawthorne and Ingrid Pitt. Dir: Mike Figgis. No Screenplay credit. Channel 4, 27 September 1984.

The House Possessed (1981). More devils taking possession – this time of a pop star's mountain hideout where his companion/nurse tries to find out who they are and what they want and gets horribly scared in the process. Featuring Parker Stevenson, Lisa Eilbacher, Joan Bennett and Slim Pickens. Dir: William Ward. Screenplay: David Lewinson. BBC1, 19 November 1984.

A Howling in the Woods (1971). Chiller-thriller with that yelping cur in the trees helping to enhance the atmosphere as Barbara Eden returns to her Nevada birthplace and finds it a ghostly and threatening place. Also featuring Larry (pre-*Dallas*) Hagman, Vera Miles and Tyne Daly. Dir: Daniel Petrie. Screenplay: Richard DeRoy. ITV, 6 January 1985.

The Hunchback of Notre-Dame (1982). Only two to go now in order to reach double figures in movie (and TV movie) versions of the Victor Hugo classic; this time a reasonably competent adaptation with Anthony Hopkins splendid in the title role. And look at his support including: Derek Jacobi, Lesley-Anne Down, Robert Powell and John Gielgud. Dir: Michael Tuchner. Screenplay: Jon Gay; based on the Hugo novel. ITV, 28 August 1984.

Hunters Are for Killing (1970). A younger Burt Reynolds as the unjustly jailed footballer who finds he is not exactly welcome back home and so when a local nighterie owner is murdered and suspicion falls on him he takes off . . . with the cops hot on his trail. Also featuring Martin Balsam, Melvyn Douglas, and Suzanne Pleshette. Dir: Bernard Girard. Screenplay: Charles Kuenstle. BBC1, 3 November 1984.

In the Matter of Karen Ann Quinlan (1977). A dilemma which crops up again and again: should a person who has become a vegetable be allowed to die? In 1975 Joe and Julie Quinlan had to make this agonizing decision about their daughter and two years later this TV film feature was based on that case. With Brian Keith, Piper Laurie and Mary Anne Grayson as the family. Also featuring Stephanie Zimbalist, David Spielberg and Bert Freed. Dir: Glen Jordan. Screenplay: Hal Sitowitz. ITV, 25 February 1985.

In This House of Brede (1975). Nicely toned down adaptation of the Rumer Godden story of a nun (Diana Rigg) who finds a handsome young novitiate devilishly attractive! Good performances, polished direction, above-average TV movie. Also featuring Judi Bowker, Pamela Brown, Gwen Watford and Denis Quilley. Dir: George Schaefer. Screenplay: James Costigan; based on the Godden novel. Channel 4, 25 September 1984.

The Incredible Rocky Mountain Race (1977). A pleasantly entertaining visual adaptation of one of Mark Twain's stories; about his and a friend's long race from their home town in Missouri to the Pacific Ocean; with much happening along the way to keep you amused and entertained. Featuring Christopher Connelly, Forrest Tucker, Jack Kruschen, Mike Mazurki and Dan Haggerty. Dir: J.L. Conway. Screenplay: David O'Marley and Thomas Chapman. BBC2, 15 May 1985.

Intimate Agony (1983). Fictional film built on a very topical problem: herpes disease. The new young doctor on Paradise Isle finds the people of the Eden up against an epidemic of the illness and not, in all cases, receptive to his publicizing the fact. Featuring Robert Vaughn, Anthony Geary and Mark Hannon. Dir: Paul Wehdkos. Screenplay: J. Henderson and J. Hirsch. Channel 4, 16 April 1985.

Ironside (1967). A feature-length episode about the famous wheelchair detective (Raymond Burr, who graced the outstanding series of crime stories of that title) which is so good that one wonders why we are not still getting additions to the series. On his first vacation for many years, Ironside is shot down by a mystery assailant. Also featuring Geraldine Brooks, Gene Lyons, Don Galloway and Barbara Anderson. Dir: James Goldstone. Screenplay: D.M. Mankiewicz. ITV, 9 August 1984.

Jennifer – A Woman's Story (1979). Elizabeth Montgomery as the widow who is determined to prove her business prowess in her late husband's boat-building organization and finding it not all that easy. The film is like a large segment from one of the glossy American soap operas. Featuring Bradford Dillman, Scott Hylands and James Booth. Dir: Guy Green. Screenplay: Richard Gregson. BBC2, 22 September 1984.

Killer by Night (1971). Virtually a TV-tailored remake of the 1950s movie *Panic in the Streets* – a thriller about a doctor trying to track down a diphtheria carrier before he triggers off an epidemic, and while so doing quite incidentally helping the police to catch up with the killer of two patrolmen. Featuring Robert Wagner, Diane Baker, Theodore Bikel, Mercedes McCambridge and Pedro Armandariz, Jr. Dir: Bernard McEveety. Screenplay: David Harmon. BBC1, 7 August 1984.

Killer on Board (1973). Routine, familiar little suspense movie about a killer germ threatening the 500 passengers on board a cruise liner in the Pacific. Who goes next? Featuring Claude Akins, Patty Duke Austin, George Hamilton, Frank Converse, Susan Howard and Jane Seymour. Dir: Philip Leacock. Screenplay: Sandor Stern. BBC1, 15 January 1985.

The Killing of Randy Webster (1980). Based on court records and the investigations of a Texas journalist, this is the story of a father's dogged search for the truth about his son's death while in the custody of the Houston police. Featuring Hal Holbrook, Dixie Carter, James Whitmore Jr, Nancy Malone and Jennifer Jason Leigh. Dir: Sam Wanamaker. Screenplay: Scott Swanton. BBC1, 22 October 1984.

Kim (1984). Peter O'Toole in the unlikely role of a 'saintly old Buddhist lama', with Ravi Sheth as the Lahore youngster he befriends. Dir: John Davies. Screenplay: James Brabazon. ITV, 26 December 1984.

The Last Days of Pompeii (1984). A new version of that spectacular old war-horse, split here into two parts and decorated with a large cast including Lesley-Anne Down, Olivia Hussey, Brian Blessed, Ernest Borgnine, Ned Beatty, Siobhan McKenna, Franco Nero, Anthony Quayle and Laurence

Olivier. Celluloid ancient history with a vengeance! Dir: Peter Hunt. Screenplay: Carmen Culver. ITV, 30 and 31 December 1984.

The Last Tenant (1978). Drama about filial responsibilities. Famous Actors' Studio boss Lee Strasberg finds a conflict of loyalties when he takes his old father into his home on the eve of his marriage. Also featuring Tony Lo Bianco and Christine Lahti. Dir: Jud Taylor. Screenplay: George Rubino. BBC2, 9 August 1984.

The Lazarus Syndrome (1979). Pilot feature for what was to turn out to be but a brief series. Medical drama about a doctor determined to expose the corruption in his local hospital. Featuring Louis Gossett Jr, Ronald Hunter and E.G. Marshall. Dir: Jerry Thorpe. Screenplay: Bill Blinn. Channel 4, 31 July 1984.

Legend of the Golden Gun (1979). Western about a young man whose parents have been killed by Quantrill's infamous Raiders during the American Civil War, helped by a great gunfighter to get his revenge and fulfil his vow. Featuring Hal Holbrook, Keil Dullea and Jeff Osterhage. Dir: Alan J. Levi. Screenplay: J.D. Parriott. BBC2, 3 April 1985.

Little Mo (1978). The true story of tennis star Maureen Connolly who reached the heights of the game (Wimbledon, American, Australian and French grand slam titles) only to be dethroned by the cancer that killed her at the age of 34. Featuring Glynnis O'Connor, Michael Learned, Anne Baxter and Claude Akins. Dir: Dan Heller. Screenplay: John McGreevy. BBC1, 20 June 1985.

The Long Journey Back (1979). Quite affecting story of a teenage girl involved in an accident which maims her physically and mentally, and her subsequent struggle to build a new life under difficult conditions. Nice performance by Stephanie Zimbalist as the girl and a quite astonishingly serious one from comedienne Cloris Leachman as the mother. Also featuring Mike Connors and Katy Kurtzman. Dir: Mel Damski. Screenplay: Audrey Davis Levin. ITV, 15 April 1985.

The Magician (1974). Bill Bixby as a theatrical magician working in a night club who turns detective to help a lady solve a mystery; and this was the feature film introduction to the series that followed. Featuring Keene Curtis, Joan Caulfield, Kim Hunter, Elizabeth Ashley, Barry Sullivan and Signe Hasso. Dir: Martin Chomsky. Screenplay: Laurence Heath. ITV, 25 August 1984.

Mandrake the Magician (1979). This feature movie about the comic-strip magic man was hoped to serve as an introduction to a series about him but the project failed to materialize. Here magician Anthony Herrera, bringing mysterious powers from Old World Tibet to New World America, brings to justice a murderer and blackmailer by his rather special methods. Also featuring Simone Griffith, David Hollander and Harry Blackstone Jr. Dir: Harry Falk. Screenplay: Rick Husky. ITV, 6 April 1985.

Maneater (1973). Wild animal trainer Richard Basehart being really base in this thriller by luring a vacationing quartet into the vicinity of his two starving tigers – hoping to save a bit of money on their meat ration. Also featuring Ben Gazzara, Sheree North and Kip Niven. Dir: Vince Edwards. Screenplay: Edwards, Marcus Demain and Jimmy Sangster. ITV, 12 July 1984.

Maneaters are Loose! (1978). Routine, familiar 'terror' movie about a couple of hungry tigers set loose in one of California's National Forests by their bankrupted owner, and the terror that follows until they are made harmless. Featuring Tom Skerritt, Steve Forrest and Harry Morgan. Dir: Timothy Galfas. Screenplay: Robert W. Lenski; based on the book by Ted Willis. BBC1, 17 August 1984.

Marriage is Alive and Well (1980). During a rough passage in his own marriage a professional wedding photographer recalls some of the couples he has snapped at their nuptials, and their stories – like his own generally having a happy ending. Romantic! Featuring Joe Namath, Jack Albertson and Susan Sullivan. Dir: Russ Mayberry. Screenplay: Lee Kalcheim. ITV, 11 March 1985.

Mary Jane Harper Cried Last Night (1977). Indignant TV tract about battered children and mentally shaky mothers, seen through the sad tale of a 4-year-old victim. Featuring Susan Dey, John Vernon and Tricia O'Neal. Dir: Allen Reisner. Screenplay: Joanna Lee. BBC2, 19 June 1985.

The Mask of Death (1984). Peter – Sherlock Holmes – Cushing gets John Mills as his Doctor Watson in this N.J. Crisp-written story about the retired sleuth persuaded to return to harness by the Home Secretary. Featuring Ray Milland, Anne Baxter, Anton Diffring, Gordon Jackson, Susan Penhaligon and Jenny Laird. Dir: Roy Ward Baker. Channel 4, 23 December 1984.

Mayflower: The Pilgrims' Adventure (1979). Captain Anthony Hopkins steers the gallant old *Mayflower* and its cargo of Pilgrim Fathers – and Mothers and lovers, too – toward the hoped-for Eden of the New World across the Atlantic. Also featuring Richard Crenna, Jenny Agutter and Michael Beck. Dir: George Schaefer. Screenplay: J.Lee Barrett. Channel 4, 10 July 1984.

Mazes and Monsters (1982). An out-of-the-rut adventure movie about a quartet of young students whose games become a dangerous reality – the characters are more fleshed out and credible than usual in this kind of movie. Featuring Tom Hanks, Wendy Crewson, David Wallace, Peter Donat and Susan Strasberg. Dir: S.H. Stern. Screenplay: Tom Lazarus; based on the novel by Rona Jaffe. Channel 4, 14 August 1984.

Missing Children: A Mother's Story (1982). Sad little story about an uneducated – and very unlucky! – girl with three children, abandoned by her husband and unable to sort out the problems of obtaining help – until she meets up with the Children's Rescue Mission and begins to get somewhere. Featuring Marie Winningham, Polly Holliday, Kate Capshaw, Jane Wyatt, John Anderson, Scatman Crothers and Richard Dysart. Dir: Dick Lowry. Screenplay: Nancy Sackett and Jim Lawrence. ITV, 17 March 1985.

Mistress of Paradise (1981). The 'Paradise' of the title is the Voodoo-atmosphered plantation home in the American Deep South to which a sea captain's daughter from New England is taken by her Creole husband after their marriage in the 1800s. The strange new life does not come easy for her. Featuring Genevieve Bujold and Chad Everett. Dir: Peter Medak. Screenplay: Bennett Foster. ITV, 31 July 1984.

Moonlighting (1982). Though made primarily for TV exposure this delightful movie became a big cinema success when shown in September 1982. Full details in 'Releases of the Year' section of the 1983–4 *Film Review*. Channel 4, 13 December 1984.

Murder by the Book (1972). 'Tec Peter Falk breaking down the alibi of thriller writer Jack Cassidy and so solving the puzzle of who it was who killed the suspect's partner. Also featuring Rosemary Forsyth and Martin Milner. Dir: Steven Spielberg. Screenplay: Steve Bochco. ITV, 26 August 1984.

My Body, My Child (1982). Vanessa Redgrave takes on the dramatic role of a mother whose reaction to the death of her mother is to decide to have a fourth child, a decision which brings tragedy. Also featuring Joseph Campanella, Jack Albertson, Stephen Elliott, James Naughton and Gail Strickland. Dir: Marvin Chomsky. Screenplay: Lousia Burns-Bisogno. Channel 4, 2 October 1984.

The New Maverick (1978). This was the feature which was intended to launch a new series similar to that starring James Garner (which ran from 1957 to 1962). But having lost something in the interval – though not the delightful star – it did not have the previous long-running success. Also featuring Charles Frank, Jack Kelly and Susan Blanchard. BBC1, 13 April 1985.

The Night the Bridge Fell Down (1979). Extra long – split into two parts – TV feature; a choice example of Irving Allen's uninhibited and hilarious thrillers. This one is about a broken bridge and the trapped victims. Featuring James McArthur, Desi Arnaz Jr, Barbara Rush and Char Fontane. Dir: George Fenady. Screenplay: Arthur Weiss, Ray Goldstone and M.R. David. BBC1, 21 and 22 August 1984.

November Night (1978). Andrzej Wajda's exciting made-for-TV (Polish) spectacle based on a famous Polish verse drama; highly original and very personal. Featuring Jan Nowicki, Teresa Budzisz-Krzyzanowska and Jerzy Stuhr. Dir: Andrzej Wajda. Screenplay: Stanislaw Wyspianski. BBC2, 16 March 1985.

The November Plan (1976). Private eye thriller about crooked politics which is actually a combination of the initial three episodes from the short-lived TV series *City of Angels*. Featuring Wayne Rogers (as Jake, the 'eye'), Diane Ladd, Dorothy Malone, Lloyd Nolan and G.D. Spradlin. Dir: Don Medford. Screenplay: S.J. Connel. BBC1, 29 January 1985.

Nowhere to Run (1978). David Janssen as the engineer so shocked by President Kennedy's assassination, and his own wife's cool reception of the news, that he decides to make a new life for himself. And the routine thriller goes up a notch when it comes to the well-knit climax. Also featuring Stefanie Powers, Allen Garfield, Linda Evans, James Keach and Charles Siebert. Dir: Richard Lang. Screenplay: Jim Byrnes, based on the James Einstein novel. ITV, 9 April 1985.

O'Hara, United States Treasury: Operation Cobra (1971). A gloomy David Janssen (understandably so, after his home has been burnt to ashes) joins the USA Customs Investigation Dept and soon proves himself to be a very dogged agent indeed. Also featuring Lana Wood, Gary Cresby, Stacy Harris and William Conrad. Dir: Jack Webb. Screenplay: J.B. Moser. ITV, 6 August 1984.

OHMS (1980). The battle that builds up between the small farmers of Freedom Plains and the giant electric power company which is determined to run its pylons and its millions of volts across the plains. Exciting . . . well, yes, until a somewhat unsatisfactory ending. Featuring Ralph Waite, David Birney and Cameron Mitchell. Dir: Dick Lowry. Screenplay: Gene Case. Channel 4, 17 July 1984.

One of Our Spies is Missing (1967). Another batch of TV's *UNCLE* series collected into a feature-movie parcel.

The old struggle between the tough goodies and the even tougher THRUSH baddies, and all over – good heavens! – an elixir of youth. All good clean – and simple – fun. Featuring Robert Vaughn, David McCallum, Leo G. Carroll, Vera Miles and Maurice Evans. Dir: E. Darrell Hallenbeck. Screenplay: Howard Bodman; from a story by Henry Slesar. BBC2, 9 July 1984.

Orphan Train (1979). Tear-jerker based on the true story of Emma Symns, who in the 1850s packed a group of poor children from New York into a westward-bound train hoping she would be able to get them adopted along the way – a remarkable and unusual story well told in cinematically visual terms. Featuring Jill Eikenberry, Kevin Dobson, John Femia and Peter Neuman. Dir: W.A. Graham. Screenplay: Millard Lampell. BBC2, 27 May 1985.

The Other Woman (1983). Lots of sharp Jewish humour and not a little wit, allied to some smart performances, make this fast-moving comedy about a man who nearly drives himself into the ground in order to satisfy a wife who is a quarter of a century younger than he is: first-class entertainment. And Anne Meara as that Other Woman of the title gives a quite marvellous performance in a screenplay she helped to write. A small-screen film of large-screen status. Featuring Hal Linden, Madeleine Smith, Warren Berlinger, Janis Paige, Selma Diamond and Jane Dulo. Dir: Melville Shavelson. Screenplay: Anne Meara and Lila Garrett. Channel 4, 23 April 1985.

Overboard (1978). A disastrous vacation for happily wed Angie Dickinson and Cliff Robertson (excellent performances) when in the Hawaiian islands the wife becomes enamoured of a handsome Frenchman . . . and then goes overboard! Also featuring Lewis Van Bergen, Andrew Duggan and Skip Homeier. Dir: John Newland. Screenplay: Hank Searles. ITV, 17 June 1985.

The People v. Jean Harris (1981). Ellen Burstyn doing a splendid job in portraying real-life character Jean, who in 1980 was sentenced to 18 years in jail for murdering her former lover. Also featuring Martin Balsam and Richard

Dysart. Dir: George Schaefer. Screenplay: George Lefferts. Channel 4, 30 October 1984.

Perfect Gentleman (1978). Star-flashing cast – Lauren Bacall, Sandy Dennis, Ruth Gordon and Robert Alda – decorating a rather superior, amusing heist story about the wives of some jailbirds who decide that while their hubbies are in clink they will carry out their own million-dollar hold-up! Unlikely? Yes, but what *fun!* Dir: Jackie Cooper. Screenplay: Nora Ephron. BBC1, 18 August 1984.

Praying Mantis (1982). Two-part British thriller set in Normandy and centred on a professor who has a lot of assets, including hard cash, on which some other less professorial folk would like to get their hands. And for once the thriller category is well earned. Featuring Jonathan Pryce, Cherie Lunghi and Carmen du Sautoy. Dir: Jack Gold. Screenplay: Philip Mackie; based on the book by Hubert Monteilhet. Channel 4, 7 and 8 November 1984.

The President's Mistress (1978). Spies under – and in – the bed in Washington. And the bed is the President's! Highly unlikely but excellently made espionage thriller with some very professional performances including those of Beau Bridges, Karen Grassie, Susan Blanchard – and all the way from *Dallas* – Larry Hagman. Dir: John Llewellyn Moxey. Screenplay: Tom Lazarus. ITV, 22 April 1985.

The Prince of Central Park (1977). Very off-beat story about a couple of kids who run away from their horrid foster-mother and take up residence in a tree in New York's Central Park! And their unlikely ally is Ruth Gordon, a sweet old girl with grit. A quite neat balance between humour, sentiment and adventure in a very unlikely plot. Also featuring T.J. Hargrave, Lisa Richards, Marc Vahanian, Eda Reiss Merin and Carol Gustafson. Dir: Harvey Hart. Screenplay: Jeb Rosebrook. BBC2, 13 April 1985.

A Question of Guilt (1978). Another American TV feature based on facts, and it carries a real K.O. wallop as it goes to work showing up the more unpleasant side of the American legal system. It tells a story about a woman

accused of the murder of her two small daughters who finds her actual crime in the court is her loose-living style rather than anything else more concrete. Tuesday Weld repeatedly steals scenes as the accused. Also featuring Ron Leibman, Viveca Lindfors, M. Emmet Walsh, Lana Wood and Peter Masterson. Dir: Robert Butler. Screenplay: Jack and Mary Willis. BBC1, 2 March 1985.

A Question of Honour (1981). An ex-New York cop co-wrote and produced this story about one of the Force's patrolmen whose ambition it is to bring off the big cop (of the crooks) as the culmination of his career but finds himself in opposition to his mates when he finally gets the chance to achieve this ambition. (The producer – writer Sonny Grosso – was actually the man who smashed the infamous 'French Connection' drugs ring.) Featuring Ben Gazzara, Paul Sorvino, Robert Vaughn, Tony Roberts and Danny Aiello. Dir: Jud Taylor. Screenplay: Budd Schulberg; from the book by Sonny Grosso and Philip Rosenberg. BBC1, 16 July 1984.

A Question of Love (1978). Based carefully, and thoughtfully, on a true story of the legal custody battle by a lesbian divorcée to keep her child. Featuring Gena Rowlands, Jane Alexander, Ned Beatty, Clu Gulaher, Bonnie Bedelia and Keith Michell. Dir: Jerry Thorpe, Screenplay: William Blinn. Channel 4, 9 October 1984.

Rage (1980). David Soul as a man accused of rape, convicted in spite of his protestations of innocence and then subjected to ordeal by group therapy for sex offenders. Also featuring James Whitmore, Yaphet Kotto and Caroline McWilliams. Dir: Bill Graham. Screenplay: George Rubino. Channel 4, 16 October 1984.

Reflections (1983). Irish-made – with plenty of authentic atmosphere – tale of a writer who rents a country cottage for the summer to complete his book but finds too many local distractions to achieve it. Shown on the large screen before shown on the small one, though made for the latter (for full details see 'Releases of the Year' section of the 1984–5 *Film Review*). Featuring Gabriel Byrne, Fionnulla Flanagan and

Harriet Walter. Dir: Kevin Billington. Screenplay: John Banville; based on his novella *The Newton Letter*. Channel 4, 5 July 1984.

Rosie: The Rosemary Clooney Story (1982). To the uninitiated, the somewhat surprising true story of the dance-band vocalist and soloist of the title, revealing her unhappy girlhood, marital disasters, complete breakdown and finally her brave climb back to comeback. Featuring Sondra Locke, Tony Orlando, Penelope Milford and John Karlen. Dir: Jackie Cooper. Screenplay: Katharine Coker; based on the book by Clooney and Raymond Strait. Channel 4, 28 May 1985.

Sacred Hearts (1984). Comedy with lots of tugging at the heart-strings, set at the beginning of World War II, in an orphanage, and based on the true experiences of writer-director Barbara Rennie and her mother. And because of that basis of fact it is well above the routine treatment of this kind of story. Featuring Anna Massey, Catrin Cartlidge, Oona Kirsch and Fiona Shaw. Dir. and Screenplay: Barbara Rennie. Channel 4, 16 May 1985.

Sam Hill: Who Killed the Mysterious Mr Foster? (1970). The answer to that question is finally revealed in this somewhat unusual – and welcome – western about a sheriff with a drink problem and the three mysterious strangers who suddenly appear on the scene. Featuring Ernest Borgnine, Judy Geeson, Bruce Dern, J.D. Cannon, Will Geer, Sam Jaffe, Slim Pickens and Jay C. Flippen. Dir: Fielder Cook. Screenplay: Richard Levinson and William Link. ITV, 3 August 1984.

The Scarlet and the Black (1983). Gregory Peck as priest Hugh O'Flaherty who when the Nazis took over in Rome managed continually to thwart the Germans by hiding Allied POWs on the run; in particular his duel of wits with Gestapo Colonel Kappler, played by Christopher Plummer. Nice acting from the duo, and from a starry supporting cast including John Gielgud, Raf Vallone, Walter Gotell, T.P. McKenna, Barbara Bouchet and Ken Colley. Dir: Jerry London. Screenplay: David Butler. ITV, 29 May 1985.

Scout's Honour (1980). Amusing lightweight comedy about a middle-aged child-detesting woman who is forced by her ex-Scout boss into organizing a local Scouts group – with all the predictable results. Featuring Gary Coleman, Katharine Helmond, Wilfrid Hyde White, Pat O'Brien and Joanna Moore. Dir: Henry Levin. Screenplay: Bennett Fletcher. ITV, 20 December 1984.

Scruples (1981). The feature-length movie which it was hoped would launch a TV series based on the novel by Judith Krantz. It depicts the troubles of a filthy-rich boutique-owner who returns to Beverly Hills with a new husband to find a major takeover crisis on her hands. Maybe the failure to take off was due to one's difficulty in feeling sorry for the characters. Featuring Shelley Smith, Priscilla Barnes, Dirk Benedict, James Darren and Elizabeth Edwards. Dir: Robert Day. Screenplay: Camille Marchetta. BBC1,12 June 1985.

The Seeding of Sarah Burns (1979). Though made five years and more back, this movie about surrogate motherhood was acutely topical when shown in Britain, with writer-director Sandor Stern exploring the several sides of the problem. Nice work from Kay Lenz as the girl willing to be implanted with another woman's embryo. Also featuring Martin Balsam, Cliff de Young and Cassie Yates. Dir. and Screenplay: Sandor Stern. Channel 4, 11 September 1984.

Side Show (1979). The most interesting thing about this routine story – about a 16-year-old lad with a flair for puppetry who, lured to the Big Top, finds life under it less glamorous than expected, especially when he becomes a killer's target for tonight – is that it was directed by TV's stout (in every way) private eye William (Frank Cannon) Conrad. Featuring Lance Kerwin, Connie Stevens, Tony Franciosa and Red Buttons. Dir: William Conrad. Screenplay: George Kirgo. Channel 4, 28 August 1984.

The Silence of Donald Lang (1979). Apparently based on the true story of a deaf and dumb young black, charged with the murder of a Chicago prostitute, who is judged unfit to plead and is committed to incarceration for life and becomes the subject of a five-year-long struggle by his (deaf) attorney to free him. Strong stuff, fine performances. Featuring Paul Sorvino, Le Var Burton and Brian Dennehy. Dir: Frank Perry. Screenplay: Ernest Tidyman. BBC2, 23 August 1984.

Sole Survivor (1969). Superior TV drama about the investigation of the mystery of the crashed US bomber found 17 years after the war in the Libyan desert, some 700 miles from where it was supposed to have gone down. (Major) Vince Edwards eventually uncovers the solution to that discrepancy. Also featuring Richard Basehart and William Shatner. Dir: Paul Stanley. Screenplay: Guerdon Trueblood. BBC2, 10 August 1984.

Some Kind of Miracle (1979). Care-free becomes caring when the bridegroom-to-be is crippled while surfing and the bride-to-be finds life has suddenly become a very serious business. Featuring David Dukes, Andrea Marcovicci and Art Hindle. Dir: Jerrold Freedman. Screenplay: Mary and Jack Wills. ITV, 15 March 1985.

Something about Amelia (1984). A carefully constructed, non-sensational treatment which explores that controversial and painful subject: incest. The devastating effect on a family when the 13-year-old daughter reveals that her father is having sex with her. The restraint and power of the film brought it a well deserved award. Featuring Ted Danson, Glenn Close, Roxana Zal and Olivia Cole. Dir: Randa Haines. Screenplay: William Hanley. BBC2, 12 June 1985.

A Song for Europe (1984). Echoes of historical fact are given off by this fictional tale about a man with integrity who reports his multi-national drugs firm employers to the Common Market authorities for breaking the rules, with unexpectedly horrific consequences to himself and family. Absorbing drama: a good example of Anglo-German collaboration. Featuring David Suchet, Maria Schneider, Laura and Vincent Jansen and Anne-Marie Blanc. Dir: John Goldschmidt. No screenplay credit shown. Channel 4, 23 May 1985.

Sophia Loren – Her Own Story

(1980). Careful – *too* careful (perhaps understandably) account of the pretty eventful life of the star. Confusingly, she plays both herself and her mother! Other players assay other star roles such as John Gavin as Cary Grant, Edmund Purdom as Vittorio de Sica, etc., never a very satisfactory ploy. Also featuring Armand Assante, Rip Torn and Veronica Wells. Dir: Mel Stuart. Screenplay: Joanna Crawford; based on the A.E. Hotchner book. BBC1, 25 January 1985.

Stand by Your Man (1981). Biopic about the early life and career of Country and Western warbler Tammy Wynette – played and actually sung here by Annette O'Toole. Fine stuff for C-and-W fans. Also featuring Tim McIntire, Cooper Huckabee and James Hampton. Dir: Jerry Jameson. Screenplay: John Gay. Channel 4, 14 May 1985.

A Step out of Line (1970). A movie that sets out to find some sort of excuse for three Vietnam war veterans who decide the best way to the good life they want is to rob a bank. And quite a bit of humour is mixed with the action. Featuring Peter Falk, Vic Morrow, Peter Lawford and Jo Ann Pflug. Dir: Bernard McEveety. Screenplay: Steve Shagen and S.S. Schweitzer. BBC1, 10 August 1984.

The Suicide's Wife (1979). The problems of the young wife of a failed teacher who takes the suicide's way out and leaves his widow to bring up their somewhat difficult young son. Featuring Angie Dickinson, Gordon Pinsent, Peter Donat and Todd Lookingland. Dir: John Newland. Screenplay: Dennis Nemec. Channel 4, 18 September 1984.

Summer Lightning (1984). Nicely made and warmly acted story of love and jealousy – in fact Ivan Turgenev's story *First Love* transposed to Ireland in the 1940s. Top-class TV film. Featuring Tom Bell, Leonie Mellinger, Dearbhla Molloy, David Warner and Paul Scofield. Dir: Paul Joyce. Screenplay: Joyce and Derek Mahon. Channel 4, 30 May 1985.

Summer Solstice (1981). Moving story of life-long devotion between a man and a woman, with Henry Fonda giving his last-ever acting performance and doing it in splendid *On Golden Pond* style. Also featuring Myrna Loy, Stephen Collins and Lindsay Crouse. Dir: Ralph Rosenblum. Screenplay: Bill Phillips. Channel 4, 7 October 1984.

Survival of Dana (1979). About a nice American high-school girl who falls in with bad company and joins a gang of 'middle-class misfits'. Featuring Melissa Sue Anderson, Robert Carradine, Marion Ross and Talia Balsam. Dir: Jack Starrett. Screenplay: Frank Norwood. BBC1, 7 June 1985.

Sweet Hostage (1975). Highly unusual TV feature about an escaped mental patient who abducts a teenage girl he fears may lead his pursuers to his secret hide-out and then finds himself falling in love with her during their enforced shared experiences. Featuring Martin Sheen (excellent), Linda Blair, and Jeanne Cooper. Dir: Lee Phillips. Screenplay: Ed Hume; based on the novel *Welcome to Xanadu* by Nathaniel Benchley. BBC1, 8 September 1984.

A Tattered Web (1971). Lots of difficult decisions to be taken by Los Angeles cop Lloyd Bridges when he finds himself torn between his duty and his filial obligations and the dangers of his own continued existence. Also Frank Converse, Sally Shockley, Broderick Crawford and Anne Helm. Dir: Paul Wendkos. Screenplay: Art Wallace. ITV, 19 July 1984.

Terrible Joe Moran (1984). The legendary James Cagney in his TV-movie debut, as an old fighter now isolated in his vast mansion, shows all his old command of the medium and gives a memorable performance in spite of everything his advanced age can do to defeat him. They do not make them like this any more, alas! Also featuring Art Carney, Ellen Barkin and Peter Gallagher. Dir: Joseph Sargent. Screenplay: Frank Cucci. Channel 4, 7 May, 1985.

They Call It Murder (1971). A shot! A body in the swimming pool. Who'sit and whodunnit? And at the centre of the mystery is a very smart impersonation. Featuring Jim Hutton, Edward Asner, Jessica Walter, Leslie Nielsen and Jo Ann Pflug. Dir: Walter Grauman. Screenplay: Sam Rolfe; based on the novel by Erle Stanley Gardner. ITV, 30 July 1984.

Toma (1973). Tony Musante as the real-life detective of the title who infiltrated and smashed a gambling crime ring. And the actual detective involved, Dave Toma, himself appears in a small role. Also featuring Simon Oakland and Susan Strasberg. Dir: R.T. Heffron. Screenplay: Edward Hume and Gerald Dipego. ITV, 2 August 1984.

True Grit: A Further Adventure (1978). Nobody can ever replace John Wayne, so this attempt to re-create (by Warren Oates) one of his most successful characterizations in a pilot feature for a suggested series was always doomed to failure. Also featuring Lisa Pelikan and Lee Meriwether. Dir: R.T. Heffron. Screenplay: Sandor Stern. BBC1, 29 August 1984.

A Very Missing Person (1972). Routine detection thriller with the oddity that the private eye involved is female and she assists the cops in their search for a missing heiress. And the fact that Eve Arden plays the lady sleuth lifts the whole thing on to a far higher plane than it might otherwise have reached. Also featuring Julie Newmar and James Gregory. Dir: Russ Mayberry. Screenplay: Philip Reisman Jr. ITV, 23 August 1984.

Wait 'Til Your Mother Gets You Home (1982). Paul Michael Glaser – a fugitive from *Starsky and Hutch* – involved in the old plot about a man and wife switching roles and both finding it not that easy. Supposedly based on truth in this case. Also featuring Dee Wallace and Peggy McKay. Dir: Bill Persky. Screenplay: Persky and D. Eyre. Channel 4, 27 November 1984.

Weekend of Terror (1970). As spent by three nuns (Carol Lynley, Lois Nettleton and Jane Wyatt, three very good performances) when they become the unfortunate victims of a kidnap plot. This goes sour when, by accident, a hostage is killed and the crooks decide notwithstanding to press ahead with their plot to obtain the ransom. Also featuring Robert Conrad and Lee Majors. Dir: Jud Taylor, Screenplay: Lionel E. Siegel. ITV, 22 July 1984.

Welcome Home, Johnny Bristol

(1971). Martin Landau as the Vietnam POW who returns to find that his home town has apparently vanished off the face of the earth! Also featuring Jane Alexander, Brock Peters, Forrest Tucker, Martin Sheen, Pat O'Brien and Mona Freeman. Dir: George McCowan. Screenplay: S.R. Greenberg. BBC2, 3 November 1984.

When Michael Calls (1972). The caller is a character presumed long dead and the called-on is an increasingly terrified woman, the caller's aunt. When the killings start the aunt soon begins to suspect she is fairly high on the killer's list of victims. Well directed, neat and densely textured thriller. Featuring Elizabeth Ashley, Ben Gazzara, Karen Pearson and Michael Douglas. Dir: Phillip Leacock. Screenplay: James Bridges. ITV. 29 July 1984.

White Mama (1980). The great Bette Davis as impressive as ever as the elderly lady who befriends the black youth (Ernest Harden) she takes as a lodger in order to help out with her pecuniary problems. Also featuring Eileen Heckart and Virginia Capers. Dir: Jackie Cooper. Screenplay: Robert C.S. Downs. Channel 4, 11 December 1984.

Wilma (1977). The true story of a girl polio victim who grew up and through her determination and dedication became a gold medal-holding sprinter in the 1960 Olympics. Cicely Tyson plays the girl, Blanche Rudolph. Also featuring Shirley Jo Finney, Jason Bernard and Joe Seneca. Dir. and Screenplay: Bud Greenspan. ITV, 4 March 1985.

Winter Flight (1984). Romance between RAF flyer Reece Dinsdale and barmaid Nicola Cowper, the handsome lass who serves all that NAAFI beer. Also featuring Gary Olsen and Sean Bean. One of the Enigma/Goldcrest TV features. Dir: Roy Battersby. Screenplay: Alan Janes. Channel 4, 20 December 1984.

The Woman's Room (1980). Lee Remick mightily impressive as the heroine of Marilyn French's best-selling feminist novel about a 38-year-old divorcée looking back at the past as she embarks on a more hopeful future. Also featuring Colleen Dewhurst and Patty Duke Austin. Dir: Glenn Jordan, Screenplay: Carol Sobieski. BBC2, 6 August 1984.

You Lie So Deep My Love (1974). Value-for-money thriller which includes murder, the lust for cash, and lust for the lovely lady by an errant husband. A mixture stirred with style by the aptly named helmsman D.L. Rich! Cast includes Don Galloway, Barbara Anderson and Walter Pidgeon. Dir: David Lowell Rich. No screenplay credit listed. ITV, 26 July 1984.

You'll Never See Me Again (1973). That is what young wife Jess Walton says when she walks out on hubbie David Hartman, who, when he starts to track her down, finds himself piling up evidence against himself as her murderer! Familiar enough; but most neatly done. Also featuring Joseph Campanella, Jane Wyatt and Bo Svenson. Dir: Jeannot Szwarc. Screenplay: William Wood and Gerald Dipego; from a story by Cornell Woolrich. ITV, 13 January 1985.

The Young Maverick (1978). Pilot feature for the series that followed, with Charles Frank as the son of Maverick Senior (James Garner) following in dad's gambling footsteps by becoming deeply involved in a poker game with a $20,000 pot. Also featuring Susan Blanchard, John Dehner, Donna Mills, James Woods, John McIntire and Howard Duff. Dir: Hy Averback. Screenplay: Robert Van Sooyk. BBC1, 8 August 1984.

The Young Visiters (1984). Delightful screen adaptation of nine-year-old Daisy Ashford's book, for which J.M. Barrie's enthusiasm resulted in publication 25 years after it was written. Featuring Tracey Ullman, Alec McCowen, Kenny Ireland and John Standing. Dir. and Screenplay: James Hill; based on Daisy Ashford's inimitable book. Channel 4, 25 December 1984.

The following TV films were shown at the end of June 1984, too late to be included in last year's feature. For the record they were:

The Cracker Factory (1979). The late Natalie Wood as a woman fighting addiction to the bottle. Also featuring Juliet Mills and Vivian Blaine. Dir: Richard Shapiro. Screenplay: R. Sha-piro; from the book by Joyce Rebeta and R Burditt. BBC, 29 June 1984.

Disaster in the Sky (1977). A star-bright list of passengers facing up to what appears to be the inevitable crash of their plane. Featuring Doug McClure, Peter Graves, Burgess Meredith, Susan Strasberg, Tina Louise and Brock Peters. Dir: David Lowell Rich. Screenplay: R.L. Joseph, M. Dolinsky and W. Robert. ITV, 24 June 1984.

A Few Days in Weasel Creek (1981). A young couple's eventful trek by road from Georgia to Texas. Winning! Featuring Marie Winningham and Joan Hammond. Dir: Dick Lowry. Screenplay: Durrell Royce Grays; based on the book by Joanna Brent. Channel 4, 26 June 1984.

Golden Girl (1979). The never released (in Britain) cinema feature about a girl athlete struggling to get to the Olympics, blown up to a two-part TV movie, with Susan Anton, James Coburn, Robert Culp, Curt Jurgens and Leslie Caron. Dir: Joseph Sargent. Screenplay: John Kohn; based on the novel by Peter Lear. ITV, 23 and 25 June 1984.

Mayday 40,000 Ft (1976). Pilot David Janssen facing the problem of a gun-toting villain on the loose in his plane and giving the orders. Also featuring Ray Milland, Broderick Crawford, Shani Wallis, Jane Powell and Lynda Day George. Dir: Robert Butler. Screenplay: Austin Ferguson, Dick Nelson and A.J. Fenady; based on the book by Ferguson. BBC. 23 June 1984.

Risko (1976). Ex-'Dead End Kid' Gabriel Dell as a private eye ignoring the DA's orders in order to bring a young girl's killer to court. Dir: Bernard Kowalski. ITV, 27 June 1984.

Sky Heist (1975). Feature introduction to a series that never was, planned to show off the prowess of the Los Angeles Aero Bureau. With Don Meredith, Joseph Campanella, Stefanie Powers and Frank Gorshin. Dir: Lee H. Katzin. Screenplay: W.F. Nolan. BBC, 30 June 1984.

Releases of the Year

In this section you will find details of films released in Great Britain from 1 July 1984 to the end of June 1985 – the period covered by all the reference features in the book. The precise dating of some of these releases is a little tricky in view of the current lack of any rigidity in the release pattern, but dates given refer to the general release and not pre-release.

When it comes to films which are sent out on a 'floating' release I have added, wherever possible, the date of the film's first London showing because usually this is also the first British showing.

The normal abbreviations operate as follows: Dir – for Director; Pro – for Producer; Assoc Pro – for Associate Producer; Ex Pro – for Executive Producer; Pro Ex – for Production Executive; Pro Sup – for Production Supervisor; Pro Con – for Production Controller; Co-Pro – for Co-Producer; Pro Co-Ord – for Production Co-Ordinator; Ph – for Photographer; Ed – for Editor; Art – for Art Director; Pro Des – for Production Designer; M – for Music; and a few others which will be obvious.

Abbreviations for the name of film companies are also pretty obvious when used, such as Fox for 20th Century-Fox, Rank for Rank Film Distributors, and UIP for Universal International Pictures. Where known, the actual production company is given first, the releasing company last.

When it comes to nationality of the film you will find that this is noted wherever possible – those films without any mention of country of origin can be taken as being American – but in these days of increasing international co-productions between two, three and even four countries it is sometimes a little difficult to sort out where the premier credit is due.

Finally, unless otherwise specified (e.g. in black-and-white), it can safely be taken that the film is made in Technicolor or some similar colour process.

Censorship certificates: the position now is that *U* represents films suitable for persons of any age; *PG* (Parental Guidance) represents films which some parents might consider unsuitable for their children; *15* means no persons under that age will be admitted and films certified with an *18* means that nobody under that age will be admitted to the cinema while that film is showing.

Note: 'No cert' means that no certificate had been issued by the initial showing of the film but one may be issued at a later date.

The Act. (Made in 1982 with the title *Bless 'Em All*.) A minor exposé movie searchlighting crooked politics and crooked politicians in America: about a 'bent' lawyer who asks for, and gets, a two million dollar reward from a union leader for freeing another union leader from a jail sentence for corruption. But the payee then orders his underlings to recover the cash by hook, crook or murder, once that freedom is obtained. A lot of real baddies and hardly a goodie in sight! Cast: Robert Ginty, Sarah Langenfeld, Nick Surovy, John Aprea, John Tripp, Eddie Albert, James Andronica, John Cullum, Roger Davis, Pat Hingle, David Huddleston, Jill St. John, Arika Wells and Tom Hunter. Dir and Co-Pro (latter with David Greene): Sig Shore. Ex Pro: Ron Gorton. Screenplay: Robert Lipsyte. Ph: Benjamin Davis. Ed: Ron Kalish. Pro Des: Steve Wilson. M: John Sebastian and Phil Goldston. (Artists Releasing Corp./Film Ventures International–Ciné US Products-Entertainment Films) Rel: floating; first shown London (Studio), 5 Oct 1984. 94 mins. Cert PG.

All of Me. Generally hilarious crazy comedy about a dead woman's 'soul' taking half possession of a living man's body and giving him all the problems that one might imagine from such a ludicrous situation: for instance, the difficulties of making love, washing, shaving and even spending pennies when the male and female halves are in conflict about the action to be taken! Outstanding comedy performances by Steve Martin and Lily Tomlin with good backing from the rest of the cast including: Victoria Tennant, Madeleine Smith, Richard Libertini, Dana Elcar, Jason Bernard and Selma Diamond. Dir: Carl Reiner. Pro: Stephen Friedman. Screenplay: Phil Alden Robinson; from the Henry Olek adaptation of the Ed Davis book, *Me Too*. Ph: Richard Kline. Ed: Bud Molin. Pro Des: Edward Carfagno. M: Patrick Williams. (King's Road/Universal–EMI) Rel: 18 Jan 1985. 91 mins. Cert 15.

Amadeus. Elaborate and musically splendid adaptation of the Peter Shaffer stage play based on the life of Wolfgang Amadeus Mozart; more particularly on the jealousy between the Austrian Court composer Antonio Salieri and his far more gifted young rival: con-

Tom Hulce (right) expressing his gratitude to F. Murray Abraham in *Amadeus*.

troversially suggesting that the latter was to some extent involved in Mozart's early death and at the same time presenting the supposition he was partly responsible for Mozart's completion on his deathbed of his great *Requiem*. But that leaves out the heart of the matter: Salieri's frenzied blaming of God for the different levels of the two composer's musical gifts. A fine (Oscar-winning) performance by F. Murray Abraham as Salieri; plus a disastrous piece of miscasting in the title role, which presents Mozart as a musically gifted, coarse buffoon. Rest of cast including: Tom Hulce (Mozart), Elizabeth Berridge, Simon Callow, Roy Dotrice, Christine Ebersole, Jeffrey Jones, Charles Kay, Kenny Baker, Lisabeth Bartlett, Barbara Bryne, Martin Cavani, Roderick Cook, Milan Demjanenko, Peter Digesu, Richard Frank, Patrick Hines, Nicholas Kepros, Philip Lenkowsky, Herman Meck-

ler, Jonathan Moore, Cynthia Nixon, Brian Pettifer, Vincent Schiavelli, Douglas Seale, Miroslav Sekera, John Strauss and Karl-Heinz Teuber. Dir: Milos Forman. Pro: Saul Zaentz. Ex Pro: Michael Hausman and Bertil Ohlsson. Screenplay: Peter Shaffer; based on his stage play. Ph: Miroslav Ondricek. Ed: Nena Danevic and Michael Chandler. Assoc Ed: Debra McDermott. Art: Karel Cerny and Francesco Chianese. Pro Des: Patrizia von Brandenstein. M Co-Ord: John Strauss. M Sup: Neville Marriner with the Academy of St. Martin-in-the-Fields, Academy Chorus, Ambrosian Opera Chorus and the Choristers of Westminster Abbey. (Saul Zaentz Co. – Thorn EMI). Rel: 8 March 1985. 159 mins. Cert PG.

The Ambassador. Fast-moving, not entirely credible, but amusing and nicely tense thriller set against a realistic background of the Israeli-Palestinian pother, with Robert Mitchum as the US Ambassador doing his best to bring peace between the factions. He fails disastrously, finding himself the victim of a political blackmail plot which puts himself, his marital happiness and even the maintenance of peace in the Middle East at risk. Handling the affair with a nice sense of pace is that steady old British director J. Lee Thompson; with Ellen Burstyn (wife), Rock Hudson (security chief), Fabio Testi (lover) and a reasonably restrained Donald Pleasence as the Israeli defence boss. Rest of cast: Heli Golden-Berg, Michal Bat Adam, Ori Levy, Uri Gavriel, Zachi Noy, Yossi Shiloah, Shmuelik Kraus, Yossi Virginsky, Iftah Katzur, Yaacov Banai, Avi Kleinberger, Haim Banai, Peter Freistadt, Danny Noiman,

33

Robert Mitchum (left), Ellen Burstyn and Donald Pleasence and (left) Rock Hudson with Mitchum in *The Ambassador*.

Rachel Steiner, Dana Ben Yehuda, Zehava Keilos, Esther Zabco, Avi Pnini and Yosef Bee. Dir: J. Lee Thompson. Pro: Menahem Golan, Yoram Globus and Issac Kol. Pro Co-Ord: Henia Mendelbaum. Screenplay: Max Jack. Ph: Adam Greenberg. Art: Yoram Barzillai. M: Dov Seltzer. (Golan Globus for Northbrook Films–Cannon Group) Rel: 23 Nov 1984. 95 mins. Cert 18.

American Dreamer. Often looking uncannily like the late Natalie Wood, JoBeth Williams plays a housewife in a rut, with a workaholic and neglectful husband. When she wins a literary prize of a week in Paris, a knock on the head makes her think she is, and causes her to act outrageously like, her favourite pulp-fiction heroine, sometimes to amusing effect – more especially when the author, Tom Conti, is involved. It is all mildly amusing. Rest of cast including: Giancarlo Giannini, Coral Browne, James Staley, C. B. Barnes, Huckleberry Fox, Pierre Santini, Pierre Olaf, Jean Rougerie, Brian Eatwell, Guy Montagne, Fernand Guiot, Yanou Collart, Michael Bardinet, Leon Zitrone, Jerzy Rogulski, Eugeninzc Priwiezencew, Marius Pusjzo, Vlodek Press, Beatrice Camurat, Genevieve Omini, Gikberte Geniat, Alexandra Sikorska, Katia Tchenko, Alain Janey, Victir Heutschy, Eleanor Heutschy, Rick Rosenthal, Jeffrey Kramer, Alan Haufrect and Robin Coleman. Dir: Rick Rosenthal. Pro: Doug Chapin. Ex Pro: Barry Krost. Screenplay: Jim Kouf and David Greenwalt; from a story by Ann Biderman. Ph: Giuseppe Rotunno. Ed: Anne Goursaud. Pro Des: Brian Eatwell (CBS Theatrical Films-Rank Film Dist) Rel: 14 June 1985. 105 mins. Cert PG.

Annie's Coming Out. A remarkably moving film from Australia which is based on newspaper headlines of some years back; about a therapist's struggle to get her intelligent spastic charge (who suffered brain damage at birth) released from the Institution which treats the inmates as little more than vegetables. Angela Punch McGregor gives a brilliant performance as the young woman who takes her case to court and persuades the judge (Charles Tingwell, superb) *her* judgement is correct. Other fine performances by Drew

A highly dangerous moment for JoBeth Williams and Tom Conti in *American Dreamer.*

Forsythe as the long-suffering therapist's boyfriend and Simon Chilvers as her astute lawyer; and a remarkable performance by Tina Arhondis, a bright-eyed teenaged spastic who is horribly crippled. Altogether a most unusual, thought-provoking and yet amusing movie. Rest of cast: Monica Maughan, Mark Butler, Philippa Baker, Liddy Clark, Wallis Eaton, John Frawley, Alistair Duncan, Brett Reynolds, James Wright, Joy Westmore, Lyn Collingwood, Laurie Dobson, Carl Bleazby, Judith Graham and Ann Sutherland. Dir: Gil Brealey. Pro: Don Murray. Ex Pro: Don Harley. Screenplay: John Patterson and Chris Borthwick. Ph: Mick von Bornemann. Ed: Lindsay Frazer. Art: Mike Hudson. M: Simon Walker. Pro Sup: Colleen Clark. Pro Co-Ord: Jo Stewart.

(Film Australia–Enterprise Pictures) Rel: floating; first shown London (Classics, Chelsea and Tott Ct Rd), 23 Nov 1984. 92 mins. Cert PG.

Another Country. Julian Mitchell's own adaptation for the screen of his highly successful stage play about life in a top English public school in the 1930s, and said to portray the beginning of the friendship between British Civil Servants and acting Russian agents (of the 1950s) Guy Burgess and Donald Maclean. The writer's suggestion seems to be that the two came together because both were outsiders, one because of his homosexuality and the other because of his Marxist convictions. In any case it is a penetrating analysis of both the public school system, and the beginning and end of a traitor, who finishes up miserably isolated in a foreign country. Fine playing from the cast: Rupert Everett, Colin Firth, Michael Jenn, Robert Addie, Rupert Wainwright, Tristan Oliver, Cary Elwes, Frederick Alexander,

Adrian Ross-Magenty, Geoffrey Bateman, Philip Dupuy, Guy Henry, Jeffrey Wickham, John Line, Gideon Boulting, Llewelyn Rees, Arthur Howard, Ivor Roberts, Crispin Redman, Nick Rowe, Kathleen St. John, Martin Wenner, Christopher Milburn, Tristram Jellinek, Tristram Wymark, Ralph Perry-Robinson and Anna Massey and Betsy Brantley. Dir: Marek Kanievska. Pro: Alan Marshall. Ex Pro: Robert Fox and Julian Seymour. Screenplay: Julian Mitchell; based on his own stage play. Ph: Peter Biziou. Ed: Gerry Hambling. Pro Des: Brian Morris. Art: Clinton Cavera. M: Michael Storey. (Goldcrest in assoc. with National Film Finance Corp./ Virgin Films/Fox/UK Film Dist. Ltd.) Rel: 24 Aug 1984. 90 mins. Cert 15.

Anou Banou or The Daughters of Utopia. A documentary financed by German TV made by the left-leaning, Paris-based, Lebanon-born Israeli Edna Politi, who manages to keep a reasonably fair balance through interviews

Rosanna Arquette gives up her all for Vincent Spano in *Baby, It's You.*

with six women who went to Palestine (as it was then) in the '20s and did not find the life of wine, honey and roses they fondly imagined they would enjoy there. Dir and Screenplay: Edna Politi. Ph: Nurith Aviv. Ed: Elisabeth Waelchli and Politi. (Archangel/ZDF–Circles) Rel: floating; first shown London (Everyman), 8 March 1985. 85 mins. Cert U. (Winner of 1st Prize at the International Festival of Women's Films, France and a special Jury Prize at the Mannheim International Film Festival 1980.)

Baby It's You. A rather sad little tale of an American high school girl pursued by an insufferable and pretty stupid young egotist who does his selfish and sometimes violent best to ruin her promising academic career. And the ambiguous ending makes you wonder if the silly girl will let him do it! Well made movie with plenty of popular music on the soundtrack and some nice performances, including a most appealing one by Rosanna Arquette as the

girl. Rest of cast: Vincent Spano, Joanna Merlin, Jack Davidson, Nick Ferrari, Dolores Messina, Leora Dana, Matthew Modine, William Joseph Raymond, Sam McMurray, Liane Curtis, Claudia Sherman, Marta Kober, Tracy Pollan, Rachel Dretzin, Susan Derendorf, Fisher Stevens and Robin Geller. Dir and Screenplay: John Sayles; based on a story by Amy Robinson. Pro: Griffin Dunne and Amy Robinson. Assoc Pro: Robert F. Colesberry. Ph: Michael Ballhaus. Ed: Sonya Polonsky. Pro Des: Jeffrey Townsend. (Double Play/Paramount–Mainline Pictures) Rel: floating; first shown London (Screen-on-the-Hill), 26 Oct 1984. 104 mins. Cert 15.

Baby Love – Roman Zair (Lemon Popsicle 5). Continuation of the series of Israeli movies about sex-obsessed youth, mixing surfing with rock numbers in a story about a young beau who while chasing all the girls objects to anyone chasing *his* sister. Cast: Yiftach Katzur, Zachi Noy, Jonathan Segal, Devorah Keidar, Menashe Warshawsky, Stefanie Petsch, Sabrina Cheval, Avi Hadash, Bea Fiedler, Dolly Dollar,

Misha Nathan, Rachel Shor, Ruth Davidson, Karol Markovich, Miri Toledano, Slaughter Jones, Reneta Langer, Orit Cohen, Shmuel Aizer, Zinger David, Marta Levis and Rachel Titlman. Dir: Dan Wolman. Pro: Menahem Golan and Yoram Globus. Ex Pro: Sam Waynberg. Assoc Pro: Amonon Globus and Rafi Adar. Pro Co-Ord: Henia Mendelbaum. Screenplay: Boaz Davidson and Eli Tabor. Ph: Ilan Rosenberg (2nd Unit Ph: Yachin Hirsch). Ed: Mark Helfrich. Assoc Ed: Uri Katoni. Art: Ariel Roshko. M: Jack Fishman. (Golan/Globus Productions, Tel Aviv Kinofilm, W. Berlin-Cannon) Rel: 21 Sept 1984. 84 mins. Cert 18.

Baby . . . Secret of the Lost Legend. For the most part, a simple, pleasing comedy about a young couple who come upon a brontosaurus family in the African jungle and then find themselves fighting off an evil professor's attempts to gain fame by taking mother and baby (after daddy B has been killed) back to Britain, leading to a quite out-of-key violent battle climax. Remarkable technical know-how makes the creatures entirely credible and baby B is quite irresistible! Cast: William Katt, Sean Young, Patrick McGoohan, Julian Fellowes, Kyalo Mativo, Hugh Quarshie, Olu Jacobs, Eddie Tagoe, Edward Hardwicke, Julian Curry, Alexis Meless, Susie Nottingham, Stephane Krora, Anthony Sarfoh, Jeannot Banny, Rogert Carlton and Theresa Taba. Dir: B. W. L. Norton. Pro: Jonathan T. Taplin. Ex Pro: Roger Spottiswoode. Screenplay: Clifford and Ellen Green. Assoc Pro: E. D. Hallenbeck. Ed: Howard Smith and David Bretherton. Ph: John Alcott. Pro Des: Raymond G. Storey. M: Jerry Goldsmith. (Touchstone Films/Disney – UK Film Dist) Rel: 29 March 1985. 93 mins. Cert PG.

Bachelor Party. The less endearing, rough and rude American type of comedy built around the occasion of the title, with the considerable saving grace of the performance of a pleasing actor called Tom Hanks, who plays the long-suffering bridegroom-to-be. Rest of cast: Tawny Kitaen, Adrian Zmed, George Grizzard, Barbara Stuart, Robert Prescott, William Tepper, Wendie Jo Sperber, Barry Diamond, Gary Grossman, Michael Dudikoff,

Mother brontosaurus is reunited with baby – watched (inset) by their human guardian angels, William Katt (left) and Sean Young in *Baby . . . Secret of the Lost Legend.*

Bradford Bancroft, Martina Finch, Deborah Harmon, Tracy Smith, Florence Schauffler, Sumant, John Bloom, Kenneth Kimmins, Gerald Prendergast, Brett Clark, Ji-Tu Cumbuka, Rosanne Katon, Dani Douthette, Katie Mitchell, Christopher Morley, Tony Alessandrini, Monique Gabrielle, Angela Aames, Richard Lorenzo Hernandez, Jonathan Tyler Trevillya, Billy Beck, Jim Hudson, Dean Dittman, Ben Slack, Milt Cogan, Greg Norberg, Coleen Maloney, Arlee Reed, Donald Thompson, Gregory Brown, Marcelino Razo, Pat Proft, Rebecca Perle, Elizabeth Arlen, Dorothy Bartlett, Annie Gaybis, Peaches Johnson, Sheri Shortt, Michael Yama, George Sasaki, Tad Honrio, W. T. Yamadera, Michele Starck, Renee Breault, Kim Robinson, Elizabeth Carter, Cynthia Kania, Bruce Block, Paul Angelo, Lisa Purcell, Hugh McPhillips, Angel, Lovey, Julia and Ginger ('Angel and the Reruns'). Dir: Neal Israel. Pro: Israel and Ron

Moler. Ex Pro: Joe Roth. Assoc Pro: Gautam Das. Screenplay: Israel and Pat Proft. Ph: Hal Trussell. (Add Ph: Tim Suhrstedt). Ed: Tom Walls. Art: Kevin Conlin and Martin Price. M and M Dir: Robert Folk. 2nd Unit Dir: Bruce Block. (Bachelor Party Productions/ Aspect Ratio Twin Continental Productions–Fox) Rel: 14 Aug 1984. 105 mins. Cert 18.

The Ball – Le Bal. Ettore Scola's award-winning (1984 Césars for Best Film, Best Direction, Best Music; 1984 Berlin Film Festival's Silver Bear for Best Direction; also an Oscar nomination) adaptation of the smash hit French stage musical; set against a background of a typical 1930s Paris Dance Hall of the Art Deco era, it tells a wordless – there is no dialogue whatsoever – history of France between 1936 and 1983, holding up a metaphorical mirror to life with all its small riches, victories, defeats, happinesses and miseries: a terpsichorean tapestry woven with wit, satire, humour and sadness adding up to a film of tremendous originality and imagina-

tion. Cast: Étienne Guichard, Régis Bouquet, Francesco de Rosa, Arnault Lecarpentier, Liliane Delval, Martine Chauvin, Danielle Rochard, Nani Nöel, Aziz Arbia, Marc Berman, Geneviève Rey-Penchenat, Michel van Speybroeck, Rossana di Lorenzo, Michel Toty, Raymonde Heudeline, Anita Picchiarini, Olivier Loiseau, Monica Scattini, Christophe Allwright, François Pick, Chantal Capron, Jean-François Perrier and Jean-Claude Penchenat. Dir: Ettore Scola. Pro: Giorgio Silvagni. Ex Pro: Franco Committeri. Assoc Pro: Mohamed Lakhdar Hamina. Screenplay: Ruggero Maccari, Jean-Claude Penchenat and Furio Scarpelli; after the show created by the Théâtre du Campagnol and based on an idea by Jean Claude Penchnat. Ph: Ricardo Aronovich. Ed: Raimondo Crociani. Pro Des: Luciano Ricceri. M: Vladimir Cosma. Choreography: D'Dee. (A Franco-Italian-Algerian Co-Production: Cinéproduction S.A. Paris/ Films A2 Paris/Massfilm, Rome/Oncic Algeria–Warner) Rel: floating; first shown London (Lumière and Gate, Notting Hill), 29 Nov 1984. 112 mins. Cert PG.

The Bay Boy. A story of adolescence set against the background of a place that Canadian director Daniel Petrie knows so well, having grown up there: Glace Bay, Novia Scotia. It is 1937, the Depression; lack of work and consequent poverty; the hard climate; a lad intended for the Church but put off it when a cleric makes a homosexual pass at him. Integral to the story is the boy's witnessing of a double murder by the local cop and for various reasons – fear of the cop and love of one of his daughters – denying he ever saw the foul deed. All this is told in a gentle manner, with a contrived happy ending: and a less than salty performance by the young actor involved in all this, Kiefer (son of star Donald) Sutherland. Rest of cast: Liv Ullmann, Peter Donat, Allan Scarfe, Mathieu Carrière, Chris Wiggins, Stephane Audran, Thomas Peacocke, Isabelle Mejias, Jane McKinnon, Leah Pinsent, Peter Spence, Josephine Chaplin, Pauline Laffont, Roy McMullin, Kathy McGuire, Robbie Gallivan, Robert Rose, Darren Arsenault, David Ferrey, Betty MacDonald, Fannie Shore, Sander Zilbert, Tom Rack, Robert Taylor, Joe MacPherson, Kevin McKenzie, Iris Currie, Francis MacNeil, Michael Egyes and Mary McKinnon. Dir and Screenplay: Daniel Petrie. Pro: John Kemeny and Denis Heroux. Co Pro: Rene Cleitman. Ex Pro: Susan Cavan and Frank Jacobs. Assoc Pro: Paulo de Oliveira. Ph: Claude Agostini. Ed: Susan Shanks (Add Ed: Daniel Petrie). Pro Des: Wolf Kroeger. Art: Richard

Beat Street a film featuring the new craze of breakdancing.

Harrison. M: Claude Bolling. (Bay Boy Pro, Montreal/Hachette–Fox Pro/Antenne 2 TV, France/Films A2 Paris in association with CTV Television–Rank Film Dist) Rel: floating; first shown London (Classic, Chelsea), 3 May 1985. 101 mins. Cert 15.

Beat Street. Consistently deafening, exhaustingly athletic (and acrobatic), largely black, beat musical for the youngsters who like this kind of thing; all about an aspiring disc jockey and a graffiti artist whose canvas for his paint-spraying prowess (?) is the New York subway trains. And the publicity has quite a bit to say about 'emerging culture', 'unique art', 'pride in the aesthetic' and all that jazz! Slickly produced and well enough acted. Cast: Rae Dawn Chong, Guy Davis, Jon Chardiet, Leon W. Grant, Saundra Santiago, Robert Taylor, Mary Alice (Smith), Shawn Elliot, Jim Borrelli, Dean Elliot, Franc Reyes, Tonya Pinkins, Lee Chamberlin, Antonia Rey, Duane Jones, Hope Clarke, Kool Here (Clive Campbell), Gina Belafonte, Kimry Smith, Jazzy Jay, Douglas Davis, Richard Thomsen, Kadeem Hardion, Tony Lopez 'Pex', Lorenso Soto 'Kuriaki', Dadi Pinero, Bill Anagnos, Pedro B. Serrano, Marvyn E. Griffith, Joseph Verhauz, Victor Magnotta, Erick Mourino, Renier Mourino, Tom Wright, Brett Smrz, Susan Roffer, Leon Stephenson, and the following Groups: Us Girls, Treacherous Three, Grand Master Melle Mel and the Furious Five, Afrika Bambaataa/Soul Sonic Force/Shango, The New York City Breakers, Rock Steady Crew and The Magnificent Force. Dir: Stan

Lathan. Pro: David V. Picker and Harry Belafonte. Assoc Pro: Mel Howard. Screenplay: Andy Davis, David Gilbèrt and Paul Golding; from a story by Steven Hager. Ph: Tom Priestley Jr. Ed: Dov Hoenig. Pro Des: Patrizia Von Brandenstein. M Pro: Belafonte and Arthur Baker. (Orion–Rank Film Dist) Rel: 6 July 1984. 106 mins. Cert PG.

Being and Doing. An Arts Council feature which sets out to show that 'Performance Art' is not just a modernistic gimmick but in fact has origins deep in our past, offering such evidence as the survival of folk rituals like Padstow's 'Hobby Horse' event. And there's a lot more to it than that – in the film. Dir: Ken McMullen. Script: Stuart Brisley. Ed: Robert Hargreaves and Clair Mussel. M: David Cunningham. (Match Films–Arts Council) Rel: floating; first shown London at the Film Festival in Nov 1984 and then for a season at the ICA from 6 March 1985. 58 mins. Cert U.

Benvenuta. A densely and not always too lucidly structured Franco-Belgian film from Flemish André Delvaux (whose few previous films include the award-winning *Rendezvous à Bray*) which confronts fiction with reality and then ambiguously mixes both in the story of a scriptwriter tracking down the author of a novel once considered scandalous in order to clear up some of the problems that face him in translating the book into a screenplay; his main object, to find out how close the novelist is to her fictional heroine, a professional pianist who falls madly in love with a philandering, older Italian magistrate. The ambiguity includes the screenwriter meeting both the author and her heroine creation in the same street! All beautifully played by Fanny Ardant, Vittorio Gassman and Françoise Fabian against lovely backgrounds of the city of Ghent. Rest of cast: Mathieu Carrière, Claire Wauthion, Phillipe Geluck, Anne Chappuis, Aramando Marra, Renato Scarpa, Franco Trevisi, Giufrida, Franco Agrisono, Goddart, Tamara Trifez, Beatrice Palme, Franz Joubert, Franco Bruno, Bert André, Muriel Buentinck, Muriel Lefèvre, Christina Borgogni, Jenny Tanghe and Toon Carette. Dir and Screenplay: André Delvaux; based on the novel *La Confession Anonyme* by

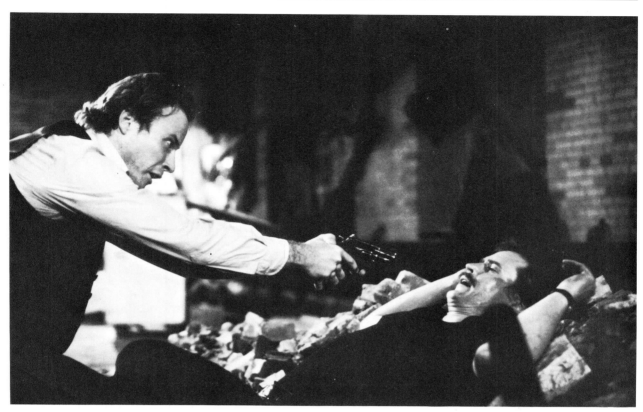

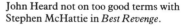

John Heard not on too good terms with Stephen McHattie in *Best Revenge*.

Suzanne Lilar. Pro: Jean-Claude Batz. Ph: Charlie Van Damme. Ed: Albert Jurgenson and Jean Goudier. Art: Claude Pignot. M: Frédéric Devresse; *Il maestro e la principiante* by Armando Marra and F. Chiaravalle and *Fenestra vascia* by the latter. (UGC/La Nouvelle Imagerie/FR3/Opera Films–Artificial Eye) Produced with the help of the

Ministry for the French Community of Belgium. Rel: floating; first shown London (Camden Plaza), 20 July 1984. 105 mins. Cert 15. (Winner of the Special Jury Prize at the Montreal Film Festival 1983.)

Best Revenge. A complicated thriller about a young drugs dealer who is blackmailed into undertaking a major dope-smuggling exercise, is crossed and double-crossed and is finally lucky to get away with his life – as well as quite a

bit of the loot! Lots of scenic backgrounds in Spain, the US and Morocco. Cast: John Heard, Levon Helm, Alberta Watson, Stephen McHattie, Moses Znaimer, John Rhys-Davies, Benjamin Gordon, Hrant Alianak, Tim McCauley, Angus MacInnes, Rob Garrison and John Evans. Dir: John Trent. Pro: Michael M. Lebowitz, in association with Pen Densham and John Watson. Ex Pro: David M. Perlmutter. Ph: John Coquillon. Screenplay: David Rothberg, Rick Rosenthal and Logan N. Danforth. Sup Ed: James Symons. Ph: John Coquillon. Pro Des: William Beeton. M: Keith Emerson. Assoc Pro: Richard Barton Lewis. (Black Cat Films in association with Polygram) Rel: floating; first shown London (The Studio and Cinecenta), 19 Oct 1984. 90 mins. Cert 18.

Beverly Hills Cop. Eddie Murphy (the black star so good in *Trading Places*) as a sometimes over-enthusiastic and headstrong young Detroit cop who when his dubiously employed pal is murdered by a couple of out-of-town hit men takes a Californian vacation in

Eddie Murphy (left) joins forces with Lisa Eilbacher and Judge Reinhold in *Beverly Hills Cop*.

order, against orders, to track down the crime boss who gave the order to slay, and with reckless bravado walks into the criminal headquarters to fight it out with all concerned. Nice performances, good pace, a fair quota of chuckles and a battle ending which stretches credibility beyond all limits as Murphy and his two aides armed only with a couple of revolvers overcome a whole arsenal of machine guns! Rest of cast: Judge Reinhold, John Ashton, Lisa Eilbacher, Ronny Cox, Steven Berkoff, James Russo, Jonathan Banks, Stephen Elliott, Gilbert R. Hill, Art Kimbro, Joel Bailey, Bronson Pinchot, Paul Reiser, Michael Champion, Frank Pesce, Gene Borkan, Michael Gregory, Alice Cadogan, Philip Levien, Karen Mayo-Chandler, Gerald Berns, William Wallace, Israel Juarbe, Randy Gallion and Damon Wayans. Dir: Martin Brest. Pro: Don Simpson and Jerry Bruckheimer. Ex Pro: Mike Moder. Screenplay: Daniel Petrie Jr; from a story by him and Danilo Bach. Ph: Bruce Surtees. Ed: Billy Weber and Arthur Coburn. Pro Des: Angelo Graham. Art: J. T. Murakami. M: Harold Faltermeyer. Assoc Pro: Linda Horner. (Paramount–UIP) Rel: 25 Jan 1985. 105 mins. Cert 15.

Birdy. Extremely interesting and pretty brave effort to bring this (cinematically) unlikely William Wharton novel to the cinema: a story about friendship and the devastating effects of war on some of those taking part in it, in particular the main character who, logged originally as 'missing in action' is now something of a nutcase confined to an asylum for the deranged, spending much of his time naked and curled up in a very birdlike posture. Flawed yet fascinating; one for those who like to venture out of the celluloid rut. Fine, sensitive performances from Matthew Modine and Nicolas Cage as the pals. Rest of cast including: John Harkins, Sandy Baron, Karen Young, Bruno Kirby, Nancy Fish, George Buck, Dolores Sage, R. L. Ryan, James Santini, Maude Winchester, Marshall Bell, Elizabeth Whitcraft, Sandra Beall, Victoria Nekko, Crystal Field, John Brumfield, Joe Lerer, Alice Truscott, Ed Taylor, Irving Selbst, Steve Lippe, William Clark, James Pruett, Priscilla Alden, Howard Kinsley, Robert Diamond and Bud Seese. Dir: Alan Parker. Pro: Alan Marshall. Ex Pro: David

Michael Caine with Michelle Johnson in *Blame it on Rio*.

Manson. Screenplay: Sandy Kroopf and Jack Behr; based on the William Wharton novel. Ph: Michael Seresin. Ed: Gerry Hambling. Pro Des: Geoffrey Kirkland. M: Peter Gabriel. Assoc Pro: Ned Kopp. (Tri-Star Pictures) Rel: floating; first shown London (Odeon, Haymarket), 14 June 1985. 120 mins. Cert 15. (Winner of Special Grand Jury Prize at the Cannes Film Festival 1985.)

Bitter Cane. A quite outstanding documentary feature – with obvious political implications – about the island of Haiti, filmed in secret by a crew who have opted to remain discreetly anonymous. It shows how Haiti, originally a French colony, achieved independence in 1800. It stayed that way, more or less, until the US's occupation, from 1915 to 1934. The island regained its freedom from foreign domination until in 1971 it came under the iron dictatorship of the ill-famed 'Papa Doc' Duvalier, whose methods caused the vast influx of Haitian refugees into the US – more than 300,000 are said to be in Brooklyn alone! Dir: Jacques Arcelin. Commentary by Jean-Claude Martineau. No other credits listed. (Haiti Films–The Other Cinema) Rel: floating; first shown London (Rio), 20 July 1984. 75 mins. No cert.

Blame it on Rio. Very reminiscent of a French film which presented the same situation with far greater subtlety and taste, a comedy about two fathers (and great friends) who take their two nubile teenage daughters on a holiday in Rio and the situation that arises when one dad is seduced by the other's daughter! The whole shaky affair is held together by another outstanding performance by Michael Caine as the conscience-stricken, reluctant lover. Rest of cast: Joseph Bologna, Valerie Harper, Michelle Johnson, Demi Moore, Jose Lewgoy and Lupe Gigilotti. Dir and Pro: Stanley Donen. Ex Pro: Larry Gelbart. Screenplay: Charlie Peters and Gelbart. Ph: Reynaldo Villalobos. Ed: George Hively and Richard Marden. Art: Marcos Flaksman. M: Ken Wannberg and Oscar Castro Neves. Assoc Pro: Robert Relyea. (Sherwood Productions Inc.–Orion–Thorn EMI) Rel: 7 Sept 1984. 97 mins. Cert PG.

Bleak Moments. Claimed by the ICA as 'the most wholly original film to be made in Britain in the last 20 years' (a claim backed up by several reviewers at the time) this 1971 movie, the only one ever to be made by Mike Leigh, was revived in the summer of 1984 for a five-week season by the ICA. Full details of the movie appeared in the 1973-4 *Film Review* .

Blood Simple. The film is anything but simple: a macabre, stylish, claustrophobic chiller in which four characters dance a deadly measure around each other, never understanding – rather, misunderstanding – what is happening to and around them but caught up in a net of violence and passion: the heavy, jealous bar-owner husband, the wayward wife, the barman lover and the sleazy, seedy private eye paid by the husband to kill the lover but double-crossing his employer. The action lags only temporarily before leaping to the horrific climax which pays homage, intentionally or otherwise, to Hitchcock. Cast: John Getz, Frances McDormand, Dan Hedaya, M. Emmet Walsh, Samm-Art Williams, Deborah Neumann, Raquel Gavia, Van Brooks, Senor Marco, William Creamer, Loren Bivens, Bob McAdams, Shannon Sedwick, Nancy Ginger and Rev. W. P. Robertson. Dir: Joel Coen. Pro: Ethan Coen. Ex Pro: Daniel F. Bacaner. Assoc Pro: Mark Silverman. Pro Co-Ord: Alma Kuttsuff. Screenplay: Joel and Ethan Coen. Ph: Barry Sonnenfeld. Ed: Roderick Jaynes, Peggy Conolly and Don Wiegmann. Pro Des: Jane Musky. M: Carter Burwell. (River Road Productions–Palace Pictures) Rel: 1 March 1985. 98 mins. Cert 18.

BMX Bandits. Thanks largely to their newfangled BMX fun bikes – the latest youth craze – three lively teenagers manage to outwit the pretty dim crooks when they stumble on their cache of hidden loot and subsequently dodge the police net thrown out for them when they start selling the stolen walkie-talkie sets, which are tuned to the cops'

BMX Bandits featured the versatility of these acrobatic new two-wheeled vehicles, and their riders.

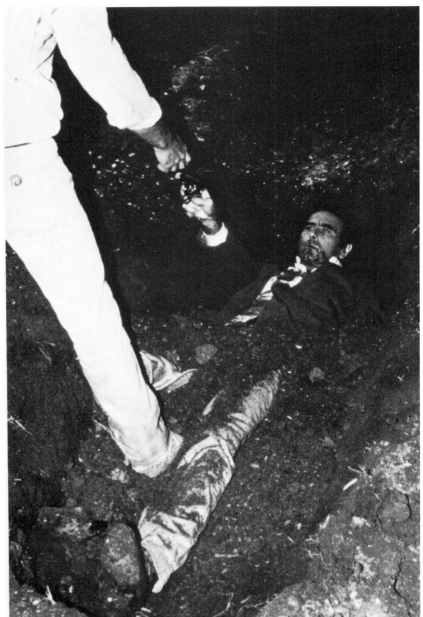

Dan Hedaya as the dead man who just won't lie down in *Blood Simple*.

own wavelength! An Australian equivalent, if plusher, of the British Children's Film Foundation movies; and jolly good stuff for the youngsters too. Cast: David Argue, John Ley, Bryan Marshall, Angelo d'Angelo, James Lugton, Nicole Kidman, Brian Sloman, Peter Browne, Bill Brady, Linda Newton, Bob Hicks, Guy Norris, Chris Hession, Norman Hodges, Tracy Wallace, Michael Gillette, Brian Best, Jerry d'Angelo, Malcolm Day, Ray Marshall, Patrick Manfield, Alan McQueen, Anthony Alafaci, Craig Hopcroft, Mary Irwin, Fiona Gage and Paul Flaherty. Dir: Brian Trenchard-Smith. Pro: Tom Broadbridge and Paul Davies. Screenplay: Patric Edgeworth; based on a screenplay by Russell Hagg. Assoc Pro: Brian D. Burgess. Ph: John Seale. Ed: Alan Lake. No Art credit. M: Colin Stead and Frank Stangio. (Nilsen Premiere–Rank Film Dist) Rel: 10 August 1984. 191 mins. Cert PG.

Bo Derek shows her form in *Bolero*.

Body Rock. The title is self-explanatory. Another movie in the *Breakdance* mould about a group of teenage graffitists and dance nuts; more particularly about one lad who is persuaded to turn professional. Cast includes: Lorenzo Lamas, Vicki Frederick, Cameron Dye, Michelle Nicastro, Ray Sharkey, Joeph Whipp and La Ron A. Smith. Dir: Marcelo Epstein. Pro: Jeffrey Schechtman. Ex Pro: Phil Ramone, C. J. Weber and John Feltheimer. Screenplay: Des-mond Nakano. Ph: Robby Muller. Ed: Richard Halsey. Pro Des: Guy Comtois. Art: Craig Stearns. Assoc Pro: Chuck Russell. (New World/Angeles Entertainment Group/Inverness Pro–Columbia) Rel: 8 Feb 1985. 93 mins. Cert 15.

Bolero. (Sub-titled *An Adventure in Ecstasy*.) Largely a celluloid exploration, and exploitation, by husband John Derek (screenplay, direction, and photography) of wife Bo Derek's very feminine body, with plenty of nudity, quite a lot of writhing couplings and, alas, very little else. Miss Derek plays a (surprisingly mature) virgin offering the gift of her state to a sheik (who falls asleep before he can accept it) and then to a bullfighter, who takes it with pleasure-giving expertise. Scenes of erotica 'the like of which the cinema has never before seen . . .' Rest of cast: George Kennedy, Andrea Occhipinti, Ana Obregon, Olivia d'Abo, Greg Bensen, Ian Cochrane, Mirta Miller, Mickey Knox, Paul Stacey, James Stacey. Dir, Screenplay and Ph: John Derek. Pro: Bo Derek. Ex Pro: Menahem Golan and Yoram Globus. Ed: No credits. Pro Des: Alan Roderick-Jones. M: Peter Bernstein. M Sup: Elmer Bernstein. Assoc Pro: Rony Yacov. (Golan/Globus for City Films–Cannon Film Dist) Rel: 2 Nov 1984. 104 mins. Cert 18.

Borowczyk's Dr. Jekyll. It is highly doubtful if Robert Louis Stevenson would have found anything even vaguely familiar about this made-in-France version of his oft-filmed story – somewhere around 44 times, apparently, since the first film was made in the early 1900s – *Dr Jekyll and Mr Hyde*, the classic tale of the potential for good and evil, and their everlasting struggle for supremacy in Man. Mr Borowczyk's creepy and unpleasant movie concentrates on male and female rape and other sexual aberrations. In this version Stevenson's mysterious phial of character-altering medicine becomes a whole bathful of murky fluid in which it is necessary to thrash about in to achieve the change! Gosh – what a slosh! Cast: Udo Kier, Marina Pierro, Patrick Magee, Howard Vernon and Clément Harari. Dir, Screenplay and Designer: Walerian Borowczyk. Pro: Robert Kuperberg and Jean-Pierre Labrande. Ex Pro: Ralph Baum. Ph: Nöel Very. Ed: Kadicha Bariha. M: Bernard Parmegiani. (Whodunit Pro Allegro Pro Multimedia–New Realm) Rel: floating; first shown London (ICA), 8 Feb 1985. 92 mins. Cert 18.

The Bostonians. Another of the James Ivory team's masterly adaptations to the screen of a Henry James novel – which Ivory likes to call 'a 19th-century human triangle story' – about a young woman lecturer on woman's rights being wooed by a rich young man of impeccable character and a penniless young Boston Lawyer, who, while de-

Madeleine Potter (left) and Vanessa Redgrave in *The Bostonians*. Miss Potter (inset) with Christopher Reeve.

testing her suffragette message, relentlessly pursues and finally carries her off. Subtle direction, a polished literate screenplay and fine acting and photography add up to a leisurely, largely dialogue-developed, reflection of civilized nineteenth-century life in Boston and New York. Cast: Christopher Reeve ('Superman' of course!), Vanessa Redgrave, Madeleine Potter, Jessica Tandy, Nancy Marchand, Wesley Addy, Barbara Bryne, Linda Hunt, Nancy New, John Van Ness Philip, Wallace Shawn, Maura Moynihan, Martha Farrar, Peter Bogyo, Dusty Maxwell, Charles McCaughan, J. Lee Morgan, Lee Doyle, De French, Jane Manners, Janet Cicchese, Scott Kradolfer and June Mitchell. Dir: James Ivory. Pro: Ismail Merchant. Screenplay:

Mel Gibson (left) protects Anthony Hopkins from harm in *The Bounty*.

Ruth Prawer Jhabvala; based on the book by Henry James. Ex Pro: Michael Landes and Albert Schwartz. Ph: Walter Lassally. Ed: Katharine Wenning and Mark Potter. Pro Des: Leo Austin. M: Richard Robbins. (Merchant Ivory Productions–Curzon Film Dist) Rel: floating; first shown London (Curzon), 28 Sept 1984. 122 mins. Cert PG.

Bounty. The fourth, and almost certainly the most balanced, translation to the screen of the famous, and factual, story of the mutiny by the crew of Captain Bligh's ship 'The Bounty'

which led to his being cast adrift with a few loyal crew members and making a remarkable 40-day voyage (without compass or other aids) to land; while the mutineers, refused refuge on Tahiti, journey on to find the then uninhabited Pitcairn islands, and settle there, undiscovered for years. A handsome, decorative production with fine setpieces made all the more memorable by the outstanding performance of Anthony Hopkins as Bligh, showing for the first time what was almost certainly his real character: a fine seaman, a magnificent navigator, a strict disciplinarian and a very courageous man, with only a lack of any psychological understanding leading to the mutiny. Rest of cast: Mel Gibson (Christian),

Laurence Olivier, Edward Fox, Daniel Day-Lewis, Bernard Hill, Philip Davis, Liam Neeson, Wi Kuki Kaa, Tevaite Vernette, Philip Martin-Brown, Simon Chandler and Malcolm Terris. Dir: Roger Donaldson. Pro: Bernard Williams, Screenplay: Robert Bolt; based on Richard Hough's book, *Captain Bligh and Mr Christian*. Ph: Arthur Ibbetson. Ed: Tony Lawson. Pro Des: John Bloomfield. M: Vangelis. (Dino de Laurentiis–Thorn EMI) Rel: 28 Sept 1984. 133 mins. Cert 15.

Brazil. A commendable, original and inventive British black comedy, with a serious underbelly, which really defies encapsulation as the film follows

Jonathan Pryce's searching for his dream girl (Kim Greist) through 'the corridors of power and paperwork at Information Retrieval, where bureaucrats like Kurtzman (Ian Holm) can survive despite stupefying incompetence'. And that is only a glimpse of the bizarre world created by writer-director Terry Gilliam in this movie which, while possibly not climbing too high in the box office charts because of subject and treatment, is nevertheless another remarkable British film achievement. Rest of cast: Robert De Niro, Katherine Helmond, Bob Hoskins, Michael Palin, Ian Richardson, Peter Vaughan, Jim Broadbent, Barbara Hicks, Charles McKeown, Derrick O'Connor, Kathryn Pogson, Bryan Pringle, Sheila Reid, John Flanagan, Ray Cooper, Brian Miller, Simon Nash, Prudence Oliver, Simon Jones, Derek Deadman, Nigel Planer, Terence Bayler, Gordon Kaye, Antony Brown, Diana Martin, Jack Purvis and Myrtle Devenish. Dir: Terry Gilliam. Pro: Arnon Milchan. Co-Pro: Patrick Cassavetti. Screenplay: Terry Gilliam, Tom Stoppard and Charles McKeown. Ph: Roger Pratt. Ed: Julian Doyle. Pro Des: Norman Garwood. Art: John Beard and Keith Pain. M: Michael Kamen. (Fox) Rel: 22 March 1985. 142 mins. Cert 15.

Breakdance 2 – Electric Boogaloo. A second celluloid slice featuring this athletic, torso-twisting dance craze with the same starring trio as in *Breakdance 1*: Lucinda Dickey, Adolfo 'Shabba-Doo' Quinones and Michael 'Boogaloo Shrimp' Chambers. This time the trio are fighting off the greedy land developers so that their Miracles local community centre can stay open. Rest of cast includes: Susie Bono, Harry Caesar, Jo de Winter, John Christy Ewing, Steve 'Sugarfoot' Notario, Sabrina Garcia, Lu Leonard, Ken Olfson, Peter MacLean, Herb Mitchell, Sandy Lipton, Bill Cort, Don Lewis, Vidal 'Coco' Rodriquez, Ice T, Jay 'Suave' Sands, Nicholas Segal, Tim Wise, Alicia Bond, Jerry Lazarus, Sam Livneh, John LaMotta, Jay Rasmuy, Daniel Riordan, Alberta Sanchez, Richard Gross, Frankie Crocker, Kimberly McCullough, Jim W. Jones, Fred Aspargus, Carol Lynn Townes, Toi Overton and Paulette McWilliams. Dir: Sam Furstenberg. Pro: Menahem Golan and Yoram Globus. Screenplay:

A bizarre scene from *Brazil* which starred Jonathan Pryce (right) seen here with Michael Palin.

Jan Venture and Julie Reichert; based on characters created by Charles Parker and Allen DeBevoise. Ph: Hanania Baer. Sup Ed: Marcus Manton. Pro Des: J. T. Garrity. Art: P. E. Tagliaferro. M Sup: Russ Regan. Song Sup: Olloe E. Brown. Ex in charge of Pro: Pieter Jan Brugge. (Golan/Globus Pro–Cannon Film Dist) Rel: 1 March 1985. 90 mins. Cert PG.

Noisy, athletic action from breakdance performers in *Breakdance 2*.

The Breakfast Club. Another of those irritating movies which suggest that if Junior is a nauseous brat it's mum and dad's fault. Let's hope this, as so many other movies of its ilk, is a gross libel, slander and whatever on the majority of today's kids: who are not, we know, like the unlikeable group of cross-section scholars (sic) attending Shermer High, Chicago. Cast: Emilio Estevez, Judd Nelson, Molly Ringwald, Anthony Michael Hall, Ally Sheedy, Paul Gleason, John Kapelos, Mary Christian, Perry Crawford, Ron Dean, Tim Gamble, Fran Gargano and Mercedes Hall. Dir and Screenplay: John Hughes. Pro: Hughes and Ned Tannen. Ed Pro: Gil Friesen and Andrew Meyer. Co-Pro: Michelle Manning. Pro Sup: Richard Hashimoto. Ph: Thomas del Ruth and George Bouillet. Ed: Dede Allen. Assoc Ed: J. W. Miller. Pro Des: J. W. Corso. M: Keith Forsey. (A & M Films/Channel/Universal–UIP) Rel: floating; first shown London (Plaza), 3 June 1985. 97 mins. Cert 15.

Mia Farrow made a fine foil to Woody Allen in *Broadway Danny Rose*.

Broadway Danny Rose. Slight Woody Allen comedy about a small-time New York theatrical agent whose one, suddenly successful, client's girlfriend is also the mistress of a poetry-writing mobster, who involves him with the Mafia, to the extent of his becoming the target of a couple of hit-men! A typical Allen movie, made in black-and-white, with the occasional funny situation and witty line, which switches to Chaplinesque sentiment – and becomes quite moving – towards the climax. A splendid out-of-character performance by Mia Farrow as a gangster's moll. Rest of cast: Nick Apollo Forte, Sandy Baron, Monica Corbett, Jackie Gayle, Morty Gunty, Will Jordan, Howard Storm, Jack Rollins, Milton Berle (the last octet playing themselves; real-life characters), Craig Vandenburgh, Herb Reynolds, Paul Greco, Frank Renzulli, Edwin Bordo, Gina Deangelis, Peter Castellotti, Sandy Richman, Gerald Schoenfeld, Olga Barbato, David Kissell, Gloria Parker, Bob and Etta Rollins, Bob Weil, David Kieserman, Mark Hardwick, Alba Ballard, Maurice Shrog, Belle Berger, Herschel Rosen, Joe Franklin, Cecilia Amerling, Maggie Ranone, Charles D'Amodio, Joie Gallo, Carl Pistilli, Lucy Iacono, Julia Barbuto, Anna Sceusa, Nicholas Pantano, Rocco Pantano, Tony Turca, Gilda Torterello, Ronald Maccone, Antoinette Raffone, Michael Badalucco, Richard Lanzano, Dom Matteo, Camille Saviola, Sheila Bond, Betty Rosotti, Howard Cosell, John Doumanian, Gary Reynolds, Sid Winter, Diane Zolten, William Paulson, George Axler and Leo Steiner. Dir and Screenplay: Woody Allen. Pro: Robert Greenhut. Ex Pro: Charles H. Joffe. Ph: Gordon Willis. Ed: Susan E. Morse. Pro Des: Mel Bourne. M (Sup., Arr. and Orchestrator): Dick Hyman ('Agita' and 'My Bambina' written and performed by Nick Apollo Forte). (Orion–Rank Film Dist) Rel: 17 Aug 1984. 85 mins. Cert PG.

Broken Mirrors – Gerbroken Spiegels. A Dutch film about life in an Amsterdam brothel, impressive in its restraint and realism; more particularly in the way that two of the girls, friends, finally decide that they can no longer live this type of life and walk out. Woven into this is a subsidiary story

about a pervert (one of the customers) who abducts women, chains them up and photographs them in the various horrible stages of their lingering death, then dumps the bodies in the river, before going off to find another victim. The second film from Marleen Gorris, whose debut movie *A Question of Silence* won the Best Dutch Film of 1982 and many other international awards. Cast: Lineke Rijxman, Henriette Tol, Edda Barends, Coby Stunnenberg, Carla Hardy, Marike Veugelers, Arline Renfurm, Anke Van't Hoff, Hedda Tabet, Elja Pelgrom, Johan Leyssen, Rolf Leendeerts, Eddy Brugman, Beppie Melissen and Wim Wama. Dir and Screenplay: Marleen Gorris. Pro: Matthijs Van Heijningen. Ph: Frans Bromet. Ed: Hans Van Dongen. Art: Harry Ammerlaan. M: Lodewijk De Boer. (Tuschinski Film Dist/Sigma Films–Thorn EMI) Rel: floating; first shown London (Cinecenta, Electric and Screen-on-the-Green), 5 April 1985. 111 mins. Cert 18.

The Brother from Another Planet. Lightweight, meandering but mildly amusing comedy about a black alien (a survivor of a – presumably – crash-landed spacecraft) who is without the power of speech (but has detachable eyes!). He arrives in Harlem, where he observes life with curiosity and, in the case of the drug peddlers, with active distaste. Pursued by two bounty hunters from his own world, our hero gets the better of them, to continue his exploration of the mores and mysteries of this new, and to him, strange world. As the visiting 'brother' Joe Morton gives a first-class performance. Rest of cast: Rosanna Carter, Ray Ramirez, Yves Rene, Peter Richardson, Ginny Yang, Darryl Edwards, Steve James, Leonard Jackson, Bill Cobbs, Maggie Renzi, Olga Merediz, Tom Wright, Minnie Gentry, Ren Woods, Reggie Rock Bythewood, Alvin Alexis, Caroline Aaron, Herbert Newsome, John Sayles, David Strathairn, Rosetta Le Noire, Michael Albert Mantel, Jaime Tirelli, Liane Curtis, Fisher Stevens, Chip Mitchell, David Babcock, Randy Frazier, Dee Dee Bridgewater, Sidney Sheriff Jr, Copper Cunningham, Marisa Smith, Ishmael Houston-Jones, Kim Staunton, Dwania Kyles, Carl Gordon, Leon W. Grant, Anthony Thomas, Andre Robertson Jr, John Griesemer, Ellis Williams, Edward

Joe Morton in *The Brother from Another Planet.*

Baran, Josh Mostel, Deborah Taylor and Herb Downer. Dir, Screenplay and Ed: John Sayles. Pro: Peggy Rajski and Maggie Renzi. Ph: Ernest Dickerson. Pro Des: Nora Chavooshian. Art: Steve Lineweaver. M: Mason Daring. (Train Films–Virgin Films) Rel: floating; first shown London (Classics at Chelsea, Tott Ct Rd and Electric Screen), 30 Nov 1984. 108 mins. Cert 15.

Cal. A finely directed melancholy, depressing and sadly convincing film about the situation in Northern Ireland, made actually in the South but carefully balanced between the Catholic and Pro-

John Lynch and Helen Mirren as the lovers in *Cal.*

Left to right, Dean Martin, Sammy Davis Jr, Shirley MacLaine and Frank Sinatra in *The Cannonball Run II*.

testant outlooks. In particular, the story of a shy and pathetic young man who, although he hates violence, is drawn unwillingly into the IRA, who refuse to let him 'out', as he wants; his desire to escape grows stronger when he meets and falls in love with the pretty young widow of a part-time policeman in whose murder he has had a part, an experience that has increasingly obsessed him ever since. A sad performance in the title role by John Lynch, a very strong and good one by Helen Mirren as the girl. Rest of cast: Donal McCann, John Kavanagh, Ray McAnally, Stevan Rimkus, Catherine Gibson, Louis Ralston, Tom Hickey, Gerard Mannix Flynn, Seamus Ford, Edward Byrne, J. J. Murphy, Audrey Johnston, Brian Munn, Daragh O'Malley, George Shane, Julia Dearden, Yvonne Adams, Lawrence Foster, Scott Frederick and Gerard O'Hagan. Dir: Pat O'Connor. Pro: Stuart Craig and David Puttnam. Ex Pro: Terence A. Clegg. Screenplay: Bernard MacLaverty; based on his own novel. Ph: Jerzy Zielinski. Ed: Michael Bradsell. Pro Des: Stuart Craig. M: Mark Knopfler. Art: Josie MacAvin. Pro Assoc: Susan Richards. (Enigma–Goldcrest–Warner) Rel: floating; first shown London (Warner), 14 Sept 1984. 103 mins. Cert 15.

Cannonball Run II. A star-flecked comedy which like its predecessor *CR1*, is about a crazy car race across America, spacing out some good gags and some jokey lines from the stars, who generally appear to have had more amusement in making the movie than there is in the movie itself. But who could resist a line-up of players headed by Burt Reynolds, Dean Martin, Frank Sinatra, Shirley MacLaine, Dom DeLuise, Telly Savalas, Sammy Davis Jr, Jack Elam, Jamie Farr, Marilu Henner and many other familiar names and faces, no matter what might be the quality of their material on hand? Rest of cast: Mel Tillis, Charles Nelson Reilly, Doug McClure, Henry Silva, Molly Picon, Michael Gazzo, Alex Rocco, Abe Vigoda, Joe Theismann, Tony Danza, Richard Kiel, Susan Anton, Catherine Bach, Arte Johnson, Jilly Rizzo, Lee Kolima, Shawn Wetherly, Jack Smith, Tim Conway, Don Knotts, Marty Allen, Avery Schreiber, Dub Taylor, Ricardo Montalban, John See, George Lindsey, Fred Dryer, John Worthington Stuart, Debi Greco, C. James Lewis, Harry Gant, Hal Needham, Robert B. Chandler, Frank O. Hill, Regina Parton, Kathleen M. Shea, Sid Caesar, Foster Brooks, Louis Nye, Jackie Chan, Mario Roberts, Jim Nabors, Patricia Bolt, Jim Cassett Anderson, Beverly Budinger, Marian Issacks, Suzynn Herzog, Caroline Reed, Ralph S. Salcido, Budd Stout, Frieda Smith and Robert Shelton. Dir:

Hal Needham. Pro: Albert S. Ruddy. Ex Pro: Raymond Chow and André Morgan. Screenplay: Needham, Ruddy and Harvey Miller. Ph: Nick McLean. Ed: William Gordean and Carl Cress. Art: Theo E. Azzani. M: Al Capps (M Sup: Snuff Garrett). Pro Co-Ord: Judith Gill. (Golden Harvest/Warner-Videoform Pictures – Heron Corp. Co. – in association with Miracle Films) Rel: 24 Aug 1984. 108 mins. Cert PG.

Caravan of Courage – An Ewok Adventure. Remember those Ewoks – the small bear-like charmers – George (*Star Wars*) Lucas introduced in *Return of the Jedi*? Well, now they get a whole – kids' – feature to themselves, along with two small children and their parents, survivors of their crashed 'starcruiser' on the forested moon of the planet Endor, home of the Ewoks. Obviously made for the Christmas panto season. Cast: Eric Walker, Warwick Davis, Fionnula Flanagan, Guy Boyd, Aubree Miller, Burl Ives (narrator), Dan Frishman, Debbie Carrington, Tony Cox, Kevin Thompson, Margarita Fernandez, Pam Grizz, Bobby Bell. Dir and Ph: John H. Korty. Pro: Thomas G. Smith. Ex Pro: George Lucas. Screenplay: Bob Carrau; from a story by George Lucas. Ed: John Nutt. Pro Des: Joe Johnston. M: Peter Bernstein. Assoc Pro: Patricia Rose Duignan. (Lucas Film/Korty Films–Fox) Rel: 14 Dec 1984. 97 mins. Cert U.

Carmen. Francesco Rosi's (French/Italian) adaptation to the screen in neo-realistic terms of Bizet's operatic war-horse, with much fine singing but with other qualities which brought a quite extraordinarily divided critical response on both sides of the Atlantic, ranging from love to hate. Truth (in this reviewer's opinion) lies somewhere midway between those rather ridiculous extremes. Cast: Julia Migenes-Johnson, Placido Domingo, Ruggero Raimondi, Faith Esham, Françoise Le Roux, Jean-Philippe Lafont, Gérard Garino, Lilian Watson, John-Paul Bogart, Julien Guiomar, Susan Daniel, Accursio Di Leo, Maria Campano, Cristina Hoyos, Juan Antonio Jiminez, Enrique El Cojo and Santiago Lopez. Dir & Art: Francesco Rosi. Pro: Patrice Ledoux. Ex Pro: Alessandro von Normann. Screenplay: Francesco Rosi and Tonio Guerra; based on the story by Prosper

Merimée and the opera by Bizet. Ph: Pasqualino de Santis. Ed: Ruggero Mastroianni and Colette Semprun. Pro Des: Enrico Job. M Dir: Lorin Maazel. Choreography: Antonio Gades. (Gaumont/Productions Marcel Dassault, France/Opera Film Produzione, Rome–Virgin) Rel: floating; first shown London (Lumière), 14 Mar 1985. 152 mins. Cert PG.

The Chain. The title and the theme is about moving; the traumas of packing up and leaving one's old residence for the new one, as someone else moves from their old address to take your place. Mild little British comedy which in its record of seven 'movings' manages to associate them with the seven deadly sins. Cast: Herbert Norville, Denis Lawson, Rita Wolf, Maurice Denham, Nigel Hawthorne, Billie Whitelaw, Judy Parfitt, Leo McKern, Tony Westrope, Bernard Hill, Warren Mitchell, David Troughton, Phyllis Logan, Anna Massey, Ann Tirard, Gary Waldhorn, Ron Pember, Carmen Munroe, Patsy Smart, Bill Thomas, Jade Magri, Robin Summers, Ben Onwukwe, James Coyle, George Rossi, Graham Jarvis, Darliah Wood, Kim Clifford, Alex Tetteh-Lartey, Paddy Joyce, Matthew Blaksted, Charlotte Long, John Rowe, Christopher Ettridge, Mark Dignam, Michael Mulkerrin, Vicky Licorish, Steven Woodcock and Bob Holness. Dir: Jack Gold. Pro: Victor Glynn. Ex Pro: David Deutsch. Screenplay: Jack Rosenthal. Ph: Wolfgang Suschitzky. Ed: Bill Blunden. Pro Des: Peter Murtori. M: Stanley Myers. (Quintet Films – Rank Film Dist) Rel: 21 June 1985. 96 mins. Cert PG.

Chaos–Kaos. Marvellous portmanteau picture from the Taviani brothers, made from five diverse stories by Luigi Pirandello, giving a memorable picture of a hard, cruel, and then suddenly unexpectedly amusing, insight into life in the Sicilian countryside of not so long ago. Episode one (*The Other Son*) is about a mother neglected by her two sons, who have emigrated to America. She hates her third son, who has stayed on and loves her but whom she cruelly rejects because he is the result of a triple raping when she was a young wife. The second segment (*Moonstruck*) is about a bride who finds her husband goes mad on every night of the full

Aubree Miller (left) and Eric Walker with the Ewoks (also right), in *Caravan of Courage – An Ewok Adventure*.

moon. *The Jar* is a comedy about a rich and feudalistic landowner taught a lesson by 'the best jar-repairer in all Sicily'. *Requiem*, the fourth story, is a tragi-comedy about some villagers and their fight against the authorities who want to stop them taking over some land for a new cemetery. And in the Epilogue, *Conversing with Mother*, author Pirandello returns home and converses with his recently departed mother's spirit, which reminds him of a girlhood adventure he has long tried, and failed, to turn into a story. Combining beautifully photographed sunny and moonlit backgrounds, integrity and imagination in the translating of the stories to visual terms, superbly controlled direction and fine performances; the result an unforgettable picture of Sicilian peasant life with all its earthiness, brutality and mordant humour. Casts: (1) Margarita Lozano as the mother. (2) Claudio Bigagli, Maria Modugno, Massimo Bonetti. (3) Ciccio Ingrassia, Franco Franchi – as the sly restorer. (4) Biagio Barone, Salvatore Rossi, Franco Scaldati, Pasquale Spadola. (5) Omero Antonutti, Regina Biachi. Dir: Paolo & Vittorio Taviani. Pro: Giuliani de Negri. Screenplay: the Taviani Brothers and Tonio Guerra. Ph: Giuseppe Lanci. Ed: Roberto Perignani. Art: Francesco Bronzi. M:

Nicola Piovani. (RAI TV Channel 1/ Filmtre Productions – Gala–Cannon) Rel: floating; first shown London (Academy), 4 Oct 1984. 190 mins. Cert 15.

Children of the Corn. A minor thriller about a community of kids who, having murdered the adults, set up their own religious community in the wilds of Nebraska and there worship a deity in the corn fields. With an undercurrent of supernatural suggestion, and plenty of superficial action at the end, the pace is too slow and there are too many holes in its credibility to flesh out satisfactorily what is obviously an adaptation of a short story. Cast: Peter Horton, Linda Hamilton, R. G. Armstrong, John Franklin, Courtney Gains, Robby Kiger, Anne Marie McEvoy, Julie Maddalena, Jonas Marlowe and John Philbin. Dir: Fritz Kiersch. Pro: D. P.

advice, her landlady who is also owner of a city bar ('Eve's Bar') (Lesley Ann Warren) and the drifter who enters the bar and their lives (Keith Carradine). It is often very reminiscent (in spirit anyway) to the writer/director's former off-beat success *Welcome to L.A.* The minority are going to find it among their most treasured movies of the year. Rest of cast: Patrick Bauchau, Rae Dawn Chong, John Larroquette, Edward Ruscha, Gailard Sartain, Robert Gould, John Considine, Jodi Buss, Sandra Will, Mike E. Kaplan, Russell Parr, Teresa Velarde, Henry G. Sanders, Margery Bond, Debra Dusay, Minnie Lindsay, Richard Marion, Albert Stanislaus, Karyn Isaacs, Elizabeth Lloyd Shaw, Edward C. Lawson, Chase Holiday, Patricia McFadden and Greg Walker. Dir and Screenplay: Alan Rudolph. Pro: Carolyn Pfeiffer and David Blocker. Ex Pro: Shep Gordon and Chris Blackwell. Ph: Jan Kiesser. Ed: Mia Goldman. Pro Des: Steven Legler. M: Luther Vandross. (CBS Theatrical Films – Island Alive Pro–Tartan Films) Rel: floating; first shown London (Plaza), 19 April 1985. 106 mins. Cert 15.

A Christmas Carol. A good, straightforward British cinematic adaptation – the third (previous *Carols* were made in 1938 and 1951) – of the famous Charles Dickens moral tale of the Christmas season about the redemption of the miser Scrooge. Made this time with plenty of good Victorian atmosphere, it has an enjoyable performance by George C. Scott as the man shown his sins by the ghosts of the Past, Present and Future. Rest of cast: Nigel Davenport, Frank Finlay, Lucy Gutteridge, Angela Pleasence, Roger Rees, David Warner, Edward Woodward, Susannah York, Michael Carter, Anthony Walters, Caroline Langrishe, Joanne Whalley, Derek Francis, John Sharp, Danny Davies, Michael Gough, John Quarmby, Sasha Wells, Keiro Hughes, Sara Moore, Orlando Wells, Nancy Dodds, Cathryn Harrison, Tim Munro, Brian Pettifer, Catherine Hall, Timothy Bateson, Pat Rose, Spencer Banks, Peter Settelen, Peter Woodthorpe, Liz Smith, Rebecca Burrill, Gavin Asher, Daniel Chatto, Louise Gasser, Joe Blatchley, Ian Giles, Alan Bodenham and Mark Strickson. Dir: Clive Donner. Pro: William F. Storke and Alfred R. Kelman. Ex Pro: Robert

Two women and a fancy-free man – recipe for trouble in the very off-beat *Choose Me*. Genevieve Bujold (above) with Keith Carradine who played the man. Lesley Ann Warren (left) was the other woman.

Porchers & Terrence Kirby. Ex Pro: Earl Glick and Charles Weber. Screenplay: George Goldsmith; based on a story by Stephen King. Ph: Raoul Lomas. Ed: Harry Keramidas. Art: Craig Stearns. M: Jonathan Elias. Assoc Pro: Max W. Anderson. (Gatlin Pro. in association with Angeles Group Inc. and Inverness Pro. Inc./Hal Roach Studios and New World Pictures–EMI) Rel: 27 June 1984. 92 mins. Cert 18.

Choose Me. Too original ever to be popular, this off-beat triangular story encompasses love, fun and violence as it centres on a radio 'Love Line' talk-show personality (Genevieve Bujold) who gives (but finds it difficult to take)

George C. Scott in *A Christmas Carol*.

E. Fuisz. Screenplay: Roger O. Hirson. Ph: Tony Imi. Ed: Peter Tanner. Pro Des: Roger Murray-Leach. M: Nick Bicat; arr. & con. Tony Britten. Pro Sup: Norman Foster. (Entertainment Partners–Enterprise Pictures) Rel: early Jan 1985. 100 mins. Cert U.

A Christmas Story. An adult looks back at his childhood in an American suburb during one Christmas period in the 1940s, when he so badly wanted an airgun – and eventually got it. A patchwork of his own and his family's day-to-day life; a mixture of nostalgia, black humour, coarseness, gimmicky technical qualities and very valid feeling of a time and place, and convincing childhood character. Cast: Peter Billingsley (the boy), Melinda Dillon (mother), Darren McGavin (the old man), Ian Petrella, Scott Schwartz, R. D. Robb, Tedde Moore, Yano Anaya, Zack

Ward, Jeff Gillen, Colin Fox, Paul Hubbard, Les Carlson, Jim Hunter, Patty Johnson, Drew Hocevar, David Svoboda, Dwayne McLean, Helen E. Kaider, John Wong, Johan Sebastian Wong, Fred Lee, Dan Ma, Rocco Bellusci, Tommy Wallace. Narrator: Jean Shepherd. Dir: Bob Clark. Pro: Clarke and René Dupont. Assoc Pro: Gary Goch. Pro Co-Ord: Suzanne Lore and David Craig. Screenplay: Jean Shepherd, Leigh Brown and Bob Clark; based on the novel *In God We Trust, All Others Pay Cash* by Jean Shepherd. Ph: Reginald H. Morris. Ed: Stan Cole. Pro Des: Reuben Freed. Art: Gavin Mitchell. M: Carl Ziffrer and Paul Zaza. (MGM/UA–UIP) Rel: 30 Nov 1984. 93 mins. Cert PG.

City Heat. A lightly amusing fun-film, a gangster-era send-up with cop Clint Eastwood and ex-partner, now private eye Burt Reynolds becoming involved in the latter's black partner's suicidal effort to play two of the town's leading mobsters against each other and double-cross both, leading to murder and other mayhem, kidnappings, and deadly confrontations ending in the usual cloud of flying lead as the three points of the triangle shoot it out in the

Peter Billingsley (below) explains his wish to Santa Claus in *A Christmas Story*.

Burt Reynolds (left) and Clint Eastwood are threatened with a gangster's gun in *City Heat*. Below, a fearless Eastwood walks unscathed through a hail of bullets.

street, the baddies falling like balletic autumn leaves while the goodies cheerfully walk into and survive even a machine gun barrage. And both Eastwood and Reynolds, in their first movie together, seem to be enjoying themselves immensely. Rest of cast: Jane Alexander, Madeline Kahn, Rip Torn, Irene Cara, Richard Roundtree, Tony Lo Bianco, William Sanderson, Nicholas Worth, Robert Davi, Jude Farese, John Hancock, Tab Thacker, Gerald S. O'Loughlin, Bruce M. Fisher, Art La Fleur, Jack Nance, Dallas Cole, Lou Filippo, Michael Maurer, Preston Sparks, Ernie Sabella, Christopher Michael Moore, Carey Loftin, Harry Caesar, Charles Parks, Hamilton Camp, Jack Thibeau, Gene LeBell, Nick Dimitri, George Fisher, Bob Herron, Bill Hart, Arthur Malet, Fred Lerner, George Orrison, Beau Starr, Anthony Charnota, Walter Robles, Richard Foronjy, Joan Shawlee, Minnie Lindsey, Darwyn Swalve, Wiley Harker, Bob Maxwell, Tom Spratley, Bob Terhune, Holgie Forrester, Harry Demopoulos, Jim Lewis, Edwin Provost, Alfie Wise, Hank Calia, Alex Plasschaert, Daphne Eckler and Lonna Montrose. Dir: Richard Benjamin. Pro: Fritz Manes. Screenplay: Sam O. Brown (Blake Edwards) and Joseph C. Stinson; based on a story by Brown. Ph: Nick McLean. Ed: Jacqueline Cambas. Pro Des: Edward Carfagno. M: Lennie Niehaus. (Malpaso/Deliverance–Warner) Rel: 1 March 1985. 97 mins. Cert 15.

City of Pirates – La Ville des Pirates. A quite unique, surrealistic, obscure, visually intriguing and generally controversial Raul Ruiz French-Portuguese production: a 'twisting tale of the blood-soaked relationship between a demon child, his spiritual mother, and the cursed murderer who haunts the bizarre island of pirates . . .' All, in fact, typical Ruiz experimental stuff. Cast: Hughes Quester, Anne Alvaro, André Engel, Duarte de Almeida, Clarisse Dole, André Gomes, Melvil Fouquad. Dir and Screenplay: Raul Ruiz. Pro: Anne-Marie La Joison. Ex Pro: Paulo Branco. Ph: Acacio de Almeida. Ed: Valeria Sarmiento, Rudolfo Wedeles, Monique Soussan and Claudio Martinez. M: Jorge Arriagada. (Les Films du Passage, Paris/Metro Films, Lisbon – The Other Cinema) Rel: floating; first shown London (ICA), 19 April 1985. 111 mins. No cert.

Codename Wildgeese – Geheimcode Wildganse. A mite misleading title maybe for this German/Italian co-production has no observable connections with the original *Wild Geese* movie. The scene is Hong Kong and Thailand and the story concerns the efforts of British mercenary captain Wesley (Lewis Collins) to smash up a vast dope depot hidden in the jungle, an adventure leading to lots of bloodletting and brutality and rough justice. Rest of cast: Lee Van Cleef, Ernest Borgnine, Klaus Kinski, Manfred Lehmann, Mimsy Farmer, Thomas Danneberg, Frank Glaubrecht, Wolfgant Pampel, Hartmut Neugebauer, Bruce Barow, Rene Arbadesa, Alan Walker. Dir: A. M. Dawson. Pro: Erwin C. Dietrich. Screenplay: Michael Lester. Ph: Peter Baumgartner. No Ed Credit. M: Jan Nemec. (Ascot Films, Berlin/Gico Cinematografica, Rome–Entertainment Films) Rel: floating; first shown London (Prince Charles), 1 March 1985. 101 mins. Cert 15.

Comfort and Joy. Another outstanding British (in fact Scots) comedy in the classic old Ealing Studios tradition from Bill (*Gregory's Girl* and *Local Hero*) Forsyth about an Edinburgh disc-jockey who becomes involved in a hilarious local ice cream war, from which he emerges after some considerable travail a wiser – and potentially wealthier – man. Simple, without any cinematic frills, but witty and subtle and consistently chuckly. One of the year's outstanding screen entertainments and another triumph for British

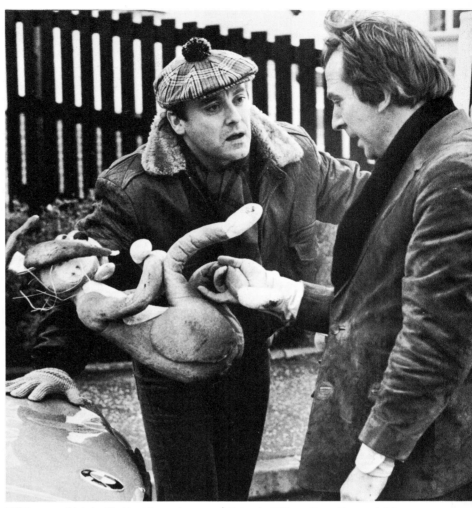

Bill Paterson (right) with Alex Norton in *Comfort and Joy*.

film. Marvellously acted, especially by Bill Paterson in the main role. Rest of cast: Eleanor David, C. P. Grogan, Alex Norton, Patrick Malahide, Rikki Fulton, Roberto Bernardi, George Rossi, Peter Rossi, Billy McElhaney, Gilly Gilchrist, Caroline Guthrie, Ona McCracken, Elizabeth Sinclair, Katie Black, Robin Black, Ron Donachie, Arnold Brown, Iain McColl, Billy Johnstone, Douglas Sannachan, Billy Greenless, Robert Buchanan, Alan Tall, Bob Starrett, David O'Hara, Allan Wylie, Alistair Campbell, Charles Kearney, Martin Currie, Elspet Cameron, Teri Lally, Pearl Deans, Ray Jeffries, Patrick Lewsley, Ronald McCleod Veitch, Johnny Irving, Johnny Mac, Clive Parsons. Dir and Screenplay: Bill Forsyth. Pro: Davina Belling and Clive Parsons. Assoc Pro: Paddy Higson. Ph: Chris Menges. Ed:

Michael Ellis. Pro Des: Adrienne Atkinson. M: Mark Knopfler. (Thorn EMI) Rel: 14 Aug 1984. 106 mins. Cert PG.

Committed. A second film based on the life and career of actress/film star Frances Farmer (first: *Frances*), this time following in a far less polished, more disjointed and openly feminist-angled style her downward slide from Hollywood studios to mental asylum, shock treatment and, finally, lobotomy. A dense mixture of events, implications, analysis, feminism – and lots more. Cast: includes Sheila McLaughlin, Victoria Boothby, Lee Breuer, John Erdman, Heinz Emigholz, Lucy Sanger, John Nesci, Peter Walker, Jim Meu, Diana White, Clove Breuer, Lute Breuer, Devon Meade, Tose Dreyer, Bob Fleischner, John McGuire, Milton Lansky, Peter Blagvad, Maryette Charlton, Paul Gibson, Jim Krell, Allen Robertson, Helen Adam, Susan

Left to right, Tusse Silberg, David Warner, Graham Crowden and Angela Lansbury in *The Company of Wolves*. Micha Bergese (below right) as the man who turns into wolf and Sarah Patterson (below left) as charming little Red Riding Hood.

Berkson, Michelle Hurst, Lillian Kiesler, Lorraine Kennedy, Cynthia Kolbowski, Barbara Wise, Kirsten Bates, Patricia Bates, Dorman Birmingham and Peter Bruno. Dir, Pro and Screenplay: Sheila McLaughlin and Lynne Tillman. Ph: Heinz Emigholtz. Ed: McLaughlin and Tillman. M: Philip Johnston. (Story Films in association with Channel 4 and various others – Cinema of Women) Rel: floating; first shown London (Electric Screen), 24 May 1985. 77 Mins. No cert.

The Company of Wolves. One of the most individual, imaginative and sometimes horrific (British) films of the year, mixing wolves, werewolves, witches and other wonders in the framework of a girl's dreams – well, mostly nightmares – and finishing up with a visually rich, poetic and subtle version of the Red Riding Hood fairy story. Full of visual splendours and literary allusions and a film for many reasons memorable and even unique.

Cast: Sarah Patterson (dreaming Rosaleen-Red Riding Hood), Angela Lansbury, David Warner, Graham Crowden, Brian Glover, Kathryn Pogson, Stephen Rea, Tusse Silberg, Micha Bergese, Georgia Slowe, Susan Porrett, Shane Johnstone, Dawn Archibald, Richard Morant, Danielle Dax, Vincent McClaren, Ruby Buchanan, Jimmy Gardner, Roy Evans, Terence Stamp. Dir: Neil Jordan. Pro: Chris Brown and Stephen Woolley. Ex Pro: Woolley and Nik Powell. Screenplay: Angela Carter and Neil Jordan; from the former's story. Ph: Bryan Loftus. Ed: Rodney Holland. Pro Des: Anton Furst. M: George Fenton. Dir of Effects Ph: Rodney Holland. (Palace Pictures–ITC) Rel: 23 Nov 1984. 95 mins. Cert 15. (Winner of Award for Best Direction from British Critics' Circle 1984.)

Conan the Destroyer. Miles better than the first Conan movie, and a real fun piece: a lavishly budgeted, spectacular and amusing comicstrip fairy story with the grace to laugh at itself. Conan (mighty-muscled world champion strong man Arnold Schwarzenegger) battling against all sorts of evil magic to finally sit pretty little Princess, Olivia D'Abo, firmly back on her usurped throne. Terrific stuff for children from less than ten to more than a hundred! Rest of cast: Grace Jones, Wilt Chamberlain, Mako, Tracey Walter, Sarah Douglas, Pat Roach, Jeff Corey, Sven Ole Thorsen, Bruce Fleischer, Ferdinand Mayne. Dir: Richard Fleischer. Pro: Raffaella de Laurentiis. Ex Pro: Stephen F. Kesten. Screenplay: Stanley Mann; from a story by Roy Thomas and Gerry Conway; based on the character created by Robert E. Howard. Ph: Jack Cardiff. Ed: Frank J. Urioste. Pro Des: Pier Luigi Basile. M: Basil Poledouris. (Dino de Laurentiis/Universal–UIP) Rel: 19 Oct 1984. 101 mins. Cert 15.

Constance. The unveiling of a very promising New Zealand film talent in the directing by Bruce Morrison of a movie about a lovely young Auckland primary schoolteacher whose life is influenced by the movies which are her great passion. Restless and exploratory, she gives up her job and embarks on a more adventurous life, always dreaming of Hollywood but finding more and more that in contrast to Tinseltown

Fiction reality is hard, cold and unrewarding. A nice performance by castheader Donagh Rees. Rest of cast includes: Shane Bryant, Judie Douglass, Martin Vaughan, Donald MacDonald, Mark Wignall, Graham Harvey, Hester Joyce, Dana Purkis, Lee Grant, Don Kjestrup, Susan Tainer, Jules Regal, Miranda Pritchard, Roman Watkins, Beryl Te Wiata, Elric Hooper, Lenore

Arnold Schwarzenegger and his redoubtable female aide, Grace Jones, in *Conan the Destroyer*.

Trustcott, Stephen Taylor, Mark Hadlow. Dir: Bruce Morrison. Pro: Larry Parr. Pro Sup: Dorthe Scheffman. Screenplay: Morrison and Jonathan Hardy. Ph: Kevin Hayward. Ed: Phil-

Donagh Rees in *Constance*.

Gangster's moll Diana Lane (above) and Richard Gere (right) as the 1920s jazzband leader in *The Cotton Club*.

lip Howe. Pro Des: Richard Jeziorny and Judith Crozier. Art: Ric Kafoed. M: John Charles and Dave Fraser. (Mirage Films–Enterprise Pictures) Rel: floating; first shown London (Screen, Baker St, Odeon, Kensington and Cinecenta), 18 Jan 1985. 103 mins. Cert 15.

The Cotton Club. Francis Ford Coppola's expensive, modestly successful blending of 1920s jazz and gangsters in a four-stories mixture centred on the career of jazz cornettist Dixie Dwyer (Richard Gere) and his association with gangster Dutch Schultz (James Remar) and the latter's girlfriend (Diane Lane). There are plenty of other threads woven into the overall pattern, which sometimes gets a little too complicated for its own good. But at least there is plenty of assorted entertainment here. Rest of cast: Gregory Hines, Lonette McKee, Bob Hoskins, Nicolas Cage, Allen Garfield, Fred Gwynne, Gwen Verdon, Lisa Jane Persky, Maurice Hines, Julian Beck, Novella Nelson, Larry Fishburne, John Ryan, Tom Waits, Wynonna Smith, Charles (Honi) Coles, Larry Marshall, Joe Dallesandro, Woody Strode, Ron Karabatsos, Glenn Withrow, Jennifer Grey, Thelma Carpenter, Ed O'Ross, Frederick Downs Jr, Diane Venora, Tucker Smallwood, Bill Graham, Dayton Allen, Kim Chan, Ed Rowan, Leonard Termo, George Cantero, Brian Tarantina, Bruce MacVittie, James Russo, Giancarlo Esposito, Bruce Hubbard, Rony Clanton, Damien Leake, Bill Cobbs, Joe Lynn, Oscar Barnes, Edward Zang, Sandra Beall, Zane Mark,

Tom Signorelli, Paul Herman, Randle Mell, Steve Vignari, Susan Meschner, Gregory Rozakis, Marc Coppola, Norma Jean Darden, Robert Earl Jones, Vincent Jerosa, Rosalind Harris. Dir: Francis Ford Coppola. Pro: Robert Evans. Ex Pro: Dyson Lovell. Co-Pro: Silvio Tabat and Fred Ross. Screenplay: Coppola and William Kennedy; based on a story by Kennedy, Coppola and Mario Puzo; suggested by James Haskins. Ph: Stephen Goldblatt. Ed: Barry Malkin and Robert Lovett. Pro Des: Richard Sylbert. M: John Barry (M recreations: Bob Wilbur). (Zoetrope Studios–Orion Pictures–Rank Dist) Rel: 30 May 1985. 128 mins. Cert 15.

Country. The trauma that apparently occurred quite recently in Iowa and elsewhere in the US when the farmers in the Middle West with governmental encouragement over-borrowed from the banks, and subsequently faced ruin when, unable to meet the interest payments because of low prices and other difficulties, the banks started to foreclose – until eventually the government

stepped in to relieve the situation. A surprising picture of poverty and pain in the normally rich farming plains of America's grain bowl. Such is the background to this story of one of these farmers – in this instance a not very efficient one – and his tougher wife, who is grimly determined to hold on to their land and keep the family together. . A film-stealing performance by Jessica Lange (who co-produced and initially set up this warm and winning movie) as the brave little woman, with sturdy support from Sam Shepard who plays her husband and Wilfrid Brimley, her old father. Rest of cast: Matt Clark, Therese Graham, Levi L. Knebel, Jim Haynie, Sandra Seacat, Alex Harvey, Stephanie-Stacie Poyner, Jim Ostercamp, Robert Somers, Frank Noek Jr., Rev. Warren Duit, Conrad Doan, James Harrell, Dean French, Betty Smith, Vern Porter, Sandra J. Hughes. Dir: Richard Pearce. Pro: William D. Wittliff and Jessica Lange. Screenplay: Wittliff. Ph: David M. Walsh (add Ph: Roger Shearman). Ed: Bill Yahraus. Pro Des: Ron Hobbs. M: Charles Gross (Touchstone Films/Disney–UK Film

Sam Shepard and Jessica Lange in *Country*.

Dist) Rel: 22 March 1985. 110 mins. Cert PG.

Crackers. Louis Malle casting his Gallic spell over another of his American productions: a lightweight comedy with a number of chuckly characterizations and a story about a group of off-beat pals who decide to rob their old Jewish pawnbroker-exploiter-friend while he is on a visit to his old mother, a heist planned with military timing which soon gets hours behind schedule as the inept robbers come up against snags, ending up by being discovered in the act by the old man, who shows them that in this case crime could *not* have paid – more than a single penny! Beautifully acted and delightfully far out of the cinematic rut. Cast includes: Jack Warden, Donald Sutherland, Sean Penn, Wallace Shawn, Larry Riley, Trinidad Silva, Christine Baranski, Irwin Corey, Charlaine Woodard, Tasia Valezza, Edouard de Soto, Anna Maria Horsford, Mitchell Lichtenstein, Marjorie Eaton, Edward Call, Joseph Hindy, Charles Bouvier, Dick Bright, Paul Drake. Dir: Louis Malle. Pro: Edward Lewis and Robert Cortes. Screenplay: Jeffrey Fiskin; suggested by the film *Big Deal on Madonna Street*. Ph: Laszlo Kovacs. Ed: Susanne Baron. Pro Des: John J. Lloyd. M: Paul Chihara. (Universal–Miracle Films) Restricted rel: 25 Jan 1985. 91 mins. Cert 15.

Left to right, Sean Penn, Larry Riley and Donald Sutherland in *Crackers*.

Miranda Richardson with Rupert Everett in *Dance with a Stranger*.

Dance with a Stranger. A British film telling the – apparently factually accurate – story of Ruth Ellis, the platinum blonde nightclub hostess with less than strict morals who repeatedly betrayed the man who loved her (and financed her son's education) for the sake of a passionate, fiery and finally distraught love affair with a drunken layabout racing driver. It ends with her shooting him as he comes out of a pub with another girl, and Miss Ellis making history by being the last woman to be sent to the gallows in Britain – on 13 July 1955. A little too long and a little too uninvolving but otherwise commendably interesting movie perfectly played by Miranda Richardson (looking sometimes like an early-period Monroe) as Ruth, Rupert Everett as the cad and Ian Holm the incurably smitten lover of the lady. Rest of cast: Matthew Carroll,

Tom Chadbon, Jane Bertish, David Troughton, Paul Mooney, Stratford Johns, Joanne Whalley, Susan Kyd, Lesley Manville, Sallie-Anne Field, David Beale, Martin Murphy, Tracy-Louise Ward, Michael Jenn, Alan Thompson, Nicholas McArdle, Miki Iveria, Lizzie McKenzie, Ian Hurley, Charles Cork, Patrick Field, Colin Rix, Tony Mathews, Charon Bourke, Elizabeth Newell. Dir: Mike Newell. Pro: Roger Randall-Cutler. Assoc Pro: Paul Cowan. Screenplay: Shelagh Delaney. Ph: Peter Hannan. Ed: Mick Audsley. Pro Des: Andrew Mollo. Art: Adrian Smith. M: Richard Hartley. Pro Co-Ord: Laura Julian. (First Film Co for Goldcrest in association with National Film Finance Corp and Film Four International–Fox) Rel: 12 April 1985. 102 mins. Cert 15.

Dark Enemy. A Children's Film Unit production; an imaginative and technically efficient feature almost entirely acted by children, and with children behind the camera, lighting and other facets of technical production. A story set in some future time when in a post-atomic era, life has reverted to

Douglas Storm (left) in one of the few adult roles in *Dark Enemy*, a film about and made largely by children.

simplicity and vegetarianism, but human nature, or rather greed, has begun to re-assert itself – the moral being underlined by the closing shot when the sole youngster left after the rest of the colony has gone off to seek a 'better' life has for company only a talking doll that cries, 'more, more, more' incessantly. The third feature made by the unit which grew out of the Forest Hill School's film society after it had made a series of shorts and, finally, in 1980, the feature film *The Custard Boys*. Cast: David Haig, Douglas Storm (the elders), Martin Laing, Chris Chescoe, Jennifer Harrison, Helen Mason, Rory MacFarquhard, Cerian Van Doorninck, James Guest, Isobel Mason, Oliver Hicks, Bethan van Doornick, James Mills, Philip Dragoumis, Mark Wallace, Elissa Phipps, Alan Chapman. Dir: Colin Finbow. Ph: Amos Richardson. Editing Assistants: Matthew Landauer and Charles Robertson. M: David Hewson. (Children's Film Unit–ICA Projects) Rel: floating; first shown London (London Film Festival – ICA), 17 Nov 1984. 85 mins. No cert.

The Dogs – Les Chiens. A 1978 French thriller now seen in Britain for the first time. A new doctor arriving in one of France's ugly New Towns finds he is treating more dog bites than seems reasonable and soon uncovers some flesh-creeping – and flesh-biting – facts. Cast includes: Victor Lanoux, Gérard Dépardieu, Nicole Calfan, Pierre Vernier, Gérard Séty, Pierre Londiche, Stéphane Bouy, Henri Labussière, Gérard Caillaud, Philippe Mareuil, Anna Gaylor, Guy Saint-Jean, Fanny Ardant, Denyse Roland, Marc Chapill, Philippe Klébert, Régis Porte. Dir: Alain Jessua. Pro: Laurent Meyniel. Ex Pro: Daniel Deschamps. Assoc Pro: Serge Cohen. Screenplay: André Ruellan and Alain Jessua, based on an idea by the latter. Ph: Etienne Becker. Ed: Hélène Plemiannikov. Art: Jean-Louis Poveda. M: René Koering and Michel Portal (song by, and sung by Djiby). A.J. Films/AMS Productions/Les Films de la Drouette, Paris/Pacific Films, Tahiti–Connoisseur) Rel: floating; first shown London (Minema), 8 Jan 1985. 99 mins Cert 15.

Dreamscape. Far-fetched but wholly professional sci-fi thriller about a young man (Dennis Quaid) with psychic powers who somewhat reluctantly collaborates with scientist Max Von Sydow's experiments into dreams, more particularly into the potential of getting one man into another's dreams and organizing them for him! It comes in useful when US President Eddie Albert's nightmares are about to topple him from the White House, and villainous politician Christopher Plummer is taking deadly advantage of the situation. Good performances. Cast includes: Kate Capshaw, David Patrick Kelly, George Wendt, Larry Gelman, Cory 'Bumper' Yothers, Redmond Gleeson, Peter Jason, Larry Cedar, Chris Mulkey, Jana Taylor, Madison Mason, Kendall Carly Browne, Kate Charleson. Dir: Joe Ruben. Pro: Bruce Cohn Curtis. Screenplay: Ruben, David Loughery and Chuck Russell. Ex Pro: Stanley R. Zupnik and Tom Curtis. Co-Pro: Jerry Tokofsky. Ph: Brian Tufano. Ed: Richard Halsey. No Art credits. M: Maurice Jarre. (Bella Pro. Inc. – Thorn EMI) Rel: 26 Oct 1984. 98 mins. Cert 15.

The Dress. Beautifully moulded half-hour movie (like a very good short story) from a new female director-producer team. Michael Palin is the errant husband who by a lucky – or unlucky, as you care to see it – coincidence is compelled to give the daring

Eddie Albert (left) and Dennis Quaid in *Dreamscape*.

red dress he is buying for his mistress to his wife, with traumatic results for the trio when the wife causes a sensation with the gown when all three attend the same party. Rest of cast: Phyllis Logan, Derrick Branche, Dave Hill, Vivienne Ritchie, John Westbrook, Elisabeth Croft. Dir: Eve Sereny. Pro: Clare Downs. (Paramount/National Film Finance Corp.–UIP) Rel: 25 Jan 1985. 25 mins. Cert PG.

Michael Palin in *The Dress*.

The spectacular sci-fi film *Dune* with the hero Kyle MacLachlan (*left*). Far left are shaven beauties (left to right) Sian Phillips, Francesca Annis and Silvano Mangano.

Herbert. Pro: Raffaella de Laurentiis. Assoc Pro: José Lopez Rodero. Ph: Freddie Francis. Ed: Antony Gibbs. Pro Des: Anthony Masters. M: Toto (Prophecy theme by Brian Eno). Special Mechanical Effects: Kit West. Special Photographic Effects: Barry Nolan. Add. Special Visual Effects: Albert J. Whitlock. Creatures created by Carlo Rambladi. (Dino de Laurentiis/ Universal Pictures–UIP) Rel: 11 Jan 1985. 136 mins. Cert PG.

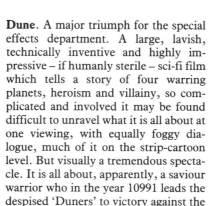

Dune. A major triumph for the special effects department. A large, lavish, technically inventive and highly impressive – if humanly sterile – sci-fi film which tells a story of four warring planets, heroism and villainy, so complicated and involved it may be found difficult to unravel what it is all about at one viewing, with equally foggy dialogue, much of it on the strip-cartoon level. But visually a tremendous spectacle. It is all about, apparently, a saviour warrior who in the year 10991 leads the despised 'Duners' to victory against the nasties of the other planets who covet the 'spice power' hidden beneath Dune's surface. Cast: Francesca Annis, Leonardo Cimino, Brad Dourif, José Ferrer, Linda Hunt, Freddie Jones, Richard Jordan, Kyle MacLachlan, Virginia Madsen, Silvano Mangano, Everett McGill, Kenneth McMillan, Jack Nance, Sian Phillips, Jurgen Prochnow, Paul Smith, Patrick Stewart, Sting, Dean Stockwell, Max Von Sydow, Alicia Roanne Witt, Sean Young. Dir and Screenplay: David Lynch; based on the book by Frank

Eddie and the Cruisers. A story about a teacher and former pop song composer for the group of the title who, when interest in his music of the 'sixties is revived, finds himself facing a dual mystery: did the group's leader really die when he made his plunge over the bridge? And what has happened to the missing master-tapes of what was planned to be the group's second album? Against a background of early, authen-

Lenny Von Dohlen with the computer that begins to take over his home and make a play for his girlfriend in *Electric Dreams*.

tic rock'n'roll, Tom Berenger, as teacher Ridgeway, solves the mysteries and finds romance with the girl who once didn't want to know . . . Rest of cast includes: Michael Paré, Helen Schneider, Matthew Laurence, David Wilson, Michael 'Tunes' Antunes, Ellen Barkin, Jo Pantoliano. Dir: Martin Davidson. Pro: Joseph Brooks and R. K. Lifton. Ex Pro: Rich Irvine and James L. Stewart. Screenplay: Martin and Arlene Davidson; based on the book by P. F. Kluge. Ph: Fred Murphy. Pro Des: Gary Weist. No Ed credit. M: Kenny Vance. Songs by John Cafferty. (Aurora/Lorimer–Media Releasing) Rel: floating; first shown London (Odeon, Marble Arch), 26 April 1985. 92 mins. Cert PG.

Edith and Marcel – Edith et Marcel. A Claude Lelouch film based on the tragic love affair between 'Little Paris Sparrow' *chanteuse* Edith Piaf and world champion French pugilist Marcel Cerdan; plus another, fictional, parallel (and largely irrelevant) story about a wartime pen-pal romance which hiccups violently upon physical meeting and ends on an uncomfortable note of compromise. A superbly convincing performance by Evelyne Bouix as Piaf (and as the other girl) and a stunning background of the singer's recordings of her often heart-aching numbers. Rest of cast: Jacques Villeret, Francis Huster, Jean-Claude Brialy, Jean Bouise, Charles Gérard, Marcel Cerdan Jr, Charlotte de Turckheim, Micky Sebastian, Maurice Garrel, Ginette Garcin, Philippe Khorsand, Jany Gastaldi, Candice Patou, Tanya Lopert, Jean Rougerie, Beata Tyszkiewicz, Charles Aznavour. Dir and Screenplay: Claude Lelouch. Pro: Tania Zazulinsky. Ph: Jean Bofféty. Pro Sup: Eugène Bellin. Ed: Hughes Darmois and Sandrine Péry. Art: Jacques Bufnoir. M: Francis Lai – lyrics by Charles Aznavour. Script Collaborators: Aznavour and Gilles Durieux. (Cannon/Gala) Rel: floating; first shown London (Berkeley, Tott Ct Rd and Arts, Chelsea), 18 Jan 1985. 140 mins. Cert PG.

Electric Dreams. A warning to all home computer nuts! The story of a young man who sets up one in his home and quickly finds it is not only interfering in his life but actually taking it over when the thing falls in love with his new girlfriend. A pretty silly story (excused as a 'fairy tale for computers') but sometimes lightly amusing and with nice performances from the two young leading players: Lenny Von Dohlen as the shy wooer and Virginia Madsen as the pretty cello-playing girlfriend, far more assured and confident than her wooer. And a nice mixture of classic and pleasant pop numbers on the sound-track. Rest of cast: Maxwell Caulfield, Bud Cort, Don Fellows, Alan Polonsky, Wendy Miller. Dir: Steve Barron. Pro: Rusty Lemorande and Larry de Waay; with story and screenplay by former. Ph: Alex Thomson. Ed: Peter Honess. Pro Des: Richard MacDonald. (Virgin Films–Fox–UK Film Dist) Rel: 5 Oct 1984. 111 mins. Cert PG.

The Element of Crime. Lars Von Trier in introducing this, his first feature film wrote: 'We won't settle for

Me Me Lei and Michael Elphick in *The Element of Crime.*

well-meaning films with a humanistic message. We want more . . .' And *more* he has certainly given us in an *avant garde* movie made in Denmark, in English, with English leading players, which Von Trier has so far steadfastly refused to allow to be dubbed in his native tongue! A weird sort of detective story set in a bombed, post-war, rotting Europe; photographed throughout in a sort of golden gloom; with sudden sidetracks into philosophical discussions and strange logical excursions. It leaves one stunned and numb; yet somehow impressed by its oddities. Cast: Michael Elphick, Me Me Lei, Esmond Knight, Jerold Wells, Preben Lerdorff Rye, Astrid Henning-Jensen, Ghota Andersen. Dir and Screenplay (latter with Niels Vorsel): Lars von Trier. Pro: Per Holst. Ph: Tom Elling. Ed: Thomas Gislason. M: Bo Holten. (Per Holst Filmproducktion in co-op with Danish Film Institute–Palace Pictures) Rel: floating; first shown London (Electric Screen), 7 June 1985. 104 mins. Cert 15.

Every Picture Tells a Story. An unremarkable but pleasing little British film by James Scott about, and made as a tribute to, his artist father, William Scott, R.A., reconstructing the latter's life from his Clydeside birth, to youthful work in Enniskellan with his signwriter father (who tragically dies trying to rescue people in a fire) and his

struggle to attain artistic recognition. Cast: Alex Norton, Phyllis Logan, Leonard O'Malley, John Docherty, Mark Airlie, Paul Wilson, Willie Joss, Natasha Richardson, Jack McQuaid. Dir: James Scott. Pro: Christine Oestreicher. Screenplay: Shane Con-

Timothy Hutton (left) and Sean Penn in *the Falcon and the Snowman.*

naughton. Ph: Adam Barker Mill. Ed: Chris Kelly. Art: Andrew Harris. Pro Des: Louise St. Jernsward. M: Michael Storey. (Flamingo Pictures in association with TSI Films Ltd. for Film Four International) Rel: floating; first shown London (Minema), 22 Mar 1985. 85 mins. Cert U.

Exterminator 2. A somewhat weak follow-up to *E1* with Robert Ginty again killing off the street-punk gangs in revenge for their having beaten, crippled and finally killed his girlfriend. Rest of cast includes: Mario Van Peebles, Deborah Geffner, Frankie Faison, Scott Randolph, Reggie Rock Bythewood, Bruce Smolanoff, David Buntzman. Dir, Pro and Screenplay: David Buntzman, with William Sachs. Ex Pro: Menahem Golan and Yoram Globus. Ph: Bob Baldwin and Joseph Mangine. Ed: Marcus Nanton and George Norris. Art: Mischa Petrow and Virginia Field (Cannon Group–Cannon Film Dist) Rel: 16 Nov 1984. 89 mins. Cert 18.

The Falcon and the Snowman. Based on fact; the story of two young American friends who for various reasons, mostly financial, decide to become spies for the Soviet Union, one of them having access to Top Secret documents. Although both end up in prison with life sentences, a possibly unintended impression is given that sometimes there can be some excuse for selling your country down the river! An uneven but often tense thriller, once again showing fact can be stranger than any fiction, the film leaves an impression of all sorts of things hidden beneath the surface which never clearly emerge. Nice performances in the demanding roles of the two odd agents by Timothy Hutton and Sean Penn, with splendid support from David Suchet as the KGB man and Pat Hingle as an unhappy parent. Rest of cast: Joyce Van Patten, Richard Dysart, Priscilla Pointer, Chris Makepeace, Dorian Harewood, Mady Kaplan, Macon McCalman, Jerry Hardin, Nicholas Pryor, Betty Lou Henson, Stanley Grover, Bob Arbogast, Boris Leskin, George C. Grant, Anatoly Davidov, Lori Singer, Jennifer Runyon, Dan McDonald, Marvin McIntyre, Dan Ingraffia, Tom Nolan, James Hardie, Burke Byrnes, Vic Polizos, Drew Snyder, Michael Ironside, Bob Nelson, Arthur Taxier, Philip Corey, Martha Campos, Herbie Wallace, Steven Miller, Jeff Seyfried, Steve Duffy, Carlos Romano, Valerie Wildman, George Belanger, Leopoldo Frances, Abel Franco, Raul Martinez, Guillermo Rios, Kamie Garza. Dir: John Schlesinger. Pro: Gabriel Katzka and John Schlesinger. Ex Pro: John Daly. Co-Pro: Edward Teets. Screenplay: Steven Zaillian, based on the book by Robert Lindsey. Ph: Allen Daviau. Ed: Richard Marden. Pro Des: J. D. Bissell. M: Pat Metheny and Lyle Mays. Assoc Pro: Michael Childers. (Orion–Rank Film Dist) Rel: 17 May 1985. 131 mins. Cert 15.

Falling in Love. Strangely reminiscent of the classic *Brief Encounter*, this lightweight piece is about a couple who, both settled in routine, normal marriages, are attracted to each other but cannot for all the obvious reasons kick over the traces and embark on the dangerous seas of an illicit affair. And the train schedules play a big part in their meetings and partings. Thanks more to the acting than the script it emerges as a pleasantly entertaining movie, with Meryl Streep (the less favoured of the two by her lines) and Robert De Niro both turning in fine performances. Rest of cast: Harvey

Keitel, Jane Kaczmarek, George Martin, David Clennon, Dianne Wiest, Victor Argo, Wiley Earl, Jesse Bradford, Chevi Colton, Richard Giza, Frances Conroy, James E. Ryan, Sonny Abagnale, George Barry, Paul Herman, Kenneth Welsh, L. P. McGlynn, John H. Reese, Yanni Sfinias, Clem Caserta, Rev. Donald Goodness, Florence Anglin, Gerald Kline. Dir: Ulu Grosbard. Pro: Marvin Worth. Screenplay: Michael Cristofer. Ph: Peter Suschitzky. Ed: Michael Kahn. Pro Des: Santo Loquasto. M: Dave Grusin. Art: Speed Hopkins (Paramount–UIP) Rel: 17 May 1985. 106 mins. Cert PG.

Fast Talking. Yet another excellent Australian feature; an amiable, sympathetic portrait of a lively 14-year-old Sydney lad whose background is a disaster (a broken home, a sot of a dad, a brother in the drugs business, etc.). But he remains cheerful in the face of a future which looks distinctly threatening. And beneath all the warmth and humour there is a serious message about the less pleasant side of modern society: for example schoolteachers are pilloried (interesting in view of the fact that director-writer Ken Cameron is himself a former teacher). Cast: Rod Zuanic, Toni Allaylis, Chris Truswell, Steve Bisley, Tracy Mann, Peter Hehir, Denis Moore, Gary Cook, Gail Sweeney. Dir and Screenplay: Ken Cameron. Pro: Ross Matthews. Ph: David Gribble. Ed: David Huggett. Pro Des: Neil Angwin. M: Sharon Calcraft (Oldata–Merchant Ivory/Century Filmtrax) Rel: floating; first shown London (Classics, Chelsea and Tott Ct Rd), 29 March 1985. 93 mins. Cert 18.

Favourites of the Moon – Les Favoris de la Lune. An inventive, confusing, amusing and fast-moving movie which with a touch of Tati here (especially in the police station sequences) and a glimpse of Clair there, manages to go flying off in all directions at once while seeming to maintain some sort of logical progression, and sticking close to its central theme about Time and the way we all waste it. A classic French crazy comedy directed by a Georgian Russian! Cast: Jean-Pierre Beauviala, Christine Bailly, Mathieu Amalric, Alix de Montaigu, Pascal Aubier, Bernard Eisenschitz, Hans Peter Cloos, René Vo Van Mindh, Katia Rupe, François Michel, Fanny Dupin, Vincent Blan-

chet, Gabriella Scheer, Marie-Claude Pouvesle, Marie Parra Aledo, Gaspard Flori, Emilie Aubry, Maité Nahyr, Julie Aubier, Laszlo Szabo, Baptiste Blanchet. Dir: Otar Yosseliani. Pro: Philippe Dussart. Ex Pro: Michel Choquet. Assoc Pro: Pierre André Boutang. Screenplay: Yosseliani and Gérard Brach. Ph: Philippe Theaudière. Ed: Dominique Bellfort. Pro Des: Claude Sune. M: Nicolas Zourabichvili. (Philippe Dusart/FR 3 Co-Pro with participation of Centre National de la Cinématographie Ministre de la Culture and RAI TV–Artificial Eye) Rel: floating; first shown London (Chelsea Cinema and Camden Plaza), 28 March 1985. 101 mins. Cert 15.

Finders Keepers. Typically uneven, crazy, and intermittently very funny (sometimes witty, too) Richard Lester comedy about a coffin travelling on a train which, instead of a body, contains lots and lots of 'greenback' loot (a 'greenback' is a dollar bill). Travelling with it, several characters anxious to get their hands on the cash, including a dizzy blonde with a four-letter-word

Rod Zuanic and Toni Allaylis take refuge from the chasing cops in *Fast Talking*.

A tense moment for Michael O'Keefe in *Finders Keepers*.

Ralph Bakshi's animated feature *Fire and Ice*.

vocabulary (Beverly D'Angelo), a sharp young man who falls in love with her (Michael O'Keefe), a smooth black con-man (Louis Gossett Jr), an heiress (Pamela Stephenson) who originally dreamed up the plot to do her rich daddy down, and a real nasty character who shares her greed (Ed Lauter)! And, as an example of the kind of fun it is, it all ends with a climax fought out on a travelling house! Yes, that's correct – *house*. Rest of cast includes: David Wayne, Brian Dennehy, Jack Riley, John Schuck, Timothy Blake, Jim Carrey, Robert Clothier, Jayne Eastwood, Alf Humphreys, Barbara Kermode, Paul Jolicoeur, Larry Reese, Blu Mankuma, Lloyd Berry, Ernie King, Richard Newman, Frances Flanagan, Campbell Lane, Wayne Robson, Margaret Martin, Judy Leigh-Johnson, Kevin Cork, John Stocker, Harvey Atkin, J. C. Roberts, Peter Haworth, The Unholy Rollers. Dir and Ex Pro: Richard Lester. Pro: Sandra and Terence Marsh. Assoc Pro: Dusty

Symonds. Screenplay: Ronny Graham, Terence Marsh and Charles Dennis; based on the latter's book *The Next to Last Train Ride*. Ph: Brian West. Ed: John Victor Smith. Art: J. Dennis Washington. M: Ken Thorne. (Theatrical Films–Rank) Rel: floating; first shown London (Plaza), 11 Jan 1985. 96 mins. Cert 15.

Fire and Ice. Comic-strip style Ralph Bakshi animated feature which once again is concerned with the everlasting struggle between Good (Fire) and Evil (Ice), continued in a future age when the advancing ice has pushed man into his last volcanic refuge. Frosted Lord Nekron and his mum, Juliana, obviously need the psychiatric treatment they cannot get as they send their Subhumans to wipe out the Humans, but are finally foiled by gallant young Larn and the mysterious warrior hero Darkwolf, plus the surprisingly resilient, brief-bikini-clad, very sexy Princess Teegra. Cast of voices: Randy Norton, Cynthia Leake, Steve Sandor, Sean Hannon, Leo Gordon, William Ostrander, Eileen O'Neill, Elizabeth Lloyd Shaw, Micky Morton, Tamarah Park, Big

Yank, Greg Elam, James Bridges, Shane Callan, Archie Hamilton, Michael Kellogg, Dale Park, Douglas Payton, Holly Frazetta. Dir and Pro (latter with Frank Frazetta): Ralph Bakshi. Ex Pro: John W. Hyde and Richard R. St. John. Screenplay: Roy Thomas and Gerry Conway (characters created by Bakshi and Frazetta). Ph: Francis Grumman. Ed: A. David Marshall. M: William Kraft. Animation Pro Sup: Michael Svayko. Assoc Pro: Lynne Betner. (Bakshi–Thorn EMI) Rel: floating; first shown London (ABC Shaftesbury Ave) 27 July 1984. 81 mins. Cert PG.

Firestarter. A confusingly confected thriller about a father with some sort of psychic powers (the result of a medical experiment) and his small daughter, who has the greater power of being able to conjure up at will anything from a flame capable of incinerating a man to a fireball powerful enough to demolish a large mansion; and the duo's flight from the government agents who would like to harness that power to official ends! Lots of brilliant special effects, an excellent performance by the small fire-raiser, Drew Barrymore. But a film which needs more than a couple of pinches of salt. Rest of cast: David Keith, Heather Locklear, Freddie Jones, Martin Sheen, George C. Scott, Art Carney, Louise Fletcher, Moses Gunn, Antonio Fargas, Drew Synder, Curtis Credel, Keith Colbert, Richard Warlock, Jeff Ramsey, Jack Magner, Lisa Anne Barnes, Larry Sprinkle, Cassandra Ward-Freeman, Scott R. Davis, Nina Jones, William Alspaugh,

Art Carney (left) and wife Louise Fletcher protect 'fiery' refuge-seeking guests Drew Barrymore and David Keith, in *Firestarter*.

Laurens Moore, Anne Fitzgibbon, Steve Boles, Stanley Mann, Robert Miano, Leon Rippy, Carole Francisco, Wendy Womble, Etan Boritzer, Joan Foley, John Sanderford, Orwin Harvey, George Wilbur, Carey Fox. Dir: Mark L. Lester. Pro: Frank Capra Jr. Assoc Pro: Martha Schumacher. Screenplay: Stanley Mann; based on the novel of same title by Stephen King. Ph: Giuseppe Ruzzolini. Ed: David Rawlins. Art: Giorgio Postiglione. M comp. and perf. by Tangerine Dream. (Dino de Laurentiis–Universal–UIP) Rel: 6 July 1984. 115 mins. Cert 15.

Forever Young. A mild, minor but pleasant enough British movie about – says its writer, Ray Connolly – 'broken dreams, remembered betrayals and the loss of innocence'. (And very nicely put, too!) The story is about a young man with a vocation for the priesthood and with a taste for pop music who in his youth seduced his best friend's girl.

Twenty years on, he – now a priest – turns up again and seduces the young and attractive mother of the young lad who is the priest's protégé – an event which, seen by the boy, sends the lad into shock and makes the priest come to

Nicholas Gecks as a pop-playing priest teaching Liam Holt how to handle a guitar in *Forever Young*.

terms with the fact that he loves the woman. This realization sends his previously cosy world crumbling. The film was partly financed by, and has every sign of being aimed at, the small screen. Cast: James Aubrey, Nicholas Gecks, Alec McCowen, Karen Archer, Liam Holt, Joseph Wright, Jane Forster, Jason Carter, Oona Kirsch, Eileen Fletcher, Carol MacReady, Julian

Firth, Jimmy Mac, Stanley Lloyd, Philip McGough, Robin Wentworth, Kate Percival, Anje Byer, Ruth Davies, Robert Hamilton, James Wynn, Martin Duncan, Pamela Miles, Robert Stagg, Peter Scott Harrison, Shelley Borkum, Kathy Burke, Michael Sundin. Dir: David Drury. Pro: Chris Griffin. Ex Pro: David Puttnam. Assoc Pro: David Bill. Screenplay: Ray Connolly. Ph: Norman Langley. Ed: Max Lemon. Art: Jeffrey Woodbridge. Theme Music: Peter Maxwell-Davies (Enigma/Goldcrest–Fox) Rel: floating; first shown London (Classic), 28 Sept 1984. 84 mins. Cert 15.

The Fourth Man – De Vierde Man. An intriguing and unusual film from Holland; a thriller which mixes suggestions of the occult, something of an obsession, scenes of bloody death and an eroticism approaching the pornographic which leaves the viewer with many questions unanswered. On the surface it tells the story of a homosexual writer who earns extra cash by lecturing and through this meets a lovely girl who immediately invites him to bed, where he finds her lover is a boy he lusts after. Every so often the writer has visions or nightmares, warnings of things to come . . . he swears Our Lady protects him and he is finally wheeled away by her to Peace! Certainly all *very* unusual, but showing exciting control and intelligent use of the medium. Cast: Jeroen Krabbé, Renee Soutendijk, Thom Hoffman, Dolf de Vries, Geert de Jong, Hans Veerman. Dir: Paul Verhoeven. Pro: Rob Houwer. Screenplay: Gerard Soeteman; from the novel by G. Reve. Ph: Jan de Bont. Ed: Ineke Schenkkan. Art: Roland de Groot. M: Moek Dikker. (Mainline Pictures) Rel: floating; first shown London (Chelsea Classic and Screen on the Hill), 13 July 1984. 95 mins. Cert 18.

Full Moon in Paris – Les Nuits de la Pleine Lune (Comedies et Proverbes). A typical Eric Rohmer conversation piece, and something of a moral tale about a young Parisian who, refusing to commit herself to her ardent lover and live with him in his suburban house – preferring to spend some nights in her Paris apartment after going out on the town – eventually loses him to another just at the moment she decides to move in with him on a permanent basis. A wry 'comedy' indeed, based on the

'proverb': 'A man with two women loses his soul, a man with two homes loses his mind.' A film made all the more movingly memorable by the fact that a few days before it was premiered in Britain its star, Pascale Ogier, who won the best actress award at the Venice Film Festival for her performance, died at the age of 24 from a heart attack. Rest of cast: Tchéky Karyo, Fabrice Luchini, Virginie Thévenet, Christian Vadim, Laszlo Szabo, Lisa Garneri, Mathieu Schiffman, Anne-Séverine Liotard, Hervé Grandsart. Noël Coffman. Dir and Screenplay: Eric Rohmer. Pro: Margaret Ménégoz. Ph: Jean-Paul Toraille and Gilles Arnaud. Ed: Cécile Decugis. Pro Des: Pascale Ogier. M: Elli & Jacno. (Les Films du Losange/Les Films Ariane–Artificial Eye) Rel: floating; first shown London (Chelsea Cinema and Camden Plaza), 8 Nov 1984. 102 mins. Cert 15.

A Funny, Dirty Little War. An Argentinian film set in the closing years of the Peronist regime telling how the government's decision to sack a leftist small town official leads to a revolt. Moulded into a black comedy. Cast includes: Federico Luppi, Hector Nidonde, Victor Laplace. Dir and Co-Screenplay (latter with Robert Cossa): Hector Olivera. Ph: Leonardo Rodriguez Solis. (ICA) Rel: floating; first shown London (ICA), 10 May 1985. 80 mins. Cert 18.

The Future of Emily. This Franco-German film with shades of Ibsen tells the story of the tortured love-hate relationship between a film star mother, *her* mother and father, and the child she has to park with them while she is filming. During a winter visit it is agonizingly revealed that while the mother envies the daughter her career and free lifestyle the daughter, in fact, would prefer to be the domesticated wife with home, husband and child. A lot (too much!) of painful talk but four excellent performances from star Brigitte Fossey, mother Hildegarde Knef, father Ivan Desny, child Tamille Raymond and lover Hermann Treusch. No other cast listed. Dir: Helma Sanders-Brahms. Ph: Sacha Vierney. Ed: Ursula West. M: Jurgen Knieper. (Mainline) Rel: floating; first shown London (Electric Screen), 26 April 1985. 107 mins. Cert 15.

Gabriella. A sexy little movie from Brazil which is considerably concerned with the various luscious charms of its leading lady, Sonia Braga, the most popular star of that South American country. She plays a girl who captivates bar-owner Marcello Mastroianni, who in spite of her faithlessness just cannot give her up. A novelty to prove it is not only nuts that they have in Brazil. Rest of cast: Antonio Cantafora, Paulo Goulart, Nelson Xavier, Nuno Leal Maia, Fernando Ramos, Nicole Puzzi, Tania Boscoli, Joffre Soares, Paulo Pilla, Claudia Gimenez, Ricardo Petraglia, Antonio Pedro, Yvan Mesquita, Zeni Pereira, Flavio Galvao, Myriam Pires, Iris Nascimento, Mauricio do Valle, Luthero Luiz. Dir: Bruno Barreto. Pro: Harold Nebenzal and Ibrahim Moussa. Pro Assoc: Helio Paulo Ferraz. Pro Sup: Jose Joaquim Salles, Vanni Ferrara and Terri Miller. Pro Co-Ord: Giuseppe Niglio and Mario Mearelli. Screenplay: Leopoldo Serran and Bruno Barreto; based on the novel *Gabriella, Cravo e Canela – Gabriella, Clove and Cinnamon* by Jorge Amado. Ph: Carlo di Palma. Ed: Emmanuelle Castro. Art: Helio Eichbauer. M: Antonio Carlos Jobim (The Sultana Corp., MGM/UA–UIP). Rel: floating; first shown London (Classic, Tott Ct Rd) 25 Oct 1984. 102 mins. Cert 18.

Ghostbusters. Taking more than $100 million at the US box office before it even reached Britain for a Christmas airing (one of only six films in the cinema's history to reach this figure), this expensively produced comedy features three ex-collegians (played by Bill Murray, Dan Aykroyd and Harold Ramis) who, having been tossed off campus, set up in business as de-haunters and find their first client (delightful lady possessed Sigourney Weaver) leads them into some very odd and occasionally funny adventures – with lots of most able contributions in the way of ghostliness by the special effects department. Rest of cast: Rick Moranis, Annie Potts, William Atherton, Ernie Hudson, David Margulies, Steven Tash, Jennifer Runyon, Slavitza Jovan, Michael Ensign, Alice Drummond, Jordan Charney, Timothy Carhart, John Rothman, Tom McDermott, Roger Grimsby, Larry King, Joe Franklin, Casey Kasem, Norman Matlock, Joe Cirillo, Joe Schmieg, Reggie Vel Johnson, Rhoda Gemignani, Mur-

Ghostbusters, starring (from left to right) Dan Aykroyd, Bill Murray and Harold Ramis as an intrepid trio who develop their own methods of dealing with spectres. Sigourney Weaver (right) is their first client.

ray Rubin, Larry Dilg, Danny Stone, Patty Dworkin, Jean Kasem, John Ring, Lenny Del Genio, Frances E. Nealy, Sam Moses, Christopher Wynkoop, Winston May, Tommy Hollis, Eda Reis Merin, Ric Mancini, Kathryn Janssen, Stanley Grover, Carol Ann Henry, James Hardy, Frances Turner, Nancy Kelly, Paul Trafas, Cheryl Birchenfield, Ruth Oliver, Kym Herrin, Bill Couch. Dir and Pro: Ivan Reitman. Ex Pro: Bernie Brillstein. Assoc Pro: Joe Medjuck and Michael C. Gross. Screenplay: Dan Aykroyd and Harold Ramis. Ph: Laszlo Kovacs and Kate Guinzberg. Ed: Sheldon Kahn with David Blewitt. Pro Des: John de Cuir. Visual Effects: Richard Edlund. M: Elmer Bernstein ('Ghostbusters' written and performed by Ray Parker Jr). (Black Rhino/Bernie Brillstein–Columbia Delphi Pro–Columbia) Rel: 7 Dec 1984. 105 mins. Cert PG.

Ghoulies. Minor, low-budget horror movie about some small but horrid little Satanistic creatures doing their nasty business against a background of a run-down-old-dark-house sort of building in Hollywood. Cast: Peter Liapis, Lisa Pelikan, Michael Des Barres, Jack Nance, Peter Risch, Tamara de Treaux, Scott Thomson, Ralph Seymour, Mariska Hargitay, Keith Joe

Dick, David Dayan. Dir: Luca Bercovici. Pro: Jeffery Levy. Ex Pro: Charles Band. Screenplay: Bercovici and Levy. Ph: Mac Ahlberg. Ed: Ted Nicolaou. Pro Des: John Carl Beuchler. M: Richard Band and Shirley Walker. Assoc Pro: Debra Dion. (Ghoulies Pro/Empire Pro-Entertainment) Rel: 28 June 1985. 84 mins. Cert PG.

Give My Regards to Broad Street. Paul McCartney's offering to his ego in a minor (though not in terms of budget and scale of production) piece showcasing three new and nine of his old numbers in a thin little story about a bad dream in which he imagines the master tapes of his proposed new album have been stolen by a crooked character who plans to take over his business. Cast includes: Paul McCartney, Bryan Brown, Ringo Starr, Barbara Bach, Linda McCartney, Tracey Ullman, Ralph Richardson, Ian Hastings. Dir: Peter Webb. Pro: Andros Epaminon-

das. Screenplay: Paul McCartney. Ph: Ian McMillan. Ed: Peter Beston. Pro Des: Anthony Pratt. Art: Adrian Smith. M (pro and dir): George Martin. (Fox) Rel: floating; first shown London (Empire and Odeon, Marble Arch), 30 Nov 1985. 108 mins. Cert PG.

The Glitterdome. James Garner as the cop suffering impotence as a result of his divorce, and John Lithgow as his haunted Catholic partner assigned the problem of discovering who killed the boss of a big film studio. An involved and difficult investigation that leads down several wrong roads before Garner – his partner having committed suicide along the way – can wearily wrap up the case. Rest of cast: Margot Kidder, John Marley, Stuart Margolin, Paul Koslo, Colleen Dewhurst, Alex Diakun, Bill Kerr, William Taylor, Dusty Morean, Christianne Hirt, Tom McBeath, Dixie Seatle, Dale Wilson, Julian Munoz, Sal Lopez, Real Andrews, Stephen Chang, Dawn Luker, Claudine Melgrave, Colin Skinner, Harvey Miller, Enid Saunders, Alistair MacDuff, Clara Kamunde, William Nunn, Preston Ford, Beau Kazer,

Christopher, Michelle and Max Martini, Benson Fong. Dir & M: Stuart Margolin. Pro: Margolin and Justis Greene. Ex Pro: Frank Konigsberg. Screenplay: Stanley Kallis; based on the novel by Joseph Wambaugh. Ph: Michael Watkins and Fred Murphy. Ed: M. S. Martin. Pro Des: Douglas Higgins. Assoc Pro: Barry Jossen. (Thorn EMI) Rel: floating; first shown London (ABCs at Shaftesbury Ave, Edgware Rd and Bayswater), 23 Nov 1984. 94 mins. Cert 18.

Gremlins. Steven Spielberg's sci-fi comedy-thriller (with a very black underlining!) relating a story about an eccentric inventor who brings home, as a Christmas present to his teenage son, a cuddly little muppet-like creature he has bought in Chinatown from a somewhat reluctant seller who warns him about the little chap's dangers. His warnings are not heeded and soon there is a whole army of vicious little monsters who proceed to create havoc in the small town of Kingston Falls, including the killing of the local police force, and various other inhabitants, and are only finally defeated by the bright young lad

James Garner (left) plays the worried cop, Margot Kidder a film star and John Lithgow his suicidal partner in *The Glitterdome*.

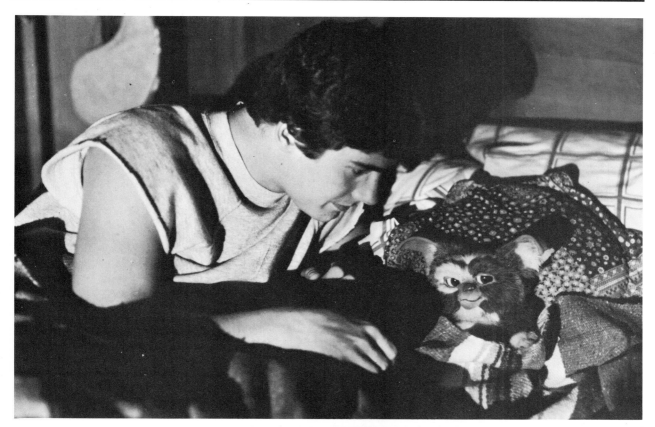

Above: a delighted Zach Galligan with his father's Christmas gift in *Gremlins*.

and his pretty girlfriend in the explosive climax. A deft mixture of youthful charm, horrors (though even these are sometimes given comic twists), humour, spectacle, arguable taste – in parts – and a marvellous contribution by monster-maker and cuddly toy creator Chris Walas. Cast: Zach Galligan, Hoyt Axton, John Louie, Keye Luke, Don Steele, Susan Burgess, Scott Brady, Arnie Moore, Corey Feldman, Harry Carey Jr., Dick Miller, Phoebe Cates, Polly Holliday, Don Elson, Belinda Belaski, Daniel Llewelyn, Edward Andrews, Judge Reinhold, Lois Foraker, Chuck Jones, Kenny Davis, Frances Lee McCain, Glyn Turman, Nick Katt, Tracy Wells, John C. Becher, Gwen Willson, Jonathan Banks, Jackie Joseph, Joe Brooks, Jim McKrell. Dir: Joe Dante. Pro: Michael Finnell. Ex Pro: Steven Spielberg, Frank Marshall and Kathleen Kennedy. Screenplay: Chris Columbus. Ph: John Hora. Ed: Tina

Hirsch. Pro Des: James H. Spencer. M: Jerry Goldsmith. Gizmo and the Gremlins designed, created and operated by Chris Walas Inc. Musical numbers: 'Christmas' perf. Darlene Love; 'Make It Shine' by Quarterflash; 'Do You Hear What I Hear' by Johnny Mathis; 'Out, Out', perf. and written by Peter Gabriel; 'Gremlins . . . Mega-Madness' perf. (and co-written) by Michael Sembello. (Amblin Entertainment-Warner) Rel: 7 Dec 1984. 106 mins. Cert 15.

The Grey Fox. Fascinating and in its modest way quite outstanding off-beat western based on fact: the story of Bill Miner, an ageing, gentle character who after 33 years in San Quentin for robbing stage coaches cannot resist trying the game with trains when he is released. He is eventually caught but he gets the final laugh. A picture-stealing performance by veteran actor Richard Farnsworth as the old Fox. Rest of cast: Jackie Burroughs, Ken Pogue, Timothy Webber, Gary Reineke,

Richard Farnsworth as the delightfully polite stagecoach/train robber in *The Grey Fox*.

Wayne Robson, David Petersen, Don Mackay, Samatha Langevin, Tom Heaton, James McLarty, George Dawson, Ray Michal, Stephen E. Miller, David L. Crowley, David McCulley, Gary Chalk, Jack Leaf, Isaac Hislop, Sean Sullivan, Bill Murdock, Jack Ackroyd, Nicholas Rice, Frank Turner, Bill Meilan, David Raines, Paul Jolicoeur, Mel Tuck, Peter Jobin, David Ackridge, Paul Whitney, Murray Ord, Tom Glass, Anthony Holland, Jon York, John Owen, Lisa Westman. Dir: Phillip Borsos. Pro: Peter O'Brian. Ex Pro: David H. Brady. Co-Pro: Barry Healey and Borsos. Screenplay: John Hunter. Ph: Frank Tidy. Ed: Frank Irvine. Pro Des: Bill Brody. M: Michael Conway Baker. (Peter O'Brian/Mercury Pictures Pro, with Canadian Film Development Corp–Palace Pictures) Rel: 17 May 1985. 92 mins. Cert PG.

Hambone and Hillie. With a winning mongrel dog as co-star to the ever-youthful Lillian Gish (in her 103rd film!) this highly sentimental, Disneyish (shades of that maestro's *The Incredible Journey*) comedy-drama could hardly fail to soften the hardest heart and amuse and entertain the entire family. It follows the journey of more than 3000-miles across country by the canine adventurer Hambone as he determinedly seeks his beloved mistress, lost to him because of a mischance at the airport when her New York plane takes off for Los Angeles. The trek involves Hambone in getting drunk, fighting off wolves, freeing some unfortunate, imprisoned fellow curs, and coming through a desperate desert ordeal: passing en route through city, ghetto, town slum, mountain range, quiet rural countryside and typical American suburbia. Suspend belief – this doggy delight appears on occasion even to be able to read! – and you'll adore this canine charmer and his adventures. Rest of cast: Timothy Bottoms, Candy Clark, O. J. Simpson, Robert Walker, Jack Carter, Alan Hale, Anne Lockhart, William Jordan, Paul Koslo, Nancy Morgan. Dir: Roy Watts. Pro: Gary Gillingham and Sandy Howard. Co-Pro: Roger La Page. Ex Pro: Mel Pearl and Don Levin. Screenplay: Sandra K. Bailey, Michael Murphy and Joel Soisson; based on a story by Ken Barnett. Ph: Jon Kranhouse. Ed: Robert J. Kizer. Pro Des: Helena Reif. M: George Garavarentz. (Sandy Howard Pro./Adams Apple Film Co./New World Pictures in assoc with Cinemamerica Pictures Corp, VTC and Grahame Jennings–ITC) Rel: floating; first shown London (Premier), 20 July 1984. 89 mins. Cert U.

Hamsin. Israeli production with a sad story about an ill-starred love affair between a Jewish girl and a handsome young Arab working for her liberal-minded farmer dad. This story is set against a moralistic background about the friction between the two races in Galilee (1982) caused by Jewish appropriation of the Arab land, thus causing a gulf between the races who for many years have lived side by side in comparative harmony. Cast: Shlomo Tarshish, Hemda Levy, Ruth Geler, Yassin Shawaf. Dir: Daniel Wachsmann. Pro: Jacob Lifshin. Screenplay: Wachsmann, Lifshin and Danny Verete. Ph: David Gurfinkel. Ed: Levi Zini. M: Raviv Gazit. (Contemporary) Rel: floating; first shown London (Phoenix, East Finchley), 9 Nov 1984. 87 mins. Cert 15.

Harry and Son. Taking on the direction as well as the star part, together with co-writing and co-producing, Paul Newman never manages to tie into a neat bundle the various threads of this father-and-son piece, although it has some good sequences here and there. Newman plays a building worker who loses his job when he – temporarily – loses his sight, and he takes out his irritation on his son. Rest of cast: Robby Benson, Ellen Barkin, Wilford Brimley, Judith Ivey, Ossie Davis, Morgan Freeman, Katherine Borowitz, Maury Chaykin, Joanne Woodward. Dir: Paul Newman. Pro and Screenplay: Newman and Ronald L. Buck; suggested by the novel *A Lost King*, by Raymond De Carpite. Ph: Donald McAlpine. Ed: Dede Allen. Pro Des: Henry Bumstead. M: Henry Mancini. (Orion–Rank Film Dist) Rel: floating; first shown London (Odeon, Haymarket), 11 May 1984. 117 mins. Cert 15.

Heimat – Homeland. Edgar Reitz's gargantuan, 15½-hour-plus West German movie took some 15 months to prepare and 18 months to shoot (in all, with post-production work, the time spent was 5 years and 4 months to complete). It is a partly autobiographical story of a village and the villagers (and also something of the story of Germany itself) between 1919 and 1982. Leisurely told, filled with incident, the film is consistently and completely absorbing, and so well made that it does not seem a minute too long, though the constant switching from black-and-white to colour photography appears irritatingly pointless. The film is without doubt a unique and tremendous achievement, unequalled in ambition and resultant attainment since Erich von Stroheim's *Greed* and Fassbinder's less important yet artistically successful 15½-hour *Berlin Alexanderplatz*. Cast includes: Marita Breuer, Willi Burger, Gertrud Bredel, Rüdiger Weigang, Karin Rasenack, Dieter Schaad, Michael Lesch, Peter Harting, Jörg Richter, Johannes Lobewein, Gertrud Sherer, Hans Jürgen Schatz, Wolfram Wagner, Eva-Maria Schneider, Eva Maria Bayerwaltes, Karin Kienzler, Arno Lang, Mathias Kniesbeck, Markus Reiter, Rolf Roth, Sabine Wagner, Michael Kausch, Roland Bongard, Inge Hoffman, Kurt Wagner, Gabriele Blum, Anke Jandrychowski, Jörg Hube, Johannes Metzdorf, Alexander Scholz, Marlies Assmann, Gudrun Landgrebe, Helga Bender, Joachim Bernhard, Hans-Günter Kylau, Gerd Riegauer, Otto Henn, Virginie Moreno, Rudolf Wessely, Kurt Wolfinger, Roswitha Werkheiser, Heike Macht, Alexandra Katins, Andreas Mertens. Dir and Pro: Edgar Reitz. Ex Pro: Inge Richter. TV Co-Pro: Joachim von Mengershausen (WDR) and Hans Kwiet (SFB). Screenplay: Reitz and Peter Steinbach. Ph: Gernot Roll. Ed: Heidi Handorf. Art: Franz Bauer. M: Nikos Mamangakis. (Reitz Film Pro in association with Westdeutscher Rundfunk – WDR – Cologne and Sender Fries SFB – Berlin-Artificial Eye) Rel: floating; first shown London, in four parts (Lumière), from 16 Feb 1985. 15 hours 36 mins. Cert 15.

The Highest Honour. Australian/Japanese co-production: Australian title, *Southern Cross*: Japanese title, *Minami Jujisei*. A pruned and revamped 108-minute version of the original 143-minute movie about the Japanese Occupation of Singapore during the last war and the efforts of the local Nippon Welfare Officer to mitigate his own countrymen's brutality and excesses. Cast: John Howard, Atsuo Nakamura, Stuart Wilson, Steve Bisley, Michael Aitkens, George Mallaby, Tony Bonner, John Ley, Harry Hopkins, Garry Waddell, Tim Elston, Neil Redfern, Michael Harris, Hu Inn Mong, Ken Goodlet, Hohsei Komatsu, Miziuho Suzuki, Allan Cassell, Slim Degrey, Baz Luhrmann, Mark Hembrow, Jonathan Sweet, Andrew Inglis, Warren Coleman, Noel Hodda, Takuya Fujioka, Bancho Tsuji, James Belton, Craig Ballard, Vincent Ball, Trevor Summers, John Griffiths, George Duff, Hassain Abu Hassan, You Numazaki, Taroh Shigaki, Riki Harada, Minori Terada, Takeshi Ohbayashi, Katshuhiro Oyama, Hajime Tawara, Jiro Sakagami, Kinya Kitaohji, Kojiro Kusanagi, Shoiehiro Sakata. Dir: Peter Maxwell. Pro: Lee Robinson. Ex Pro: John McCallum. Assoc Pro: Katsuya Suzaki and Takeo Ito. Pro Sup: Betty Barnard. Assoc Dir: Seiji Maruyama. Screenplay: Lee Robinson in association with Suzaki and Ito. Ph: John McLean. Ed: David Stiven. Pro Des: Bernard Hides. Art: Virginia Bieneman. M: Eric Jupp. (Southern Enterprise Films–Enterprise Pictures) Rel: floating; first shown London (Classics and Odeon, Kensington), 12 Oct 1984. 108 mins. Cert 15.

Highway to Hell. (*Running Hot* in America, where it was originally titled *Lucky 13*.) A sort of minor 'Road' film with Eric Stoltz as the teenager on the run – accompanied by a helpful prostitute (Monica Carrico) – after he has been condemned to death for the murder of his dad, a crime of which he is, it turns out, innocent. The many rock songs on the soundtrack cannot disguise the weakness of the film's motivation; however there is the (perhaps unintentional) occasional laugh along the way between the death throes of the various characters. Rest of cast: Stuart Margolin, Virgil Frye, Richard Bradford, Louise Baker, Joe George, Laurel Patrick, Sorrells Pickard, Ben Hammer, Juliette Cummins. Dir and Screenplay: Mark Griffiths. Pro: David Calloway. Ex Pro: Dimitri T. Skouras. Ph: Tom Richmond. Ed: Andy Blumenthal. Pro Des: Katherine Vallin. Art: Anthony Cowley. Co-Pro: Zachary Feuer. (Highroad Pro in association with Westcom Pro/New Line Cinema–Anglo American) Rel: floating; first shown London (Scene), 27 July 1984. 90 mins. Cert 18.

The Hit. A stylish if pretty consistently unconvincing movie about a crook (Terence Stamp, his best work in years) who, after ten years of the good life in Spain following his 'grassing' on his companions in crime, is abducted by a hit man (John Hurt, playing the role as a woodenly sardonic satire) whose assignment is to take him back through Spain and France to his execution in Paris. This itinerary goes awry, thanks to the potential victim's cheerful acceptance of his fate, the killer's amateur assistant (Tim Roth) and the pretty little spitfire (Laura del Sol) who is forced to go along after witnessing an early killing. Superb scenic backgrounds and an explosive, unexpected finale. All quite fascinating; and British, too. Rest of cast: Fernando Rey, Bill Hunter, Freddie Stuart, Ralph Brown, A. J. Clarke, Lennie Peters, Bernie Searle, Brian Royal, Albie Woodington, Willoughby Gray, Jim Broadbent, Manuel de Benito, Juan Calot, Quique San Francisco, Joaquin Alonso, José Luis Fernandez, Camilo Vilanova, Tim Roth, Carlos Lucena, Miguel Garmendia, Carlos Zabala,

Eneko Olazagasti, Patxi Barko, Xavier Aguirre, Carlos Tristancho. Dir: Stephen Frears. Pro: Jeremy Thomas. Assoc. Pro: Joyce Herlihy. Pro Sup: Denise O'Dell. Screenplay: Peter Prince. Ph: Mike Molloy. Ed: Mick Audsley. Pro Des: Andrew Sanders. M: Paco de Lucia (Title music by Eric Clapton). (Glinwood Films/Central Productions/Recorded Picture Co. – Zenith Productions–Palace Pictures) Rel: 13 Sept 1984. 97 mins. Cert 18.

The Home and the World – Ghare-Baire. A long, leisurely paced Satyajit Ray film with a human triangle story set against an important Indian historical event: the Bengal Moslem-Hindu riots of 1908, caused by the 'Divide and Rule' policy of Lord Curzon, the then Governor General of India, giving birth to the 'Swadeshi' movement which sought to ban the sale of all British and other foreign goods. The film follows the problem this causes for a liberal-minded lord (Victor Banerjee) who, while supporting the idea in theory, sees it as likely to harm the poor Moslems under his jurisdiction, and so comes into open conflict with his charismatic friend (Soumitra Chatterji) who stirs up a campaign of terrorism while wooing his host's wife (Swatilekha Chatterji). The last film to be made by Jennifer (Kapoor) Kendal prior to her death in September 1984. Rest of cast: Gopa Aich, Manoj Mitra, Indrapramit Roy, Bimala Chatterjee. Dir, Screenplay (based on the novel by Rabindranath Tagore) and M: Satyajit Ray. Ph: Soumendi Roy. Ed: Dulal Dutt. Art: Ashoke Bose. (National Development Corp. of India–Artificial Eye) Rel: floating; first shown London (Academy), 13 Sept 1984. 140 mins. Cert U.

The Hotel New Hampshire. An odd but occasionally effective patchwork quilt of black humour, sex (both normal and immoral: incest, homosexuality), other nastiness, and plenty of foul language in Tony Richardson's adaptation of John Irving's sprawling novel which has quite a lot in common with *The World According to Garp*. It concerns a family whose motto for existence is to 'pass by open windows' – not heeded by its smallest member, who after a big literary success and then a flop stops by one and jumps! In a pageant of life, love, sorrow, happiness

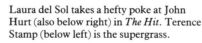

Laura del Sol takes a hefty poke at John Hurt (also below right) in *The Hit*. Terence Stamp (below left) is the supergrass.

Family and friends line-up in *The Hotel New Hampshire*, including Jodie Foster (left) Beau Bridges (third from left) and Nastassja Kinski (second from right).

and death, the family move from American failure to equal lack of success in Vienna (where they are joined by Nastassja Kinski, who actually lives in a bearskin!) and finally return to smoother, happier days in their smart new US 'Hotel Arbuthnot'. And that's only one little bit of the incident overfilled story. Cast: Jodie Foster, Rob Lowe, Paul McCrane, Beau Bridges, Lisa Banes, Jennie Dundas, Seth Green, Nastassja Kinski, Wallace Shawn, Wilford Brimley, Wally Aspell,

Joely Richardson, Jobst Oriwal, Linda Clark, Nicholas Podbrey, Norris Domingue, Matthew Modine, Cali Timmins, Dorsey Wright, Richard Jutras, Johnny O'Neil, Colin Irving, Anthony Ulc, Nick Nardi, Charles Fournier, Anita Morris, Fred Doederlein, Walter Massey, Young Sup Chung, Inhi Chung, Ada Fuoco, Joan Heney, Robert Thomas, Gayle Garfinkle, Jonelle Allen, Elie Oren, Roger Blay, Timothy Webber, Janine Manatis, Jean-Louis Roux, Amanda Plummer, Sharon Noble, Lorena Gale, Jade D. Bari, Adrian Aron, Arthur Grosser, Tara O'Donnell, Louis de Bianco, Jyanna Honey, Michele Scarabelli, Jeffrey Cohen, Benoit Laberge, Jon Hutman, James V. Mathews, Prudence Emery. Dir and Screenplay: Tony

Richardson (from a novel by John Irving). Pro: Neil Hartley, Pieter Kroonenberg and David Patterson. Co-Pro: Jim Beach. Ex Pro: George Yaneff, Kent Walwin and Grahame Jennings. Ph: David Watkin. Ed: Robert K. Lambert. Pro Des: Jocelyn Herbert. Art: John Meighen. M: Offenbach, arr. and con. by Raymond Leppard. Assoc Pro: Bill Scott and Norman Twain. Pro Co-Ord: Daniele Rohrbach. (Woodfall Inc. for Orion–Thorn EMI) Rel: 4 Jan 1985. 108 mins. Cert 18.

Improper Conduct. A provocative documentary from France which attacks Castro's social policies, more especially his lack of sympathy for homosexuals and the like (hippies,

Harrison Ford (left) in *Indiana Jones and the Temple of Doom*. (Above) The fun and danger is shared by Ke Huy Quan and Kate Capshaw.

long-hairs, etc.). It pulls no punches – and sometimes slips into some dubious body blows! With: Renaldo Arenas, Guillermo Cabrera Infante, Susan Sontag, Armando Valladares, Harberto Padilla, Caracol, Fidel Castro. Dir and Screenplay: Nestor Almendros and Orlando Jiminez Leal. Pro: Margaret Menegoz, Barbet Schroeder and Michel Thoulouze. Ph: Dominique Merlin. Ed: Michel Pion and Alain Tortevoix. (ICA) Rel: floating; first shown London (ICA), Jan 1985. 115 mins. No cert.

Indiana Jones and the Temple of Doom. A pacey, violent, thrilling, amusing and consistently entertaining all-action melodrama (reminiscent of about ten old silent serials all crammed into two hours) that continues the unlikely adventures of that unlikely archaeologist Jones (Harrison Ford, continuing the characterization he created in this film's forerunner, *Raiders of the Lost Ark*). The action moves rapidly from Shanghai to Macau and on to India as our intrepid hero seeks the magic stone – along with a blonde nightclub singer Kate Capshaw and small Chinese aide Ke Huy Quan. Rest of cast: Amrish Puri, Roshan Seth, Philip Stone, Roy Chiao, David Yip, Ric Young, Chua Kah Joo, Rex Ngui, Philip Tann, Dan Aykroyd, Akio Mitamura, Michael Yama, D. R. Nanayakkara, Dharmadasa Kuruppu, Stany de Silva, Ruby de Miel, D. M. Denawake, I. Serasinghe, Dharshana Panagala, Raj Singh, Frank Olegario, Ahmed El-

Shenawi, Art Repola, Nizwar Karanj, Pat Roach, Moti Makan, Mellan Mitchell, Bhasker Patel, Arjun Pandher, Zia Gelani. Dir: Steven Spielberg. Pro: Robert Watts. Ex Pro: George Lucas and Frank Marshall. Screenplay: Willard Huyck and Gloria Katz; from a story by Lucas. Ph: Douglas Slocombe. Ed: Michael Kahn. Pro Des: Elliot Scott. M: John Williams. Assoc Pro: Kathleen Kennedy. 2nd Unit Dir: Michael Moore. UK Crew Pro Sup: John Davis. London Unit Dir: Frank Marshall. Macau Pro Sup: Vincent Winter. Sri Lanka Pro Sup: Chandran Rutnam. Aerial Unit Dir: Kevin Donnelly. (Lucasfilm Ltd/Spielberg-Paramount-UIP) Rel: 13 July 1984. 117 mins. Cert PG.

The Innocent. A heart-warming, beautifully tailored British film about a boy growing up in the Yorkshire Dales during the Depression of the 1930s. It is a film of sunlit countryside and worried townsfolk, as the local mill closes down. A movie which, in parts, reminds one irresistibly of *Kes*. Cast: Tom Bell, Liam Neeson, Kika Markham, Miranda Richardson, Clive

Wood, Denis Lil, Kate Foster, Andrew Hawley, Patrick Daley, Richard Hope, Jack Carr, Richard Laxton, Alison Lloyd, Bill Rodgers. Dir: John Mackenzie. Pro: Jackie Stoller. Ex Pro: Dickie Bamber. Screenplay: Ray Jenkins; based on the novel *The Aura and the Kingfisher* by Tom Hart. Ph: Roger Deakins. Ed: Tony Woollard. Pro Des: Andrew Mollo. Art: Philip Elton. M: Francis Monkman. (Tempest Films for TVS–Curzon) Rel: floating; first shown London (Curzon West End), 31 May 1985. 96 mins. Cert 15.

Into the Night. A carefully tailored construction of gore and (some) guffaws in a good old chase comedy-thriller; with Jeff Goldblum as the insomniac who becomes increasingly involved with the pretty girl who lands on his car's bonnet during a midnight jaunt to the local airport. It is soon revealed she is fleeing from a gang of trigger-happy Iranians who, along with sundry other crooked characters, are after the fortune in precious stones she's smuggled into the country, and so she and her initially accidental protector cannot go to the police to save them from all the nastiness that is always hot on their heels. Michelle Pfeiffer as the girl with the gems is gorgeous enough to recruit any normal male to her side, especially our hero, who has just found out his wife is having an affair. Rest of cast includes: Stacey Pickren, Carmen Argenziano, Dan Aykroyd, Richard Farnsworth, Kathryn Harrold, David Bowie, Irene Papas, Paul Mazursky, Paul Bartel, Don Siegel, Roger Vadim, Vera Miles, Clu Gulager, Carl Gottlieb, Robert Paynter, David Cronenberg, Robert Moberly, John Hostetter, Dick Balduzzi, Richard Franklin, Cal Worthington, Wes Dawn, Christopher George, Ali Madani, Michael Zand, Hadi Sadjadi, Beruce Gramian, John Landis, Hope Clarke, Eric Lee, Jake Steinfeld, Sue Bowser, Waldo Salt, Viola Kate Simpson, Bruce McGill, Jon Stephen Fink, Deedee Pfeiffer, Rick Baker, Colin Higgins, Daniel Petrie, David Sosna, Mark Levine, William Kaplan, Jonathan Kaufer, Saul Kahan, Jonathan Lynn, Bill Taylor, Jim Bentley, Pete Ellis, Jack Arnold, Hassan Ildari. Dir: John Landis. Pro: George Folsey Jr and Ron Koslow. Ex Pro: Dan Allingham. Screenplay: Ron Koslow. Ph: Robert Paynter. Ed: Malcolm

Andrew Hawley as *The Innocent*, growing up in the Yorkshire Dales in the 1930s.

Campbell. Pro Des: John Lloyd. M: Ira Newborn (featuring B. B. King). Assoc Pro: David Sosna. (Universal–UIP) Rel: 26 April 1985. 115 mins. Cert 15.

Jeff Goldblum comes to the aid of pretty Michelle Pfeiffer in *Into the Night*.

Irreconcilable Differences. The examination of one more marriage that has gone sour, and how it went that way; with the novel angle that it is the 9-year-old daughter of the pair (Drew Barrymore) who decides to sue her parents (Ryan O'Neal and Shelley Long) for divorce! She reckons she is the adult and the parents the children not responsible enough to bring her up, a premise agreed by the court, who put

Shelley Long and Ryan O'Neal fight over possession of Drew Barrymore (also left) in *Irreconcilable Differences*.

her into the care of her comfy old nurse. Behind all this is the failure to success story of the mother, with a best-selling book, and the success to failure story of the father, whose musical, movie version of *Gone with the Wind* dies the death at the box office. An old, familiar storyline decorated with some goodies like witty lines, a moral undertone, amusing performances and a nicely ironic look at Hollywood and its life-style. Rest of cast: Sam Wanamaker, Allen Garfield, Sharon Stone, Hortensia Colorado, Richard Michenberg, Lorinne Vozoff, Stuart Pankin, David Graf, Jenny Gago, David Paymer, Beverlee Reed, Charlotte Stewart, Rex Reed, Kelly Lange, Steffen Zacharias, Ken Lerner. Dir: Charles Shyer. Pro: Arlene Sellers and Alex Winitsky. Ex Pro: Nancy Meyers. Assoc Pro:

Richard Hashimoto. Screenplay: Shyer and Meyers. Ph: William A. Fraker. Ed: John F. Burnett. Pro Des: Ida Random. Art: Jane Bogart. M: Paul de Senneville and Olivier Toussaint. (Piano solos played by Richard Clayderman.) (Lantana–Warner/Guild International) Rel: floating; first shown London (Leicester Square Theatre), 15 Feb 1985. 113 mins. Cert 15.

Jazzin' for Blue Jeans. A 22-minute short which started out as a promotional video for David Bowie's single of that title but emerged good enough for the decision to be taken to give it a big-screen airing. Bowie plays the double role of an innocent trying to impress the girl of his dreams (Louise Scott) and a wild pop performer (a wonderful guying of his own stage act) and shows a nice sense of self-parody. Dir: Julien Temple. Screenplay: Terry Johnson. Conceived by David Bowie. (Nitrate Films) Rel: 5 Oct 1984. 22 mins. Cert U.

The gunman (Jo Piscopo), the suave gangster boss (Michael Keaton) and the girl (Marilu Henner) in *Johnny Dangerously*.

Johnny Dangerously. In spite of the occasional lapse into bad taste, a very amusing farce-comedy which sends up the 1930s American gangster era by presenting the story of a smart young man who rises from paper-boy to gangster boss (forced into the business by the constant need to raise money for the string of illnesses suffered by his apparently always fit washer-woman Ma). A neat performance in the title role by Michael Keaton. Rest of cast: Jo Piscopo, Marilu Henner, Maureen Stapleton, Peter Boyle, Griffin Dunne, Glynnis O'Connor, Dom DeLuise, Richard Dimitri, Danny DeVito, Ron Carey, Ray Walston, Dick Butkus, Byron Thames, Alan Hale, Scott Thomson, Sudie Bond, Mark Jantzen, Gary Watkins, Mike Bacarella, Hank Garrett, Leonard Termo, Troy W. Slaten, Alexander Hertzberg, George Olden, Cynthia Szigeti. Dir: Amy Heckerling. Pro: Michael Hertzberg. Ex Pro: Bud Austin and Harry Colomby. Screenplay: Norman Steinberg, Bernie Kukoff, Harry Colomby and Jeff Harris. Ph: David M. Walsh. Ed: Pem Herring. Pro Des: J. R. Jennings. M: John Morris. Assoc Pro: Neil A. Machlis. (Fox–U.K. Film Dist) Rel: 17 May 1985. 90 mins. Cert 15.

The Karate Kid. A sort of junior – but more tender – *Rocky* (actually directed by John G. Avildsen, the guiding hand of the first of those several movies). A story about a young lad (Ralph Macchio) from New Jersey who finds life pretty tough when he emigrates with his Mum to California, where he becomes the target for a gang of bullies. But thanks to the expert tuition, both mental and physical, of an Oriental janitor, who just happens to be a Karate expert, he learns to fight back – and how! Rest of cast: Noriyuki 'Pat' Morita, Elisabeth Shue, Martin Kove, Rande Heller, William Zabka, Ron Thomas, Rob Garrison, Chad McQueen, Tony O'Dell, Israel Juarbe, William Bassett, Larry B. Scott, Juli Fields, Dana Andersen, Frank Burt Avalon, Jeff Fishman, Ken Daly, Tom Fridley, Pat E. Johnson, Bruce Malmuth, Darryl Vidal, Frances Bay,

Left to right, Elisabeth Shue, Ralph Macchio and William Zabka in *The Karate Kid*.

Christopher Kriesa, Bernard Kuby, Joan Lemmo, Helen J. Siff, Larry Drake, David Abbott, Molly Basler, Brian Davis, David de Lange, Erik Felix, Peter Jason, Todd Lockinland, Clarence McGee, Jr, William Noren, Sam Scarber, Scott Strader. Dir: John G. Avildsen. Pro: Jerry Weintraub. Ex Pro: R. J. Louis. Screenplay: Robert Mark Kamen. Ph: James Crabe. Ed: Bud Smith, Walt Muconery and Avildsen. Pro Des: William J. Cassidy. M:

Sam Waterston and Dr Haing S. Ngor in
The Killing Fields. Right, the fields of the
title.

Bill Conti. Assoc Pro: Bud Smith. (Columbia) Rel: 31 Aug 1984. 127 mins.
Cert PG.

The Key – La Chiave. A highly erotic,
almost pornographic, Italian film set in
Venice just prior to the war and concerning an English husband's physical
obsession with his younger Italian wife.
His – and the camera's – eye is constantly exploring the woman's luscious
body in minute detail, with its exciting
curves; hollows, hills and forests! Cast:
Frank Finlay, Stefania Sandrelli, Franco Branciaroli, Barbara Cupisti,
Armando Marva, Maria Grazia Bon,
Gino Cavalieri, Piero Bortoluzzi, Enzo
Turrin, Irma Veithen. Dir, Ed and
Screenplay: Tinto Brass; based on the
novel *Kagi* by Junichiro Tanizaki. Pro:
Giovanni Bertlucci. Ph: Silvano Ippoliti. Art: Paolo Biagetti. M: Ennio Morricone. (San Francisco Film/Selenia
Cinematografica S.r.l/International
Video Service S.r.l–Enterprise Pictures) Rel: floating; first shown London (Odeon, Haymarket), 25 Jan 1985.
109 mins. Cert 18.

The Killing Fields. Another outstanding British film (produced by the
adventurous David Puttnam) which
misses greatness only because it lacks
the final magic touch of warmth in its
true story of a remarkably deep and
sacrificial friendship between an American reporter in Cambodia and his local
guide and interpreter, seen against the
brilliantly realized horrific, often harrowing background of the brutal and
inhuman struggle in that country with
the Khmer Rouge. And there is an
outstanding Oscar-winning performance by Haing S. Ngor (actually a
Cambodian doctor and not a profes-

sional actor) as the interpreter. Rest of cast: Sam Waterston, John Malkovich, Julian Sands, Craig T. Nelson, Spalding Gray, Bill Paterson, Athol Fugard, Graham Kennedy, Katherine Kragum Chey, Joanna Merlin, Jay Barney, Mark Long, Sayo Inaba, Mow Leng, Chinsaure Sar, Hout Ming Tran, Thach Suon, Neevy Pal, Oliver Pierpaoli, Edward Entero Chey, Tom Bird, Monirak Sisowath, Lambool Dtangpaibool, Ira Wheeler, David Henry, Patrick Malahide, Nell Cambell, John Harris. Dir: Roland Joffé. Pro: David Puttnam. Assoc Pro: Iain Smith. Pro Sup: Robin Douet. Screenplay: Bruce Robinson; based on the 1980 New York *Times* article by Pulitzer prize-winning Sydney Schanberg. 'The Death and Life of Dith Pran'. Ph: Chris Menges. Ed: Jim Clark. Pro Des: Roy Walker. Art: Roger Murray Leach and Steve Spence. M: Puccini, Paul McCartney, John Lennon and Mike Oldfield. (Goldcrest/International Film Investors–Enigma–Warner) Rel: 8 Feb 1985. 142 mins. Cert 15.

The King and Mr Bird – Le Roi et l'Oiseau. A 1979 French animated feature hitherto not shown in Britain. With an impeccable pedigree (directed and co-written by distinguished French animator Paul Grimault and poet Jacques Prévert), this delightfully amusing adaptation of a Hans Christian Andersen fairy tale (in something of the old Disney style) adds an edge of philosophical satire. The story concerns a king with a horrid squint and an enormous ego, the pretty little shepherdess who takes his fancy, the handsome young sweep the girl loves and the artful Black Bird who finally bests His Majesty. Marvellously imaginative; fine draughtsmanship and some delightful – both good and bad – characters. Dir: Paul Grimault. Screenplay: Grimault and Jacques Prévert. Ph: Gerard Soirant. Art: Grimault with Lionel Charpy and Roger Duclent. M: Wojiech Kilar; songs by Joseph Kosma (music) and Prévert (lyrics). (Les Films Paul Grimault/Les Films Gibe/Antenne 2 – ICA Projects in association with Entertainment Films) Rel: floating; first shown London (ICA), 20 July 1984. 85 mins. Cert U.

Kings and Desperate Men. Highly promising directing, writing and producing debut of French-born,

Two scenes from the delightful animated feature *The King and Mr Bird*.

Canadian-educated (and stage-trained) actor-star Alexis Kanner, who brings a certain style and individual treatment to a story about a bizarre plot by a small band of amateur 'terrorists' to abduct a TV chat-show specialist ('The Englishman's Englishman – A Man You Love to Hate') and hold him hostage against the re-trial of one of their members who has been sentenced to 15 years incarceration for killing a cop. It settles down into a duel of wills between the TV man (a nice performance by Patrick McGoohan) and the group's leader. Rest of cast: Alexis Kanner, Andrea Marcovicci, Margaret Trudeau, Budd

Knapp, David Patrick, Robin Spry, Jean-Pierre Brown, Frank Moore, Neil Vipond, August Schellenberg, Kevin

Patrick McGoohan as the hostage in *Kings and Desperate Men*.

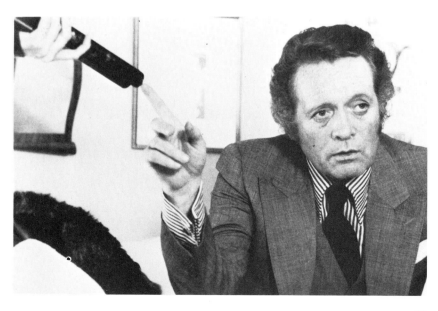

Fenlon, Peter MacNeil, Kate Nash, Frederic Smith-Bolton, Jane Hooper. Dir, Pro and Screenplay (with Edmund Ward), Ph: (with Paul Vanderlinden) and Ed: Alexis Kanner. Art: Will McGow. M: Michel Robindoux and Pierre F. Brault. (Kineversal–Blue Dolphin) Rel: floating; first shown London (Classic, Oxford St and ABC, Bayswater), 28 Dec 1984. 118 mins. Cert 15.

Ladies on the Rocks – Koks i Kulissen. A coarse comedy with a black underbelly, this Danish film is about two women (one married, with two small children, the other single) who produce a pretty outrageous show (so outrageous that when he sees it the married one's husband walks out on her) which they take on to the wintry, misty roads for a series of one-night stands in village and small-town halls. Feminist, satirical and superbly acted by the two women: Helle Ryslinge and Anne Marie Helger. Rest of cast: Flemming Quist Moller, Hans Henrik Clemmensen, Gyda Hansen, Lis Frederiksen, Aksel Erhardsen, Gotha Andersen, Peter Ronild, Bent Conradi, Lene Vasgaard, Lotte Olsen, Knud Dittmar, Arne Simsen, Asta Esner Andersen, Kim Weisgaard, Peter Boesen, Bruno Bjorn, Pernille Grumme, Rosemaria Rex, Johanne Emilie Lund. Dir: Christian Braad Thomsen. Screenplay: Thomsen, Helle Ryslinge and Anne Marie Helger. Ph: Dirk Bruel and Fritz Schroder. Ed: Grete Moldrup, M: Helle Ryslinge and the Paravion Rock Group. (Danish Film Studio for Danish Film Institute–Artificial Eye) Rel: floating; first shown London (Screen-on-the-Green), 8 Mar 1984. 100 mins. Cert 18.

The Last Battle – Le Dernier Combat. A collector's piece from France, directed by 23-year-old Luc Besson. In some future age, after some entirely unexplained catastrophe, some human, mute survivors live amid the ruins of Paris, where a supply of fresh water represents power. One young man ventures out in his home-made aeroplane to discover, and join with, a besieged doctor in a battle against a homicidal nut-case against whom he finally proves himself and returns to take over the local water-source gang and win the girl. All vaguely reminiscent of a good 'B' western told in terms of science-

fiction but done with panache, a certain style and an undercurrent of quiet, wry fun. Made without any dialogue in black-and-white and, warns the publicity, 'very loud' Dolby stereo! Cast: Pierre Jolivet, Jean Bouise, Fritz Wepper, Jean Reno, Maurice Lamy, Pierre Carrive, Jean-Michel Castanie, Michel Doset, Bernard Have, Petra Müller, Christiane Krüger, Marcel Berthomier, Garry Jode. Dir, Pro and Screenplay: Luc Besson; the last with Pierre Jolivet. Ph: Carlo Varini. Ed: Sophie Schmit. No Art credit, but 'set design' by Christian Grosrichard, Thierry Flamand and Patrick Leberre. M: Eric Serra. (Les Films du Loup–ICA Projects) Rel: floating; first shown London (ICA and Screen-on-the-Green), 10 Aug 1984. 90 mins. Cert 15.

Lassiter. A good, old-style, fast moving, increasingly incredible movie mixing hokum and several story themes (big 'caper' – i.e. theft – espionage, romance, adventure, etc.) all built around Tom Selleck's performance as the romantic hero (recall him in *High Road to China?*); a sort of up-dated Raffles blackmailed by the 'Yard's' toughest 'tec into attempting to steal £10 million's worth of uncut diamonds hidden in the Soviet Embassy in London, *circa* 1939. Rest of cast: Jane Seymour, Lauren Hutton, Bob Hoskins, Joe Regalbuto, Ed Lauter, Warren Clarke, Paul Antrim, Christopher

A tight corner for Tom Selleck in *Lassiter*.

Malcolm, Edward Peel, Harry Towb, Belinda Mayne, Barrie Houghton, Brian Coburn, Morgan Sheppard, Tristram Jellinek, Jane Wood, Elliott Johnson, Scott Johnson, David Warbeck, Nicholas Bond-Owen. Dir: Roger Young. Pro: Albert S. Ruddy. Ex Pro: Raymond Chow and André Morgan. Screenplay: David Taylor. Ph: Phil Taylor. Sup Ed: Allan Jacobs. Ed: B.A. Weissman and Richard Hiscott. Pro Des: Peter Mullins. Art: Alan Tompkins and Brian Ackland-Snow. M: Ken Thorne (Song: 'Let's Call the Whole Thing Off' sung and played by Peter Skellern). Assoc Pro: Frederick Muller. (Golden Harvest–Rank Film Dist) Rel: 21 Sept 1984. 100 mins. Cert 18.

The Last Starfighter. A rather jolly and certainly light-hearted science-fiction opus which commendably does not take anything too seriously and is cheerfully derivative (the ending, for instance, with its clear echoes of *Close Encounters*) in its story about a video games whiz-kid who takes on a whole space armada to protect the frontiers of space and knocks out every last invader with his skills. A nice performance by Lance Guest as the lad with a lot on his spacial plate, and he is extremely well backed up by girlfriend Catherine Mary Stewart and Robert Preston, as a happy salesman from another planet. Rest of cast: Dan O'Herlihy, Barbara Bosson, Norman Snow, Kay E. Kuter, Dan Mason, Chris Herbert, John O'Leary, George McDaniel, Maggie Cooper,

Lance Guest and Catherine Mary Stewart meet with some very odd characters (below) in *The Last Starfighter*.

Charlene Nelson, Bruce Abbott, John Maio, Robert Starr, Al Berry, Scott Dunlop, Vernon Washington, Peter Nelson, Peggy Pope, Meg Wyllie, Ellen Blake, Britt Leach, Bunny Summers, Owen Bush, Marc Alaimo, Cameron Dye, Geoffrey Blake, Sue Snyder, Kimberley Ross, Wil Wheaton, Bob Kenaston, Ed Berke. Dir: Nick Castle. Pro: Gary Adelson and Edward O. Denault. Assoc Pro: John H. Whitney Jr. Screenplay: Jonathan Betuel. Ph: King Baggot. Ed: C. Timothy O'Meara. Pro Des: Ron Cobb. Art: James D. Bissell. M: Craig Safan. (Heron Films in association with Miracle Films/Lorimar–Universal) Rel: 11 Jan 1985. 100 mins. Cert PG.

Laughterhouse. Another jewel in Britain's currently sparkling celluloid crown; a simple, modest-budgeted, imaginative and extremely funny comedy

about a livestock farmer who, when his 'plucking' staff go on strike just before the Christmas market deadline, decides he will revert to the ancient ways of marketing and actually drives his large flock of geese by road from Norfolk to London's Smithfield Market. He is closely followed by an intrusive TV team who are making the expedition a major item in their magazine programme. Beautifully but unobtrusively acted and splendidly directed. Cast: Ian Holm, Penelope Wilton, Stephanie Tague, Bill Owen, Richard Hope,

Stephen Moore, Rosemary Martin, Patrick Drury, Aran Bell, Tim Seely, C. J. Allen, Kenneth Macdonald, Barbara Burgess, Ben Wright, Stephen Phillips, Steve Vickers, Dave Atkins, Tommy Wright, Eric Richard, Pearl Hackney, Ken Ives, Norman Fisher, Denise Summers, Kenneth MacDonald, Johnny Golde, Gillian Barge, Tim Sterne, Patrick Connor. Dir: Richard Eyre. Pro: Ann Scott. Ex Pro: Simon Relph.

Ian Holm (centre) in *Laughterhouse* as a turkey farmer working to thwart his striking workers with Bill Owen (left) as his loyal but cantankerous old farmworker.

Screenplay: Brian Glover. Ph: Clive Tickner. Ed: David Martin. Art: Jamie Leonard. Pro Co-Ord: Roxy Glassford. (Greenpoint–Palace Pictures) Rel: floating; first shown London (Gate, ABC Fulham Rd and Classic, Oxford St), 20 July 1984. 93 mins. Cert PG.

Leila and the Wolves. A British/Lebanese film with a strong feminist slant: an examination of the status of women in several countries over a period of sixty years. A very ambitious effort, only partially successful. Cast includes: Nabila Zeitouni, Rafiq Ali Ahmed, Raja Nehme, Emilia Fowad, Ferial Abillamah. Dir and Screenplay: Heiny Srour. Ph: Curtis Clark and Charles Record. Ed: Eva Hedouva. (BFI/Hussein El Sayes, Beirut – Cinema of Women) Rel: floating; first shown London (Gate, Notting Hill), 8 April 1985. 90 mins. Cert 15.

Lies. And lots of them, too, in this slightly less than *grand guignol* thriller with a convoluted plot about an actress caught up in a web of deceit as her husband sets up a plan to have her certified insane so that he can collect her money. Murder, blackmail, chases, gunfights and the uncovering of various real baddie types help to create a consistent atmosphere of tension. Cast: Ann Dusenberry, Gail Strickland, Bruce Davison, Clu Gulager, Terence Knox, Bert Remsen, Stacy Keach Senior, Douglas Leonard, Patience Cleveland, Julie Philips, Ann Gibbs, Dick Miller, Walter Wood, Jerry Vaughn, Guy Remsen, Tony Miller, Jean Howell, B. J. Davis, Eddie Braun, Jane Lillig, Miriam Byrd Netherby, Patricia Lentz, Rebecca Robertson, Joshua Gallecros, Susann Akers, Douglas Manes, Omar Paxson. Dir, Pro (with Shelley Hermann) and Screenplay: Ken and Jim Wheat. Ex Pro: James Hart and Lawrence Taylor-Mortorff. Assoc Pro: Michael Bennett. Pro Co-Ord: Bernadette Caulfield and (2nd Unit) Ellen Freund. Ph: Robert Ebinger. Ed: Michael Ornstein and Dennis Hill. Assoc Ed: Tony Porter. Pro Des:

Christopher Henry. Art: Deborah Moreland. M: Mark Donahue. (Alpha–New Empire Films in association with Wescon Productions) Rel: 5 Oct 1984. 102 mins. Cert 18.

Lonely Hearts. Another brilliant film from Australian writer-director Paul Cox; a touching comedy in a minor key with Norman Kaye giving another outstanding performance (he first appeared on our screens in Cox's highly impressive off-beat *Man of Flowers*) as a fiftyish bachelor who when his mother dies goes to a marriage bureau and through it meets a much younger, parent-dominated, repressed young woman whose feelings for him are jelled into love when she sees him for the first time without his toupée! A completely charming, gently humorous romance full of nuances and wit, and marvellously acted by the entire cast: Wendy Hughes, John Finlayson, Julia Blake, Jonathan Hardy, Irene Inescort, Vic Gordon, Ronald Falk. Dir and Screenplay (latter with John Clarke): Paul Cox. Pro: John B. Murray. Ex Pro: Phillip Adams. Ph: Yuri Sokol. Ed: Tim Lewis. Art: Neil Angwin. M: Norman Kay. (Gala) Rel: floating; first shown London (Academy), 2 Aug 1984. 95 mins. Cert 15.

A Love in Germany – Eine Liebe in Deutschland. A somewhat ambiguous Andrzej Wajda (Franco-German) film about a German greengrocer's wife who falls in love with a Polish POW while her husband is at the front, affronting Nazi ethics. A not-so-bad local Gestapo representative is forced to take action by the attitude of the couple and when nobody else will do the hanging has to carry out the sentence on the Pole himself, while the woman is sent off to a labour camp for the duration. A rather oddly fashioned, and for several reasons an uncomfortable movie, way below some of Wajda's past work. Cast: Hanna Schygulla, Marie-Christine Barrault, Armin Mueller-Stahl, Elisabeth Trissenaar, Daniel Olbrychski, Piotr Lysak, Gérard Desarthe, Bernhard Wicki, Ralf Wolter, Otto Sander, Ben Becker, Thomas Ringelmann, Friedrich G. Beckhaus, Gernot Duda, Sigfrit Steiner, Erika Wackernagelm, Serge Merlin, Rainer Basedow, Jutta Kloppel, Heidi Joschko, Jurgen von Alten, Ilse Bahrs, Hannes Kaetner, Jurgen

Norman Kaye as the shy partner-seeking bachelor in *Lonely Hearts* and (inset) Wendy Hughes the prize he wins.

Born, Dieter Kursawe, Dietrich Mattausch, Gerd Holtenau, Dorothea Moritz, Dieter Kirschlechner, Gundula Petrovska, Herbert Weissbach, Evelyn Meyka, Christoph Beyertt, Ellen Esser Dir: Andrzej Wajda. Pro: Arthur Brauner. Ex Pro: Peter Hahne. Assoc Pro: Emmanuel Schlumberger. Screenplay: Boleslaw Michalek, Agnieszka Holland and Wajda; based on the novel by Rolf Hochhuth. Ph: Igor Luther. Ed: Halina Prugar-Ketling. Art: Allan Starski, Gotz Heymann and Jurgen Henze. M: Michel Legrand. (CCC Filmkunst, West Berlin/Gaumont/TFI/Stand'Art, Paris-Artificial Eye) Rel: floating; first shown London (Lumière), 9 May 1985. 107 mins. Cert 15.

Love on the Ground – L'Amour par Terre. A rather meaningless title, by the way, with Jacques Rivette once more indulging himself in his favourite movie theme; the complex contrasts between life and theatre, previously explored – a little more impressively – in films like *L'Amour Fu* and *Céline et Julie en Bateau*. A story about two American actresses in Paris (Jane Birkin and Geraldine Chaplin) persuaded by a rather pompous playwright (Jean-Pierre Kalfon) to take part in a dramatic presentation at his *château* and finding it a disturbing and difficult assignment, capped by the fact that the last act writes itself! A technically assured mixture of humour (more especially from Laszlo Szabo as a play-translating manservant), tension, confection and complexity. Rest of cast: André Dussollier, Facundo Bo, Sandra Montaigu, Eva Roelens, Isabelle Linnartz. Dir: Jacques Rivette. Pro: Martine Marignac. Screenplay: Rivette, Pascal Bonitzer, Marilu Parolini and Susanne Schiffman. Ph: William Lubtchansky. Ed: Nicole Lubtchansky. Art: Roberto Plate. (La Cecilia in association with the Minister of Culture–Cannon/Gala) Rel: floating; first shown London (The Everyman, Hampstead and Arts, Chelsea), 16 Nov 1984. 125 mins. Cert 15.

Love Unto Death – L'Amour à Mort. The third of Alain Resnais's trilogy of films (the first two being *Mon Oncle d'Amérique* in 1980 and *La Vie est Roman* in 1983) concerned with life, love and death, viewed from philosophical and theological angles. This time it is the story of a Jewish archaeologist who embarks on an intense love affair with a young Catholic girl but is soon stricken with a heart-attack which results in the doctor pronouncing him dead. But almost miraculously he survives; the experience, however, leaves him so obsessed with death that it gradually clouds the couple's love. On the sidelines are another couple, both Protestant pastors with differing views on love – human and godlike – and the suicide the girl finally seeks when her lover dies. An austere, intelligent but gimmicky movie with every scene irritatingly separated by varying long blackouts accompanied by some unpleasing music. Fine performances by the leading quartet of players: Sabine Azema, Fanny Ardant, Pierre Arditi and André Dussollier. Rest of cast: Jean Daste, Geneviève Mnich, Jean-Claude Weibel, Louis Castel, Françoise Rigal, Françoise Morhange. The voices of Jean Champion, Bernard Malaterre, Yvette Etievant. Dir: Alain Resnais. No Pro credit. Screenplay: Jean Gruault. Ph: Sacha Vierny. Ed: Albert Jurgenson and Jean-Pierre Besnard. M: Hans-Werner Henze, played by The Fires of London. (Philippe Dussart and Les Films Ariane/Films A2 in collaboration with the French Ministry of Culture–Cannon/Gala.) Rel: floating; first shown London (Berkeley and The Arts), 22 Feb 1985. 93 mins. Cert 15.

MS.45 – Angel of Vengeance. Zoe Tamerlis as the pretty little mute seamstress whose reaction to being raped twice in the same day is to kill the second rapist with an iron bar and then go on the rampage with his revolver, killing almost any male who comes in sight. A bit drastic maybe, but after a double rape to some extent understandable! Apparently this movie became a cult film in New York and roared to success. Rest of cast: Darlene Stuto, Jimmy Laine, Peter Yellen, Editta Sherman, Albert Sinkys, Steve Singer, Bogey. Dir: Abel Ferrara. Ex Pro: Rochelle Weisberg. Screenplay: Nicholas St. John. Ph: James Momel. M: Joe Delia. (Sunbeam Productions) Rel: floating; first shown London (Scala Club Cinema), 18 Jan 1985. 81 mins. Cert 18.

Majdhar. This was obviously intended primarily for small-screen life. It is an interesting production by some Asian moviemakers in Britain, about a lovely young Pakistani girl living in London who, when her husband leaves her for a white woman (anticipating she will return to her country and cause no further bother for him), decides to stay on, abort her baby, liberate herself, adopt Western ways and clothes and generally make a new and different kind of life for herself. Apart from Rita Wolf's thoroughly professional performance there are some moving moments in the movie. Rest of cast: Tony Wredden, Feroza Syal, Andrew Johnson, Sudha Bhuchar, Daniel Foley, Julianne Mason. Dir and Screenplay: A. A. Jamal. Pro: Mahmood Jamal. Ph: Philip Chavannes. Ed: John Dinwoodie. Art: Fay Rodrigues. M: Ustad Imrat Khan. (Retake Films/Video Collective) Rel: floating; first shown London (Ritzy, Brixton), 8 Mar 1985. 76 mins. No cert.

Making the Grade. A run-of-the-mill teenager-aimed movie based on the culture clash, with a New Jersey street urchin taking the place of a rich kid (who skips school for a European tour) and eventually making a diploma success of it. Some mild fun, break-dancing and romance add up to a harmless romp. Cast: Judd Nelson, Jonna Lee, Gordon Jump, Walter Olkewicz, Ronald Lacey, Dana Olsen, Carey Scott, Scott McGinnis, Andrew Clay, John Dye, Daniel Schneider, John Stevens, Lucille Ewing, Patrice Watson, Moses Peace, Robert Meltzer, Ray Hill, Mattie Grayson, Tim Fall, Jeri Boyle, Waldo Zimmerman, Vince Lemorrocco, Ronald Gordon, Chris Williams, Jack Ray, Marc G. Wilson, Steve Wilkerson, Edgar Orman, Treat McDonald, Pam Shirley, Gail Stone-Stanton, Teresa Nix, Mike Crews, The Revolving Band. Dir: Dorian Walker. Pro: Gene Quintano. Ex Pro: Menahem Golan and Yoram Globus. Pro Co-Ord: Jacque Zambrano and Caroline St. Clair. Screenplay: Gene Quintano. Ph: Jacques Haitkin. Ed: Daniel Wetherbee and Roy Watts. Art: Joseph E. Garrity. M: Basil Poledouris (plus various groups). (Cannon Films/Cannon Film Dist) Rel: 1 Mar 1985. 104 mins. Cert 15.

A Man Like EVA – Ein Mann Wie EVA. For 'EVA' one *could* read RWF (Rainer Werner Fassbinder) because the film with its story about a German director shooting a Dumas story (*Lady of the Camelias*) constantly provides clear reference to the recently departed West German moviemaker's career and somewhat unsavoury life. Cast: Eva Mattes, Lisa Kreuzer, Werner Stocker, Charles Regnier, Charly Mohamed Huber, Carola Regnier, Albert Kitzl, Towje Kleiner, Sybille Rauch, Lothar Borowsky, Maria Mettke, Lock Dikker, Frank Bussing, Heinz Kowalczyk, Frederike Wild, Bembe Bowakow, Mick Miekamp, Siris Motamed, Donald Arthur and dancers from the Tanzschule Richter, Munich. Dir: Radu Gabrea. Pro: Horst Schier and Laurens Straub. Screenplay: Gabrea and Straub; based on an idea by Schier and Straub. Ph: Horst Schier. Ed: Dragos-Emanuel Wittkowski. (Schier and Straub in collaboration with Trio Films, Impuls Films and Maran Films – Blue Dolphin) Rel: floating; first shown London (Screen-on-the-Hill), 3 Jan 1985. 90 mins. Cert 18.

Manifestations of Shiva. A fascinating documentary about the cult of the Indian God, written, directed and photographed (on 16mm) in fine style and great beauty by Malcolm Leigh, who made the movie in 1980 but only now gains a London showing (Orient) Rel: floating; first shown London (Barbican), 25 Jan 1985. 61 mins. No cert.

Maria's Lovers. Russian director Andrei Konchalovsky's extremely impressive first American film, set against the marvellously caught background of Pennsylvania just after the war and based on the theme of the dream obscuring and spoiling the reality; seen in the not so unfamiliar story of a returned-from-the-wars soldier who after marrying his beloved pre-war girlfriend finds himself unable to consummate the marriage, though capable with other women, which leads to his walking out on his ever-loving wife. Frustrated beyond endurance, she takes a strolling player to her virginal bed, begets a baby; ironically this leads to a re-union with her husband whose virility now returns. All this is lifted several

John Savage finds married life with Nastassja Kinski (also right) a very difficult business in *Maria's Lovers*.

notches above normal by sincere treatment, directorial skill and fine performances, notably by the ubiquitous Nastassja Kinski, who (looking incredibly like the young Ingrid Bergman) is quite magnificent as the wife. Rest of cast: John Savage, Robert Mitchum, Keith Carradine, Anita Morris, Bud Cort, Karen Young, Tracy Nelson, John Goodman, Danton Stone, Vincent Spano, Lela Ivey, Elena Koreneva, Anton Sipos, Larry John Meyers, Anna Levine, Tania Harvey, Bill Smitrovich, Nardi Novak, Eddie Steinfeld, Norman St. Pierre, Father Raphael Rozdilski, Vladimir Bibic, Gary Hileman, 'Porky' Albert Kaiser, Clayton D. Hill, Ann Caulfield, Mary Hogan, and Frankie (the 'Wonder Dog'). Dir: Andrei Konchalovsky. Pro: Bosko Djordjevic and Lawrence Taylor-Mortoff. Ex Pro: Menahem Golan and Yoram Globus. Screenplay: Gerard Brach, Andrei Konchalovsky, Paul Zindel and Marjorie David. Ph: Juan

Ruiz-Anchia. Pro Des: Humphrey Dixon. Art: David Briskin. M: Gary S. Remal. (The Cannon Group–Cannon Film Dist) Rel: 8 Jan 1985. 105 mins. Cert 15.

Mata Hari. A highly fanciful British-made story of real-life 'beautiful spy' Miss Hari, the half-Dutch, half-Javanese exotic dancer who during World War I in Paris combined her terpsichorean activities with the business of spying for the Germans and ended up in front of a firing squad when revealed with her 'front' down! Cast includes: Sylvia Kristel, Christopher Cazenove, Oliver Tobias, Gaye Brown, Gottfried John, William Fox, Michael Anthony, Vernon Dobtcheff,

Anthony Newlands, Brian Badcoe, Tutte Lemkow, Taylor Ryan, Tobias Rolt, Victor Langley, Nicholas Selby, Malcolm Terris, Carlos Sutton, Neril Robinson, Derek de Lint, Agnes David, Odon Gyalog, Ferenc Nemethy, Czaba Jakab, Erzsebet Cserhalmi, Matyas Usztics, Gabor Nagi, Ferenc Bencze, Miklos B. Szeley. Dir: Curtis Harrington. Pro: Rony Yacov. Ex Pro: Menahem Golan and Yoram Globus. Pro Co-Ord: Naomi Mayberg. Screenplay: Joel Ziskin. Ph: David Gurfankel. Ed: Henry Richardson. Art: Tivadar Bartalan. M: Wilfred Josephs and Sri Hastanto. (Cannon Pro–Cannon Film Dist) Rel: floating; first shown London (Classic, Oxford St), 10 May 1985. 108 mins. Cert 18.

The Mean Season. Philip Borsos confirms his brilliance as a director (following his outstanding debut with the western *The Grey Fox*) with this tight, exciting crime thriller about a psycho-killer who manipulates a newspaper reporter deeper and deeper into his web. Visually stunning, psychologically absorbing and finely acted. Cast includes: Kurt Russell, Richard Jordan, Mariel Hemingway, Richard Masur, Joe Pantoliano, Richard Bradford, Andy Garcia, Rose Portillo, William Smith, John Palmer, Fred Buch, Bruce McLaughlin, Jill Beach, Peter Lindquist, Connie Hicks, Bill Rutherford. Dir: Philip Borsos. Pro: David Foster and Larry Turman. Screenplay: Leon Piedmont; based on the novel *In the Heat of the Summer* by John Katzenbach. Ph: Frank Tidy. Ed: Duwayne Dunham. Pro Des: Phillip Jefferies. M: Lalo Schifrin. Assoc Pro: Steven Perry. (Turman/Foster–Orion–Rank) Rel: floating; first shown London (Leicester Square Theatre), 31 May 1985. 104 mins. Cert 15.

Memed, My Hawk. Nothing that the richly versatile and witty Peter Ustinov does is without merit and there is plen-ty of his individuality in this rather odd little comedy-drama about some amusing villains in the Anatolian region of Turkey in the 1920s (a story that has been on the production agenda ever since Darryl Zanuck took an interest in it way back in 1963). There are also some very good character cameos. Rest of cast: Herbert Lom, Simon Dutton, Denis Quilley, Michael Elphick, Leonie Mellinger, Vladek Sheybal, Michael Gough, Walter Gotell, Siobhan McKenna, T. P. McKenna, Clive Swift, Relja Basic, Marne Maitland, Jeffrey Wickham, Ernest Clark, Rosalie Crutchley, Eileen Way, Phil Rose, Barry Debnen, Edward Burnham. Dir and Screenplay: Peter Ustinov; adapted from the novel by Yashar Kemal. Pro: Fuad Kavur. Co-Pro: Brian Smedley-Aston. Pro Co-Ord: Jim Connock. Ph: Freddie Francis. Ed: Peter Honess. Art: Veljko Despotovic. M: Manos Hadjikadis. (Peter Ustinov Productions/ Jadran Films–Focus Film Dist) Rel: floating; first shown in London (ABC

Left, Peter Ustinov in *Memed, My Hawk*. Above left to right, Simon Dutton, Denis Quilley and Michael Elphick.

Shaftesbury Ave), 15 May 1984. 103 mins. Cert 15.

Metropolis. The extremely controversial re-vamping – with a certain amount of colour injection and a pop music score – of Fritz Lang's 1927 silent classic. It caused something of an uproar among film buffs when unveiled at the 1984 Cannes Film Festival, and it is likely to go on doing the same everywhere with lots of 'fors' and as many, if not more, 'againsts'. Reconstructed and adapted by Giorgio Moroder, who is also responsible for the music. (Virgin Films) Rel: floating; first shown London, 30 Nov 1984. 87 mins. Cert PG.

Micki and Maude. A comedy-cum-farce which gradually increases its pace until it reaches its very funny finale. A TV interviewer loves his very busy lawyer (about to become judge) wife but at the same time falls as deeply in love with a young girl cellist. He not only becomes a bigamist, sharing his time between his two wives, but gets into deeper trouble when both become pregnant at the same time and deliver their babies in adjoining hospital rooms, between which the distraught father frantically dashes trying to be in both places at once. Typical Blake Edwards comedy (even to its slightly self-indulgent overlength) offering extremely good laughter value for money. Cast: Dudley Moore (Dad), Amy Irving (Mum 1), Ann Reinking (Mum 2) – three excellent performances, Richard Mulligan, George Gaynes, Wallace Shawn, John Pleshette, H. B. Haggerty, Lu Leonard, Priscilla Pointier, Robert Symonds, George Coe, Gustav Vintas, Ken Olfson, Phillippe Denham, Emma Walton, Ruth Silveira, Richard Drown: and the wrestlers: Jack 'Wildman' Armstrong, André 'The Giant' Rousimmoff, 'Big' John, 'Stud' Minton, 'Chief Jay Strongbow' Joe Scarpa, 'Madman' John J. Flynn Jr. Gene Le Bell, Wiley Harker, Tina Theberge, Jim Giggins, Roger Rose, Tiiu Lee, Jamie Abbott, Christa Denton, Robby Kiger. Dir: Blake Edwards. Pro: Tony Adams. Ex Pro: Jonathan D. Krane and Lou Antonio. Assoc Pro: Trish Caroselli. Screenplay: Jonathan Reynolds. Ph: Harry Stradling. Ed: Ralph E. Winters. Pro Des: Roger Maus. Art: Alf Clausen. M: Lee Holdridge; 'Something New in My Life' by Michel Legrand with lyrics by Alan and Marilyn Bergman, performed by Stephen Bishop. (Columbia/Delphi 111 Pro–Columbia) Rel: 3 May 1985. 118 mins. Cert PG.

A Midsummer Night's Dream – Sueno de Noche de Verano. A British-Spanish co-production; a low-budget screen version of the Lindsay Kemp Co.'s campy stage production of the Shakespeare play, the text almost eliminated in favour of song-and-dance, mime and nude rompings, with charac-

Dudley Moore has two wives in *Micki and Maude*. Ann Reinking (above) played wife one and Amy Irving (right) wife two.

ters of dubious sexuality, adding up to what is almost certainly the oddest *Dream* yet, either on stage or screen. Cast: Lindsay Kemp, Manuela Vargas, Jack Birkett, Michael Matou, François Testory, David Meyer, Neil Caplan, David Haughton, Annie Huckle, Cheryl Hazelwood, Atilio Lopez, Christian Michaelson, Javier Sanz, The Incredible Orlando. Dir and Screenplay: Celestino Coronado. Pro: Miguel Angel Perez Campos. Ph: Peter Middleton. Pro Des: Lindsay Kemp with Mark Baldwin. Art: Carlos Dorremochea. M: Carlos Miranda. (Cabochon Film Pro London/TV Espanola, Madrid/Channel 4 – Mainline Pictures) Rel: floating; first shown London (Screen-on-the-Hill), 1 Feb 1985. 78 mins. No cert.

Mikey and Nicky. Re-issue of a 1978–9 film which became the bone of legal contention between writer-director Elaine May and her Paramount bosses which caused its original release to be delayed. Starring John Cassavetes and Peter Falk (both giving the impression of having made the whole thing up on

the spur of the moment), the former plays a fugitive with a gangster's 'contract' on his head who goes to his friend Falk to get help but finds that his support is hardly as firm a prop as he would have liked! (Enterprise) Rel: floating; first shown London (Minema), 25 Oct 1984. 105 mins. Cert 15.

Missing in Action. Chuck Norris as the dime novel hero Col. James Braddock in a jingoistic story about his returning to Vietnam, where he suffered torture and privation during the war. Throwing diplomatic arguments to the winds, he sets out to prove that some US military captives are still being held

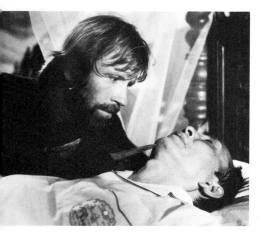

Chuck Norris persuading James Hong to disclose the location of camps illegally holding American prisoners in *Missing in Action*.

secretly in the jungle, and as a sort of one-man army tracks them down through blood and thunder to rescue them triumphantly and fly them back to Ho Chi Minh City in a captured helicopter! This can only be termed an 'action' thriller. Rest of cast: M. Emmet Walsh, David Tress, Lenore Kasdorf, James Hong, Ernie Ortega, Pierrino Mascarino, E. Erich Anderson, Joseph Carberry, Avi Kleinberger, Willy Williams, Ric Segreto, Bella Flores, Gil Arceo, Roger Dantes, Sabatini Fernandez, Renato Morado, Jim Crumrine, Jeff Mason, Stephen Barbers, Nam Moore, Kim Marriner, Deanna Crowe, Jesse Cuneta, Juliet Lee, Joonee Gamboa, Augusto Victa, Protacio Dee, Omar Camar, Jack Perez. Dir: Joseph Zito. Pro: Menahem Golan and Yoram Globus. Ex Pro: Lance Hool. Screenplay: James Bruner; from a story by Hool and John Crowther; based in turn on characters created by Arthur Silver, Larry Levinson and Steve Bing. Ph: Joao Fernandes. Ed: Joel Goodman (Co Ed: Daniel Loewenthal). Art: Ladi Wilheim. M: Jay Chattaway. Ex in charge of Pro: Christopher Pearce. Assoc Pro: Avi Kleinberger (Golan-Globus) Rel: 22 Feb 1985. 94 mins. Cert 15.

Mr Skeeter. Another – the fourth – film to be made by the Children's Film Unit (average age of the camera crew, 12 years old; all other production chores involved kids only four years older). It features two children, truants from a seaside holiday home, who meet the millionaire of the title, 'a man with frayed cuffs, a dead daisy in his hat and an invisible dog'. Cast includes: Peter Bayliss (as Mr. S), Orlando Wells, Louise Rawlings. Dir: Colin Finbow (the CFU founder). (Children's Film Unit–ICA Projects) Rel: floating; first shown London (ICA), 4 May 1985. 85 mins. Cert U.

Moments – Moments de la Vie d'une Femme. A 1979 Franco-Israeli co-production about two women, one Israeli, the other French, who meet on a train from Tel-Aviv to Jerusalem and start a friendship which becomes a passionate liaison before they part. Meeting up again five years later, when both are married, they try to find the old magic of their first meeting. Cast: Michal Bat-Adam, Brigitte Catillon, A. Dayan, Avi Pnini, Eliram Dekel, Dan Ben-Amotz. Dir and Screenplay: Michal Bat-Adam. Pro: Moshe Mizarahi. Assoc Pro: Rudi Cohen and Louis Wint. Ph: Yves Lafaye. Ed: Sophie Coussein. Art: Eytan Levi. M: arr. by Hubert Rostaing. (Rosa Productions/Mica Films, Paris/Ben Hashurot, Tel-Aviv–Cinegate) Rel: floating; first shown London (Gate, Bloomsbury), 12 Jan 1985. 92 mins. Cert 18.

Morons from Outer Space. An occasionally mildy comic British movie about the adventures of a quartet of vacationing aliens from another planet (Blob!) who force-land their craft on the M1 motorway and have to evade a lynch mob before becoming pop stars. Eventually three are ferried off home, leaving the fourth to face an earthly career. Cast: Mel Smith, Griff Rhys Jones, Joanne Pearce, Jimmy Nail, Paul Bown, James B. Sikking, Dinsdale Landen, Tristram Jellinek, George Innes, John Joyce, Mark Jones, Leonard Fenton, André Maranne, Joanna Dickens, R. J. Bell, Peter Whitman, Olivier Pierre, Edward Riley, Robert Austin, John Barcroft, Bill Stewart, Joss Buckley, Roger Hammond, Des Webb, Derek Deadman, Angela Crow, Jimmy Mulville, Lesley Grantham, Barbara Hicks, Tim Barker, Graham Fellows, Bob Sessions, Shane Rimmer, Diane Ricardo, Miriam Margolyes, Ian East, M. J. Jackson, James Taylor, Christopher Northey, Jo Ross, Susan Denaker, Lesa Lockford, Edward Arthur, Shelley Thompson, John Clamp, Richenda Carey, David Haig, Robert Henderson, Karen Lancaster, Ronnie Stevens, Pamela Mandell, David James, Thick Wilson, David Whitaker, John O'Toole, Peter Straker, Robin Driscoll. Dir: Mike Hodges. Pro: Barry Hanson. Ex Pro: Verity Lambert. Pro Ex: Graham Easton. Pro Sup: David Ball. Pro Co-Ord; Lorraine Goodman. Screenplay: Griff Rhys Jones and Mel Smith; developed by Bob Mercer. Ph: Phil Meheux. Ed: Peter Boyle. Pro Des: Brian Eatwell. Art: Terry Gough and Bert Davey. M: Peter Brewis. M Dir: John Cameron. (Thorn EMI) Rel: floating, first shown London (Warner, Classics Haymarket and Oxford St and Minema), 22 Mar 1985. 97 mins. Cert PG.

Moscow on the Hudson. A warm, generally winning Paul Mazursky film about a Russian circus-band saxophonist who defects during a tour of America, where he has to come to terms with his new life and win over a somewhat reluctant Italian immigrant girlfriend. This gives writer-director Mazursky a chance to compare New York life with life in Moscow; and though the balance may be strained towards the latter a little it does show some of the New World's flaws viewed through an immigrant's eyes. (And with its touches of patriotism and sentimentality one cannot help but remember it in relation to Frank Capra's movies.) Cast includes: Robin Williams, Maria Conchita Alonso, Cleavant Derricks, Alejandro Rey, Savely Kramarov, Elya Baskin, Oleg Rudnik, Alexander Beniaminov, Ludmila Kramrevsky, Ivo Vrzal, Natalie Iwanow, Tiger Haynes, Edye Byrde, Robert Macbeth, Donna Ingram Young, Olga Talyn, Alexander Narodetzky, Pierre Orcel, Stephanie Cotsirilos, Fred Strother, Anthony Cortino, Betsy Mazursky, Kaity Tong, Royce Rich, Christopher Wynkoop, Lyman Ward, Joe Lynn, Joy Todd, Paul Mazursky, Thomas Ikeda, Barbara Montgomery, Dana Lorge, Adalberto Santiago, Sam Moses, Yakov Smirnoff, Sam Stoneburner, Michael Greene, Rosetta le Noire, Sal Carollo, Filomena Spanguolo, Annabella Turco, George Kelly, Yury Olshansky, Jacques Sandulescu, Emil Feist, Vladimir Tukan, Mark Rutenberg, Yury Belov, Igor Panich, Jurij Gotowtschikow. Dir, Pro and Screenplay (the last with Leon Capetanos): Paul Mazursky. Co-Pro

Savely Kramarov (left) as a KGB agent confronting store guard Cleavant Derricks who is defending defector Robin Williams in *Moscow on the Hudson.*

and Pro Des: Pato Guzman. Ph: Donald McAlpine. Ed: Richard Halsey. Assoc Pro: Geoffrey Taylor. M: David McHugh. (Columbia Delphi–Columbia) Rel: floating, first shown London (Warner), 5 Oct 1984. 117 mins. Cert 15.

My Best Friend's Girl. A uniquely French comedy about two pals, working in the ski resort of Courcheval, whose long and close relationship is brought near to disaster by the advent of a pretty little tramp who enters their beds, their lives and almost – but not quite – breaks them up and sets them against each other. Wholly immoral, wholly chuckly and not without a certain degree of solid philosophical sense. And all so well played, by: Isabelle Huppert, Coluche, Thierry Lhermitte, Farid Chopel, François Perrot, Daniel Colas. Dir and Screenplay (latter with Gerard Brach): Bertrand Blier. Pro: Alain Sarde. Ex Pro: Pierre Grunstein. Ph: Jean Penzer. Ed: Claudine Merlin. Sets (no Art credits): Theo Meurisse. M: J. J. Cale. (Sara Films/Renn Productions–Cannon Gala) Rel: floating; first shown London (Berkeley and Chelsea Arts), 7 June 1985. 99 mins. Cert 15.

My Brother's Wedding. That rarity, a Black film, made by independent black American director Charles Burnett and set in the largely black Los Angeles suburb of Watts, where Burnett grew up. A tragi-comedy about a 30-year-old man who works in his parent's laundry business and loves his surroundings, detesting the bourgeois ambition of his lawyer brother, and reluctantly agreeing to be the best man at the latter's wedding, only to find that he has agreed at the same time to attend his best pal's funeral! A warm and loving look at the community the direc-

Left to right, Gaye Shannon-Burnett, Monte Easter and Jessie Holmes in *My Brother's Wedding.*

tor knows, and portrays with rare integrity and incidental humour. Cast includes: Everette Silas, Jessie Holmes, Gaye Shannon-Burnett, Ronald E. Bell, Dennis Kemper, Sy Richardson, Frances Nealy, Garnett Hargrave etc. Dir, Screenplay and Ph: Charles Burnett. Pro: Burnett and Gaye Shannon-Burnett. Assoc Pro: Brigitte Kramer. Ed: Thomas M. Penick. Assoc Ed: Christine Renee Penick. No Art credits listed. M: Johnny Ace and John Briggs. (Charles Burnett Productions–Blue Dolphin Films) Rel: floating; first shown London (Ritzy, Brixton), 28 March 1985. 90 mins. No cert.

My Own Country – Bayan Ko. A highly explosive Philippino/French political thriller with quite as interesting a story behind it as that which appears on the screen: its maker, Lino Brocka, having been arrested by the Marcos regime for his anti-government activities and facing life imprisonment at the time of the film's British debut. The movie is a well-made feature based on two actual historical incidents, a general strike and an abduction which led to a gangsters *v* cops shootout in Manilla. It was only after the film was shown at Cannes that the government began to see the political criticism that was implied by the action. Cast: Phillip Salvador, Gina Alajar, Claudia Zobel, Raoul Aragonn, Rez Cortez, Venchito Galvez, Aristo Reyes Jr, Lorli Villenueva, Normer Son, Gloria Guinto, Lucita Soriano, Joe Taruc and PETA Kalinangan Ensemble. Dir: Lino Brocka. Pro: Toni Gonzalez and Vera Belmont. Ex Pro: Jeric Soriano. Screenplay: Jose F. Lacaba. Ph: Conrado Baltazar. Ed: George Jarlego, Robert Yugeco and Hero Reyes. No Art but 'Sets' credit to Joey Luna. (Malay Films, Philippines/Stephan Films, Paris–ICA Projects) Rel: floating; first shown London (ICA), 29 Mar 1985. 108 mins. No cert.

Nadia. An American-Yugoslav co-production, made entirely in Yugoslavia, which with only minor fictional trimmings relates the story of the Rumanian gymnast prodigy who won three gold medals at the 1976 Olympic Games in Montreal. And very nice entertainment it proves to be, too, with special appeal to fledgling gymnasts. Cast includes: Leslie Weiner, Talia Balsam, Jonathan Banks, Joe Bennett,

Simone Blue, Johann Carlo, Conchata Ferrell, Carrie Snodgress, Carl Strano, Karrie Ullman, Sonja Kereskenji including gymnasts. Dir: Alan Cooke. Pro: James E. Thompson. Ex Pro: Sheldon Cooper, Dave Bell. Assoc Pro: Marilyn Hall. Screenplay: J. McGinn. Ph: Frank Beascoechea. Ed: Raymond Bridgers. Pro Des: George Becket. Art: Seljko Senecic. M: Christopher L. Stone, perf. by Zagreb Studio Orchestra. (Dave Bell Pro/Tribune Entertainment Co in association with Jadran Films, Yugoslavia–Odyssey Films) Rel: floating; first shown London (Scene, Leicester Sq), 26 Oct 1984. 99 mins. Cert U.

Robert Redford as the gifted baseball player in *The Natural*.

The Natural. Most films about American baseball have proved something like British box-office poison (not *all*, though, for example *Bad News Bears*) but this one at least deserves a far better break, thanks largely to the fact it is about people rather than the game. Robert Redford is superb as the silent, secretive character who appears on the scene at normal retiring age and proceeds to inspire the previously failing New York Knights team to triumph. The Great American Dream again, marred this time only by the evil woman who comes into the player's life to spoil it for the years before a good one enters to inspire success. Sir Galahad with a bat confuting all evil – bribes, blackmail and threats – to score that winning hit, for game and life. Lots of fine supporting performances, too. Rest of cast: Robert Duvall, Glenn Close, Kim Basinger, Wilford Brimley, Barbara Hershey, Robert Prosky, Richard Farnsworth, Darren McGavin, Joe Don Baker, John Finnegan, Alan Fudge, Paul Sullivan Jr, Rachel Hall, Robert Rich III, Michael Madsen, Jon Van Ness, Mickey Treanor, George Wilkosz, Anthony J. Ferrara, Philip Mankowski, Danny Aiello III, Joe Castellano, Eddie Cipot, Ken Grassano, Robert Kalaf, Barry Kivel, Steven Kronovet, James Meyer, Michael Starr, Sam Green, Martin Grey, Joseph Mosso, Richard Oliveri, Lawrence Couzens, Duke McGuire, Steve Poliachik, Keven Lester, Joseph Charboneau, Robert Rudnick, Ken Kamholz, Sibby Sisti, Phillip D. Rosenberg, Christopher D. Rehbaum, Nicholas Koleff, Jerry Stockman, James Quamo, Joseph Strand, James Mohr, Ralph Tabakin, Dennis Gould, Joshua Abbey, Gale Vance, George Scheitinger, Peter Poth, Bernie McInerney, Elizabeth Ann Klein, Charles Sergis, Edward Walsh, The Buffalo Swing Nightclub Band. Dir: Barry Levinson. Pro: Mark Johnson. Ex Pro: Roger Towne and Philip M. Breen. Assoc Pro: R. F. Colesberry. Screenplay: Towne and Phil Dusenberry: based on the novel by Bernard Malamud. Ph: Caleb Deschanel. Ed: Stu Linder. Pro Des: Angelo Graham and Mel Bourne. Art: James J. Murikami and Speed Hopkins. M: Randy Newman. (Tri-Star) Rel: 26 Oct 1984. 122 mins. Cert PG.

The Never Ending Story – Die Unendliche Geschichte. A delightful, marvellously visual West German adaptation by Wolfgang Petersen of his own and Herman Weigel's fairytale about a small, brave boy who goes on a dangerous mission to save the land of Fantasia and its strange, assorted inhabitants from the advance of an all-enveloping Nothing. This is framed within the story of another boy who experiences or dreams it all as he reads the book of the title. (A tale which stunned to silence a rowdy audience of kids at the film's opening press show by the magical effects, the fun, the thrills and the characters, especially the sweetest, most cuddly dragon ever to appear on the screen.) Cast: Barrett Oliver, Gerald McRaney, Drum Garrett, Darryl Cooksey, Nicholas Gilbert, Thomas Hill, Deep Roy, Tilo Prück-

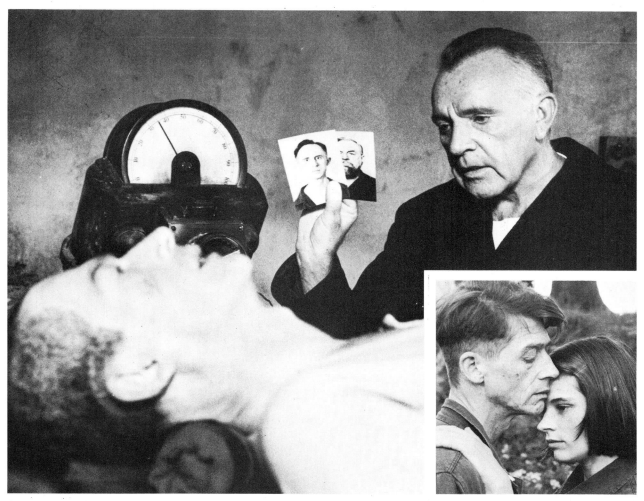

Richard Burton applying a little torture to John Hurt in *1984* and (inset) Hurt with Suzanna Hamilton as the ill-fated lovers.

ner, Moses Gunn, Noah Hathaway, Alan Oppenheimer, Sydney Bromley, Patricia Hayes, Tami Stronach. Dir and Screenplay (latter with Herman Weigel): Wolfgang Petersen. Pro: Bernd Eichinger and Dieter Geissler. Ex Pro: Mark Damon and John Hyde. Co-Pro: Gunther Rohrback. Assoc Pro: Klaus Kähler. Ph: Jost Vacano. Ed: Jane Seitz. Sup of Special and Visual Effects: Brian Johnson. Pro Des: Rolf Zeherbauer. M: Giorgio Moroder (lyrics by Keith Forsey) perf by Limahl. (Neue Constantin Pro in collaboration with Bavaria Studios and WDR-Warner) Rel: 4 April 1985. 94 mins. Cert U.

Night of the Comet. An amusingly derivative, workmanlike and finally nicely entertaining sci-fi film about nasty goings-on among the few survivors of a holocaust on another planet; periodically lit-up by funny lines and character reactions. Cast: Catherine Mary Stewart, Kelli Maroney, Robert Beltran, Geoffrey Lewis, Mary Woronov, John Achorn, Sharon Farrell, Michael Bowen, Ivan Roth. Dir and Screenplay: Thom Eberhardt. Pro: Andrew Lane and Wayne Crawford. Ex Pro: Thomas Coleman and Michael Rosenblatt. Ph: Arthur Albert. Ed: Fred Stafford. Pro Des: John Muto. M Sup: Tom Perry (Coleman/Rosenblatt/Film Dev Fund) Rel: 21 June 1985. 95 mins. Cert PG.

1984. George Orwell's pessimistic prophecy about nasty things to come (though he got the date wrong the spectre remains valid) when the Big Brother State has taken over, with a ruthless manipulation of Man into supportive Machine. This time (the story was first filmed in 1956) made with a commendable integrity but, inevitably, gloomily, with some harrowing scenes of torture as Richard Burton, looking haggard and ill (this was his last movie), brings John Hurt to heel. Rest of cast: Suzanna Hamilton, Cyril Cusack, Gregor Fisher, James Walker, Andrew Wilde, David Trevena, David Cann, Anthony Benson, Peter Frye, Roger Lloyd Pack, Rupert Baderman, Corinna Seddon, Martha Parsey, Merelina Kendall, P. J. Nicholas, Lynne Radford, Pip Donaghy, Shirley Stelfox, Janet Key, Hugh Walters, Phyllis Logan, Pam Gems, Joscik Barbarossa, John Boswall, Bob Flag, John Hughes, Robert Putt, Christine Hargreaves, Garry Cooper, Matthew Scurfield, John Golightly, Rolf Saxon, Ole Oldendorp, Eddie Stacey, Norman Bacon, John Foss, Carey Wilson, Mitzi McKenzie. Dir and Screenplay: Michael Radford. Pro: Simon Perry. Ex Pro: Marvin J. Rosenblum. Co-Pro: Al Clark and Robert Devereux. Ph: Roger Deakins. Ed: Tom Priestley. Pro Des: Allan Cameron. M: Dominic Muldowney. Assoc Pro: John Davies. Art: Martin Herbert and Grant Hicks. (Virgin Films–Fox) Rel: 25 Nov 1984. 120 mins. Cert 15.

Ninja III – The Domination. The same team that created *Ninja II* worked on this further martial arts movie; this one with *Breakin'* star Lucinda Dickey as the young lady interested in Japanese culture who on a visit to Arizona becomes occasionally possessed by the spirit of the cop-killing, villainous Ninja. For all of those who enjoyed *Ninjas I & II*! Rest of cast: Jordan Bennett, David Chung, Dale Ishimodo, James Hong, Bob Craig, Pamela Ness, Roy Padilla, Moe Mosley, John La Motta, Ron Foster, Alan Amiel, Steve Lambert, Earl Smith, Carver Barnes, Karen Pretty, Randy Mulkey, James Maher, Judy Starr, Cheryl Van Cleeve, Suzanne Collins, Rosemary Ono, Janet Marie Heil, Charly Harroway, John Perryman, Chris Micelli, Lem Cook, Howard Dean, Tom Castronova, Jay Rasumny, T. O. Goodman, Bill Helmintoller. Dir: Sam Firstenberg. Ex Pro: Menahem Golan and Yoram Globus. Assoc Pro: David Womark. Screenplay: James R. Silke; based on his own story. Ph: Hanania Baer. Ed: Michael Duthie. Pro Des: Elliot Ellentuck. M: Udi Haroaz; and others. (Golan/Globus – Cannon – MGM/UA–Cannon Film Dist) Rel: 7 Dec 1984. 95 mins. Cert 18.

The North – El Norte. A long, three-part story, based on the topical and troublesome American problem of the influx into the States, from across the Mexican border, of illegal immigrants. A young man and his devoted sister leave Guatemala when their father is killed and their mother is abducted by the military, who ravage their village. They embark on the long and arduous journey into and across Mexico to the border, which they eventually manage to cross through an old sewer, and settle in Los Angeles, where a certain success is followed by tragedy. Realistically played and directed; a story of courage and devotion and the will to survive, and even succeed, no matter what the odds. Cast: Zaide Silvia Gutierrez, David Villalpando, Ernesto Gomes Cruz, Alicia del Lago, Eraclio Zepeda, Stella Quan, Rodolfo Alexandre, Emilio del Haro, Rodrigo Puebla, Trinidad Silva, Abel Franco, Mike Gomez, Lupe Ontiveros, John Martin, Ron Joseph, Larry Cedar, Sheryl Bernstein, Gregory Enton, Tony Plana, Enrique Castillo, Diane Civita, Jorge Moreno. Dir: Gregory Nava. Pro: Anna Thomas. Screenplay: Nava and Thomas. Ph: James Glennon. Ed: Betsy Blankett. M: The Folkloristas, Melicio Martinez, Emil Richards, Linda O'Brien, Samuel Barber, Giuseppe Verdi, Gustav Mahler. (Cinecom International Films/Islands Alive–Mainline Pictures) Rel: floating; first shown London (Electric Screen), 20 July 1984. 139 mins. Cert 15.

Not for Publication. Highly original director and actor Paul Bartel's fifth feature (he made and starred in *Eating Raoul*, which was certainly 'original') has all the elements of his previous productions; black comedy, off-beat humour (of sometimes dubious taste), odd characters, and overall obvious delight in tying everything together into an amusingly unconventional package. Here it is, all in a story about a girl on a scandal sheet newspaper who dreams of her investigative reporting bringing a big scoop, while under another name she is acting as the Mayor's assistant during election year. All pretty wild, and wildly funny, with a zany climax and a happy ending. Cast: Nancy Allen, Don Peoples, Katherine Schultz, Richard Blackburn, Sonia Petrovna, Cork Hubbert, Richard Paul, Warrington Winters, Jeanne Evans, J. David Moeller, Desmond Dhooge,

Paul Bartel's highly original comedy *Not for Publication*.

Alan Rosenberg, Leslie Lyon, Laurence Luckinbill, Randy Moore, Frances Galvan, Christopher Wycliff, Bill Engvall, David Naughton, Lynn Ritchie, Alice Ghostley, Barry Dennen, Marsha McClelland, Sarah McCracken, Darcy Pulliam, Michael O'Sullivan, Mary Ann Smith, Tadeusz Mendreck, Robert Ahola, Hart Sprager, Don Wyse, Jack Robinson, Helena Humann, Susan Bayer, Robert Leinberger, Beverly Renquist, Malcolm Wittman, Polly Lou Moore, John Galt, Anne Kimmel, Paul Bartel. Dir: Paul Bartel. Pro: Anne Kimmel. Ex Pro: Mark Forstater. Screenplay: Bartel and John Meyer. Ph: George Tirl. Ed: Alan Toomayan. Pro Des: Robert Schulenberg. M: John Meyer. Assoc Pro: Lynwood Spinks and Jack Cummins. Pro Ex: Katherine Haber. Art: Michael O'Sullivan and Becky Block. (Thorn EMI) Rel: floating; first shown London (ABC Fulham Rd and Classic, Tott Ct Rd), 23 Nov 1984. 87 mins. Cert 15.

Not Quite Jerusalem. A neat collection of cinema clichés in a somewhat sentimental adaptation of a more stringent stage play about a group of assorted youngsters from all points of the compass who come for various reasons to a kibbutz in Israel and find equally various satisfactions from their stay, culmi-

Sam Robards finds romance with pretty Joanna Pacula in *Not Quite Jerusalem*.

nating in a quite farcical Arab terrorist attack which is effectually dealt with by the Israeli army. Thus is drama added to the romance and comedy bits. A charming performance by pretty Joanna Pacula. Rest of cast: Sam Robards, Kevin McNally, Todd Graff, Selina Cadell, Bernard Strother, Ewan Stewart, Kate Ingram, Gary Cady, Sawally Srinonton, Zafrir Kochanovsky, Shlomo Tarshish, Poli Reshef, Esti-Katz, Juliano Mer, Rita Shukroon, David Menachem, Gershon Sobelman, Aharon Greener, Libby Morris, Bernard Spear, Sara Aman, Peter Freistadt, Yaakov Ben Sira, Menachem Bar'am, Naomi Rosenberg, Irit Frank, Shuli Rosenberg. Dir and Pro: Lewis Gilbert. Co-Pro: William P. Cartlidge. Pro Sup: Zvi Spielmann. Ex Pro: Herbert Oakes. Screenplay: Paul Kember; based on his own play. Ph: Tony Imi. Ed: Alan Strachan. Pro Des: John Stoll. Art: Giora Porter. M: Rondo Veniziano and Gian Reverberi. (Rank Dist) Rel: 26 April 1985. 114 mins. Cert 15.

Number One. A British film reminiscent of the 'Kitchen Sink' era; a story about a gifted snooker player-cum-layabout who is persuaded to take up the game professionally and then suddenly getting the fame bug, to the irritation – to say the least – of his crooked backers. The star's (a former pop performer) and some of the other players' accents are so thick that subtitles would have helped me, at least to understand them. Some good performances, especially by Alison Steadman as the prostitute who falls in love with the fiery-tempered lad with the magic cue. Rest of cast: Bob Geldof, Mel Smith, P. H. Moriarty, Phil Daniels, Alfred Molina, James Marcus, David Howey, Ian Dury, David Squire, Ron Cook, Alun Armstrong, Tony Scott, Kate Hardie, Ray Winstone, Albie Woodington, Jack Eden, A. J. Clark, Harry Scott, Eric Richard, Jimmy Tippett, Patsy Houlihan, Keith O'Keefe, Michael Forrest, John Turner, Alan Davidson, Martin Jackson, Terry Andrews, Reg Stewart, Gene October, Jude Alderson, Stan Taylor, John Benfield, George Phillips, Norman Bacon, Vivienne Ritchie, Prunella Gee, Kenny Ireland, Robert Austin, Cassian Hall, John Salthouse, Freddie Davies, Bill Rourke, Stefan Escreet, Tony Calvert, Mark Jordan, John Reed, Adam War-

Bob Geldof played the naturally gifted snooker-playing layabout in *Number One*.

ren, Stephen Churchett, Rupert Massey, John Blundell, and Ted Lowe, John Williams and Danny Adds. Dir: Les Blair. Pro: Mark Forstater and Raymond Day. Ex Pro: Warren Goldberg. Screenplay: G. F. Newman. Ph: Bahram Manocheri. Ed: Jon Gregory. Pro Des: Martin Johnson. M: 'Savin' Face' by David Mackay and Joe Fagin sung by Fagin. Assoc Pro: Selwyn Roberts. (Mark Fortstater/Stageforum Pro–Videoform Pictures) Rel: 19 April 1985. 106 mins. Cert 15.

Once Upon a Time in America. After a dozen apparently non-productive years Sergio (spaghetti westerns) Leone returns with a vast, sprawling, overlong, indulgent, but in parts brilliant, often baffling (maybe because of cuts, even in the Leone 'approved' version of 229-minutes shown at Cannes; whole thick slices were taken out for the 150 minute American version) film. But finally it is a wearying saga of a Jewish gangster family between 1923 and 1968, leaving a final impression that within all this celluloid mountain there's a great movie trying to cut itself loose. Cast includes: Robert De Niro, James Woods, Elizabeth McGovern, Treat Williams, Tuesday Weld, Burt Young, Joe Pesci, Danny Aiello, William Forsythe, James Hayden, Darlan-

Fleugel, Larry Rapp, Amy Ryder, Scott Tiler, Rusty Jacobs, Jennifer Connelly, Mike Monetti, Adrian Curran, Brian Bloom, Julie Cohen, Noah Moazezi, James Russo, Karen Shallo, Dutch Miller, Robert Harper, Richard Bright, Gerard Murphy, Olga Karlatos, Mario Brega, Ray Dittrich, Frank Gio, Angelo Florio, Frankie Caserta, Joey Marzella, Frank Sisto, Jerry Strivelli. Dir: Sergio Leone. Pro: Arnan Milchan. Ex Pro: Claudio Mancini. Screenplay: Leone, Leonardo Benvenuti, Piero de Bernardi, Enrico Medioli, Franco Arcalli and Franco Ferrini; based on the book *The Hoods*

Robert De Niro in *Once Upon a Time in America*.

by Harry Grey. Add. dialogue by Stuart Kaminsky. Ph: Tonino Delli Colli. Ed: Nino Baragli. Art: Carlo Simi and James Singelis. M: Ennio Morricone. (Ladd Co./Warner–Thorn EMI) Rel: floating; first shown London (ABC Shaftesbury Ave), 5 Oct 1984. 229 mins. Cert 18.

One Deadly Summer – L'Eté meurtrier. Essentially a Gallic mixture of obsession leading to insanity, quiet touches of mirth, marvellously evocative backgrounds and final stark tragedy in a story – not always easy to follow, so devious are the threads – about a girl who lives to have her revenge on the three men who so brutally raped her mother and – presumably – of whom one begat her. Powerful, fascinating, complex and all lit up by the remarkable, outstanding performance as the girl by Isabelle Adjani. Directed by celebrated Jacques Becker's talented son Jean. The film won four French Academy Awards: for best actress (Adjani), best supporting actress (Suzanne Flon), best adapted screenplay (Sebastien Japrisot) and best editing (Jacques Witta). Rest of cast: Alain Souchon, Jenny Cleve, François Cluzet, Manuel Gélin, Michel Galabru, Maria Machado, Roger Carel, Jean Gaven, Max Morel, Cécile Vassort, Martin Lamotte, Jacques Dynam, Raymond Meunier, Evelyne Didi, Yves

Afonso, Jacques Nolot, Edith Scob, Daniel Langlet, Catherina le Gouey, Maiwen Lebesco. Dir: Jean Becker. Pro: Christine Beytout. Ex Pro: Gerard Beytout. Pro Sup: Alain Darbon. Pro Administrator: Nicole Lenfant. Screenplay: Sebastian Japrisot; based on his own novel. Ph: Etienne Becker. Ed: Jacques Witta. Art: Jean-Claude Gallouin. M: Georges Delerue. (Ste Nouvelle de Cinema/CAPAC/TFI Films–Cannon Films) Rel: floating; first shown London (Premier), 1 July 1984. 130 mins. Cert 18.

Ordeal by Innocence. A routine – British – adaptation of an Agatha Christie whodunit. A scientist returns to Britain after a two-year stint in the Antarctic to find that during his absence his evidence could have saved a man from hanging. With family and police adopting an uninterested stance, he begins to realize that because the convicted man was innocent, the crime must be laid at the door of another still living member of the family. Driven by his conscience, the scientist (Donald Sutherland) begins to probe into the problem. The murdered: Faye Dunaway. Suspects: Christopher Plummer, Diana Quick, Sarah Miles, Ian McShane, Michael Maloney, Phoebe Nicholls, Valerie Whittington, Annette Crosbie, Billy McColl – plenty to work on! Rest of cast: Cassie Stuart, Michael Elphick, Ron Pember. Dir: Desmond Davis. Pro: Jenny Craven. Ex Pro: Menahem Golan and Yoram Globus. Screenplay: Alexander Stuart. Ph: Billy Williams.

Assoc Pro: Michael Kagan. Ed: Timothy Gee. Pro Des: Ken Bridgeman. M: Dave Brubeck; played by his Quartet. (Cannon Group Inc.) Rel: floating; first shown London (Classic, Haymarket), 15 Feb 1985. 90 mins. Cert 15.

Our Story – Notre Histoire. A complicated – not to say extremely confusing – French film which hovers undecidedly between dream and reality as it tells the story of a beer-soaked, depressed train traveller who is casually seduced in his compartment by a nymphomaniac. An equally disillusioned girl, she then finds she cannot get rid of her latest lover who, with a supply of cans, takes up residence in her home, It is all very wordy, stylish, well acted but finally rather unsatisfying. Cast: Alain Delon, Nathalie Baye, Michel Galabru, Geneviève Fontanel, Jean-Pierre Darrossin, Gerard Darmon, Sabine Haudepin, Norbert Letheule, Vincent Lindon, Bernard Farcy, Jean-Louis Foulquier, Philippe Laudenbach, Paul Guers, Firmin, Jean-François Stevenin, Nathalie Nell, Ginette Garcon. Dir and Screenplay: Bertrand Blier. Pro: Alain Sarde. Ph: Jean Penzer. Ed: Claudine Merlin. Art: Bernard Evein. M: by classical composers. (Adel Productions/Sara Films–Artificial Eye) Rel: floating; first shown London (Lumière), 20 June 1985. 111 mins. Cert 15.

Over the Edge. A terrifying picture of American teenagers in a sort of US equivalent to Britain's New Towns; all the more scary in that it is claimed to be based on truth. Disdaining education, constantly needling the local cops, stealing firearms, sabotaging cars (two young thugs shoot at, and wreck, a police car), the teenagers then progress to locking-in their parents at a school meeting called to discuss their escapades and, embarking on an orgy of destruction, smashing everything within sight, setting their parents' cars alight and finally killing a cop with one of the stolen firearms. Cast: Michael Kramer, Pamela Ludwig, Matt Dillon, Vincent Spano, Tom Fergus, Harry Northup, Andy Romano, Ellen Geer, Richard Jamison, Julian Pomeroy, Tiger Thompson, Eric Lalich, Kim Kliner, Frank Mugavero, Kristina Hanson, Diane Reilly, Jeff Fleury, Lane Smith, Bill Whedbee, Molly McCarthy, Gary Tessler, Polly Shaw,

Donald Sutherland (left) and Christopher Plummer in *Ordeal by Innocence*.

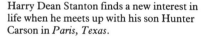

Mike Osborne, Frank Bauer, Susan von Till. Dir: Jonathan Kaplan. Pro: George Litto. Assoc Pro: Joe Kapp and Robert S. Bremson. Screenplay: Charlie Haas and Tim Hunter. Ph: Andrew Davis. Ed: Robert Barrère. Pro Des: Jim Newport. M: Sol Kaplan; performed by Cheap Trick, The Cars, Little Feat, Jimi Hendrix, Valerie Carter, The Ramones and Van Halen. (Mainline Pictures) Rel: floating; first

Cop Harry Northup frisks the kids (Michael Kramer and Matt Dillon) in *Over the Edge*.

shown London (Cinecenta and Screen-on-the-Green), 6 July 1984. 95 mins. Cert 18.

Paris, Texas. A Wim Wenders German-French (made in America) 'Road' movie, probably his best work since *Kings of the Road*, even if this particular road is far too long and too slowly travelled (apparently pruned to 140 mins from something like 5 hours). A wandering walker (Harry Dean Stanton in his first starring role) after four years missing turns up exhausted in a

Harry Dean Stanton finds a new interest in life when he meets up with his son Hunter Carson in *Paris, Texas*.

small Mexican border town, where he is picked up by his younger brother and installed in the latter's Los Angeles home. There he gradually unwinds in the company of the brother's young French wife and his own, deserted, small son, an odyssey which ends with his restoring the boy to his mother in Houston and then setting out once more on his aimless travels. A carefully tailored classic, if not a particularly credible ending. That title? He once bought a plot of ground, as yet unseen, in the place of the title, where he thinks he was conceived. A European view of America, and a view conceded by many American critics to be a highly perceptive one. Rest of cast: Dean Stockwell, Nastassja Kinski, Aurore Clément, Sam Berry, Bernhard Wicki, Claresie Mobley, Hunter Carson, Viva Auder, Socorro Valdez, Justin Hogg, Edward Fayton, Tom Farrell, John Lurie, Jeni Vici, Sally Norvell, Sharon Menzel, The Mydolls. Dir: Wim Wenders. Pro: Don Guest. Ex Pro: Chris Sievernich. Screenplay: Sam Shepard. Story

Adaptation: L. M. Kit Carson. Ph: Robby Müller (add. 2nd unit Ph: Martin Schär). Ed: Peter Przygodda. Art: Kate Altman. M: Ry Cooder. Pro 'Delegue': Anatole Dauman. Assoc Pro: Pascale Dauman. (Road Movies GmbH, Berlin and Argos Films, Paris in association with Westdeutscher Rundfunk, Cologne and Channel 4, London and Project Film, Munich–Palace Pictures) Rel: floating; first shown London (Gate, Notting Hill, Lumière and Screen-on-the-Hill), 23 Aug 1984. 144 mins. Cert 15. (Winner of best film Grand Prix at Cannes Festival 1984.)

Parker. A modest but very well made British thriller marking the cinema film debut of successful TV director Jim Goddard (*Callan* and *The Black Stuff* are among his small-screen successes). It is a very involving yarn about a British-based Australian businessman who is kidnapped while on a trip to Berlin and then unexpectedly released, and his subsequent efforts to find out why – an investigation that leads to the murder of his mistress and his abductors before he begins to find the right answers. And it grips all the way from start to final solution. Cast: Bryan Brown, Cherie Lunghi, Kurt Raab, Hannen Elsner, Bob Peck, Phil Smeeton, Gwyneth Strong, Simon Rouse, Dana Gillespie, Tom Wilkinson, Ingrid Pitt, Robert Goodale, Thomas, Rebecca and Virginia Goode, Jane Bertish, Elizabeth Spriggs, Frank Mills, Osman Ragheb, Beate Finkh, Achim Geissler, Jurgen Kuhn, Claus Fuchs, Colin Gilder, Marie-Charlotte Schuler, Alexander Duda, Klaus Menzel, Udo Weinberger, Uwe Ochsenknecht, Micha Lampert, John Huth, John Blundell, Mandy More. Dir: Jim Goddard. Pro: Nigel Stafford-Clark. Screenplay: Trevor Preston. Ph: Peter Jessop. Ed: Ralph Sheldon. (Moving Picture Co–Virgin Films) Rel: floating; first shown London (Classics), 3 May 1985. 97 mins. Cert 15.

The Party Animal. Another American male collegiate with only one thing on his mind, the pursuit of sex – and, as the character is, intentionally or not, made so wholly unappealing it's no wonder he is a frustrated fellow. For some youngsters the saving grace will be the rock music background contributed by groups like The Buzzcocks, The Untouchables and others. Cast: Matthew Causey, Tim Carhart, Robin Harlan, Suzanne Ashley, Jerry Jones, Frank Galati, Luci Roucis. Dir and Screenplay: David Baird. Pro: Bryan England and Mark Israel. Ex Pro: Alan C. Fox. Ph: Bryan England. Ed: Susan Jenkins. Pro Des: Ron Siegel. Assoc Dir: T. Cohen and C. A. Duncombe Jr. (Entertainment) Rel: 19 April 1985. 78 mins. Cert 18.

A Passage to India. David Lean's classical adaptation of E. M. Forster's literary classic set in India of the Raj; about a mysterious event that takes place in the Marabar caves when the unconventional Adela Quested accepts a young Indian doctor's invitation to a picnic there, resulting in her accusing him of attempted rape, and the court case that follows, with its surprising climax, affecting the lives of all concerned. Leisurely, atmospheric, intelligent direction by Lean and some fine performances – notably those by James Fox, Alec Guinness, Peggy Ashcroft, Victor Banerjee and Judy Davis – make this a subtle, polished and, all in all, remarkably fine and memorable movie in spite of its being a little too slow and a little too long. Rest of cast: Nigel Havers, Richard Wilson, Michael Culver, Antonia Pemberton, Art Malik, Ann Firbank, Saeed Jaffrey, Clive Swift, Sandra Hotz, Roshan Seth, Rashid Karapiet, H. S. Krishnamurthy, Ishaq Bux, Moti Makan, Mohammed Ashiq, Phyllis Bose, Paul Anil, Z. H. Khan, Ashok Mandanna, Dina Pathak, Peter Hughes, Sally Kinghorne, Mellan Mitchell, Adam Blackwood. Dir, Screenplay and Ed: David Lean; based on the novel by E. M. Forster and the play by Santha Rami Rau. Pro: John Brabourne and Richard Goodwin. Pro Sup: Barrie Melrose. Ph: Ernest Day. Pro Des: John Box. M: Maurice Jarre. Assoc Ed: Eunice Mountjoy. (Thorn EMI) Rel: 19 April 1985. 163 mins. Cert PG.

Pavlova – A Woman for All Time. A British-Russian co-production relating the (largely true) story of the comparatively short life and career of Anna Pavlova (she died in 1931 aged 49), one of the world's greatest ballerinas. Lavish production qualities with some marvellous balletic set-pieces seen against backgrounds of the grand theatres of Europe, Russia and South America. And Galina Beliaeva as Pavlova shows she can have few terpsichorean peers in today's world of ballet, even if she is unlikely ever to reach similar acting heights. Rest of cast: James Fox, Sergei Shakourov, V. Larionov, Lina Boultakova, Georgio Dimitriou, Ivan Shkyra, P. Gusev, Martin Scorsese, Bruce Forsyth, Roy Kinnear, Jacques Debari, Michael Kradunin, Alkis Kritikos, Anastasia Stakis, Svetlana Toma, Tijt Khyarm. Dir and Screenplay: Emil Lotianou (Western version supervised by Michael Powell). Ex Pro: Frixos Constantine. Assoc Pro: Eric Weissber-

Bryan Brown in the title role of *Parker*.

ger and Serafim Karalexis. Ph: Eugeni Guslinsky. Ed: I. Kalatikova, E. Galkina and J. Connock. Art: Boris Blank. M: Eugeny Dogas. Ballets staged by Pro. P. Gusev. (Frixos Constantine–Poseiden Films) Rel: floating; first shown London (Odeon, Marble Arch), 11 Mar 1985. 132 mins. Cert U.

Perfect Lives. Robert Ashley's highly original, seven-part, 3½-hour opera primarily, and obviously, created for the small screen. A mixture of classical, rock and operatic music, the film is concerned with a day in the life of a Mid-West American town, its 'surreal characters engaged in an absurdist plot'. All certainly very much out of the rut with a touch of Ashley magic. Cast: Robert Ashley, 'Blue' Gene Tyranny, Jill Kroesen, David Van Tiegham. 'Realized in collaboration with' John Sanborn (director), Carlotta Schoolman (TV producer), Tyranny (music col-

Judy Davis with Victor Banerjee (left) in *A Passage to India*. Fine performances, too, from James Fox (below left) with Banerjee, and Peggy Ashcroft (below).

Nancy Allen, Michael Paré, and Eric Christmas in *The Philadelphia Experiment*.

laborator) and Peter Gordon (music producer). Rel: floating; first shown London (ICA), 30 Oct 1984. 210 mins. No cert.

Phar Lap – Heart of a Nation. An overall warmth, deeply etched characters (presented by some very good players) and plenty of beautifully photographed horse-racing excitement distinguish this Australian film about an equine hero. (Phar Lap seems to have been very much an Aussie equivalent of Britain's much-loved Red Rum.) With its factual base about the steed's rise to glory and sad end, it is first-rate entertainment, in large part also due, too, to the sense of reality which has become the trademark of so much Australian cinema. Cast includes: Tom Burlinson, Ron Leibman, Martin Vaughan, Judy Morris, Celia de Burgh, Richard Morgan, Robert Grubb, Georgia Carr, James Steele, Vincent Ball, Peter Whitford, John Stanton, Roger Newcombe, Len Kaserman, Tom Woodcock, Steven Bannister, Richard Terrill, Warwick Moss, Henry Duvall, Pat Thompson, Redmond Phillips, Maggie Miller, Anthony Hawkins, Roger Newcombe, Brian Anderson, Len Kaserman, Paul Riley, Brian Adams, Alan Wilson. Dir: Simon Wincer. Pro: John Sexton. Ex in charge of Pro: Richard

Davis. Pro Co-ord: Peta Lawson. Screenplay: David Williamson. Ph: Russell Boyd. Ed: Tony Paterson. Pro Des: Laurence Eastwood. Art: David Bowden. M: Bruce Rowland. (John Sexton in assoc with Michael Edgley International – Fox/UK Film Dist) Restricted Rel: 15 March 1985. 107 minutes. Cert PG.

The Philadelphia Experiment. A highly imaginative sci-fi tale about a 1943 US Naval radar experiment which goes badly wrong and appears to get tied into a current one, resulting in a couple of young sailors getting caught up in a time warp and finding themselves uncomfortably 40 years in front of themselves. And if that sounds confusing it is no more so than the story, which needs quite a few pinches of salt before one can sit back and enjoy the action, romance and, yes, fun. Cast includes: Michael Paré, Nancy Allen, Eric Christmas, Bobby Di Cicco, Kene Holliday, Debra Troyer, Gary Brockette, Pamela Brull, James Crittenden, Pamela Doucette, Robin Krieger, Clayton Wilcox, Rudy Daniels, Don Dolan, Glenn Morshower, Stephen Tobolowsky, Ed Bakey, Vivian Brown, Jim Edgecomb, Louise Latham, Steve Sachs, Harry Beer, Anthony R. Nuzzo, Joe Moore, Andrew Bracken, Pat Das-

ko, Brent S. Laing, Kerry Maher, Charles Hall, Raymond Kowalski, Bo Parham, Lawrence Doll, Bill Smillie, Ralph Manza, Stephanie Faulkner, Michael Villani, Michael Currie, Lawrence Lott, Mary Lois Grantham. Dir: Stewart Raffill. Pro: Douglas Curtis and Joel B. Michaels. Ex Pro: John Carpenter. Screenplay: William Gray and Michael Janover; from a story by Wallace Bennett and Don Jakoby. Ph: Dick Bush. Ed: Neil Travis. Art: Chris Campbell. No M credit. Assoc Pro: Pegi Brotman. (New World Pictures and Cinema Group in association with New Pictures Group–Thorn EMI) Rel: 12 Oct 1984. 101 mins. Cert PG.

Places in the Heart. A thoroughly delightful, warmly remembered, carefully balanced portrait of life in the small Texas town of Waxahachie in the depressed 1930s by director/writer Robert Benton, whose family have lived there for four generations. It depicts the determined struggle of widder-woman Edna Spalding (Sally Field, an outstanding Oscar-winning performance) to keep her farm and her family together after her sheriff husband has been – accidentally – killed by a local (black) drunk's bullet. Vivid characters, convincing background, credible story and splendid atmosphere; one of the year's most memorable movies. Rest of cast: Lindsay Crouse, Ed Harris, Amy Madigan, John Malkovich, Danny Glover, Yankton Hatten, Gennie James, Lane Smith, Terry O'Quinn, Bert Remsen, Ray Baker, Jay Patterson, Toni Hud-

Sally Field as the Texas widow in *Places in the Heart* helped out (inset) by her children, Yankton Hatten and Gennie James, and a faithful worker, Danny Glover.

son, Devoreaux White, Jerry Haynes, Lou Hancock, Shelby Brammer, Norma Young. Dir and Screenplay: Robert Benton. Pro: Arlene Donovan. Ex Pro: Michael Hausman. Ph: Nestor Almendros. Ed: Carol Littleton. Pro Des: Gene Callahan. Art: S. Z. Litwak. M: John Kander (add M pro and adapted by Howard Shore). (Tri-Star Pictures) Rel: 15 March 1985. 111 mins. Cert PG.

The Pope of Greenwich Village. A slice of life, cut from Manhattan's shadier Italian community, which starts confusingly with a non-essential sequence but becomes clearer as it goes along in spite of dialogue so Italian-Brooklynese, and spoken with such accents, that for much of the time it is difficult to decipher. It is an adaptation of a best-selling novel about two unstable characters – cousins – one of whom leads the other into a heist of what turns out to be gangster's riches, with predictably uncomfortable results! Some good performances and nicely

atmospheric backgrounds. Cast: Eric Roberts, Mickey Rourke, Daryl Hannah, Geraldine Page, Kenneth McMillan, Tony Musante, M. Emmet Walsh, Burt Young, Jack Kehoe, Philip Bosco, Val Avery, Joe Grifasi, Tony Di Benedetto, Ronald Maccone, Betty Miller, Thomas A. Carlin, Leonard Termo, Marty Brill, John Bentley, Ed Setrakian, Rik Colitti, John Finn, Ger-

ry Murphy. Dir: Stuart Rosenberg. Pro: Gene Kirkwood. Screenplay: Vincent Patrick; based on his own book. Ph: John Bailey. Ed: Robert Brown. Pro Des: Paul Sylbert. M: Dave Grusin. Assoc Pro: Benjy Rosenberg.

Eric Roberts (left) and Mickey Rourke in *The Pope of Greenwich Village*.

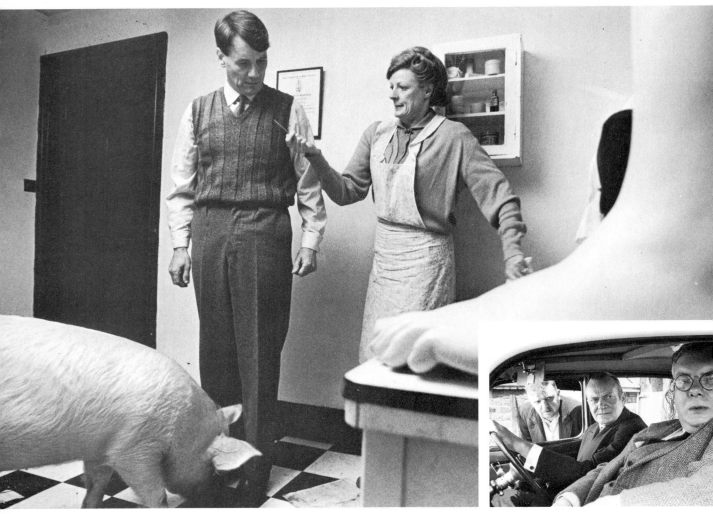

Michael Palin and Maggie Smith with stolen pig in *A Private Function*. Left to right (inset) Tony Haygarth, Denholm Elliott and Richard Griffiths.

(MGM/UA–UIP) Rel: 30 Nov 1984. 120 mins. Cert 15.

A Private Conversation. A Russian chamber-piece film with a cast of two: Irina Kupchenko and Mikhail Ukyanov. Dir: Nikita Mikhalkov. Screenplay: Mikhalkov and Sofia Prokofyeva and Ramiz Fataliyev; based on the play by Sofia Prokofyeva. Ph: Pavel Lebeshev. Ed: Zh. Praksina. Art: Alexander Adabashyan and Igor Makarov. M: Eduard Artemyev. (Contemporary) Rel: floating; first shown London (Phoenix, East Finchley), 24 May 1985. 94 mins. Cert PG.

A Private Function. The title very much gives the key for this broad, occasionally tasteless, but overall pretty hilarious British comedy set in a 1947, rationed Britain. Michael Palin plays a chiropodist in a small town in the Yorkshire Dales who discovers some of the local bigwigs are secretly fattening an illegally kept pig (for their planned banquet to celebrate the impending Royal marriage) and abducts the animal and takes it to his home, where it soon proves itself a highly unwelcome and smelly guest. Beneath all the fun a few serious notes are struck about human weaknesses. In spite of my own reservations this should be one of the biggest British comedy successes of the year. Rest of cast: Maggie Smith (delicious of course), Denholm Elliott, Richard Griffiths, Tony Haygarth, John Normington, Bill Paterson, Liz Smith, Alison Steadman, Jim Carter, Pete Postlethwaite, Eileen O'Brien, Rachel Davies, Reece Dinsdale, Philip Wileman, Charles McKeown, Susan Por-rett, Donald Eccles, Denys Hawthorne, Don Estelle, Eli Woods, Amanda Gregan, Paula Tilbrook, Bernard Wrigley, Lee Daley, Gilly Coman, Maggie Ollerenshaw, Josie Lang, David Morgan. Dir: Malcolm Mowbray. Pro: Mark Shivas. Ex Pro: George Harrison and Denis O'Brien. Screenplay: Alan Bennett; from a story by him and Mowbray. Ph: Tony Pierce-Roberts. Ed: Barrie Vince. Pro Des: Stuart Walker. Art: Judith Lang and Michael Porter. M: John du Prez. (Handmade Films) Rel: 25 Jan 1985. 94 mins. Cert 15.

Private Life – Chastnaya Zhizn. An interesting view of Soviet life in the story of a Russian workaholic businessman who, forced into early retirement, only then begins to see himself as he really has been, and has time to catch up on his private life and relationships with his family and friends. Cast: Mikhail Ulyanov, Iya Savvina, Alexei

Goldie Hawn as the cocktail bar waitress turned diplomat in *Protocol*.

Blokhin, Tatiana Dogileva, Irina Gubanova, Evgenia Lazarev. Dir: Yuli Raizman. Screenplay: Raizman and Anatoly Grebnyev. Ph: Nokolai Olonovsky. Art: Tatyana Lapshina. Ed: V. Belova. No M credit. (Contemporary Films) Rel: floating; first shown London (Phoenix, East Finchley), 2 Nov 1984. 102 mins. Cert PG.

The Prodigal. A film with a message, relating the gradual breakdown of the Stuart family as each of them finds the tradition of regular church attendance inadequate to cope with the changing values of modern life. Cast: John Hammond, Hope Lange, John Cullum, Arliss Howard, Morgan Brittany, Ian Bannen, Joey Travolta, Billy Graham. Dir and Screenplay: James F. Collier.

Pro: Ken Wales. Ex Pro: William F. Brown. Ph: Frank W. Stanley. Ed: William W. Brame. Art: William Creber. (International Films) Rel: June/July 1984. 110 mins. Cert PG.

Protocol. Though suffering a bit in comparison with her *Private Benjamin* success, Goldie Hawn is still intermittently delicious in vaguely similarly themed story about a cocktail bar waitress suddenly thrust into the world of Washington diplomacy and ruthlessly manipulated until she gets wise and turns serious on us with a little tub-thumping speech about Serving the People! Rest of cast: Chris Sarandon, Richard Romanus, André Gregory, Gail Strickland, Cliff de Young, Keith Szarabajka, Ed Begley Jr, James Staley, Kenneth Mars, Jean Smart, Maria O'Brien, Joel Brooks, Grainger Hines, Kenneth McMillan, Richard Hamilton, Mary Carver, Jack Ross Obney, Kath-

leen York, Georgianne La Pierre, la Myers, Joe George, Tom Spratley, Dorotha Duckworth, Sally Thorner, Jeanne Mori, Elizabeth Anderson, Archie Hahn, G. D. Wallace, Julie Hampton, Thom Sharp, Paul Willson, Holly Roberts, Lyman Ward, Joe Lambie, Daphne Maxwell, Michael Zand, Cece Cole, Roger Til, Marcella Saint-Amant, Ellen Tobie, Alice O'Connor, A. S. Csaky, Ken Gibbel, Ken Hill, Albert Leong, Peter Pan, Robert Donovan, Amanda Bearse, Marvie Barkin, Deborah Dutch, Lorraine Fields. Dir: Herbert Ross. Pro: Anthea Sylbert. Screenplay: Buck Henry; from a story by C. Shyer, N. Mayers and H. Miller. Ex Pro: Goldie Hawn. Ph: William A. Fraker. Ed: Paul Hirsch. Pro Des: Bill Malley. M: Basil Poledouris. Assoc Pro: Lewis J. Rachmil. (Warner) Rel: floating; first shown London (Warner), 3 May 1985. 95 mins. Cert PG.

P'tang Yang Kipperbang: a delightful comedy proving that made for television films do have a cinema life.

P'Tang Yang Kipperbang. Made in 1982, shown in 1983, this delightful British TV movie becomes the subject of an experiment with a cinema release in 1984, hoping to prove that 'there's life after death' as executive producer David Puttnam put it. As well made and entertaining as any cinema movie to be seen during the year, it is about a clumsy, shy, 14-year-old schoolboy and his pure passion for a pretty girl schoolmate which climaxes when he finds himself unable to kiss her – his dream – in the school play. Peripheral threads concern England's battle against Australia in the then current (1948) Test Match and the arrest as a deserter of the boy's hero, the young school groundsman who is having an affair with one of the schoolmistresses. Funny, moving and intensely human and so very well acted. Cast: John Albasiny, Abigail Cruttenden, Alison Steadman, Garry Cooper, Mark Brailsford, Chris Karallis, Frances Ruffelle, Maurice Dee, Nicola Prince, Robert Urquhart, Richenda Carey, Tim Seeley, Maurice O'Connell, Peter Dean, Dave Atkins, Eric Richard, Arthur Whybrow, Paul Wilson, Philip Edkins. Dir: Michael Apted. Pro: Chris Griffin. Ex Pro: David Puttnam. Screenplay: Jack Rosenthal. Ph: Tony Pierce-Roberts. Ed: John Shirley. Art: Jeffrey Woodbridge. M: David Earl. Assoc Pro: David Bill. (Enigma/Television Fox/Goldcrest–Fox) Restricted Rel: 2 Aug 1984. 80 mins. Cert PG. (Released with another TV movie, *Those Glory, Glory Days*, as a double-bill), see under that title.)

Purple Rain. One would surely have to be a fan of the exotically attired (minor Liberace style), St. Vitus-inspired, young black American pop star Prince to enjoy to the full the routine succession of his stage numbers thinly bound by a sketchy background of his home life and climb to fame as presented in this flashy musical, which gives the star the opportunity to exploit the range of his voice from quite pleasing soprano to spine-chilling shreik! Rest of cast: Apollonia Kotero, Morris Day, Olga Karlatos, Clarence Williams III, Jerome Benton, Billy Sparks, Jill Jones, Charles Huntsberry, Dez Dickerson, Brenda Bennett, Sandra Claire Gershman, Kim Upsher, Alan Leeds, Israel Gordon, Gil Jacobson, Joseph F. Ferraro, James French, Gerald E. Hubbard Jr, Paul Peterson, Jesse Johnson Dir and Ed: Albert Magnoli. Pro: Robert Cavallo, Joseph Buffalo and Steven Fargnoli. Screenplay: Magnoli and William Blinn. Ph: Donald L. Thorin. Pro Des: Ward Preston. M Score: Michael Colombier. Original songs composed by Prince. Groups taking part: The Revolution, Apollonia 6, and The Time. Numbers: 'Let's Go Crazy', 'Jungle Love', 'Take Me With U', 'Modernaire', 'The Beautiful Ones', 'God' (*Purple Rain* love theme), 'When Doves Cry', 'Father's Song',

Flamboyant pop-star Prince in *Purple Rain*.

'Computer Blue', 'Darling Nikki', 'Sex Shooter', 'The Bird', 'Purple Rain', 'Baby I'm a Star' and 'I would Die 4 U'. (Purple Films Co.–Warner) Rel: 31 Aug 1984. 111 mins. Cert 15.

Queen: We Will Rock You. A concert by the group of the title filmed with a 35,000 audience at Canada's Montreal Forum in early 1984. (Queen Films Ltd/Mobilvision and Yellowbill) Rel: 21 Sept 1984. 80 mins. Cert U.

Racing with the Moon. Swimming against the tide of a flood of raucous and rude films about American youth (shown too often as sex-mad and foul-mouthed) this movie about a few teenagers, set in the period of the middle of the last war, shows them as normal, fun-loving and loving youngsters. While two friends wait for their call-up, one falls deeply and truly in love while the other, more casual and less caring, gets his girl in the family way and rather callously organizes her abortion. A light and leisurely told story beautifully keyed to the period and mood, and a convincing pastiche of a time and place. A trio of nice performances from Sean Penn, Elizabeth McGovern and Nicolas Cage. Rest of cast: John Kar-

Sean Penn in *Racing with the Moon.*

len, Rutanya Alda, Max Showalter, Crispin Glover, Barbara Howard, Bob Maroff, Dominic Nardini, John Brandon, Eve Brent Ashe, Suzanne Adkinson, Shawn Schepps, Charles Miller, Patricia Allison, Al Hopson, Ted Grossman, Scott McGinnis, Brian Trumble, Kate Williamson, Julie Philips, Fielding Greaves, Arnold Johnson, Kevin Fraser, Gerry Gibson, Page Hannah, Shane Kerwin, Jonathan Charles Fox, Michael Madsen, Dana Carvey, Victor Rendina, Lou Butera, Michael Talbott, Philip Adams, Charlie Picerni, Philip Romano, Arlin Miller, Jan Rabson, Walter Matthews, Rebecca Pollack, Victor Paul, Sue Allen, Kathrine L. Brown, Peggy Clarke, Carol Kane. Dir: Richard Benjamin. Pro: Alain Bernheim and John Kohn. Screenplay: Steven Kloves. Ph: John Bailey. Ed: Jacqueline Cambas. Pro Des: David L. Snyder. M: Dave Grusin. (Paramount–UIP) Rel: floating; first shown London (Plaza), 14 Sept 1984. 108 mins. Cert 15.

Rat Trap – Elippathayam. Indian family piece, set in a remote locale and centred on an estate owned by a middle-aged man who increasingly neglects it as he drifts into a reclusive and uncaring state. Cast: Karamana, Sarada, Jalaja, Rajam K. Nair, Prakash, Sonan, John Samuel, Joycee, B. K.

Nair, Thampi, B. Nair, Sajit, Soha, Sindhu, Devan. Dir and Screenplay: Adoor Gopalakrishnan. Pro: Ravi. Assoc Dir: Meera. Ph: Ravi Varma. Ed: M. Mani. Art: Sivan. M: M. B. Srinivasan. (General Pictures–BFI) Rel: floating; first shown London (Everyman, Hampstead), 9 Nov 1984. 121 mins. Cert PG.

Red Dawn. A somewhat unlikely – if not downright silly – supposition is the basis of this otherwise generally well made story about a united Cuban and Russian invading force which takes the US completely by surprise by parachuting into a small town in Colorado, where it proceeds to take and kill hostages and commit all the usual wartime outrages, while a few youngsters from the ruthlessly gunned-down school take to the hills and with an astonishing amount of weaponry cause havoc among the invaders. Noteworthy that only conventional weapons are used by both sides and the war ends in at least temporary stalemate! Cast: Patrick Swayze, C. Thomas Howell, Lea Thompson, Charlie Sheen, Darren Dalton, Jennifer Grey, Brad Savage, Doug Toby, Ben Johnson, Harry Dean

Left to right, Charlie Sheen, C. Thomas Howell and Patrick Swayze in *Red Dawn.*

Stanton, Ron O'Neal, William Smith, Vladek Sheybal, Powers Boothe, Frank McRae, Roy Jensen, Pepe Serna, Lane Smith, Judd Omen, Michael D'Agosta, Johelen Carleton, George Ganchev, Waldemar Kalinowski, Sam Slovick, Radames Pera, Lois Kimbrell. Dir: John Milius. Pro: Buzz Feitshans and Barry Beckerman. Ex Pro: Sidney Beckerman. Screenplay: Milius and Kevin Reynolds; based on the latter's book. Ph: Ric Waite. Ed: Thom Noble. Pro Des: Jackson de Govia. M: Basil Poledouris. (A Valkyrie Film/Sidney Beckerman Productions–MGM/UA– UIP) Rel: 10 Nov 1984. 114 mins. Cert 15.

Repo Man. (Repo equals hire-purchase–re-possession agent.) An original mixture of fast-moving car sequences, re-possession incidents, science-fiction (a car with what appears to have a radiation-killing plant in the boot), off-beat characters and lots of foul language all mixed up in the sort of odd, fragmented whole which might easily make the movie a cult success. Cast: Harry Dean Stanton, Emilio Estevez, Tracey Walter, Olivia Barash, Sy Richardson, Susan Barnes, Fox Harris, Tom Finnegan, Del Zamora, Eddie Velez, Zander Schloss, Jennifer Balgobin, Dick Rude, Michael Sandoval, Vonetta McGee, Richard Foronjy, Bruce White, Biff Yeager, Ed Pansullo,

Emilio Estevez (centre) surrounded by glamour in *Repo Man*.

Steve Mattson, Thomas Boyd, Charles Hopkins, Helen Martin, Jon St. Elwood, Kelitta Kelly, Varnum Honey, David Chung, Cynthia Szigeti, Dorothy Bartlett, Jonathon Hugger, Sharon Gregg, Dale Reynolds. Dir and Screenplay: Alex Cox. Pro: Jonathan Wacks and Peter McCarthy. Ex Pro: Michael Nesmith. Assoc Pro: Gerald Olsen. Ph: Robby Muller. Ed: Dennis Dolan. Art: J. Rae Fox and Linda Burbank. M: Tito Larriva and Steven Hufsteter. Groups: Iggy Pop, Black Flag, Suicidal Tendencies, Burning Sensations, Fear, The Circle Jerks, The Plugz, Juicy Bananas. (Edge City Productions/Universal–Artificial Eye.) Rel: floating; first shown London (Chelsea Cinema and Camden Plaza), 10 Jan 1985. 92 mins. Cert 18.

The Return of Captain Invincible. A likeable, modestly-made Australian parody on Superman and his ilk. And great fun, with the old-time comic-strip hero of thirty years back, reduced to a penurious drunk in Sydney's less salubrious quarters, brought back to hero status – and all his former magical powers – by a clever little lady cop. And restored to Super-Super class (by hearing 'God Bless America' on the radio), he turns the villains' atomic missiles back on to their launchers. Cast: Alan Arkin, Christopher Lee, Kate Fitzpatrick, Bill Hunter, Michael Pate, David Argue, John Bluthal, Chelsea Brown, Max Cullen, Arthur Dignam, Noel Ferrier, Hayes Gordon, Chris

Haywood, Graham Kennedy, Gus Mercurio, Max Phipps, Alfred Sandor, Brian Adams, Vince Aloschi, Ron Beck, Joe Bell, Ken Bernard, Cali, Joe Catucci, Beru Cox, Robert Davis, Maggie Dence, Amanda Dole, Roger Eagle, Norman Erskine, Terry Hartshorne, Virginia Hey, Connie Hobbs, Gillian Hyde, Christine Jurisic, Ken Kruse, Madame Lash, Simon Reptile, Del Massey, Garry Mather, John McCall, Doug McGrath, Grarth Meade, Karen Michelle, Tiriel Mora, Roger Newcombe, Jerome Patillo, Virginia Rooksby, Shulmalite Rovkin, Lila V. Schreiber, Scott Smith, Bruce Spence, Henri Szeps, Consuelo Vera, Mark Wignall, Coco York, The Palm Court Orchestra. Dir: Phillipe Mora. Pro: Andrew Gaty. Assoc Pro: Brian D. Burgess. Screenplay: Steven E. de Souza and Andrew Gaty. Ph: Mike Molloy (2nd Unit Ph: Nixon Binney). Ed: John Scott. Pro Des: David Copping. Art: Owen Patterson and Ron Highfield. M: William Motzing. (Willarra/Seven Keys Pro– Media Releasing) Rel: floating; first shown London (Minema), 5 April 1985. 100 mins. Cert PG.

Reuben, Reuben. A far more than usually literate – and witty – comedy, with a heart; about a shambling, drunken, tweed-clad, womanizing Scots poet (a character drawing something from both Brendan Behan and Dylan Thomas) who has not written a line in twelve years and is making a thin living by reciting his own poems on a lecture tour of the New England college circuit. And what happens when he meets a sweet young girl who falls for him and he – for the first time in his life – finds himself sampling the mental upheaval of true love; it all leads to an ironically amusing if tragic conclusion. A movie brought to brilliant life by Tom Conti's marvellous performance as the poet with a death-wish. Rest of cast: Kelly McGillis (a nice debut), Robert Blossom, Cynthia Harris, E. Katherine Kerr, Joel Fabiani, Lois Smith, Rex Robbins, Kara Wilson, Jack Davidson, Damon Douglas, Robert Nichols, Ed Grady, Tom McGowan, Dan Doby, Scott Coffey, Barry Bell, Rene Copeland, Roger Black, Angus MacLahlan, Mary-Fran Lyman, Claudia Geraghty, Joanna Morgan, Gladys Lavitan, Mac McGuire, Paul Austin, Jamie (the dog – 'Reuben'). Dir: Robert Ellis Miller. Pro: Walter Shenson. Co Pro: Julius J.

Tom Conti with his possessive mistress Katherine Kerr in *Reuben, Reuben*.

Epstein. Screenplay: Epstein; from the novel by Peter DeVries and play *Spofford* by Herman Shumlin. Assoc Pro: Philip Epstein and Dan Allingham. Ph: Peter Stein. Ed: Skip Lusk. Pro Des: Peter Larkin. M: Billy Goldenberg. (Saltair Productions–Enterprise Pictures) Rel: 3 Aug 1984. 100 mins. Cert 15.

Revenge of the Nerds. Another somewhat off-putting look at the strange and quite frightening world of American scholastics, with the 'Nerds' – or the youngsters who seem to have some pretentions of education – suffering from and then learning to fight back against the roughly rampant ball players of the college, who when their own quarters have been burnt out evict the nerds from their dormitory and generally humiliate them. Cast: Robert Carradine, Anthony Edwards, Ted McGinley, Bernie Casey, Julia Montgomery, Tim Busfield, Andrew Cassese, Curtis Armstrong, Larry B. Scott, Brian

Tochi, Donald Gibb, Daid Whol, John Goodman. Dir: Jeff Kanew. Pro: Ted Field and Peter Samuelson. Ex Pro: David Obst and Peter Bart. Co-Pro: Peter MacGregor Scott. Screenplay: Steve Zacharias and Jeff Budhai; from a story by them plus Tim Metcalfe and Miguel Tejada-Flores. Ph: King Baggot. Ed: Alan Balsam. Pro Des: James L. Schoppe. M: Thomas Newman. (Interscope Communications–Fox) Rel: 8 Mar 1985. 90 mins. Cert 18.

Richard Pryor Here and Now. Carefully edited mixture of bits and pieces from some of Pryor's solo concert performances in Saenger Theatre, New Orleans, on 9, 10 and 11 August 1983. They add up to very much the story as before, but with a little something added, the acute sympathy Pryor shows for dope addicts and the like even when he uses them to get his laughs . . . and as an admitted former 'doper' he has earned that right. Not intended for modest ears or polite company, Pryor fills his material with all his usual foul language and over-the-edge lines – but his devoted fans remain legion and enthusiastic! Dir and Written: Richard

Pryor. Pro: Bob Parkinson and Andy Friendly. Ex Pro: Jim Brown. Ph: Vincent Singletary, K. A. Patterson, Joe Epperson, Tom Geren and John Sim-

Richard Pryor in *Richard Pryor Here and Now*.

Mel Gibson and Sissy Spacek, assisted by Shane Bailey, battle against the elements in *The River* while (right) Spacek with Betty Jo Lynch enjoy a more tranquil moment.

mons. Ed: Raymond Bush. Pro Des: Anthony Sabatino and William Harris. Assoc Pro: Linda Howard. Pro Assoc: Terri McCoy. Pro Co-Ord: Jim Moriarty. 2nd Unit Dir: Stan Lathan. In charge of Pro: Julian Bercovici. Art: Tom Melleck. (Columbia Delphi–Columbia) Rel: floating; first shown London (Dominion), 10 Aug 1984. 95 mins. Cert 18.

The River. Another in the mini-cycle of movies showing that America's Mid-West farmers are having difficult times but have the guts to pull through! This time stolid Mel Gibson is the obstinate land-lover who is struggling against a far too high overdraft, nature (with its periodic floodings of his land and crop failures) the bank's threat to foreclose and his wealthy neighbour's plan to flood the valley and create a reservoir to ease his own arid problems. It works

out as a warm-hearted, stirringly happy-ending (if temporary), victory-over-the-odds movie with two outstanding performances (from Sissy Spacek as the indomitable farmer's wife and Scott Glenn as the villain whose hard shell *can* be cracked), and some marvellously well created storm scenes. And the two children in the story are both really delightful: Shane Bailey and Becky Jo Lynch. Rest of cast: Don Hood, Billy Green Bush, James Tolkan, Bob W. Douglas, Andy Stahl, Lisa Sloan, Larry D. Ferrell, Susie

Toomey, Kelly Toomie, Frank Taylor, Ivan Green, Desmond Couch, Charles G. Riddle, Jim Antonio, Samuel Scott Osborne, Amy Rydell, David Hart, Barry Primus, Mark Erickson, Jack Starrett, Charlie Robinson, Dean Whitworth, Charles S. Hanson, Ira M. Quillen II, Matt Bearson, Timothy Shadden, Elizabeth Lane, Gary Gershaw. Dir: Mark Rydell. Pro: Edward Lewis and Robert Cortes. Screenplay: Robert Dillon and Julian Barry; from a story by Dillon. Ph: Vilmos Zsigmond. Ed: Sidney Levin. Pro Des: Charles Rosen. Art: Norman Newberry. M: John Williams. (Universal Pictures–UIP) Rel: 22 March 1985. 124 mins. Cert PG.

Romancing the Stone. A highly diverting example of good old Hollywood hokum; a romantic adventure movie always maintaining a pace, nice sense of humour, and range of spectacular backgrounds that takes it towards the top of the year's fun films tree. Kathleen Turner, giving a delightfully well judged performance as a best-selling romantic novelist living in New York otherwise

Michael Douglas with Kathleen Turner, the resilient heroine of *Romancing the Stone.*

uneventful life suddenly erupts as if into her own exciting fictional world when she receives her sister's SOS call to save her from a most unpleasant fate in Colombia, a journey which leads to her involvement with one of her typical macho heroes (Michael Douglas) and a desperate treasure hunt in the jungle. Rest of cast: Danny DeVito, Zack Norman, Alfonso Arau, Manuel Ojeda, Holland Taylor, Mary Ellen Trainor, Eve Smith, Joe Nesnow, Jose Chavez, 'Chachita', Camillo Garcia, Rodrigo Puebla, Paco Morayta, Jorge Zamoro, Kym Herrin, Bill Burton, Ted White, Manuel Santiago, Ron Silver, Mike Cassidy, Vince Deadrick Sr, Richard Drown, Joe Finnegan, Jimmy Medearis, Jeff Ramsey. Dir: Robert Zemeckis (2nd Unit Dir and Stunt Co-Ord: Terry Leonard;) 2nd Unit Ph: Richard Hart). Pro: Michael Douglas.

Screenplay: Diane Thomas. Ph: Dean Cundey. Ed: Donn Cambers and Frank Morriss. Pro Des: Lawrence G. Paull. Art: Augustin Ituarte. Co-Pro: Jack Brodsky and Joel Douglas. M: Alan Silvestri (title song written performed and produced by Eddy Grant). (El Corazon Producciones SA–Fox) Rel: 17 Aug 1984. 105 mins. Cert PG.

Runaway. Entertaining, fast-paced, generally imaginative cop thriller with sci-fi trimmings; set at some future time, when a special elite Force is detailed to dealing with runaway rogue robot killers. Built on the logical premise that as man is imperfect and can turn evil, so can the creatures he creates. But the murders that Tom Selleck and pretty assistant Cynthia Rhodes investigate here are very much at human instigation. Rest of cast: Gene Simmons, Kirstie Alley, Stan Shaw, G. W. Bailey, Joey Cramer, Chris Mulkey, Anne-Marie Martin, Michael Paul Chan, Elizabeth Norment, Carol Teesdale, Jackson Davies, Paul Batten, Babs Chulla, Marilyn Schreffler, Cec

Verrell, Natino Bellentino, Judith Johns, Betty Phillips. Dir and Screenplay: Michael Crichton. Pro: Michael Rachmil. Ex Pro: Kurt Villadsen. Ph: John A. Alonzo. Ed: Glenn Farr. Pro Des: Douglas Higgins. M: Jerry Goldsmith. (Tri-Star) Rel: 21 June 1985. 100 mins. Cert 15.

Running Brave. Another addition to the Sporting Heroes' True Tales series (sparked off by the success of Britain's Oscar-winning *Chariots of Fire*). This is the story of a young Sioux Indian from South Dakota who won a place at the University of Kansas, where he showed his running talents; continued to blossom when he joined the US Marines; and astonished everyone by winning the 10,000 metres race at the Tokyo Olympics. All pretty pat until the moving and exciting climax; but with some sly digs at the American brand of sporting spirit . . . *win*, at any cost. Cast: Robby Benson, Pat Hingle, Claudia Cron, Jeff McCracken, August Schellenberg, Denis Lacroix, Graham Greene, Kendall Smith, George Clutesi, Margo Kane, Derek Campbell, Maurice Wolfe, Albert Angus, Barbara Blackhorse, Carmen Wolfe, William Berry, Kaye Corbett, John Littlechild, Tantoo Martin, Gail Omeasoo, Billy Runsabove, Seymour Eaglespeaker, Maurice Wolfe, Merrill Dendoff, The Ermineskin Band, Michael J. Reynolds, Chris Judge, Paul Hubbard, Jack Ackroyd, Tommy Banks, Clare

Robby Benson hits the finishing tape in *Running Brave.*

Drake, Rob Roy, Graham MacPherson, Francis Damberger, Ray Kelly, Thomas Peacocke, Barbara Reese, Douglas Marquardt, Bonar Bain, Donna Devore, Wendell Smith, Daryl Menard, Greg Coyes, Kim Maser, Walter David, Bryan Hall, Greg Rogers, Christopher Gaze, William Fisher, Fred Keating, Brendan Hughes, Will Reese, Harvey Haugen. Dir: D. S. Everett. Pro: Ira Englander. Assoc Pro: Maurice Wolfe. Pro Ex: Martha Moran. Pro Co-Ord: Angela Heald. Screenplay: Henry Bean and Shirl Hendryx. Ph: François Protat. Sup Ed: Peter Zinner. Pro Des: Carol Spier. Art: Barbara Dunphy. M: Mike Post. (Englander Productions in association with The Ermineskin Band–ITC) Rel: 6 July 1984. 102 mins. Cert PG.

Savage Islands. A modestly but well-made action melodrama from New Zealand about bootleggers' rivalry in the South Pacific in the mid-19th century, with a colourful wedding, a massacre, bridal abduction, German gunboat, Samoan king, sea battle and last-minute rescue sequences to keep the pot nicely boiling. And the villain-cum-hero, 'Bully' Hayes (Tommy Lee Jones) proves to be not quite all bad. Rest of cast: Michael O'Keefe, Max Phipps, Jenny Seagrove, Grant Tilley, Peter Rowley, Bill Johnson, Kate Harcourt, Reg Ruka, Roy Billing, Bruce Allpress, David Letch, Prince Tui Teka, Pudji Waseso, Peter Vere Jones, Ton Vanderlaan, Mark Hadlow, Philip Gordon, Norman Fairley, Warwick Simmins, Paul Farrell, Frank Taurua, Norman Keesing, Robert Bruce, Timothy Lee, Peter Bell, Peter Diamond, John Rush, Grant Price, Karl Bradley. Dir: Ferdinand Fairfax. Pro: Lloyd Phillips and Rob Whitehouse. Pro Sup: Ted Lloyd. 2nd Unit Dir: Michael Horton. Screenplay: John Hughes and David Odell; from the latter's story, based on a story by Lloyd Phillips. Ph: Tony Imi. Ed: John Shirley. Pro Des: Maurice Cain. Art: Dan Hannah, Rick Kofoed and Jo Ford. M: Trevor Jones. (Phillips White-House Production–Paramount–UIP) Rel: 28 Sept 1984. 99 mins. Cert PG.

Scarred. (Originally titled *Red on Red*.) Prostitution in Hollywood is the background to this sad little story about a teenage mother, sans husband, money, job or family, who takes to the streets and finds herself up against what amounts to a closed shop run by the local pimps and hookers. And it was all shot in the streets of the celluloid city. Cast includes: Jennifer Mayo, David Dean, Jackie Berryman, Ricco Richardson. Dir, Screenplay and Ed: Rose-Marie Turko. Pro: Turko and Mark Bourde, in association with Dan Helperin. Ed Pro: Seymour Bourde. Ph: Michael Miner. Sup Ed: Miller Drake. Art: Cecilia Rodarte. M: Tim Timmermans. (Videoform Pictures in association with Black Cat Films). Rel: floating; first shown London (Prince Charles and ABC Edgware Rd), 9 Nov 1984. 84 mins. Cert 18.

Scream for Help. Michael Winner, whose big successes have generally been violent ones, seems to have had his tongue in his cheek (though maintaining his sometimes off-putting speciality) in this technically first-rate, routine thriller about a teenager who cannot convince anyone that her nasty stepfather is planning to murder her mum, so in the classic cliché manner sets out to do the detective work herself and then, when too late for prevention, equally firmly sets out on the road of revenge. Cast: Rachael Kelly, Marie Masters, David Brooks, Lolita Lorre, Rocco Sisto, Corey Parker, Sandra Clark, Tony Sibbald, Stacey Hughes, David Baxt, Leslie Lowe, Michael Corby, Ronald Fernee, Richard Oldfield, Tony Cyrus, Joel Cutrara, Jeff Hard-

The lady is about to *Scream for Help* in the film of that title.

ing, Brittain Saine Walker, Erick Ray Evans, William Roberts, Michael Fitzpatrick, Diana Ricardo, Burnell Tucker, Bruce Boa, Robyn Mandell, Morgan Deare, Sarah Brackett, Chuck Julian, Clare Burt, Matthew Peters. Dir and Pro: Michael Winner. Ex Pro: Irwin Yablans. Screenplay: Tom Holland. Ph: Robert Paynter. Ed: Christopher Barnes. Art: Tony Reading. M: John Paul Jones. Pro Sup: Malcolm Christopher. (Lorimar–Videoform Pictures/Miracle Films) Rel: 15 March 1985. 89 mins. Cert 18.

Secret Honour. Limited-appeal film version of the stage play, with a cast of one – Philip Baker Hall. Described as a 'fictional meditation', it follows, often closely, the career of former US President Nixon, coming up with the surely tongue-in-cheek suggestion that he was the tool of a group of sinister characters seeking world domination – or something like that! Certainly an item to add to any collection of cinematic curiosities. Dir and Pro: Robert Altman. Ex Pro: Scott Bushnell. Screenplay: Donald Freed and Arnold M. Stone: based on their one-act play. Ph: Pierre Mignot. Ed: Juliet Weber. Art: Stephen Altman. M: George Burt. Assoc Dir: Robert Hardres. (Sandcastle 5 Pro Inc. in association with University of Michigan Dept of Communications and Los Angeles Theatre–Blue Dolphin) Rel: floating; first shown London (Everyman), 8 Feb 1985. 90 mins. Cert 15.

Secret Places. A minor, pleasant little British film about life in a girls' school during World War II; it concerns the friendship that, springing up between a shy British pupil and a more sophisticated new German arrival, survives the sneers of some of the girls and a mistress's warning that the relationship might drift into something too close for their own good. Variably acted, pleasant backgrounds, nice atmosphere. Cast: Marie-Thérès Relin, Tara MacGowran, Claudine Auger, Jenny Agutter, Cassie Stuart, Ann-Marie Gwatkin, Pippa Hinchley, Klaus Barner, Sylvia Coleridge, Rosemary Martin, Amanda Grinling, Veronica Clifford, Adam Richardson, John Henson, Robert Kenly, Paul Ambrose, Rosamund Greenwood, Erika Spotswood, Bill Ward, Margaret Lacey, Maurice O'Connell, Zoe Caryl, Mike Haywood,

Marie-Thérès Relin (left) as a sophisticated German refugee with Tara MacGowran as a shy British pupil in *Secret Places*.

John Blundell, Lesley Nightingale, Andrew Byatt, Tony London, Georgia Slowe, Stewart Guidotti, Mark Lewis, Jessica Walker, Sian Dunlop, Alan Barry, John Segal, Lala Lloyd. Dir and Screenplay: Zelda Barron (from the novel by Janice Elliott). Pro: Simon Relph and Ann Skinner. Ex Pro: Al Clark and Robert Devereux. Ph: Peter Macdonald. Ed: Laurence Mery-Clark. Pro Des: Eileen Diss. Art: Bob Cartwright and Judith Lang. M: Michel Legrand (Song: 'Secret Places', lyrics by Alan Jay Lerner). (Skreba/Virgin Films in association with National Film Finance Corp, Redifusion and Rank Film Dist) Rel: 6 July 1984. 98 mins. Cert 15.

Sheena. A good fun film based on the comic-strip-style book *Sheena, Queen of the Jungle*, with Tanya Roberts as a kind of lovely lady Tarzan (she reveals all her statuesque charms on more than one occasion) who with the help of a couple of American film cameramen defeats the plan of Prince Otwani (the

Tanya Roberts (right) as the 'beautiful and gifted primeval woman with mystical powers' in *Sheena*.

James Mason (left) in *The Shooting Party* with John Gielgud.

local villain) to pin the murder of his brother on to Miss Tarzan's framed Ma. Rest of cast: Ted Waas, Donovan Scott, Elizabeth of Torro, France Zobda, Trevor Thomas, Clifton Jones, John Forgeham, Errol John, Sylvester Williams, Bob Sherman, Michael Shannon, Nancy Paul, Kathryn Gant, Kirsty Lindsay, Nick Brimble, Paul Gee, Dave Cooper, Tim Ward-Booth, Wil-

bury Nyabongo, Oliver Nyabongo, Oliver Litondo, Louis Mahoney, Shane Mwigereri, Tom Mwangi, Margarita Ndisi, Joseph Olita, Lenny Juma, William Allot, Lucy Wangiu Hishomo, Mick Ndisho. Dir: John Guillermin. Pro: Paul Aratow. Ex Pro: Yoram Ben-Ami. Ph: Pasqualino de Santis. Screenplay: David Newman and Leslie Stevens. Ed: Ray Lovejoy. Pro Des: Peter Murton. M: Richard Hartley. Assoc Pro: Christian Ferry and Alain Rinzler. (Columbia–Delphi 11–Columbia) Rel: 24 May 1985. 115 mins. Cert PG.

The Shooting Party. A beautifully realized film of the 1980 Isabel Colegate novel, set in the last days of the Edwardian period, just prior to the First World War. A masterly evocation of a weekend party on a country estate where the idle, socially assured guests kill vast numbers of peasants, indulge in quiet adultery, gossip, dine elegantly, dress exquisitely and are only temporarily shocked when instead of a bird they kill a man: and the key to all this is the remark of the tired and cynical, but in a crisis warmly human host: 'If you take away the proper function of the aristocracy, what can it do but play games too seriously?' A sumptuous, polished and stylish film in which fine players give fine performances; headed by James Mason, who in his last role as the world-weary host gives one of his most memorable and magnificent performances. Rest of cast: John Gielgud, Edward Fox, Dorothy Tutin, Gordon Jackson, Frank Windsor, Cheryl Campbell, Judi Bowker, Rupert Frazer, Robert Hardy, Joris Stuyk, Sarah Badel, Rebecca Saire, Aharon Ipalé, John J. Carney, Ann Castle, Daniel Chatto, Mia Fothergill, Thomas Heathcote, Barry Jackson, Jonathan Lacey, Richard Leech, Jack May, Deborah Miles, Daniel Moynihan, Patrick O'Connell, Nicholas Pietrek, Warren Saires, Lockwood West. Dir: Alan Bridges. Pro: Geoffrey Reeve. Ex Pro: Jeremy Saunders. Assoc Pro: Peter Dolman. Screenplay: Julian Bond; based on the Isabel Colegate novel. Pro Co-Ord: Tom Reeve. Ph: Fred Tammes. Ed: Peter Davies. Pro Des: Morley Smith. M: John Scott. (Curzon) Rel: floating; first shown London (Curzon), 1 Feb 1985. 98 mins. Cert 15.

Silver City. An Australian film with Polish underpinning: a passionate love story about an immigrant couple struggling to find a place in the new world. The realistic background is drawn in with refreshing honesty and fine detail, and the romance is beautifully played, especially by new Polish-born actress Gosia Dobrowolska who seems sure, from this evidence, to be heading for major international stardom. Though with some flaws, a triumph for director and co-writer Sophia Turkiewicz, herself brought to Australia by her immigrant Polish parents when she was three years old. The film won a well earned trio of top Aussie awards: for best supporting actor and actress and for

costume design. Rest of cast: Ivar Kants, Anna Jemison, Steve Bisley, Debra Lawrence, Ewa Brok, Joel Cohen, Tim McKenzie, Dennis Miller, Annie Byron, Steve Jacobs, Halina Abramowicz, Joseph Brewniak, Ron Blanchard. Dir and Screenplay (latter with Thomas Keneally): Sophia Turkiewicz. Pro: Joan Long. Ph: John Seale. Ed: Don Saunders. Art: Igor Nay. M: William Motzing (song 'Love Forgives Everything' – 'Milsoc Ci Wszystko' by Henry Wars: lyrics by M. Olden). (Limelight/Artificial Eye) Rel: floating; first shown London (Chelsea Cinema and Screen on Baker St), 13 June 1985. 100 mins. Cert 15.

Slow Moves. Another remarkable little movie from Jon Jost which he made for something around £6,000 on a 4½-day shooting schedule, wrote, directed, produced and edited and for which he composed the music himself. With all its almost inevitable faults (poor sound, for instance) it is *quite* an achievement. Using amateurs (Roxanne Rogers and Marshall Gaddis), he tells a story about two strangers who meet on the Golden Gate Bridge, team up and go off in something like the *Bonnie and Clyde* manner to end with the hero being killed during an attempt to rob a store. Rest of cast: Debbie Krant, Barbara Hammes, Geoffrey Rotwein, Bebe

Adolph Caesar (right) makes an accusation against Larry Riley while Art Evans looks on in *A Soldier's Story*.

Bright, Roger Ruffin. Dir, Screenplay, Ed, Pro and M: Jon Jost. (Jon Jost Productions–ICA) Rel: floating; first shown London (ICA), 2 Jan 1985. 93 mins. No cert.

A Soldier's Story. Black *v.* black tensions as well as black *v.* white and white *v.* black prejudices are at the heart of this (obviously stage-play-based), carefully balanced story about a black US Army Captain sent from Washington to investigate the murder of a black NCO at a Lousiana training camp; a doggedly determined search for truth which, by a series of flashbacks as the interrogations continue, gradually reveals the real, surprise killer – and it is all so similar to a black American-orientated Agatha Christie piece! Cast: Howard E. Rollins Jr, Adolph Caesar, Art Evans, David Alan Grier, David Harris, Dennis Lipscomb, Larry Riley, Robert Townsend, Denzel Washington, William Allen Young, Patti LaBelle, Wings Hauser, Scott Paulin, John Hancock, Trey Wilson, Patricia Brandkamp, Carl Dreher, Vaughn Reeves, Robert Tyler, Pat Grabe, Terry Dodd, Warren Clements, James W. Bryant, John Valentine, Ronald E. Greenfield, Anthony C. Sanders, Traftin E. Thompson, Roy Wells, Tommy G. Liggins, Calvin Franklin, Kevin T. Mosley, Michael Williams, David Ashley, Thomas Howard, Bobby McGaughey, Rick Ramey, Lacarnist Hiriams. Dir: Norman Jewison. Pro: Jewison, Ronald L. Schwary and Patrick Palmer. Assoc Pro: Charles Milhaupt. Pro Assoc: Michael Jewison.

Gosia Dobrowolska (right) gave a scintillating performance in *Silver City*, a story of Polish immigrants in Australia.

Two views of mermaid Daryl Hannah in *Splash* – at rest, with tail, and taking some *fruits de mer* nourishment, with legs.

Screenplay: Charles Fuller: based on his play *A Soldier's Play*. Ph: Russell Boyd. Ed: Mark Warner and Caroline Bigger-staff. Pro Des: Walter Scott Herndon. M: Herbie Hancock. (Columbia/Delph–Columbia) Restricted Rel: 15 March 1985. 101 mins. Cert 15.

Spinal Tap. (Also titled *This is Spinal Tap*.) Hilarious American-made 'rock-umentary' about the disastrous tour of the US by a British rock group who finally decide they'll do better in Japan, where their 'Smell the Glove' album, in contrast to otherwise notable lack of interest, is doing so well. A satirical view of some of the public house and other groups from Britain who have dared to cross the Atlantic. Flawed but funny. Cast: Christopher Guest, Michael McKean, Harry Shearer, R. J. Parnell (the Spinal Tap Group): David Kaff, Rob Reiner, June Chadwick, Tony Hendra, Bruno Kirby, Ed Begley Jr, Paul Benedict, Zane Buzby, Billy Crystal, Howard Hesseman, Patrick Macnee, Paul Shaffer, Fred Willard, Fran Drescher, Joyce Hyser, Vicki

Blue, Anjelica Huston, Kimberly Strin-ger, Chazz Dominguez, Shari Hall, Jean Cromie, Patrick Maher, Danny Kortchmar, Memo Vera, Julie Payne, Dana Carvey, Sandy Helberg, Robin Mencken, Jennifer Child, J. J. Barry, George McDaniel, Anne Churchill, Paul Shortino, Cherie Darr, Lara Cody, A. J. Lederer, Russ Kunkel, Diana Duncan, Gina Marie Pitrello, Gloria Gifford, Archie Hahn, Charles Levin, Wonderful Smith, Chris Roma-no, Daniel Rogers, Fred Asparagus, Rodney Kemerer, Robert Bauer. Dir: Rob Reiner. Pro: Karen Murphy. Pro

Ex: Lindsay Doran. Pro Controller: Jeff Stott. Pro Co-Ord: Margaret E. Fannin. Screenplay: Reiner, Christ-opher Guest, Michael McKean and Harry Shearer. Ph: Peter Smokler. Sup Ed: Robert Leighton. Ed: Kent Beyda and Kim Secrist. Pro Des: Bryan Jones. Add Art: Stan Harris. M and Lyrics: Christopher Guest, Michael McKean, Harry Shearer and Rob Rein-er. M Ed: Kenneth Karman. (Spinal Tap Productions for Embassy Pictures–Mainline) Rel: floating; first shown London (Classics, at Oxford St and Chelsea and Electric Screen), 7 Sept 1984. 83 mins. Cert 15.

Splash. A fantasy-comedy-romance about a young wholesale fruiterer who meets the girl of his dreams – suitably enough at Cape Cod! – and finds her legs are only temporary – she is in fact a mermaid he met many years ago when as a small boy he fell into the sea. And there are some splashes of real situation comedy when the girl's secret is re-vealed to the wondering world! All very pleasant, too, with nice performances by Daryl Hannah as the lady with the tail and Tom Hanks as the lover pre-pared to sacrifice his legs, presumably, for love. Rest of cast includes: Eugene Levy, John Candy, Dody Goodman,

Shecky Greene, Richard B. Shull, Bobby Di Cicco, Howard Morris, Tony di Benedetto, Patrick Cronin, Charles Walker, David Knell, Jeff Doucette, Royce D. Applegate, Tony Longo, Nora Denny, Charles Macaulay, Ronald F. Hoiseck, Lou Tiano, Joe Grifasi, Dance Howard, Corki Corman-Grazer, Fred Lerner, David Lloyd Nelson, Al Chesney, Lowell Ganz, James Ritz, Maurice Rice, Babaloo Mandel, Pierre Epstein. Dir: Ron Howard. Pro: Brian Grazer. Ex Pro: John Thomas Lennox. Screenplay: Lowell Ganz, Babaloo Mandel and Bruce Jay Friedman; from a screen story by Friedman, based on an original story by Grazer. Ph: Don Peterman. Ed: Daniel P. Hanley and Michael Hill. Pro Des: Jack D. Collis. Art: J. B. Mansbridge. M: Lee Holdridge (song 'Love Came for Me' performed by Rita Coolidge). (Touchstone–U.K. Film Distributors) Rel: 27 July 1984. 110 mins. Cert PG.

Spring Symphony – Frühlingssinfonie. A pleasing West German musical film about Robert Schumann, his passion for Clara, and his ever-increasing passion for his music, the moving ending with Felix Mendelssohn triumphantly conducting the first public performance of Robert's first symphony (an achievement prefacing what was later to become a tragic story of mental decline, leading to the composer's death in an insane asylum at the age of 46). Cast: Herbert Grönemeyer (Schumann), Nastassja Kinski (Clara), Rolf Hoppe, Anja-Christine Preussler, Edda Seippel, André Heller, Gidon Kremer, Bernard Wicki, Sonja Tuchmann, Margit Geissler, Wolfgang Gresse, Gunter Kraa, Uwe Muller, Gisela Rimpler, Helmut Oskamp. Dir and Pro: Peter Schamoni. Pro Sup: Horst Hartwig and Lilo Pleimes. Screenplay: Schamoni and Hans A. Neunzig. Ph: Gerard Vandenberg. Ed: Elfie Tillack. Pro Des: Alfred Hirschmeier. (Blue Dolphin Films) Rel: floating; first shown London (Queen Elizabeth Hall and Minema), 14 Sept 1984. 105 mins. Cert PG.

Starman. Routine visitor-from-another-planet sci-fi movie with Jeff Bridges as the 'visitor' (though *why* he's here remains a mystery!) who falls in love with the pretty widow whose late husband's appearance he assumes while he's here. Familiar stuff, but made entertaining by the performances, and

Jeff Bridges as a very human-looking alien with hostage Karen Allen in *Starman*.

the direction of John Carpenter. Rest of cast: Karen Allen, Charles Martin Smith, Richard Jaeckel, Robert Phalen, Tony Edwards, John Walter Davis, Ted White, Dirk Blocker, M. C. Gainey, Sean Faro, Buck Flower, Russ Benning, Ralph Cosham, David Wells, Anthony Grumbach, Jim Deeth, Alex Daniels, Carol Rosenthal, Mickey Jones, Lu Leonard, Charles Hughes, Byron Walls, Betty Bunch, Victor McLemore, Stevan Brennan, Pat Lee,

Left to right, James Doohan, Walter Koenig and William Shatner share a tense scene in *Star Trek III – The Search for Spock*.

Judith Kim, Ronald Colby, Robert Stein, Kenny Call, Jeff Ramsey, Jerry Gatlin, David Daniell, Randy Tutton. Dir: John Carpenter. Prod: Larry J. Franco. Co Pro: Barry Bernardi. Ex Pro: Michael Douglas. Screenplay: Bruce A. Evans and Raynold Gideon. Ph: Donald M. Morgan. Ed: Marion Rothman. Pro Des: Daniel Komino. M: Jack Nitzsche (Columbia/Delphi Pro–Columbia) Rel: 24 May 1985. 115 mins. Cert PG.

Star Trek III – The Search for Spock. The continuation of the spatial adventures of gallant space-fleet Admiral Kirk (William Shatner) and his now ageing starship *Enterprise*. Grieving for his much respected Captain Spock –

Diana Dors and Patti Love in *Steaming*.

killed in *ST No. II* – Kirk's mission in No. III is to find the body of his lieutenant and return it to Spock's father, on the planet Vulcan. And it does not turn out to be all that easy, thanks to the interference of the villainous Krugea, a sort of 23rd-century Viking with nasty habits. All this and more; all pretty good sci-fi-spectacular fun. Rest of cast: Leonard Nimoy (as Spock – and he directs the adventure this time around), DeForest Kelley, James Doohan, Walter Koenig, George Takei, Michelle Nicholls, Robin Curtis, Merritt Butrick, Phil Morris, Scott McGinnis, Robert Hooks, Carl Steven, Vadia Potenza, Stephen Manley, Joe W. Davis, Paul Sorensen, Cathie Shirriff, Christopher Lloyd, Stephen Liska, John Larroquette, Dave Cadiente, Bob Cummings, Branscombe Richmond, Phillip Richard Allen, Jeanne Mori, Mario Marcelino, Allan Miller, Sharon Thomas, Conroy Gedeon, James B. Sikking, Miguel Ferrer, Mark Lenard, Katherine Blum, Dame Judith Anderson, Gary Faga, Douglas Alan Shanklin, Grace Lee Whitney. Dir: Leonard Nimoy. Pro and Screenplay: Harve Bennett; based on the *Star Trek* story by Gene Roddenberry. Ex Pro: Gary Nardino. Ph: Charles Correll. Ed: Robert F. Shugrue. Art: John E. Chilberg II. M: James Horner. Assoc Pro: Ralph Winter. (Paramount–UIP) Rel: 17 Aug 1984. 105 mins. Cert PG.

Steaming. Joseph Losey's last film – he died just after completing it in Britain – is an adaptation of a play by Nell Dunn (adapted to the screen by Losey's wife) about a group of females (the cast is entirely female) in a run-down South London Turkish bath. There amidst the steam the various ladies let off more as they lay bare their opinions about men as they bare their bodies. With the theatrical origin always obvious, the main entertainment and the fun come from the characters, and they are played with great enjoyment and considerable skill by the late Diana Dors, Sarah Miles, Felicity Dean, Brenda Bruce, Sally Sagoe, Patti Love (who squeezes the last drop out of her juicy role) and Vanessa Redgrave (who does not look all that happy in her part). Dir: Joseph Losey. Pro: Paul Mills. Ex Pro: Richard F. Dalton. Screenplay: Patricia Losey; based on the stage play by Nell Dunn. Ph: Christopher Challis. Ed: Reginald Beck. Pro Des: Maurice Fowler. Art: Michael Pickwoad. M: Richard Harvey. (Columbia) Restricted Rel: 31 May 1985. 95 mins. Cert 18.

Stop Making Sense. A pop music feature filmed over three days of performances by the group Talking Heads in Hollywood in December, 1983. A Jonathan Demme film (Palace Pictures) Rel: floating; first shown London – during London Film Festival – (Classic, Oxford St and Screen-on-the-Green), 26 Nov 1984. 88 mins. Cert U.

Stranger Than Paradise. Certainly a strange little West German/American movie, made in grainy black-and-white with nearly every scene divided by a black-out on the screen; the whole is sub-divided more definitely into three segments ('The New World', 'One Year Later' and 'Paradise'). Set in the depressing world of immigrants from Hungary, it is the story of a new girl arrival, her stay with a 10-year-established layabout cousin in New York and their attempts (along with a friend) to make their way to Miami for a holiday. America is seen from an unusual, and grey, angle. The movie won the Camera d'Or prize at the 1984 Cannes Festival, as well as the Grand Prix at Locarno. Cast: John Lurie, Eszter Balint, Richard Edson, Cecilia Stark, Danny Rosen, Rammellzee, Tom Dicillo, Richard Boes, Rockets Redglare, Harvey Perr, Brian J. Burchill, Sara Driver, Paul Sloane. Dir, Screenplay and M: Jim Jarmusch. Pro: Sara Driver. Ex Pro: Otto Grokenberger. Ph: Tom Dicillo. Ed: Jarmusch and Melody London. No Art credit. (Grokenberger Film Produktions/-Munich/Cinesthesia Productions Inc., New York–ZDF–Artificial Eye) Rel: floating; first shown London (Camden Plaza), 4 Oct 1984. 90 mins. Black-and-white. Cert 15.

Streets of Fire. Stylish, colourful comic-strip action – tough, brutal and sometimes downright sadistic – set against a sleazy, slummy American big city background, to the accompaniment of 14 variable but often excellent rock numbers. A paper-thin story about the rescue of a kidnapped pop singer-star (abducted by a moronic motorcycle

Michael Paré confronts Willem Dafoe in *Streets of Fire*.

gang's leader who lusts after her) by her one-man-army ex-boyfriend. It all has the feeling of being a video blown-up to big screen size. Cast: Michael Paré, Diane Lane, Rick Moranis, Amy Madigan, Willem Dafoe, Deborah Van Valkenburgh, Richard Lawson, Rick Rossovich, Bill Paxton, Lee Ving, Elizabeth Daily, Lynne Thigpen, Marine Jahan (the uncredited, exciting dancing double for the star in *Flashdance*), Ed Begley Jr, John Dennis Johnston, Harry Beer, Olivia Brown, Kip Waldo, Peter Jason: Stoney Jackson, Grand Bush, Robert Townsend, Mykel T. Williamson – The Sorels; Paul Mones, Vince Deadrick Jr, Paul Lane, Bernie Pock, Spiro Razatos, Jeff Smolek – The Roadmasters; William Beard II, Stuart Kimbell, Angelo, John Ryder – The Attackers; David Alvin, Philip Alvin, Lee Allen, William Bateman, John Bazz, Eugene Taylor, Steve Berlin – The Blasters. Dir: Walter Hill. Pro: Lawrence Gordon and Joel Silver. Ex Pro: Gene Levy. Screenplay: Hill and Larry Gross. Ph: Andrew Laszlo. Ed: Freeman Davies and Michael Ripps. Pro Des: John Vallone. M Score: Ry Cooder. Assoc Pro: Mae Woods. (Universal/RKO–UIP) Rel: 5 Oct 1984. 94 mins. Cert 15.

Strikebound. A painfully topical – when first shown – Australian film which dramatized the events of a strike by Victoria's coal miners (many of them actually Welsh) in 1927, when the mili-

tants struggled against both the mine owners and the police and the situation in many respects was uncomfortably close to that in Britain in 1984–5. Filmed on location in an old mine specially re-opened for the movie, with some of the actual strikers taking a part in the proceedings. And it is not difficult to see where the sympathies of the youngsters who made the film lie. Cast: Chris Haywood, Carol Burns, Hugh Keays-Byrne, Rob Steele, David Kendall, Declan Affley, John Flaus, John Howard, Tony Hawkins, Marion Edward, Nik Forster, Lazar Rodic, Reg

Chris Haywood as the militant leader of the striking coalminers in *Strikebound*.

Evans, Mary Howlett, Denzil Howson, Charles Gilroy, Ivor Bower, Kirsty Grant and Wattie and Agnes Doig. Dir and Screenplay: Richard Lowenstein; based on his mother Wendy Lowenstein's so far unpublished book, *Dead Men Don't Dig Coal*. Pro: Miranda Bain and Timothy White. Ph: Andrew De Groot. Ed: Jill Bilcock. Pro Des: Tracy Watt. M: Declan Affley. (TRM Productions in association with Film Victoria–Mainline) Rel: floating; first shown London (the Screen cinemas), 2 Nov 1984. 100 mins. Cert PG.

Success is the Best Revenge. Highly personal Jerzy Skolimowski comedy about first and second generation exiles – Polish in this case – living in Britain (London in this case) with friction between father (a stage director struggling to put on a show in London without any cash but with a host of increasingly insistent creditors) and a son who goes punk and returns to Warsaw (to be de-punked by unamused immigration officials) to try and find his birthright. A theme explored with more satire than sympathy but making for highly effective viewing. Michael York as Dad, Michael Lyndon as Son, and John Hurt as the Polish exile who has made his situation an unqualified pecuniary success. Rest of cast: Joanna Szczerbic, Jerry Skol, Michel Piccoli, Anouk Aimée, Ric Young, Claude Le Sache, Malcolm Sinclair, Hilary Drake, Jane Asher, Adam French, Sam Smart, Tim Brown, Maribel Jones, Mike Sarne, Maureen Bennett, Martyn Whitby, Bill Monks, Rory Edward, Archie Pool, Robert Whelan, Suzan Crowley, Tristram Jellinek, Ralph Nossek, Colin Bennett, Felicity Dean, Guy Degny, Eugeniusz Hczkiewicz, Stella Maris, Luis Piniꞁla. Dir, Pro and Screenplay (the last with Michael Lyndon, the director's son): Jerzy Skolimowski. Ph: Mike Fash. Ed: Barri Vince. Pro Des: Vaytek: drawings by Topolski. M: Stanley Myers and Hans Zimmer. (DeVere/Gaumont–Everyman) Rel: floating: first shown London (Everyman), 23 Nov 1984. 91 mins. Cert 15.

Sunday in the Country – Un Dimanche à la Campagne. A very personal, literate and stylish movie from Bertrand Tavernier, relating with consummate artistry and complete control the undramatic events of a Sunday in and around the country mansion of an octogenarian classical painter who is visited (as every Sunday) by his son and family and (a rare occasion) his lovely actress daughter, whose natural vivacity hides romantic troubles. The date is *circa* 1912 and it is a day of memories, gentle melancholia, regrets and flaring autumnal tints, superbly photographed and beautifully acted. Cast: Louis Ducreaux, Sabine Azema, Michel Aumont, Geneviève Mnich, Monique Chaumette, Claude Winter, Thomas Duval, Quentin Ogier, Katia Wostrkoff, Valentine Suard, Erika Faivre, Marc Perrone, Pascale Vignal, Jean-Roger Milo, Jacques Poitrenaud. Dir: Bertrand Tavernier. Screenplay: Bertrand and Colo Tavernier; based on the novel *Monsieur L'Admiral va bientôt mourir* by Pierre Bost. Ph: Bruno de Keyzer. Ed: Armand Psenny. Art: Patrice Mercier. (Artificial Eye) Rel: floating; first shown London (Chelsea Cinema), 1 July 1984. 94 mins. Cert PG. (Winner of Best Director award at the Cannes Festival 1984.)

Supergirl. After Superman's amusingly spectacular efforts to right some of the world's wrongs (or, as the publicity would have it, his 'fight for Truth, Justice and the American Way') in the three previous Superman movies, cousin Supergirl now takes the stage, and arrives on the earthly scene. Though with the same asset of being able to switch from human to high-flying superhuman at the drop of a hat, her interest in ethics comes second to her task to regain her planet Crypton's power source, which through an accident has arrived on Earth with a bump and is stolen by lovely though nasty-minded witch Faye Dunaway (delightful). Helen Slater as the charming super one, Brenda Vaccaro as her lively friend and Peter O'Toole as a very careless

Spacelord Peter O'Toole with Helen Slater in *Supergirl*.

Superlord. Rest of cast: Mia Farrow, Peter Cook, Simon Ward, Marc McClure, Hart Bochner, Maureen Teefy, David Healy, Sandra Dickinson, Robyn Mandell, Jenifer Landor, Diana Ricardo, Nancy Lippold, Sonya Leite, Linsey Beauchamp, Michelle Taylor, Nancy Wood, Virginia Greig, Julia Lewis, Matt Frewer, Bill McAllister, Sally Cranfield, Martha Parsey, Kelly Hunter, Ter Battenburg, Richard Bidwell, Desiré, Christian Fletcher, Karen Hale, Beulah Hughes, Lia, Mike Pearce, Kevin Scott, James Snell, Jane Sumner, Bailie Walsh, Elaine Ives-Cameron, Gay Baynes, Fred Lee Own, Edwin Van Wyk, Orla Pederson, Joe Cremona, April Orlich, Erick Ray Evans, Zoot Money, Ron Travis, Danique, Russell Sommers, Dulcie Huston, David Graham, Martin Serene, Keith Edwards, Bradley Lavelle, Carol Charnow, Shezwae Powell, Glory Annen, Sandra Martin. Dir: Jeannot Szwarc. Pro: Timothy Burrill. Ex Pro: Ilya Salkind. Screenplay: David Odell. 2nd Unit Dir: David Lane. Ph: Alan Hume. Ed: Malcolm Cooke. Pro Des: Richard Macdonald. Sup Art Dir: Terry Ackland-Snow. Pro Ex: Pauline Coutelenq. Special Effects Sup: John Evans. Pro Co-Ord: Marguerite Green. M: Jerry Goldsmith. (Salkind–Thorn EMI) Rel: 3 Aug 1984. 116 mins. Cert PG.

Surf II. Was there ever a *Surf I*? If so it never rippled across the Atlantic. Nor is it easy to track down on the other side. Anyway, no hassle, *SII* takes a slightly satirical look at all those teenage 'beach' movies, with a very slight story and a few topless damsels to add a touch of froth. Cast: Eddie Deezen, Linda Kerridge, Cleavon Little, Peter Isacksen, Lyle Waggoner, Eric Stoltz, Jeffrey Rogers, Corinne Bohrer, Lucinda Dooling, Morgan Paull, Ruth Buzzi, Tom Villard, Carol Wayne, Terry Kiser, Brandis Kemp, Biff Maynard. Dir and Screenplay: Randall Badat. Pro: G. G. Braunstein and Ron Hamady. Ex Pro: F. D. Tolin and Lou George. Ph: Alex Phillips Jr. Ed: Jackie Cambas. Art: Jeff Staggs. (International Film Marketing–Odyssey) Rel: floating; first shown London (Eros), 5 Oct 1984. 91 mins. Cert 18.

The Swing. A charming, meandering and inconsequential West German family piece concerning a rather vague, professorial Munich royal horticulturist, his French pianist wife and their three daughters and one son, a very 'free-minded' quartet. A beautifully and lovingly though rather confusingly drawn picture of a time and a place, with plenty of good performances and some fine photography. Cast: Rolf Illig (father), Christine Kaufmann (mother), Anja Jaenicke, Lena Stolze, Susanne Herlet and Joachim Bernhard (children). Dir and Screenplay: Percy Adlon. Ph: Jurgen Martin. M: Peer Raaben. (Artificial Eye) Rel: floating; first shown London (Everyman), 26 Dec 1984. 133 mins. Cert PG.

Teachers. A repelling picture of an American high school where eccentric and inept teachers struggle with their moronic pupils. Somewhere beneath all the supposed fun there is some sort of social document trying, apparently, to struggle out . . . in vain; in no small part due to the schmaltzy ending. Cast: Nick Nolte, JoBeth Williams, Judd Hirsch, Ralph Macchio, Allen Garfield,

Richard Mulligan putting across his own highly individual ideas about teaching history in *Teachers*.

Lee Grant, Richard Mulligan, Royal Dano, William Schallert, Art Metrano, Laura Dern, Crispin Glover, Morgan Freeman, Madeleine Sherwood, Zohra Lampert, Mary Alice, Katharine Balfour, Vivian Bonnell, Virginia Capers, Ellen Crawford, Terry Ellis, Aaron Freeman, Patricia Gaul, Anthony Heald, Ronald Hunter, Julia Jennings, Stephen Mendillo, Jeff Ware, Richard Zobel, Da Nang McKay, Virginia Smith, Ray Noch, Maria D. Magisano, Bill Marinella, Noerena Abookire, Andrew Ream, Jennifer Quilty. Dir: Arthur Hiller. Pro: Aaron Russo. Ex Pro: Irwin Russo. Assoc Pro: Art

Levinson. Screenplay: W. R. McKinney. Ph: David M. Walsh. Ed: Don Zimmerman. Pro Des: Richard Macdonald. M Ed: William Saracino. Groups: ZZ Top, Bob Seger, Joe Cocker, Night Ranger, 38 Special, The Motels, Freddie Mercury, Ian Hunter, Roman Holliday, Eric Martin and Friends (UA/MGM–UIP) Rel: floating; first shown London (Plaza), 1 Feb 1985. 106 mins. Cert 15.

The Terminator. A somewhat complicated if well-made sci-fi movie which initially is set in the post-atom-bombed year of 2029 (a time when the brainy machines have taken over from the less dependable humans). It then moves back into the present where the half-human, half-mechanized title character (played by Arnold Schwarzenegger) arrives from that future with the assignment of terminating the life of the lady who, if allowed to exist and bear her salvationist child, will spoil everything for the villains of the second millenium. Modest in budget, the film is something of a minor triumph for writer/director, former art director James Cameron. Rest of cast: Michael Biehn, Linda Hamilton, Paul Winfield, Lance Henriksen, Rick Rossovich, Bess Motta, Dick Miller, Earl Boen, Shawn Schepps, B. M. Kerner, Franco Columbu, Bix Paxton, Brad Rearden, Brian Thompson, W. Wisher Jr, Ken Frizt, Tom Oberhaus, Ed Dogans, Joe Farago, Hettie Lynn Hurtes, Tony Mirelez. Dir, Pro and Co-Screenplay (last with Gale Anne Hurd): James Cameron. Ex Pro: John Daly and Derek Gibson. Ph: Adam Greenberg.

Ed: Mark Goldblatt. Art: George Costello. M: Brad Fiedel. (Pacific Western/Orion–Rank Dist) Rel: 12 Jan 1985. 107 mins. Cert 18.

Terror in the Aisles. A compilation feature made up of 'shock bits' from a considerable number of thriller movies, ranging from Hitchcock's *To Catch a Thief* and De Palma's *Dressed to Kill* to good old *Dracula* and *Frankenstein*, all knitted together by a commentary by

A shot from *Bug* which made up part of the compilation feature *Terror in the Aisles*.

Donald Pleasence and Nancy Allen. Dir: Andrew Kuehn. Pro: Kuehn and Stephen Netburn. Written by Margery Doppelt. Ph: John A. Alonzon. Ed and Assoc Pro: Gregory McClatchy. M: John Beal, Add M: Doug Timm and

Arnold Schwarzenegger as a hitman on the job in *Terminator*.

Richard Johnston. Add Ed: Richard Goldstein. Pro Ex: Martin Wesson. (T.E.M. Programs Int/Kaleidoscope Films Ltd/Universal Pictures–Palace Pictures) Rel: floating; first shown London (Classic, Oxford St), 29 March 1985. 83 mins. Cert 18.

That's Not All, Folks. Three compilation movies: 1: *Looney Tunes and Merrie Melodies – The Best of Warner Brothers*, 2: *Tex Avery – King of Cartoons* and 3: *Cartoons Spoof Hollywood*. A review of the work of Avery and his colleagues at the old Warner Brothers cartoon studios, where such famous characters as Bugs Bunny, Roadrunner, Porky Pig, Daffy Duck and Tweety Pie were born. Many of the sequences included have been unseen on big or little screen for a very long time. (ICA/BFI) Rel: floating; first shown London (ICA), 14 Dec 1984. 154 mins. in all. Cert U.

Those Glory, Glory Days. Another 1982 (shown in 1983) TV movie to be made (along with *P'Tang Yang Kipperbang*) the subject of an experiment to see whether (executive producer David Puttnam's words) 'there is any [cinema] life after [TV] death,' by sending out these two TV movies on a double-bill release. This one is primarily for soccer fans and Spurs supporters in particular, as in light-vein comedy style it tells the story of four ardent young fans of the club, their passion for captain Danny Blanchflower and their struggle to get to Wembley to see their team complete the year's cup and league double. Cast: Zoe Nathenson, Liz Campion, Sara Sugarman, Cathy Murphy, Julia McKenzie, Elizabeth Spriggs, Julie Goodman, Rachael Meidman, Amelia Diplle, Eva Lohman, Peter Tilbury, Stephan Chase, Brian Pringle, John Salthouse. Dir: Philip Saville. Pro: Chris Griffin. Ex Pro: David Puttnam. Screenplay: Julie Welch. Ph: Phil Meheux. Series Script Ed: Jack Rosenthal. Art: Maurice Cain. M: Trevor Jones. Assoc Pro: David Bill. Pro Co-Ord. Mo Coppitters. (Enigma/Goldcrest–Fox) Restricted Rel: 2 Aug 1984. 90 mins. Cert PG.

Three Crowns of the Sailor – Les Trois Couronnes du Matelot. Chilean expatriate, Paris-based 'New Waver' Paul Ruiz's surrealistic movie about a sailor's tale of his fantastic adventures in South American ports and brothels while sailing the world in a weird and ghostly barque, as told to the student he catches murdering his tutor. All most odd, macabre and highly imaginative – qualities, which with others, brought the film high critical praise in France. Cast: Jean-Bernard Guillard, Philippe Deplanche, Jean Badin, Nadege Clair, Lisa Lyon, Claude Dereppe, Frank Ogier, Jose de Carvalho, Mostepha Djadjam, Andre Gomes, Adelaide Joao, Claudio Martinez, Marthe Reynolds, Oscar Tebar and the voices of Raoul Guillet and Hugo Santiago. Dir: Raul Ruiz. Screenplay: Ruiz with Emilio de Solar and François Ede. Pro: Jean Lefaux, Maya Feuillette and Jose-Luis Vasconselos. Ph: Sacha Vierny. Ed: Janine Verneau, Valerie Sarmiento, Jacqueline Simoni-Adamus and Pascale Sueur. Set Design: Bruno Beauge and Pierre Pitrou. M: Jorge Arriagada. (Antenne 2/L'Institut National de l'Audiovisuel/Société du Cinéma du Pantheon–BFI) Rel: floating; first shown London (ICA), 23 Nov 1984. 117 mins. No cert.

Tightrope. A tense, tightly directed but somewhat overlong (more especially in the admittedly exciting final chase and confrontation between cop and killer) murder thriller about a psychotic ex-cop who preys on prostitutes in New Orleans. With some nice touches of humour and a very welcome restraint in terms of gore; all adding up to a good example of the genre with some unusual psychological depth – a sort of superior *Dirty Harry* with Clint Eastwood facing up to some personal as well as police problems. Rest of cast: Genevieve Bujold, Dan Hedaya, Alison Eastwood, Jennifer Beck, Marco St. John, Rebecca Perle, Regina Richardson, Randi Brooks, Jamie Rose, Margaret Howell, Rebecca Clemons, Janet MacLachlan, Graham Paul, Bill Holliday, John Wilmot, Margie O'Dair, Joy N. Houck Jr, Stuart Baker-Bergen, Donald Barber, Robert Harvey, Ron Gural, Layton Martens, Richard Charles Boyle, Becki Davis, Jonathan Sacher, Valerie Thibodeaux, Lionel Ferbos, Eliott Keener, Gary Wilmot Alden, David Valdes, James Borders, Fritz Manes, Jonathan Shaw, Don Lutenbacher, George Wood, Kimberly Georgoulis, Glenda Byars, John Schluter Jr, Nick Krieger, Lloyd Nelson, David Dahlgren, Red Masterson, Glenn Wright, Angela Hill, Ted Saari, Wayne Van Horn, George Orrison. Dir and Screenplay: Richard Tuggle. Pro: Clint Eastwood and Fritz Manes. Ph: Bruce Surtees. Ed: Joel Cox. Pro Des: Edward Carfagno. M: Lennie Niehaus. (Malpaso-Warner) Rel: 2 Nov 1984. 114 mins. Cert 18.

New Orleans cop (Clint Eastwood) in an off-duty moment with daughters (Jennifer Beck and Eastwood's own daughter Alison) in *Tightrope*.

A cow with wellington boots caused considerable fun in *Top Secret!* Spy Omar Sharif and blind pedlar Ian McNeice (inset) provided further fun.

The Times of Harvey Milk. A documentary record of the career of the homosexual Milk in the 1970s, in San Francisco; a politician who managed to get a Gay Rights bill passed and was subsequently assassinated, along with the local mayor. Dir: Robert Epstein. Pro: Epstein and Richard Schmeiechen. Ph: Frances Reid. Ed: Deborah Hoffman. Narrated by Harvey Fierstein. (Black Sands/TeleCulture–Contemporary) Rel: floating; first shown London (Everyman), 26 April 1985. 87 mins. Cert 15.

Top Secret! The *Airplane* writing-directing team bring to this spy caper the same kind of inconsequential, crazy humour; relating a ludicrous story of an East German plot to take over its Western neighbour which is defeated by a visiting young American pop star (with an Elvis style) and his new German girlfriend, daughter of a scientist being blackmailed into making a horrid new atomic-mine weapon. A collection of jokes, gags and gimmicks – some laughably good, some indifferent, some rude and mostly entirely unrelated to the business on hand – tossed into an amusing if untidy whole. Cast: Val Kilmer, Lucy Gutteridge, Omar Sharif, Jeremy Kemp, Warren Clarke, Tristram Jellinek, Billy J. Mitchell, Major Wiley, Gertan Klauber, Richard Mayes, Vyvyan Lorrayne, Nancy Abrahams, Ian McNeice, John Sharp, Michael Burlington, Marcus Powell, Louise Yaffe, Charlotte Zucker, Susan Braslau, Helen Kahan, Burton Zucker, Richard Pescud, John Carney, O.T., Russell Somers, Michael Gough, Sara Montague, Gerry Paris, David Adams, Geoff Wayne, Steve Ubels, Chas Bryer, Mac McDonald, Peter Cushing, Mandy Nunn, Lee Sheward, Janos Kurucz, Sydney Arnold, Harry Ditson, Christopher Villiers, Jim Carter, Eddie Tagoe, Dimitri Andreas, Michelle Martin, Nicola Wright, Lisa Gruenberg, Daisy (the cow!), Andrew Hawkins, Richard Bonehill. Dir and Ex Pro: Jim Abrahams, David and Jerry Zucker. Pro: John Davison and Hunt Lowry. Assoc Pro: Tom Jacobson. Screenplay: Abrahams, D. and J. Zucker and Martyn Burke. 2nd Unit Dir: Jack Lowin. Ph: Christopher Challis. Ed: Bernard Gribble. Pro Des: Peter Lamont. Art: John Fenner and Michael Lamont. M: Maurice Jarre. Pro Sup: Eric Rattray. (Paramount–UIP) Rel: 27 Sept 1984. 90 mins. Cert 15.

12 Views of Kensal House. The biography of a building opened by the Gas Light & Coke Co as a model estate in 1936: examining both the ideas that brought it into existence and the changes that have occurred during its fifty years of use. The *12 Views* are those of people who have known the building from various perspectives. A valid contribution to the current debate about modern architecture and its future. Dir, Pro and Script: Peter Wyeth. Ph: Patrick Duval. Ed: William Diver. (Capitol Films–Arts Council of Great Britain) Rel: floating; first shown London (ICA), 3 April 1985. 55 mins. Cert U.

2010. The lavishly budgeted, spectacular and technically impressive sci-fi follow-up to Stanley Kubrick's *2001: A Space Odyssey* with Peter Hyams now earning the writing, directing and producing credits. Against a background

Helen Mirren and Roy Scheider confront each other on board the spacecraft in *2010*.

of Russo-American tension on Earth there is tension of another kind in the Soviet spacecraft *Leonov*, where the mixed Russian and American crew are trying to find and recover the data on board the abandoned US spacecraft *Discovery* and solve the dark mystery of the nearby orbiting black monolith which shows in deadly earnest it wants no interlopers around it. Lots of questions raised but few answered; too many extraneous political and other threads woven into a basically exciting space adventure. Cast: Roy Scheider, John Lithgow, Helen Mirren, Bob Balaban, Keir Dullea, Douglas Rain, Madeleine Smith, Dana Elcar, Taliesin Jaffe, James McEachin, Mary Jo Deschanel, Elya Baskin, Savely Kramarov, Oleg Rudnik, Natasha Shneider, Vladimir Skomarovsky, Victor Steinback, Jan Triska, Larry Carroll, Herta Ware, Cheryl Carter, Ron Recasner, Robert Lesser, Olga Mallsnerd, Delana Michaels, Gene McGarr. Dir, Ph, Pro and Screenplay: Peter Hyams; based on the novel by Arthur C. Clarke. Ed: James Mitchell and Mia Goldman. Pro Des: Albert Brenner. Visual Effects Sup: Richard Edlund. M: David Shire. Assoc. Pro: J. A. Zimbert and Neil A. Machlis. (MGM/UA–UIP) Rel: 22 March 1985. 116 mins. Cert PG.

Albert Finney (left), Jacqueline Bisset and Anthony Andrews in *Under the Volcano*.

Under the Volcano. After 30 years deliberating about bringing the famous book by British writer Malcolm Lowry to the screen, John Huston magnificently succeeds in simplifying in visual terms the author's intricate and essentially literary story about the last 24 hours in the life of a recently resigned British Consul in a Mexican town on the 'Day of the Dead' with its macabre festivities. A dedicated drunk-

ard, the Consul's tragic slide is inevitable, more especially after he rejects the last chances of redemption (his wife's return to him and his brother's arrival) and courts his end in a sleazy little bar-cum-brothel, determined to reach his personal hell. This sorry and some may find pathetic tale is given humour and absorbing strength by Huston's outstandingly fine direction and the no less impressive performance by Albert Finney, ably supported by Jacqueline Bisset (wife) and Anthony Andrews (brother). Rest of cast: Ignacio Lopez Taro, Katy Jurado, James Villiers, Carlos Riquelme, Emilio ('El Indio') Fernandez, Gunter Meisner, Alfonso Castro Valle, Isabel Vasquez, Eduardo Borbolla, Alejandra Suarez, Rodolfo de Alejandre, Mario Arevalo, Arturo Sarabia, Rene Ruiz ('Tun Tun'), Roberto Martinez Sosa, Eliazar Garcia Jr, Sergio Calderon, Salvador Sanchez, Araceli Ladewuen Castelun, Hugo Stiglitz. Dir: John Huston. Pro: Moritz Borman and Wieland Schulz-Keil. Ex Pro: Michael Fitzgerald. Pro Sup: Tom Shaw. Screenplay: Guy Gallo; based on the book by Malcolm Lowry. Ph: Gabriel Figueroa. Ed: Robert Silvi. Pro Des: Gunther Gerszo. Art: Jose Rodriguez Granada. M: Alex North. (Michael and Kathy Fitzgerald/Ithaca–Conacine Productions–Fox) Rel: floating, first shown London (Odeon, Haymarket), 31 Aug 1984. 112 mins. Cert 15.

Unfaithfully Yours. Polished remake of one of Preston Sturges's later (1948) – and, regrettably, less brilliant – comedies, with Dudley Moore having a ball in the old Rex Harrison role of a famous orchestral conductor who, thinking his young wife (Nastassja Kinski) has been unfaithful, literally dreams up a perfect plot for revengeful killing of her lover while he is conducting a symphony. But it all goes horribly – and uproariously – wrong when he actually goes ahead with the plan. Always amusing, there are some marvellous farcical moments, and for this one must give a lot of credit to the hard-working little Dudley. Rest of cast: Armand Assante, Albert Brooks, Cassie Yates, Richard Libertini, Richard B. Shull, Jan Triska, Jane Hallaren, Bernard Behrens, Leonard Mann, Estelle Omens, Penny Peyser, Nicholas Mele, Benjamin Rayson, Art La Fleur, Magda Gyenes, Frederic Franklyn, Alison Price, Frank

Dudley Moore (centre) looks on as Armand Assante compliments the former's wife, Nastassja Kinski, in *Unfaithfully Yours*.

Di Elsi, Edward Zammit, Tony Abatemarco, Daniele Jaimes Worth, Alexander B. Reed, Ralph Buckley, Steven Hirsch, Murray Franklyn, Dr. Betty Shabazz, Ed van Nuys, Robin Allyn, Ricky Paull Goldin, Evan Hollister Miranda, Elana Beth Rutenberg, Rochelle L. Kravit, Gabriel E. Gyorffy, Linda Stayer, Bob Larkin, Kim Leslie, Camille Hagen, Mary Alan Hokanson, Jacque Foti. Dir: Howard Zieff. Pro: Marvin Worth and Joe Wizan. Ex Pro: Daniel Melnick. Assoc Pro: Jack B. Bernstein. Screenplay: Valerie Curtin, Barry Levinson and Robert Klane, based on a screenplay by Preston Sturges. Ph: David M. Walsh. Ed: Sheldon Kahn. Pro Des: Albert Brenner. M: Bill Conti: played by the Los Angeles Philharmonic Orchestra conducted by Leonard Slatkin, with Pinchas Zukerman as solo violinist in the Tchaikovsky concerto. (Fox) Rel: 7 Sept 1984. 96 mins. Cert 15.

Utu. A western in nearly everything but locale, this confusingly edited New Zealand movie is about the country's turbulent history, *circa* the 1870s. Some pre-reading up of the New Zealand story of the period is needed if it is to make much sense. But to give the production its due, even without that prerequisite the mixture of violent

death, constant action, examination of the Maori character and traditions, along with the deft touches of humour, gives the movie a constant fascination, augmented by the background scenery and some top-class performances (enough to merit a two-page *New Yorker* review!). Cast: Anzac Wallace, Wi Kuki Kaa, Bruno Lawrence, Kelly Johnson, Tim Elliott, Tania Bristowe, Merata Mita, Faenza Reuben, Ilona Rodgers, Tom Poata, Martyn Sanderson. Dir: Geoff Murphy. Pro: Murphy and Don Blakeney. Ex Pro: Don Blakeney, Kerry Robins and David Carson-Parker. Screenplay: Murphy and Keith Aberdein. (Miracle) Rel: floating; first shown London (Classic, Tott Ct Rd and Odeon Kensington), 26 April 1985. 104 mins. Cert 15.

Anzac Wallace in *Utu*.

Valley Girl. A sort of Romeo and Juliet teenage romance between a Valley Girl (San Fernando Valley, with its odd teenage 'Valspeak' language) and a punk from Hollywood across the ridge. A strange youthful world pictured with some sympathy and therefore less off-putting than many of its predecessors. Cast: Nicolas Cage, Deborah Foreman, Elizabeth Daily, Michael Bowen, Cameron Dye, Heidi Holicker, Michelle Meyrink, Tina Theberge, Lee Purcell, Richard Sanders, Colleen Camp, Frederic Forrest, David Ensor, Joanne Baron, Tony Plana, Tony Markes, Christopher Murphy, Robby Romero, Camille Calvert, Lisa Antille, Theresa Hayes, Andrew Winner, Betsy Bond, Laura Jacoby, Karl Johnson, Joyce Heiser, Michael Wyle, Stephen Sayre, Wayne Crawford. Dir: Martha Coolidge. Pro and Screenplay: Wayne Crawford and Andrew Mane. Ex Pro: Thomas Coleman and Michael Rosenblatt. Pro Co-Ord: Bruce Schwartz and Nancy Battaglia. Ph: Frederick Elmes (2nd Unit Ph: Don Cirillo). Ed: Eva Gardos. Pro Des: Marya Della Javier. Art: Carl Adana. M: Scott Wilk and Marc Levinthal. M Ed: Bob Biggart. (Valley–9000 Productions–New Realm) Rel: floating; first shown London (ABCs Edgware Rd and Bayswater), 30 Nov 1984. 000 mins. Cert 15.

A Very Moral Night. A comedy-drama period piece from Hungary set in a small town brothel, at the beginning of the century, in which the decor, the handsome girls and even the 'guests' are all drawn with a rich, and unreal, nostalgic charm. The night in question occurs when the staid, out-of-town mother of the (surely too old?) medical student living in the establishment arrives on the scene and the warm-hearted madame cancels trade for the evening in order to entertain the innocent old lady for dinner with her young lady 'boarders'. All very much a crop of ripe and rich and nicely presented corn. Cast includes: Iréne Psota, Margit Makay, György Cserhalmi, Györgyi Tarjan, Carla Romanelli, Edith Lehrer, Mari Kiss, Ildiko Kishouti, Zsuzsa Manyai, Edith Soos. Dir: Karoly Makk. No Pro credit listed. Screenplay: István Örkeny and Peter Bacso; based on the short story *The House With the Red Light* by Sandor Hunyady. Ph: János Toth. Ed: György Sivó. Art: Tamas P. Balassa. M: (various) played

by T. P. Balassa. (Dialog Studio Budapest–Cannon/Gala) Rel: floating; first shown London (Berkeley), 12 April 1985. 103 mins. Cert 15.

Vigil. An impressive debut for a new New Zealand director, Vincent Ward. A bleak, hard and yet human story of a family living in a remote valley farm and the events that follow the father's accidental death when he defends his stock against the action of a poacher, who then takes up residence in the farmhouse. All this is seen almost magi-

Little Fiona Kay through whose eyes the whole story is seen in *Vigil*.

cally through the not-unprejudiced eyes of the dead man's daughter as she reaches womanhood. Marvellous backgrounds, superb atmosphere, remarkable imagery. Cast: Penelope Stewart, Frank Whitten, Fiona Kay, Bill Kerr, Gordon Shields, Arthur Sutton, Snow Turner, Bill Liddy, Maurice Trewern, Eric Griffin, Emily Haupapa, Debbie Newton, Bob Morrison, Lloyd Grundy, Joseph Ritai, Josie Herlihy, Sadie Marriner, Bill Brocklehurst, Rangi-toheriri Teupokopakari. Dir: Vincent Ward. Pro: John Maynard. Screenplay: Ward and Graeme Tetley. Ph: Alun Bollinger. Ed: Simon Reece. Pro Des: Kai Hawkins. (John Maynard Productions in association Film Invest Corp of NZ and NZ Film Comm–Enterprise Pictures/ICA) Rel: floating; first shown London (ICA), 25 Jan 1985. 89 mins. Cert 15.

The Wall (Duvar) – Le Mur. A disturbing, depressingly brutal and often harrowing film about life in a modern Turkish prison, made in France by the Kurdish actor turned film director Yilmaz Güney. He died two days after the film opened in London. He knew a lot about the subject, having served several terms in Turkish jails for his stoutly maintained radical views. Cast: Saban, Sisko, Ziya, Garip, Zapata, Mankafa, Malik Berrichi, Nicholas Hossein, Tuncel Kurtiz, Selahattin Kuzuoglu, Jean-Pierre Colin, Isabelle Tissandier, Ali Berktay, Sema Kuray, Habes Bounabi, Ahmet Ziyrek, Jacques Dimanche, Bernard Certeaux, Ali Dede Altuntas, Aicha Arouali, Ayse Emel Mesei. Dir and Screenplay: Yilmaz Güney. Pro: Marin Karmitz. Ph: Izzet Akay. Ed: Sabine Mamou. M: Ozan Garip Sahin and Setrak Bakirel. (Contemporary) Rel: floating; first shown London (Phoenix, East Finchley and ICA) 7 Sept 1984. 117 mins. Cert 18.

What Makes David Run? – Qu'est-ce qui fait courir David? A noisy, somewhat untidy French farce about a young Jewish film director whose reaction to every problem is to run away from it and who tries to cover every difficult situation with an often forced laugh. But in spite of this he does finally complete his film – maybe *this* one? Cast: Francis Huster, Nicole Garcia, Charles Aznavour, Magali Noel, Michel Jonasz, Nathalie Nell, Anouk Aimée, André Dussollier, Katia Tchenko, Charles Gérard, Annie Noel, Maurice Benichou, Geneviève Mnich, Nicolas Hossein, José Yanne, Alexis Hazera, Eric Magnan, Nicolas Wolf, Sophie Lifshitz, Caroline Varon, Alexandre Buenos. Dir and Screenplay: Elie Chouraqui. Pro: Xavier Gelin. Ex Pro: Daniele Delorme and Yves Robert. Pro Sup: Jean-Claude Bourlat. Ph: Robert Alazraki. Ed: Georges Klotz. No Art credit as such. M: Michel Legrand. (lyrics by Charles Aznavour). (Productions de la Gueville/7 Films/FR3–Warner) Rel: floating; first shown London (Gate, Notting Hill), 5 July 1984. 99 mins. Cert 15.

Water. A stingless but sometimes very laughable British satire about the end of colonialism, seen in a farcical story about a small Caribbean island where the discovery of a mineral water spring

Michael Caine (left) and Fulton Mackay in *Water*, and (inset) Leonard Rossiter with Brenda Vaccaro.

leads to US efforts to exploit and market it, French efforts to destroy it, and British Governor Michael Caine's determination that it continue to gush for the good of the soon-to-be liberated island population. And in the rather frenzied interaction there are very faint echoes from the great days of the Ealing Studio comedies like *Whisky Galore*. Caine, as usual, holds it all together with his polished performance. Rest of cast: Valerie Perrine, Brenda Vaccaro, Leonard Rossiter, Billy Connolly, Dennis Duggan, Fulton Mackay, Jimmie Walker, Dick Shawn, Fred Gwynne, Trevor Laird, Chris Tummings, Stephan Kalipha, Alan Igbon, Kelvin Omard, Oscar James, Charles Thomas Murphy, Felicity Dean, William Hootkins, Alan Shearman, Bill Bailey, Richard Pearson, Maureen Lipman, Paul Heiney, Glory Annen, Bruce Boa, Danny Brainin, Jacqueline de Peza, Harry Ditson, Ben Feitelson, Darcy Flynn, Christopher Gilbert, Rashid Karapiet, Sabu Kimura, Julie Legrand, Lucita Lijertwood, Alfred Molina, Bill Persky, Manning Redwood, Bill Reimbold, Bob Sessions, Ruby Wax, Eric Clapton, George Harrison, Ringo Starr. Dir: Dick Clement. Pro: Ian La Frenais. Ex Pro: George Harrison and Denis O'Brien. Co-Pro: David Wimbury. Screenplay: Dick Clement, Ian La Frenais and Bill Persky; from latter's story. Ph: Douglas Slocombe. Ed: John Victor Smith. Pro Des: Norman Garwood. Art: Keith Pain and A. Cartledge. M Score: Mike Moran; songs by Moran, Eddy Grant, George Harrison and Eric Clapton. (Handmade Films–Rank Film Dist) Rel: 8 Feb 1985. 100 mins. Cert 15.

Wetherby. A cold, complex British movie hardly likely to knock 'em in the Old (or New!) Kent Road but an obvious contender for honours at international film festivals, with its original and clever construction, its dark emotional underpinning and its fine performances. It tells of a young university student who commits bloody suicide in front of a repressed spinsterish lady teacher and the subsequent gradual revelation of what triggered off the tragedy. Vanessa Redgrave superb of course (though shame on her teacher, who goes into class with a fag in her mouth) and fine support from the rest of the cast: Ian Holm, Judi Dench, Marjorie Yates, Tom Wilkinson, Tim

Vanessa Redgrave as the repressed spinsterish Yorkshire teacher in *Wetherby*.

McInnerny, Suzanna Hamilton, Stuart Wilson, Joely Richardson, Robert Hines, Penny Downie, Brenda Hall, Marjorie Sudell, Patrick Blackwell, Diane Whitley, Mike Kelly, Howard Crossley, Matthew Guinness, Ted Beyer, Katy Behean, Bert King, Paula Tilbrook, Christopher Fulford, David Foreman, Stephanie Noblett, Richard Marris, Jonathan Lazenby, Nigel Rooke, John Robert, Norman Mills, Vanessa Rosenthal, Trevor Lunn, Guy Nicholls, Ian Bleasdale, Peter Martin. Dir and Screenplay: David Hare. Pro: Simon Relph. Assoc Pro: Patsy Pollock. Ph: Stuart Harris. Ed: Chris Wimble. Pro Des: Hayden Griffin. Art: Jamie Leonard. M: Nick Bicat; arranged and conducted by Tony Britten. (Film Four International/Zenith–Greenpoint Films–Palace Pictures) Rel: floating; first shown London (New Curzon), 8 March 1985. 102 mins. Cert 15.

Where the Boys Are, '84. Not just a straight remake of the 1960 film ('Youthful comedy-drama about students on the loose, obsessed with sex, on their Easter vacation in Florida' – *1961–2 Film Review*) but based on the same literary source and very much a lookalike. It concerns a crowd of youngsters disporting themselves in the sun ('all you'll need is a bikini and a diaphragm') and being very modern; but in fact most of them are looking for old-fashioned love. Cast includes: Lisa Hartman, Russell Todd, Lorna Luft, Wendy Schaal, Howard McGillin, Lynn-Holly Johnson, Louise Sorel, Alana Stewart, Christopher McDonald,

Daniel McDonald. Dir: Hy Averback. Pro: Allan Carr. Ex Pro: Terry Donnelly and Jeff Apple. Screenplay: Stu Krieger and Jeff Burkhart; suggested by the Glendon Swarthout novel. Ph: James A. Contner. Ed: Melvin and Bobbie Shapiro. Pro Des: Michael Baugh. M: Sylvester Levay. Assoc Pro: Denis Pregnolato. (Tri-Star Pictures–ITC) Rel: 13 July 1984. 94 mins. Cert 15.

Where the Green Ants Dream – Wo die Grünen Ameisen Traümen. German Werner Herzog's Australian/English speaking movie which is basically concerned with the confrontation of modern, advancing technology (a large mining firm looking for uranium) and the ancient beliefs and culture of the Aborigines, whose ownership of the land becomes the subject of a High Court case. Thematically fascinating; at times wilfully obscure (with incongruous excursions into unrelated incidents), visually memorable with some fine performances (including those of the Aborigines) and always cinematically interesting. (Shot in 4 weeks at Coober Pedy and Melbourne.) Cast: Bruce Spence, Wandjuik Marika, Roy Marika, Ray Barrett, Norman Kaye, Colleen Clifford, Ralph Cotterill, Nicolas Lathouris, Basil Clarke, Ray Marshall, Dhungala I. Marika, Gary Williams, Tony Llewellyn-Jones, Marraru Wunungmurra, Robert Brissenden, Susan Greaves, Michael Glynn, Michael Edols, Noel Lyon, Max Fairchild, Bob Ellis, Trevor Orford, Hugh Keays-Byrne, Andrew Mack, Maria Stratford, Michael Mandalis, Anastasios Chatzidimpas, Maria Chatzidimpas, Paul Cox, Philip Radke, Ricky and Ronnie, James Ricketson, Christopher Cain, Paul Donazzan, Tim Cartwright, Michael Glynn. Dir and Screenplay: Werner Herzog. Script consultant and addit. dialogue: Bob Ellis. Pro: Lucki Stipetic. Ph: Jorg Schmidt-Reitwein. Ed: Beate Mainka-Jellinghaus. Art: Ulrich Bergfelder. M: Faure, Bloch, Wiese, Wagner and (aboriginal music on the didgeridoo) Wandjuik Marika.

White Men represented by Bruce Spence (second left) and Ray Barrett with the local Aborigines' spokesman, Wandjuik Marika, in *Where the Green Ants Dream*.

(Werner Herzog Filmproduktion-ZDF–Artificial Eye) Rel: floating; first shown London (Chelsea Cinema), 18 Oct 1984. 100 mins. Cert 15. (Winner of German Best Film award.)

Wild Flowers – Les Fleurs Sauvages. French/Canadian film recording in intimate detail and at great – far too great – length the lives of a family in the Montreal countryside, following their day-to-day experiences during the week in July when the wife's mother pays her annual holiday visit to her daughter, her second husband and their two children. Though they all love the old lady she causes a certain tension in her daughter, largely because the two women are apparently unable to express their true feeling for each other. Beautifully done and marvellously well acted but far, far too long for comfort. Cast: Marthe Nadeau, Michèle Magny, Pierre Curzi, Eric Beauséjour, Claudia Aubin. Dir and Screenplay: Jean Pierre Lefebvre. Pro and Ed: Marguerite Duparc-Lefebvre. Ph: Raoul Duguay. M: Raoul Duguay (theme song, 'Le Queteux'; M: Claude Fonfrède; Lyrics: Raoul Duguay). (Cinegate) Rel: floating; first shown London (Gate, Bloomsbury), 10 Jan 1985. 155 mins. Cert 15. (Winner of the International Critics Prize at the Cannes Film Festival 1982.)

Wild Geese II. Far from the African adventures of *WGI*, this *WGII* is about a plot to snatch Hess from Spandau prison by a brother-and-sister TV team, with the assistance of a soldier of fortune and his recruits. All very efficiently done if highly unlikely, leaving several questions unanswered and a hint of 007 in the air. Cast: Scott Glenn, Barbara Carrera, Edward Fox, Laurence Olivier, Robert Webber, Robert Freitag, Kenneth Haigh, Stratford Johns, Derek Thompson, Paul Antrim, John Terry, Ingrid Pitt, Patrick Stewart, Michael Harbour, David Lumsden, Frederick Ward, Malcolm Jamieson, Billy Boyle, David Sullivan, Dan Van Husen, James Monaghan, Michael Buttner, Herbert Chwoika, Carl Price, Ronald Nitschke, Wilfried Gromau, Shaun Lawton, Peter Kybart, Amelie zur Muhlen, Gabriel Kastner. Dir: Peter Hunt. Pro: Euan Lloyd. Co-Pro: A. E. Scotoni. Pro Ex (Germany): Willy Egger. Ex Pro: Chris Chrisafis. Pro Sup: Norman Foster.

Pro Co-Ord: Beryl Harvey. Screenplay: Reginald Rose; based on the Daniel Carney book *The Square Circle*. Ph: Michael Reed. Ed: Keith Palmer. Pro Des: Syd Cain. Art: Peter Williams. M: Roy Budd. (Frontier Films–Thorn EMI) Rel: 30 May 1985. 124 mins. Cert 15.

Winter Kills. Revival of William Richert's black comedy based on Richard Condon's *Kennedy Conspiracy* satirical novel, originally released in America in 1979. Cast: Jeff Bridges, Anthony Perkins, Eli Wallach, Tomas Milian, Toshiro Mifune, Elizabeth Taylor, John Huston, Sterling Hayden, Dorothy Malone, Ralph Meeker, Richard Boone, Belinda Bauer. Dir and Screenplay: William Richert. Pro: Fred Caruso. Ph: Vilmos Zsigmond. M: Maurice Jarre. (ICA Projects–Rank Film Dist) Rel: floating; first shown London (ICA), 8 March 1985. 95 mins. No cert.

Witness. Though trying to cover too much diverse ground, as part thriller, part romance, part moralistic examination and part character study, Australia's outstanding director Peter Weir's first American production was more than good enough to stand out from the run-of-the-mill movies. About a Philadelphia honest cop (Harrison Ford) hunted by his crooked superior and henchmen after he uncovers the Deputy Commissioner's guilt and taking refuge (after being plugged by one of his pursuers) in a peace-loving, violence-eschewing Amish community where he falls in love with his pretty young

Scott Glenn carries Barbara Carrera to safety, watched by Edward Fox, in *Wild Geese II*.

widow-nurse (Kelly McGillis). It is all wonderfully visual, often highly amusing, generally absorbing (if weak on the wild side) as it contrasts the pacifist sect with the violent and crooked world outside. Rest of cast: Josef Sommer, Lukas Haas, Jan Rubes, Alexander Godunov, Danny Glover, Brent Jennings, Patti LuPone, Angus MacInnes, Frederick Rolf, Viggo Mortensen, John Garson, Beverly May, Ed Crowley, Timothy Carhart, Sylvia Kauders, Marian Swan, Maria Bradley, Rozwill Young, Paul S. Nuss, Emily Mary Haas, Fred Steinharter, John D. King, Paul Goss, Annemarie Vallerio, Bruce E. Cambern. William Francis, Tom W. Kennedy, Ardyth Kaiser, Thomas Quinn, Eugene Dooley, Victoria Scott

Harrison Ford in *Witness*.

Left to right, Gene Wilder, Joseph Bologna, Charles Grodin and Michael Huddleston, the four female-obsessed pals who are fascinated by Kelly le Brock (left) in *The Woman in Red*.

marie Henize, Thomas Voborka, Shawn Lawton. Dir and Pro: Robert Van Ackeren. Screenplay: Ackeren and Catharina Zwerenz. Ph: Jurgen Jurges. Ed: Tanja Schmidtbauer. M: Peer Raben. Assoc Pro: Dieter Geissler. (PIK 7 Film Produktions und Vertriebs GMBH–Cannon Film Dist) Rel: floating; first shown London (Premiere), 31 Aug 1984. 100 mins. Cert 18.

The Woman in Red. Gene Wilder's lightly amusing version of a very funny French farce film of the mid-1970s called *Pardon Mon Affair* in which Jean Rochefort gave an outstanding comedy performance. Wilder's script and performance is almost inevitably less funny by comparison as it tells the story of four firm pals and their largely sexual adventures; more especially, Wilder's infatuation for a delicious model girl when he sees her shapely attractions revealed as the wind lifts her skirt. And the climax, with the would-be lover shooed out of bed on to a ledge far above the ground by the advent of his beloved's big husband, is still very funny. Rest of cast: Charles Grodin, Joseph Bologna, Judith Ivey, Michael Huddleston, Kelly le Brock, Gilda Radner, Kyle T. Heffner, Michael Zorek, Billy Beck, Kyra Stempel, Robin Ignico, Viola Kates Stimpson, Danny Wells, Buddy Silberman, Monia Parker, Ernest Harada, Julann Griffin, Sandra Wilder, Tammy Brewer, Noni White, John McKinney, Barbara Schweke, Larry Gilman, Milt Kogan, Rob Balhatchet, Dan Magiera, Catherine Schreiber, Barbara Andrews, Sharon Moore, Allen Gebhardt, Sheldon Feldner, George Johnson, Ann Waterman, Steven Kravitz, Dale Kusch, Kelly Andrus, Deborah Dalton, Elissa Leeds, Stevie Myers, Freddie Dawson, Robert Krantz, Maureen O'Connor, James Higgins, Elizabeth Norment, James Cavan, Roberta J. Smith, Deborah May. Dir and Screenplay: Gene Wilder (based on the screenplay *Un Elephant Ça Trompe Enormément* by Jean Loup Dabadie, and Yves Robert, who directed *Pardon Mon Affair*). Pro: Victor Drai. Ex Pro: Jack Frost Sanders. Ph: Fred Schuler. Ed: Christopher Greenbury. M: John Morris. Songs written by Stevie Wonder and sung by Wonder and Dionne Warwick. (Orion Pictures International–Rank Film Dist) Rel: 12 Oct 1984. 86 mins. Cert 15.

D'Angelo, Richard Chaves, Tim Moyer, Nino del Buono, James Clark, Joseph Kelly, Norman Carter, Craig Clement, Robert Earl Jones, Michael Levering, Cara Giallanza, Anthony Dean Rubes, Bernie Styles, Blossom Terry, Jennifer Mancuso, Gary Epper, Bob Minor, Anderson Martin. Dir: Peter Weir. Pro: Edward S. Feldman. Co-Pro: David Bombyk. Assoc Pro: Wendy Weir. Screenplay: Earl W. Wallace and William Kelley; from a story by Kelley and Earl and Pamela Wallace. Ph: John Seale. Ed: Thom Noble. Pro Des: Stan Jolley. M:

Maurice Jarre. (Paramount–UIP) Rel: floating; first shown London (Plaza), 24 May 1985. 112 mins. Cert 15.

A Woman in Flames. (German.) A powerful performance by Gudrun Landgrebe literally lights up this story about an outwardly normal middle-class woman who suddenly leaves her bourgeois life and husband to become a superior sort of prostitute; she rooms with a male prostitute (later her lover) who turns out to also have bourgeois ideas by investing their money in a restaurant. Shocked by this revelation she decides to leave, whereupon he throws a bottle of spirits over her and lights her up – hence that title. Rest of cast: Mathieu Carrière, Hans Zischler, Gabriele Làfari, Matthias Fuchs, Christiane B. Horn, René Schonenberger, Magdelena Montezuma, Klaus Mikoleit, Georg Tryphon, Walther Busch, Carola Regnier, Johannes Grutzke, Salome, Catharina Zwerenz, Ute Gerhard, Joachim Von Ulmann, Roland Von Schulze, Ursula Tahiri, Achim E. Ruppel, Kalus Hoser, Rose-

Video Releases

ANTHONY HAYWARD

Steven Spielberg's blockbuster *Raiders of the Lost Ark* became, by December 1984, the first video to sell a million copies worldwide. It had been available on video for a year and sold 800,000 copies in America alone. *Raiders* reached the magic million by leapfrogging over *Making Michael Jackson's Thriller*, which remains the best-selling music cassette. In Britain, pre-Christmas video sales in 1984 were very buoyant. Music videos did best, but some feature films, such as *Trading Places*, also sold well.

More films are now appearing on video even before – and often at the same time as – their cinema release, but there appears to be a decline in cassette rental. Sales of video recorders, too, are falling – 1,500,000 in 1984 compared with 2,200,000 the previous year, say the British Radio and Electronic Equipment Manufacturers' Association.

The British video industry is now coming to terms with the Video Recordings Act, which became law on 1 September 1985. The previous year was particularly traumatic, for dealers and distributors, because the Director of Public Prosecutions' (DPP) guidelines on horror tapes that risked police seizure under the Obscene Publications Act caused confusion. The DPP's monthly list of such cassettes included some that had been awarded British Board of Film Censors certificates for cinema release. Various videos, such as *Possession* – cleared of obscenity charges by a court – were eventually removed from the list. In just two months, five tapes were dropped.

Also, a study by the Oxford Polytechnic Television Research Unit showed that police were confiscating cassettes not included in the DPP's list. Some of these tapes were found to contravene the Obscene Publications Act. Parliament hopes the confusion will disappear as videos are gradually classified by the British Board of Film Censors under the terms of the Video Recordings Act.

Amid the controversy over the new laws, the fight against video piracy has continued. By the autumn of 1984, the Federation Against Copyright Theft estimated that illegally produced cassettes accounted for only 1 in 5 tapes available in Britain, compared with 3 in 5 18 months earlier. But the British video market had also increased.

Almost all illegal tapes now come from abroad and their quality is often very poor. Worldwide, piracy is costing film and video companies, as well as cassette dealers, at least two billion dollars a year, according to the report by the International Federation of Phonogram and Videogram Producers.

June 1984

The Angry Breed (Videoform)
And Now for Something Completely Different (RCA/Columbia)

Balboa (Quadrant/VideoSpace)
The Band Reunion Concert (Videoform Music)
Battletruck (Guild)
Benji (Vestron)
The Birds (re-release) (CIC)
The Black Stallion Returns (Warner)
Blue Skies Again (Guild)
Blue Thunder (RCA/Columbia)
Breakfast at Tiffany's (CIC)
The Bridges at Toki-Ri (CIC)

Confessions of a Pop Performer (RCA/Columbia)
Conquest (Merlin/CBS/Fox)
Cool It Carol (Alpha/CBS/Fox)
The Corrupt Ones (Embassy)

The Dark Crystal (RCA/Columbia)
The Day of the Jackal (CIC)
Dracula (CIC)

The Escape Artist (PolyGram)

Fatal Games (Merlin/CBS/Fox)
Forbidden World (Embassy)
For Whom the Bell Tolls (CIC)
Frenzy (re-release) (CIC)

Game for Vultures (RCA/Columbia)

Having it All (Arcade/VideoSpace)
It Came from Outer Space (CIC)

Killpoint (Videoform)

Lonesome Cowboys (Virgin)
The Lords of Flatbush (RCA/Columbia)
Luggage of the Gods (CBS/Fox)

The Man with Bogart's Face (CBS/Fox)

Never Say Never Again (Warner)

Odds and Evens (RCA/Columbia)

An Officer and a Gentleman (CIC)
The Other Woman (Alpha/CBS/Fox)

Porky's II (CBS/Fox)
Psycho (re-release) (CIC)
Psycho II (CIC)
The Pyx (Brent Walker)

Return of the Evil Dead (Precision)
The Reward (PolyGram)
Rip Off (Alpha/CBS/Fox)
Road to Utopia (CIC)
Roll Over (Warner)

Savages (Guild)
The Secret Policeman's Other Ball (VideoSpace)
Spring Fever (Odyssey)
The Squeeze (Warner)
The Streetwalker (Palace)

The Tempest (RCA/Columbia)
Tombs of the Blind Dead (Precision)

The Toy (RCA/Columbia)
Trash (Virgin)
21 Hours at Munich (Videoform)

Utopia (Virgin)

Vigilante Force (Warner)

Wilde's Domain (Precision)
Without a Trace (CBS/Fox)

July

Airwolf (CIC)
Amityville III (Thorn EMI)
Attica (Videoform)

Barry McKenzie Holds His Own (Alpha/
    CBS/Fox)
Betrayal (Virgin)
The Big Bus (CIC)
Bill on His Own (Odyssey)
Blind Ambition (VTC)
Blind Date (Videomedia)
Bury Me an Angel (VCL)

Can She Bake a Cherry Pie? (Virgin)
The Cradle Will Fall (Videoform)

Deadly Impact (EV)
Doctor in Clover (Rank)
Dracula (Mountain)

The Elephant Man (re-release) (Thorn EMI)

Family Plot (CIC)
Fanny by Gaslight (Rank)
Footloose (CIC)

The Great Gatsby (CIC)

A Hard Day's Night (Vestron/PVG)

The Italian Connection (Palace)

Jaws 3 (CIC)

The Jazz Singer (re-release) (Thorn EMI)
The Kid from Left Field (VTC)
Kim (Embassy)
The King of Comedy (Thorn EMI)

Last Plane Out (re-release) (VCL)
La Traviata (VideoSpace)
Let's Break (Warner)

The Man Who Fell to Earth (re-release)
    (Thorn EMI)
Maroc 7 (Rank)
Memed My Hawk (VTC)
Monty Python's The Meaning of Life (CIC)
Murder on the Orient Express (re-release)
    (Thorn EMI)

Ninja's Force (VTC)
Nobody's Boy (Mountain)

Once Upon a Scoundrel (Precision)

Paradise Alley (CIC)

Rentadick (Rank)
Ringo Goes West (Mountain)
Rottweiler – The Dogs of Hell (Thorn EMI)

Sahara (Guild)
Savage Islands (CIC)
Scarface (CIC)
The Seven Per Cent Solution (CIC)
Skokie (Vidoeform)
Smokey and the Bandit (CIC)
Spaceship (EV)

S.P.Y.S. (re-release) (Thorn EMI)
Staying Alive (CIC)
Steps (Precision)

Techno Police (Mountain)
Terms of Endearment (CIC)
Trading Places (CIC)
The Trespassers (VCL)

Uncommon Valour (CIC)
Under Fire (Rank)

Waterhole 3 (CIC)

Zapped (Embassy)

August

Aces High (re-release) (Thorn EMI)
All the Right Moves (CBS/Fox)
American Heartbeat (CBS/Fox)
The Antagonists (CIC)
The Archies (re-release) (Select/Videoform)

The Babysitter (Videoform)
Beach House (CBS/Fox)
Blackstar (re-release) (Select/Videoform)
Bloodbath at the House of Death (Thorn
    EMI)
Bloodline (CIC)
Breathless (Rank)
The Buddy System (CBS/Fox)

Carry On Follow That Camel (Rank)
Charlie's Balloon (Odyssey)
Cold River (CBS/Fox)
Cross Country (Thorn EMI)

Dangerous Cargo (PolyGram)
Death on the Nile (re-release) (Thorn EMI)
The Deer Hunter (re-release) (Thorn EMI)
The Devil Within Her (Arcade/VideoSpace)
A Dream of Passion (PolyGram)

The Eiger Sanction (CIC)

Getting Out Alive (Prime Time)
The Go-Between (re-release) (Thorn EMI)
Going Down (Prime Time)
Gorky Park (Rank)

Jaws 3 (CIC)
Jungle Warriors (Videoform)

La Balance (CBS/Fox)
Lassie (re-release) (Select/Videoform)

Man of Flowers (Palace)
Meatballs (CIC)
Motel (Odyssey)

Nickelodeon (re-release) (Thorn EMI)

Plaza Suite (CIC)
The Power (EV)

Real Life (EV)
The Return of Martin Guerre (Palace)
The Rocky Horror Picture Show (CBS/Fox)
R.S.V.P. (Avatar/CBS/Fox)

The Sign of Four (Embassy)
SOS Titanic (re-release) (Thorn EMI)
Streethawk (CIC)
Streets of Fire (CIC)

That Man Bolt (CIC)
Together (CBS/Fox)
To Kill a Stranger (VCL)
The Train Killer (Thorn EMI)
240 Robert (Videoform)

Villa Rides! (CIC)

We of the Never Never (Odyssey)
Why Shoot the Teacher? (Rank)

Zorro (re-release) (Select/Videoform)

September

The Assassination of Trotsky (PolyGram)
The Boat (re-release) (RCA/Columbia)

Cross Creek (Thorn EMI)
Cujo (Guild)

The Dark Crystal (re-release) (RCA/
    Columbia)
The Dead Zone (Thorn EMI)
Don't Look Now (re-release) (Thorn EMI)
Dracula's Revenge (Guild)

Emmanuelle 4 (Thorn EMI)

Footloose (CIC)
Foxes (Warner)

Gandhi (re-release) (RCA/Columbia)
The Golden Seal (Thorn EMI)

Hammersmith Is Out (Brent Walker)
Hearts of the West (MGM/UA)
Highway to Hell (Videomedia/Relay)
Homeward Bound (Pyramid/21st Century
    Entertainments)
Howzer (PolyGram)

It Shouldn't Happen to a Vet (re-release)
    (Thorn EMI)

Killing Machine (Embassy)
Kramer Vs. Kramer (re-release) (RCA/
    Columbia)

Lady Caroline Lamb (re-release) (Thorn
    EMI)
The Lady from Yesterday (Odyssey)
Laurel and Hardy's Laughing Twenties
    (MGM/UA)

Mad Mission Three (Thorn EMI)
The Man Who Loved Women (RCA/
    Columbia)
Mr Majestyk (Warner)
My Old Man (IPC/ VideoSpace/Arcade)

Obsessive Love (Precision)

The Right Stuff (Warner)
Risky Business (Warner)
The Ritz (Warner)
Running Brave (PolyGram)

Say Hello to Yesterday (Brent Walker)
Secret Squirrel (Guild)
Spider-Woman (Guild)
Stranger's Kiss (Embassy)
Stuck on You (PolyGram)
Sudden Impact (Warner)
Sweeney! (re-release) (Thorn EMI)

Tootsie (RCA/Columbia)
Towser (Longman)
Toy Soldiers (VTC)

Villain (re-release) (Thorn EMI)

The Whacky Secret Weapon (Guild)
Warlords of Atlantis (re-release) (Thorn
    EMI)

Yanks (Warner)

October

Angel (US) (Thorn EMI)
The Apple Dumpling Gang Rides Again (Walt Disney)

Baby Love (Guild)
The Ballad of Gregorio Cortez (Embassy)
The Bears and I (Walt Disney)
Blackbeard's Ghost (re-release) (Walt Disney)
Breakdance (Guild)
Breaking Up (VTC)

Children of the Corn (Thorn EMI)
The Choice (Videoform)
Cross of Iron (re-release) (Thorn EMI)

Death Collector (VTC)
The Devil and Max Devlin (re-release) (Walt Disney)
Dragonslayer (re-release) (Walt Disney)
Dr Syn Alias the Scarecrow (Walt Disney)

The Empire Strikes Back (CBS/Fox)
The Endless Summer (Pacific Arts/VideoSpace)
Escape from El Diablo (Arcade/VideoSpace)

Far from the Madding Crowd (re-release) (Thorn EMI)
Fire and Ice (Thorn EMI)
The First Deadly Sin (Warner)
Five Guns West (Rank)
Flash Gordon (re-release) (Thorn EMI)
The Fourth Man (Embassy)

Going Berserk (CIC)
Greystoke: The Legend of Tarzan, Lord of the Apes (Warner)
Gunfight at the OK Corral (CIC)
Gwendoline (Embassy)

Hands Off! (Guild)
The Happiest Millionaire (Walt Disney)
Heart Like a Wheel (Embassy)
Honey (CBS/Fox)
The Honorary Consul (Thorn EMI)
House of the Dark Shadows (MGM/UA)

In God We Trust (CIC)
In Love with an Older Woman (VideoSpace)

The James Dean Story (Pacific Arts/VideoSpace)

Katy (CBS/Fox)
The Killing Hour (Ariel Films/CBS/Fox)

Lenny (Warner)
Lonely Hearts (FilmTown/VideoSpace)

Mark I Love You (Videoform)
Midnight Cowboy (Warner)
Miracle of Love (Videoform)
The Mirror Crack'd (Thorn EMI)

North Dallas Forty (CIC)

Partners (CIC)
Paris, Texas (Palace)
Pete's Dragon (re-release) (Walt Disney)
Private School (CIC)

The Rise of the Third Reich (MGM/UA)
Risky Business (Warner)
Roger Ramjet (Mountain/Graphic)
Romance with a Double Bass (CIC)

Samson and Delilah (CBS/Fox)
Schizo (Warner)
Sessions (VCL)
Silkwood (Rank)
Something Wicked This Way Comes (Walt Disney)
Song and Dance (RCA/Columbia)
Space Riders (Thorn EMI)
Star 80 (Warner)
Suburbia (Vestron)
Surf II (Odyssey)

Terms of Endearment (CIC)
To Catch a King (Videoform)

Uncommon Valour (CIC)

The Watcher in the Woods (re-release) (Walt Disney)
Welcome to Blood City (re-release) (Thorn EMI)
Where the Boys Are (Precision)
The Wicker Man (re-release) (Thorn EMI)

November

The Adventures of Sinbad (VCL)
Alice in Wonderland (Walt Disney)
Americana (CBS/Fox)
An American Christmas Carol (IPC/VideoSpace)
Annie (re-release) (RCA/Columbia)
The Apple Dumpling Gang (re-release) (Walt Disney)
Arabian Adventure (re-release) (Thorn EMI)
At the Earth's Core (re-release) (Thorn EMI)
The Awakening (re-release) (Thorn EMI)

Bananaman (Thorn EMI)
Benji's Very Own Christmas Story (Vestron)
The Blue Lagoon (re-release) (RCA/Columbia)
Britannia Hospital (re-release) (Thorn EMI)

Chained Heat (Thorn EMI)
Champions (Embassy)
The Comedy of Terrors (Rank/Orion)
Condorman (re-release) (Walt Disney)
Countdown (Warner)
Curse of the Pink Panther (Warner)

Dangerous Traffic (VTC)
Deadly Force (Embassy)
Driver (re-release) (Thorn EMI)

Educating Rita (Rank)
Eskimo Nell (Movietime)
The Evil that Men Do (Precision)

Forbidden Love (PolyGram)
Freaky Friday (re-release) (Walt Disney)
The Freedom Force (Select)

Gone in 60 Seconds II (VTC)

Hey Good Lookin' (VTC)
High Road to China (Guild)
Hill's Angels (re-release) (Walt Disney)
The Hit (Palace Premiere)
Hundra (Thorn EMI)

In Love with an Older Woman (IPC/VideoSpace)

The Jungle Book (Embassy)

Kelly's Heroes (MGM/UA)

Laughterhouse (Palace)
Longshot (CBS/Fox)
Love Letters (Vestron)

Master of the World (VCL)
Midnight Express (re-release) (RCA/Columbia)
Monkey Grip (FilmTown/VideoSpace)
Monty Python's Life of Brian (re-release) (Thorn EMI)
Mr Mum (Thorn EMI)
My Favourite Martians (Select)
Mysterious Island (VCL)

Napoleon and Samantha (Walt Disney)
Never Cry Wolf (Walt Disney)
Now That's What I Call Music Four (Virgin/PMI/PVG)

One Blow Too Many (CBS/Fox)
1001 Rabbit Tales (Warner)
Only One Winner (CBS/Fox)
The Osterman Weekend (Thorn EMI)
The Outsiders (Warner)

Paris, Texas (re-release) (Thorn EMI)
Passione d'Amore (Vestron)
Percy (re-release) (Thorn EMI)
Phantasm (VCL)
Playing with Fire (CBS/Fox)
Popeye (re-release) (Walt Disney)
Popeye – Days Gone By (Select)
The Prince and the Pauper (VCL)
Prince Jack (VCL)
P'Tang Yang Kipperbang (Thorn EMI)

The Railway Children (re-release) (Thorn EMI)
Riel (Saturn/21st Century/Videoform)
The Right Stuff (Warner)

Scandalous (Guild)
Scum (re-release) (VCL)
Separate Tables (MGM/UA)
The Seventh Date of Hell (PolyGram)
Silver Bears (re-release) (Thorn EMI)
Slapstick of Another Kind (Virgin)
The Small One (re-release) (Walt Disney)
Smash Palace (CBS/Fox)
Snowball Express (re-release) (Walt Disney)
The Song Remains the Same (Warner)
Split Image (PolyGram)
Street of the Damned (Embassy)
Stripes (re-release) (RCA/Columbia)
Swallows and Amazons (re-release) (Thorn EMI)
Sweeney 2 (re-release) (Thorn EMI)

That's Entertainment I/That's Entertainment II (MGM/UA)
This Man Stands Alone (VCL)
Thrillkill (CBS/Fox)
Tiger Town (Walt Disney)
Two of a Kind (CBS/Fox)
The 2000 Year Old Man (Videoform)

Valley Girl (Avatar/CBS/Fox)

The Wanderers (VCL)
Watership Down (re-release) (Thorn EMI)
Willy Wonka and the Chocolate Factory (Warner)

Yentl (Warner)

December

The Amazing Adventures of Sherlock Holmes (CIC)
Big Red (Walt Disney)
The Black Hole (re-release) (Walt Disney)
The Cat from Outer Space (re-release) (Walt Disney)
Cheech and Chong's Next Movie (CIC)
The Day the Women Got Even (VTC)
Deaf Smith and Johnny Ears (MGM/UA)
Dempsey (Media Home Entertainment/Videoform)
The Digital Kid (VCL)
Fabulous Funnies (Mountain)
The Fighter (Videoform)
Harry and Son (Rank)
Heidi (Select)
Hellbenders (Embassy)
Herbie Goes to Monte Carlo (Walt Disney)
KGB – The Secret War (VTC)
Kum Kum (CIC)
Marciano (re-release) (Videoform)
Secrets of a Married Man (Precision)
See How She Runs (Capricorn)
Silent Kill (PolyGram)
The Time Crystal (VTC)
Tin Man (VCL)
Underboss (PolyGram)
Voltron, Defender of the Universe (CBS/Fox)
Where the Boys Are (MGM/UA)
The Wind of Jarrah (IPC/VideoSpace)
Would I Lie (MGM/UA)

January 1985

Absence of Malice (re-release) (RCA/Columbia)
Ace High (CIC)
Act of Passion (CBS/Fox)
Against All Odds (RCA/Columbia)
The Baby Maker (re-release) (Videomedia/Relay)
Beat Street (Rank)
The Bible . . . In the Beginning (re-release) (CBS/Fox)
The Big Bus (CIC)
Blame it on Rio (Thorn EMI)
Bluebeard (re-release) (Thorn EMI)
Blue Hawaii (Videoform)
Breaking with the Mighty Poppalots (Vestron/PVG)
Bring Me the Head of Alfredo Garcia (Warner)
Cannonball Run II (Heron)
Carnal Knowledge (Embassy)
Confessions of a Driving Instructor (re-release) (RCA/Columbia)
Dawn – Portrait of a Teenage Runaway (Emco/Videoform)
Daydreamer (Embassy)
The Day of the Dolphin (Embassy)
Death Wish II (re-release) (RCA/Columbia)
Dixie Changing Habits (Videomedia/Relay)

Doctor Detroit (CIC)
Evil Under the Sun (re-release) (Thorn EMI)
Exodus (Warner)
Framed (CIC)
Fun in Acapulco (Videoform)
GI Blues (Videoform)
Girls, Girls, Girls (Videoform)
Gnomemobile (re-release) (Walt Disney)
Herbie Goes Bananas (re-release) (Walt Disney)
Herbie Rides Again (re-release) (Walt Disney)
Her Life as a Man (IPC/VideoSpace)
The Hills Have Eyes Part 2 (Thorn EMI)
Hopscotch (re-release) (Thorn EMI)
The Hospital (Warner)
Hostage Tower (Warner)
How to Murder Your Wife (Warner)
How to Succeed in Business Without Really Trying (Warner)
It Happened at the World's Fair (MGM/UA)
Kes (Warner)
Last Touch of Love (Gem/Ruby)
Leave 'Em Laughing (re-release) (Videoform)
The Life and Times of Judge Roy Bean (Warner)
The Little Prince (Vestron/PVG)
The Lonely Guy (CIC)
The Long Good Friday (re-release) (Thorn EMI)
The Lord of the Rings (re-release) (Thorn EMI)
The Love Bug (re-release) (Walt Disney)
Love's Savage Fury (IPC/VideoSpace)
The Man from Snowy Mountain (re-release) (CBS/Fox)
The Man with Two Brains (Warner)
McVicar (re-release) (PolyGram)
The Million Pound Note (Rank)
The Mission (Palace/Motion Pictures on Video)
The Moon Stallion (BBC)
Ned Kelly (Warner)
No Deposit, No Return (re-release) (Walt Disney)
Of Unknown Origin (Warner)
One Flew Over the Cuckoo's Nest (re-release) (Thorn EMI)
Over the Brooklyn Bridge (Guild)
Paradise Hawaiian Style (Videoform)
Police Academy (Warner)
Press for Time (Rank)
Rascals and Robbers (CBS/Fox)
Reuben, Reuben (Embassy)
Roustabout (Videoform)
Running Scared (re-release) (Videoform)
The Sailor Who Fell from Grace with the Sea (Embassy)
Secret Places (Rank)
Seduced (CBS/Fox)
A Sensitive, Passionate Man (Videoform)

Something So Right (Videoform)
Speedway (MGM/UA)
Start the Revolution Without Me (Warner)
Support Your Local Gunfighter (Warner)
Support Your Local Sheriff (Warner)
This Happy Breed (Rank)
Time Bomb (CIC)
To Be or Not to Be (CBS/Fox)
Tough Enough (re-release) (CBS/Fox)
The Toy (re-release) (RCA/Columbia)
Videodrome (CIC)
Viva Las Vegas (MGM/UA)
Yol (Vestron)

February

All Night Long (Rank)
Another Country (Virgin)
Best Revenge (PolyGram)
Butterfly (re-release) (Thorn EMI)
Conduct Unbecoming (re-release) (Thorn EMI)
Crimebusters (Warner)
Deal of the Century (Warner)
Demon Murder Case (Videoform)
Escape to Witch Mountain (re-release) (Walt Disney)
Firestarter (Thorn EMI)
Galaxy of Terror (Warner)
Gangster Wars II (CIC)
The Glitter Dome (Thorn EMI)
Gone are the Dayes (Walt Disney)
The Greek Tycoon (CIC)
The House Where Evil Dwells (Warner)
Ice Pirates (MGM/UA)
Invitation to Hell (Precision)
Island at the Top of the World (re-release) (Walt Disney)
King Kong (re-release) (Thorn EMI)
The Last Waltz (Warner)
Love's Savage Fury (IPC/VideoSpace)
The Man from the High Country (Ariel/CBS Records)
Nickleodeon (re-release) (Thorn EMI)
Night Crossing (re-release) (Walt Disney)
The October Man (Rank)
Oh! What a Lovely War (CIC)
Rage of Angels (Videoform)
Ragtime (re-release) (Thorn EMI)
Rolling Thunder (Rank)
Rosemary's Baby (CIC)
Sakharov (Vestron)
Snowballing (CBS/Fox)
Star Trek III – The Search for Spock (CIC)
Success is the Best Revenge (Gem)
Swiss Family Robinson (re-release) (Walt Disney)
Tales from the Crypt (CBS/Fox)
Tell Them Willie Boy is Here (CIC)
Terminal Choice (CBS/Fox)
Testament (CIC)
The Toughest Man in the World (CBS/Fox)
Trenchcoat (Walt Disney)

Under the Volcano (CBS/Fox)

Vault of Horror (CBS/Fox)
Vertigo (re-release) (CIC)

Warrior of the Lost World (Thorn EMI)

March

Annie's Coming Out (IPC/VideoSpace)

Barbarella (re-release) (CIC)
Battlestar Galactica (re-release) (CIC)
Black Emannuelle (Warner)
Bolero (Guild)
The Bounty (Thorn EMI)
Brainstorm (MGM/UA)

Call to Glory (CIC)
The Cartier Affair (Odyssey/PolyGram)
Close Encounters of the Third Kind (Special edition) (re-release) (RCA/Columbia)
Comfort and Joy (Thorn EMI)
Condor (MGM/UA)
Conquest of the Earth (re-release) (CIC)

Darby O'Gill and the Little People (Walt Disney)
Dead Easy (Vestron)
The Deserter (CIC)
Die Laughing (Warner)
Doc (Warner)
The Dresser (RCA/Columbia)
Dumbo (Walt Disney)

Endangered Species (MGM/UA)
The Execution (Videoform)

Fallen Angel (RCA/Columbia)
Forever Young (Thorn EMI)

Hanky Panky (re-release) (RCA/Columbia)
Hard to Hold (CIC)
Hearts and Armour (Warner)

The Incredible Journey (re-release) (Walt Disney)
In Praise of Older Women (Warner)

Jimi Plays Berkeley (Palace)
Jinxed (Warner)

The Keep (CIC)

Lady Chatterley's Lover (re-release) (RCA/Columbia)
Lassiter (Rank)

The Man Who Knew Too Much (CIC)
Mission Galactica – The Cylon Attack (re-release) (CIC)
Monster (Warner)

Nairobi (Embassy)
The Natural (CBS/Fox)

The Philadelphia Experiment (Thorn EMI)

Racing with the Moon (CIC)
Richie (Odyssey/PolyGram)

Samson and Delilah (CIC)
Second Time Lucky (Gem)
Silent Rage (re-release) (RCA/Columbia)
So Long at the Fair (Rank)
Soup for One (Warner)
Stand Up Virgin Soldiers (Warner)
Star Trek – The Motion Picture (re-release) (CIC)
Star Trek II – The Wrath of Khan (re-release) (CIC)

The Survivors (RCA/Columbia)

Tank (CIC)
Texas Across the River (CIC)
This is Spinal Tap (Embassy)
Toy Soldiers (CBS/Fox)

Ugly Dachshund (re-release) (Walt Disney)

Very Important Person (Rank)
Victims for Victims (MGM/UA)

Walking the Edge (CBS/Fox)
The War of the Worlds (re-release) (CIC)
Weekend Pass (Vestron)
White Line Fever (re-release) (RCA/Columbia)
Winning (CIC)

April

Broadway Danny Rose (Rank)
Buffalo Bill and the Indians (re-release) (Thorn EMI)

Cagney and Lacey (Heron)
Cal (Warner)
The Company of Wolves (Vestron)
Conan the Destroyer (RCA/Columbia)
The Conqueror of Maracaibo (Precision)
Covergirl (CBS/Fox)

The Daughter of Mata Hari (Precision)
Death Ride to Osaka (Odyssey)
Diner (re-release) (MGM/UA)
Dirty Dingus Magee (MGM/UA)

49th Parallel (Rank)

Going in Style (Warner)
Goliath Against the Giants (Precision)

Heaven with a Gun (MGM/UA)
High School USA (Ariel/CBS Records)
Hoffman (re-release) (Thorn EMI)
Honky Tonk Freeway (re-release) (Thorn EMI)

In Love with an Older Woman (IPC/VideoSpace)

Juggernaut (Warner)

The Legend of the Seven Golden Vampires (Warner)
The Long Goodbye (Warner)

Making the Grade (Guild)
The Man with the Deadly Lens (RCA/Columbia)

Purple Hearts (Warner)
Purple Rain (Warner)

Rhinestone (CBS/Fox)
Romancing the Stone (CBS/Fox)

St Ives (Warner)
Salem's Lot (Warner)
Scarred (Heron)
Scorpio (Warner)
Splash (Touchstone)
The Stonekiller (RCA/Columbia)
Street Killing (Heron)
Superdad (Walt Disney)

Taxi Driver (RCA/Columbia)
Terror in the Aisles (Palace)
Thunder and Lightning (CBS/Fox)
Time Bandits (re-release) (Thorn EMI)

To the Devil a Daughter (re-release) (Thorn EMI)
The Valachi Papers (re-release) (Thorn EMI)
The Wilby Conspiracy (Warner)
The Winds of Jarrah (IPC/VideoSpace)

May

And Justice for All (RCA/Columbia)
Anne of the Thousand Days (CIC)
Around the World in Eighty Days (Warner)
Aurora (IPC/VideoSpace)

Badge 373 (CIC)
Beyond the Door (Sun/Carey)
Borsalino (CIC)

Charlie's Balloon (Odyssey/PolyGram)
The China Syndrome (RCA/Columbia)
CHUD (Medusa/CBS/Fox)
City Killer (Embassy)
Cloak and Dagger (CIC)
The Computer Wore Tennis Shoes (Walt Disney)

Daniel (PolyGram)
The Don is Dead (CIC)

Easy Rider (RCA/Columbia)

Family Secrets (Precision)
The Final Terror (Thorn EMI)
From Disney with Love (Walt Disney)
The Front (RCA/Columbia)

Go for It (Warner)

Hercules (Guild)
Hot Potato (Warner)

Just the Way You are (MGM/UA)

Khartoum (Warner)

The Last Run (MGM/UA)
Law and Disorder (PolyGram)
Lawrence of Arabia (RCA/Columbia)
The Lone Ranger (MGM/UA)
Love Child (Warner)

Mean Dog Blues (Vestron)
Moscow on the Hudson (RCA/Columbia)
Moving Violation (CBS/Fox)

Not for Publication (Thorn EMI)

Oliver! (RCA/Columbia)
Once Upon a Time in America (Thorn EMI)

Pandemonium (Warner)

Repo Man (CIC)
Rock and Rule (Embassy)
Rosie Dixon – Night Nurse (RCA/Columbia)

Secrets of the Phantom Caverns (Rank)
The Shaming (Carey)
Shattered Vows (IPC/VideoSpace)
South Pacific (CBS/Fox)
The Streetfighter (RCA/Columbia)
Stroker Ace (CIC)
Suffer, Little Children . . . (Films Galore)

Tightrope (Warner)
Topkapi (Warner)
The Trouble with Harry (CIC)

The Undergrads (Walt Disney)
Utu (MGM/UA)

Walking Tall (Vestron)
Watch on the Rhine (Warner)
Where the Buffalo Roam (CIC)

June

And Now for Something Completely
   Different (RCA/Columbia)
Au-Pair Girl (Naughty But Nice/Heron)

Bachelor Party (CBS/Fox)
The Barefoot Executive (Walt Disney)
The Beast Within (Warner)
Between Friends (Vestron)
Big Shot (PolyGram)
Body Rock (Thorn EMI)

Constance (MGM/UA)
Crackers (CIC)

Digital Dreams (MGM/UA)
Double Play (Embassy)
Dracula AD 1972 (Warner)
Dune (Thorn EMI)
Dutch Girls (Thorn EMI)

Fast Forward (RCA/Columbia)

The Girls in the Office (Naughty But Nice/
   Heron)
Go Tell the Spartans (Warner)
The Greatest Show on Earth (CIC)

The Great Northfield Minnesota Raid (CIC)

Hawaiian Heat (CIC)
The Hound of the Baskervilles (Warner)

If I Ever See You Again (PolyGram)
The Incredible Melting Man (RCA/
   Columbia)
It Lives Again (Warner)

Jabberwocky (RCA/Columbia)

The Land that Time Forgot (re-release)
   (Thorn EMI)
Legs (Naughty But Nice/Heron)
Lots of Luck (Walt Disney)

Model Behaviour (Embassy)
My Darling Slave (Naughty But Nice/
   Heron)

Never give an Inch (CIC)
Nice Dreams (RCA/Columbia)
Ninja III – The Domination (Guild)
No Sex Please – We're British (RCA/
   Columbia)

The One that Got Away (Rank)
Operation Daybreak (Warner)
Ordeal by Innocence (MGM/UA)

Party, Party (re-release) (PVG)
Percy's Progress (re-release) (Thorn EMI)

Phar Lap (CBS/Fox)
Portrait of a Stripper (Naughty But Nice/
   Heron)
Pumping Iron (re-release) (Thorn EMI)
Pursuit (PolyGram)

Raid on Entebbe (re-release) (Thorn EMI)
Red Dawn (Warner)
The River Rat (CIC)
Rope (CIC)

The Satanic Rites of Dracula (Warner)
Scandal in the Family (Naughty But Nice/
   Heron)
Sex with a Smile (Naughty But Nice/Heron)
Shalako (re-release) (Thorn EMI)
She (Avatar)
Sheena, Queen of the Jungle (RCA/
   Columbia)
Sky High (PolyGram)
Smorgasbord (CBS/Fox)
Southern Comfort (re-release) (Thorn EMI)
Special Delivery (Vestron)
Success (Odyssey)

Top Secret (CIC)
Trial Run (Embassy)
200 Motels (Warner)

Up the Creek (Rank)

When Dinosaurs Ruled the Earth (Warner)

Letter from Hollywood

ANTHONY SLIDE

While others have talked – a favourite occupation in this city – of opening a Hollywood Museum, John LeBold has done what seemed the impossible. He has actually opened a tasteful, entertaining and informative Hollywood Museum in a building which formerly housed a bank only a block from the Chinese Theatre on Hollywood Boulevard.

LeBold's own collection, gathered together over the past thirty years, makes up most of the exhibits, with additional items loaned primarily by Paramount Pictures and Western Costume. The emphasis here is on costumes, including those worn by Charlie Chaplin in *The Great Dictator* (1940), Judy Garland in *The Wizard of Oz* (1939), Rudolph Valentino in *Blood and Sand* (1922), Hedy Lamarr in *Samson and Delilah* (1949), Marlene Dietrich in *Shanghai Express* (1932), Katharine Hepburn in *Mary of Scotland* (1936), Betty Grable in *Coney Island* (1943), Claudette Colbert in *Cleopatra* (1934), Julie Andrews in *The Sound of Music* (1965), Alice Faye in *Hello, Frisco, Hello* (1943) and Gloria Swanson in *Sunset Boulevard* (1952). A favourite item for the younger fan is the pair of shorts worn by Sylvester Stallone in *Rocky* (1976).

Also of appeal to younger visitors is a special section of Bruce Lee memorabilia, which sits adjacent to one of Carmen Miranda's outrageous hats, and across the room from a fascinating sample of Harold Lloyd material. There is a handwritten questionnaire completed by Alfred Hitchcock for the Directors' Guild. The time machine, in working order, from *Time after Time* (1979) is on display. There is even a section devoted to horror, science fiction and fantasy films, including the grotesque clown doll from *Poltergeist* (1982) and the

head of one of the aliens from *Close Encounters of the Third Kind* (1977). (Much of this material was on loan for the 1985 Berlin Film Festival.)

The oldest item on display in the museum is a fan used by Theda Bara in her 1917 vehicle *Cleopatra*. It is in

The gallery of the Hollywood Museum.

beautiful condition, as are all of the items on display. LeBold says the Museum handles a certain amount of restoration, but utilizing only fabric and materials from the same period, matching sequins, etc. Restoration *is* a major problem. For example, one of the gowns on display was worn by Bette Davis in *The Private Life of Elizabeth*

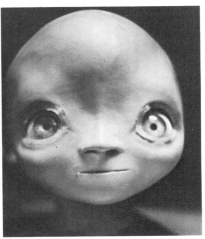

Above: Charlton Heston's costume from *Ben-Hur* (1959). Left, one of the aliens from *Close Encounters of the Third Kind*.

Ken Wlaschin seems to lack the flair for generating an exciting and controversial 'Filmex', which was the mark of his predecessor Gary Essert. Both the 1984 and 1985 'Filmex' screenings were lacklustre events.

The opening night film, *A Private Function*, was promoted as the opening of British Film Year in America. Despite its being a very entertaining work, the audience at 'Filmex' was not overly impressed, and there were a number of walk-outs during the film. The size of the theatre – 1,500 seats – did not help the film, and nor did the poor sound. Everything was somehow a little shabby and a little shoddy (which, one hopes, is not the state of Britain or the British film industry). There were four rather seedy-looking horsemen outside the theatre dressed in the manner of the Household Cavalry, and they were supported by a Los Angeles high school marching band, wearing kilts; a strange lady carrying a basket of flowers and singing English music hall songs with a distinctly American pronunciation; and two individuals whom one assumed were supposed to be a Pearly King and Queen. Perhaps the presence of such an ill-advised group kept away the stars? Only Michael Caine, Sidney Poitier, Cher and Michael York were glimpsed in the audience. They heard the British Ambassador, Sir Oliver Wright, make an entertaining, welcoming speech, which would have been better received had the microphone been working.

This may have been the start of British Film Year, but the British were evident in Los Angeles the previous summer when the British Academy of Film and Television Arts hosted 'A Royal Day of British Film and Television' at the Academy of Motion Picture Arts and Sciences. Princess Anne opened the event – on 10 July 1984 – and there was an interesting assortment of film screenings, including *An Englishman Abroad*, without charge for anyone who had the time and inclination. That evening Princess Anne was again on hand for the American premiere of *Comfort and Joy*. When not at the Academy or at the Olympic Games, Princess Anne was attending the opening of the British section of the 1984 'Filmex', and creating unfortunate controversy because her presence meant

and Essex (1939), and was made by designer Orry Kelly – whom LeBold hails as one of the industry's finest – from 100-year-old fabric. It is impossible to duplicate such material today.

Down the street from the Hollywood Museum is the Chinese Theatre, which was the site for the opening ceremonies of the 1985 edition of 'Filmex', the Los Angeles International Film Exposition. Despite his experience with the London Film Festival and the National Film Theatre, the new artistic director

Opposite: Frank Capra at the start of his career with Columbia.

Claudette Colbert and Clark Gable in *It Happened One Night*. A new 35mm print was donated to the UCLA Film Archives.

that the theatre had to be cleared and checked by security guards before the opening film. Angry moviegoers arrived to find the film preceding the royal event had been started at an earlier and unannounced time to allow for these security measures, and the Royal Family came in for considerable and unfair criticism.

'Filmex' founder and former director Gary Essert meanwhile announced plans, in January of 1985, for an American Cinematheque to be part of the restored Pan Pacific Center in the heart of Los Angeles. The landmark Pan Pacific building opened in 1935 and has long been empty. Essert plans to reopen it as a ten-million dollar screening facility, along the lines of the National Film Theatre in London and the Cinémathèque Française in Paris.

One of the major sources of films for Essert's new project will be the UCLA Film and Television Archives, which is the largest archival film institution in the Western United States and second only to the Library of Congress in terms of the amount of film and television programmes which it houses. Amazingly the Archives now have a collection of some 90,000 films, television programmes and radio broadcasts. They are particularly rich in nitrate prints of Paramount, 20th Century-Fox and Warner Bros. features from the 'thirties and 'forties, and in Republic films. The Archives also has the Hearst Metrotone Newsreel library as well as many short subjects.

Robert Gitt has been in charge of the Archives' preservation programme since its inception. He is one of the few archivists who does not sit behind a desk shuffling papers, but actually works with the films themselves. For too long his dedication has gone unnoticed, but late in 1984 much of America became aware of his efforts, along with those of Richard Dayton of YCM Laboratories, to restore *Becky Sharp*, the first three-strip, or full-colour, Technicolor feature from 1935, which is, as Gitt has remarked, as important to the history of the colour motion picture as *The Jazz Singer* is to the history of sound in film.

Directed by Rouben Mamoulian and with Miriam Hopkins in the title role, *Becky Sharp* has only been available for viewing in poor, two-colour Cinecolor versions until the present. With its lush colours restored, *Becky Sharp* has lost much of its dullness and suddenly become a witty and entertaining work. The Gitt-Dayton restoration proved the first film to sell out at the New York Film Festival, and played to an equally appreciative and capacity crowd at its West Coast re-premiere at the Academy of Motion Picture Arts and Sciences.

Following the success of *Becky Sharp*, the UCLA Film and Television Archives presented a two-month series of films preserved by Robert Gitt on the UCLA campus from 11 January to 17 March 1985. The opening night film was *The Animal Kingdom*, a newly rediscovered film from 1932, directed by Edward H. Griffith and starring Ann Harding, Leslie Howard and Myrna Loy. Other films in the series were *The Royal Family of Broadway* (1932), *Street Scene* (1931), *North Star* (1943), and *Arch of Triumph* (1948). All were screened in sparkling new 35mm prints. Canadian Club Whiskey entered the preservation field by making money available for the preservation of twelve classic features by US archives, including three – *Death Takes a Holiday* (1934, *Dark Command* (1940) and *Road to Rio* (1947) – by UCLA.

I had the pleasure of introducing 'An Evening with André de Toth', at which two of his films – *Dark Waters* (1944) and *Pitfall* (1948) – were screened in newly restored prints. André and I also travelled up to the Pacific Film Archive at Berkeley, just outside of San Francisco, for a four-film tribute, which also included *None Shall Escape* and *Monkey on My Back*. André de Toth is a director deserving of wider recognition for his realistic approach to melodrama – for too long he has been known simply as the one-eyed director who made the most famous of 3-D epics, *House of Wax*.

UCLA Film and Television Archives was the recipient of a new 35mm print of *It Happened One Night* (1934), along with a check for $75,000 from Columbia Pictures to 'safeguard' a collection of its films. The occasion – on 23 January 1985 – was a special luncheon at Chasen's honouring Frank Capra on the 50th anniversary of his film's winning the top five Academy Awards, hosted by Columbia. Among the Capra performers on hand were Viola Dana, James Stewart, Ralph Bellamy, Alexis Smith, Hope Lange, Lionel Stander, Frank Faylen, Coleen Gray, Margo Albert, Ann Doran, and Peter Falk. Viola Dana told an amusing tale of being hired by Capra to star in *That Certain Thing* (1928) because of her wiggle. According to Miss Dana, during the making of the film she fell down on her wiggle and it has never been the same since. It was one of those wonderfully genuine testimonials, thanks to the warmth of the participants, the lack of irritating flash bulbs and video cameras, and because it was hosted by Columbia, a studio so closely linked with Capra, but for whom, of course, he no longer works. At its close, Capra asked fellow director John Huston to stand, and remarked, 'As long as we've got guys like you around, we're going to be okay'. For some thirty years Columbia might have said exactly the same thing of Frank Capra.

One group which also claims to be preserving films is the National Film Society. In reality it preserves interest in 'old' films rather than the films themselves, through its magazine, *American Classic Screen*, and its Artistry in Cinema Awards, the most recent edition of which was held at the new Sheraton Premiere Hotel in Universal City on 21 October 1984. The winners this year included Lyle Talbot, Clarence Nash (the voice of Donald Duck), art director Lyle Wheeler, Richard Farnsworth, Leonard Nimoy, Alex North, Lizabeth Scott and Sydney Guilaroff. The last received his award from a svelte, very glamorous and extremely well-spoken Elizabeth Taylor, who, along with Esther Williams, flanked Guilaroff at his table. The book of the year award went to Richard Koszarski for his Erich von Stroheim autobiography, *The Man You Loved To Hate*, and it was presented by this writer – the first time (and probably the last) I have shared a stage with Elizabeth Taylor!

Miss Taylor was also very visible in Hollywood at the annual Golden Globes Awards, presented by the Hollywood Foreign Press Association on 26 January 1985. She received the Cecil B. DeMille Award, for a lifetime's achievement in films, from Liza Minnelli. The Hollywood Foreign Press Association performed a delicate balancing act by having both *Amadeus* and *A Passage to India* win top awards, with the former being voted Best Motion Picture – Drama and the latter Best Foreign Film. (The Association subsequently changed its rules, and, in future, the Best Foreign Film must be in a foreign language.)

Aside from the National Film Society, the other major film buff-oriented American group is the Society for Cinephiles, whose members are chiefly film collectors. It holds its convention each Labor Day weekend (the American equivalent of the British August Bank Holiday). The 1984 convention was held in San Francisco, was well organized by Jon Mirsalis and Rob McKay, and included tributes and awards to Priscilla Bonner, Mary Brian, Bernice Clair, Nell O'Day, and Esther Ralston. Kit Parker received a special award for his efforts in the field of 16mm, non-theatrical film distribution.

The two best-known, but not necessarily the best, awards events in any Hollywood year are the presentations of

Silent star Priscilla Bonner at the Cinecon convention.

Above: Two of Paramount's top stars of the 'twenties, Esther Ralston and Mary Brian at the Cinecon convention.

Below: Bernice Clair at the Cinecon convention.

Former western leading lady Nell O'Day at the Cinecon convention.

the Emmys and the Oscars. The former, presented by the Academy of Television Arts and Sciences, honour the best programmes and personalities (both in front of and behind the camera) from television. The big winner at the 24 September 1984 event at the Pasadena Civic Auditorium was NBC, thanks to its two most popular shows, *Cheers* and *Hill Street Blues*.

Myrna Loy received a long overdue tribute from the Academy of Motion Picture Arts and Sciences.

The Academy Awards presentation on 25 March 1985 was fairly predictable, with *Amadeus* garnering eight awards, including Best Picture, and *The Killing Fields* and *A Passage to India* trailing far behind with three and two awards respectively. This year's show lacked spontaneity and warmth. Jack Lemmon's remarks were a little too clichéd, with only Steve Martin displaying genuine wit in a presenter's speech, which made one realize how much Johnny Carson was missed. By trying to force the winners to limit their remarks to a few seconds, the producers took away much of the sparkle and surprise one has come to expect at an Academy Awards presentation. The highspot was unquestionably the presentation, by Cary Grant, of an Honorary Award to James Stewart, who took a cue from the title of one of his best-known films and remarked that it had indeed been a wonderful life.

The non-Oscar related aspects of the Academy are often more interesting than the Awards presentation. Certainly one of the most exciting events in the Academy's year was the presentation of Alfred Hitchcock's papers, by his daughter Patricia Hitchcock O'Connell, to the Academy's Margaret Herrick Library. Although there is not too much material from the 'forties and earlier, the collection does include the hand-written script by Thornton Wilder for *Shadow of a Doubt* (1943), stills and newspaper clippings from the director's British silent films, and evaluations by Hitchcock of actresses being considered for the title role in *Rebecca* (1940). Of tremendous historical importance are the original audio tapes of the François Truffaut-Alfred Hitchcock interviews, all 52 hours of them. Interestingly, the only two British films of which Hitchcock owned prints – in 35mm – are *Juno and the Paycock* (1930) and *Rich and Strange* (1932). Could it really be that these were Hitchcock's favourite British films? One hopes not!

To celebrate the donation, the Academy hosted a star-studded tribute to Alfred Hitchcock on 5 December 1984, with guests including Anthony Perkins, Tippi Hedren, Janet Leigh, Robert Cummings, Eva Marie Saint, Gregory Peck and James Stewart. Peter Bogdanovich introduced a selection of film clips from Hitchcock's career.

The Academy presented a major star tribute not in Los Angeles but in New York, where, on 15 January 1985, it presented a special salute to Myrna Loy, with guest appearances by Lauren Bacall, Lillian Gish, Lena Horne, Sidney Lumet, Joseph L. Mankiewicz, Robert Mitchum, Maureen O'Sullivan, Tony Randall, Burt Reynolds, Sylvia Sidney, Maureen Stapleton and Teresa Wright. Aside from the Academy, there was another link with Hollywood; the film screened in its entirety was the newly restored UCLA Film and Television Archives print of *The Animal Kingdom*.

'It was a lot of work, but we had fun. We had the best of times,' said Gene Kelly, as he received the 13th annual American Film Institute Life Achievement Award on 7 March 1985. On hand to pay tribute to Kelly, at an event hosted by Shirley MacLaine, were Gregory Hines, Cyd Charisse, the Nicholas Brothers, Donald O'Connor, Debbie Reynolds and Fred Astaire.

A year which began with the opening of a Hollywood Museum and included major recognition for a local film archive was not a bad year. All in all, there seemed evidence that Hollywood *is* working to recognize and preserve its past.

In Memoriam

Luther Adler, who died on 8 December 1984 at the age of 81, was a member of a family who founded and played an important part in New York's Yiddish Theatre. Commencing his acting career at the age of 5, Adler had a distinguished and busy theatrical career prior to his screen debut in *Lancer Spy* in 1937. Playing Hitler in both *The Magic Face* and *The Desert Fox*, he was often cast as the villain of the piece. His other film appearances included *The Last Angry Men*, *Cast a Giant Shadow*, *The Three Sisters*. For nine years – 1938–47 – he was married to Sylvia Sidney.

Richard Basehart suffered the first of a series of heart attacks on the morning of 13 August 1984, after he had read a poem at the closing ceremony of the Los Angeles Olympics. These were finally to kill him a month later, on 19 September, at the age of 70. Born in Ohio in 1914, the son of a newspaper editor, he did odd jobs about the paper

Richard Basehart.

until he became a reporter and local radio announcer. He switched career to acting in 1938, playing some 40 roles in repertory before his Broadway debut in 1943. Two years later he made a big hit and won the New York Drama Critics' award for his performance in *The Hasty Heart*. He made his screen debut in 1947 in *Cry Wolf* and quickly established himself as a versatile performer in such films as *The Titanic*, *The Good Die Young*, *The Brothers Karamazov*, *Chato's Land*, *The Island of Dr. Moreau* and a considerable number of foreign movies including *La Strada*, *Il Bidone* and *L'Ambitieuse*. One of his greatest successes was in the role of Ishmael in John Huston's *Moby Dick*. His last film, made in 1979, was *Being There*. Apart from his many movies – between 40 and 50 according to various records – he did an immense amount of work in TV movies, series and documentaries, and was in great demand as a commentator and narrator because of his sonorous voice.

Edmond O'Brien, who died in California on 9 May 1985 at the age of 69, started his showbiz career early in life when at the age of 10 he began to give magic shows in the basement of his parents' house, presenting tricks learned from his next-door neighbour Harry Houdini. Later, after appearing in Columbia University stage productions, he landed a small role in a Broadway production and soon he was appearing regularly on the New York stage, notably with Ruth Chatterton, Laurence Olivier, Kathleen Cornell and John Gielgud. After a period with Orson Welles's Mercury Theatre Company, he made his film debut in *The Hunchback of Notre-Dame*. After war service he returned to Hollywood to appear in a considerable number of

films including *White Heat*, *Julius Caesar*, *The Great Imposter*, *Birdman of Alcatraz*, *The Man Who Shot Liberty Valance* and *The Wild Bunch*. O'Brien also directed and produced and in between filming did a lot of TV work. In 1954 he won the Supporting Actor Oscar for his performance in *The Barefoot Contessa* and ten years later was again nominated (unsuccessfully) for the same award for his work in *Seven Days in May*.

Hugh Burden, who died at the age of 72 at his London home on 17 May 1985, was one of those constantly busy actors whose name never becomes well known by the public. In his 50-year showbiz career, which started with a role in the play *Singing Gold* in 1933 and ended with a part in the recent James Mason film *Dr Fischer of Geneva*, Burden appeared in a large number of plays, movies (including *One of Our Aircraft is Missing*, *Funeral in Berlin*, *Fame is the Spur*, *The Ruling Class*, etc.), radio and TV productions and documentaries as well as writing a number of plays. His great asset was his beautiful speaking voice, which made him a favourite radio reader.

Richard Burton, who died from a cerebral haemorrhage, aged 58, in a Swiss hospital close by his village home near Geneva on 5 August 1984, was a great natural actor who passed by his chances to become a greater one for the sake of the cash, the life-style and the headline-hitting existence of a millionaire superstar. (There is a story that Laurence Olivier, noticing the way things were going, once asked Burton if he wanted to become a great actor or a household name, and the snap reply came, 'Both'.) Born Richard Jenkins, the twelfth of thirteen children of a coal-

Richard Burton in *Absolution*.

just 50 movies, the last of which was a film of Orwell's *1984*, completed only a few weeks before his death. His extrovert, hard-drinking, hard-living lifestyle, plus an operation on his spine some while ago, brought a sad change in his appearance recently and he looked far older than his actual years. For many, apart from his several outstanding stage and screen performances, he will be fondly recalled for his speaking of the poetry of fellow Welshman (and hard-drinker!) Dylan Thomas, more especially for his reading of the poet's gloriously rich outflow of language in *Under Milk Wood*, which served to exhibit the full range of Burton's wonderful voice.

Clifford Evans, the Welsh actor who starred in a considerable number of British films and later contributed character roles, died at his home in Wales on 9 June 1985 at the age of 73. Films include *Love on the Dole*, *SOS Pacific*, *His Brother's Keeper*, *Our Brief Summer*, etc. He appeared in a considerable number of stage plays, as well as on TV and radio. He was also a Governor of the Welsh National Theatre.

Carl Foreman died – from cancer of the brain – at his Beverly Hills home on 26 June 1984 at the age of 69. Born in Chicago in 1914, he was an Anglophile who worked and lived in England from 1951 to 1975. His best memorial it is hoped will be the 1985 release of Columbia's *The Yellow Jersey*, the story of the French cycle race classic, the 'Tour de France', which gives both writing and co-producing credits to Foreman even though he died before the start of production. The son of Russian immigrants, Foreman started out as a circus and carnival producer before turning to journalism and copywriting. In 1938 he obtained a job as a reader in the MGM studios after winning a prize for his screenplay of a documentary made by the Californian Medical Association and selling his script (written by Charles Marlon) for a movie (filmed as *Spooks Run Wild*) for around £100! But he earned more for his subsequent scripts, including those for some of the *Bowery Boys* movies. After the war (in which he served with the US Army) he joined up with Stanley Kramer, for whom he produced the scripts for a number of the latter's earlier productions. Increasingly successful, he had

miner of Pontrhydfen, South Wales, Burton owed his adopted name and much of his success to the interest shown in him by his schoolteacher Philip Burton, his mentor who gave him his initial interest in and ambition for an acting career. Entering Oxford when he was only 16, in 1943, Burton at the same time won his first professional role in the West End production of the Emlyn Williams play *Druid's Rest*. From 1944 to 1947 Burton served with the RAF and it was not until 1948 that he made his screen debut in *The Last Days of Dolwyn*, on the set of which he met his first wife Sybil Williams. After considerable stage success on both sides of the Atlantic in *The Lady's Not for Burning*, Burton made his first American film, *My Cousin Rachel*, in 1952, which brought him the first of several Oscar nominations he was to receive during his career. Alternating between stage and screen for the next few years, his film credits of the period include: *The Robe*, *The Desert Rats*, *Prince of Players*, *Alexander the Great* and the French *Bitter Victory*. It was while play-

ing in *Camelot* on Broadway that Burton was offered the co-starring part of Antony in Joseph Mankiewicz's gargantuan production of *Cleopatra*, with Elizabeth Taylor in the title role, which he accepted at the cost of the $50,000 he had to pay to bow out of the play. His subsequent constant headline-hitting romance with his co-star off the set, and his magnetic performance on it, raised him immediately to superstar status and brought him a fee of around a million dollars for each of his future performances. In 1963 he married Miss Taylor for the first time (he was to marry and divorce from her twice). Increasingly lured by the flesh-pots and the millionaire life-style he quickly came to like, Burton seems seldom to have troubled much about the quality of the roles and the films he was offered and many of them were entirely unworthy of his talent. But among the dross there were the occasional glimpses of gold and it glittered in films like *Who's Afraid of Virginia Woolf?* (a film in which Miss Taylor also gave one of her best screen performances), *The Spy Who Came in from the Cold* and *Anne of a Thousand Days*. In all, Burton made just completed the script for that classic western *High Noon* when he became a victim of the McCarthy 'witch hunt' and was blacklisted by all the American studios. He came to Britain, where he worked under various names (he wrote the script for *The Sleeping Tiger* as 'Derek Frey' – while, ironically, fellow McCarthy victim Joseph Losey used the name of 'Victor Hanbury' as director) and received no credit at all for the screenplay of *The Bridge on the River Kwai*. By 1958 things had improved enough for him to form his own company Open Road Films. Among Foreman's best scripts where those for *Champion* in 1949, *The Men* (two years later), *The Guns of Navarone* and *Young Winston*. He also produced the last two movies. In 1963 he successfully wrote and directed *The Victors*, the only time he attempted direction. In 1975, just 23 years after he left America, he returned to produce *Force Ten from Navarone* (for which he also wrote the outline script) and, in 1979, *The Day the World Ended*. Elected President of the British Writers' Guild in 1968, he was also a governor of the British Film Institute from 1965 to 1971, in 1970 being awarded the honour of becoming a Commander of the British Empire. He was Executive Producer of TV's *Born Free* series and also of *The Golden Gate Murders* TV feature. At the time of his death he had plans for at least six movies as well as a TV series about the life of China's Sun Yat Sen.

Peggy Ann Garner died from cancer at Woodland Hills, California, on 16 October 1984 at the age of 52. Ohio born, Miss Garner was a child model

Peggy Ann Garner in *Black Widow*.

before appearing in her first movie, *Little Miss Thoroughbred*, in 1938. From that date she was seldom idle for long, appearing in films like *Abe Lincoln of Illinois*, *Jane Eyre* and *The Eagle Squadron*. She is probably best remembered for her 1945 Oscar-winning performance in *A Tree Grows in Brooklyn*. After her 1945 success she starred in *Keys of the Kingdom*, *Daisy Kenyon* and *The Black Forest*. After making the last, there came a ten-year gap before her next movie, *The Cat*. There was a further gap of eleven years before she re-appeared on the screen in *A Wedding*. Between these movies she held down commercial jobs such as a real estate agent and a car sales manageress. She also appeared regularly in TV productions, both telefilm features and series.

Janet Gaynor (real name Laura Gainor) who died in Palm Springs, California, on 14 September 1984 at the age of 77, had the distinction of being the first film actress to win an Oscar – awarded in 1927/28 primarily for her performance in *Street Angel* but also reflecting her success in two other films of that period (1928), *Seventh Heaven* and *Sunrise*. Her death was attributed partly to a horrific car accident in which she was involved some two years previously (a truck hit her taxi, also injuring Mary Martin who was with her). Miss Gaynor started acting in school plays with her sister and in 1924, soon after the family moved to Los Angeles, she was accepted as an extra on the Hal Roach studio's list. In 1926 she got her first real break with an important role in *The Johnstown Flood* for Fox, as a result of which she won a $100-a-week contract from the studio, for whom she made a number of movies, including a couple directed by John Ford. She subsequently appeared in F.W. Murnau's silent classic *Sunrise* and Frank Borzage's big success *Seventh Heaven* (her first film opposite Charles Farrell, with whom she made a dozen movies). Her first talkie (a box-office record breaker in its day) was the musical *Sunny Side Up* which, with other winners, brought her a revised contract and a wage rise to $1,500 a week! Later outstanding successes included *Tess of the Storm Country*, the original *State Fair*, *The Farmer Takes a Wife* and the first *A Star is Born* movie, the last bringing her an Oscar nomination. At

Janet Gaynor, with co-star Charles Farrell.

the height of her success (she made only two movies after *A Star is Born* – *Three Loves Has Nancy* and *The Young in Heart*) she retired to go globe-trotting with her second husband (they purchased a coffee plantation in Brazil) and to paint, later staging exhibitions of her work in Los Angeles and Chicago. In 1951 she appeared with her old-time partner Farrell in a TV tribute to them and six years later played Pat Boone's mother in *Bernardine*. In 1961 she appeared on TV in what was hoped would be a showcase feature for a series called *Sweet 16* but this did not materialize. Janet Gaynor had a lot of the stuff in her of which Mary Pickford and other stars of the silent era were made; she generally played a sweet kind of character who though often suffering the slings and arrows of outrageous fortune triumphantly won through to enjoy a happy-ever-after ending.

Richard Greene died at his Norfolk home on 1 June 1985 at the age of 66 as an indirect result of a fall he had in 1982. Born in Plymouth, the son of an actor and a descendant of the British film pioneer Richard Friese-Greene, Richard was soon acting in repertory after completing his education, and at the age of 20 was lured to Hollywood by Fox, who liked his dimpled handsomeness and fed him with plenty of star roles even though for some reason he never quite achieved major stardom. After nearly 50 films his career began to tail off, but took on a new lease of life in the late 1950s when he starred in the TV series *Robin Hood*, which brought him back to peak popularity and played in many countries across the world. Some of his films: *Four Men and a*

Prayer, The Hound of the Baskervilles, Stanley and Livingstone, Flying Fortress, That Dangerous Age, Forever Amber, The Desert Hawk, Lorna Doone, Captain Scarlett and, apparently his last two large-screen roles, *Tales from the Crypt* and *The Castle of Fu Manchu* in 1972.

Yilmaz Güney, the Turkish actor turned film director, died from stomach cancer in Paris (where he had lived since escaping from a Turkish prison in 1979) on 9 September 1984 at the age of 47, just two days after his most recent film *The Wall (Duvar)* was premiered in London. Both *Duvar* and his earlier *Yol* (which won the Golden Palm, the premier award at the 1982 Cannes Film Festival) were based on his own harrowing experiences in Turkish jails, his expressed radical beliefs having led to his imprisonment. A Kurd, Güney was a very popular player in the '50s and in 1965 created some sort of record by appearing in 27 films during those twelve months! His first spell in jail came in 1961, when he was charged with publishing a communist poem. He was quickly released from his second sentence, in 1971. Four years later he was found guilty of the murder of a member of the Turkish judiciary who had apparently insulted his wife. Among the films he directed are *Bride of the Earth (Seyyit Han), Hungry Wolves (Ac Kurtlar), The Father (Baba), The Friend (Arkadas)* and *Anxiety (Endise)*.

Neil Hamilton (full name, James Neil Hamilton) who died, as a result of long-standing asthma attacks, at his Californian home on 24 September 1984 at the age of 85, started out as a male model. Born in Wynn, Massachusetts, he arrived in New York in 1917 and was soon to be seen advertising shirts and the like. His stage debut came in 1919, in a repertory production of *The Better 'Ole*. His screen career really lifted off when D.W. Griffith picked him to play opposite Mae Marsh in *The White Rose*. He went to Hollywood in 1926 on a five-year contract with Paramount (he made 26 movies for them as well as appearing in other companies' productions during the period). After this he starred in Lubitsch's *The Patriot* with Emil Jannings, *Three Weekends* opposite Clara Bow, Wyler's *The Love Trap* opposite Laura La Plante, Howard Hawks' *The*

Dawn Patrol and *Strangers May Kiss* opposite Norma Shearer. During the 1930s and 1940s he made more than 40 movies. Then for a while he opened an agency but soon returned to the stage and in 1948 began a busy and successful TV career which lasted some twenty years. His final screen appearance seems to have been in the 1970 production *Which Way to the Front?*.

Henry Hathaway (real name, Henri Leopold de Fiennes) died, aged 86, from heart failure, in Hollywood on 11 February 1985. He was one of Hollywood's most famous golden age directors. Son of an actress and lawyer-turned-stage manager, Henry started working in the theatre as a young boy and by the time he was 10 was kept busy appearing in one-reel movies. He served with the American Armed Services during World War I and after being demobilized was engaged by Frank Lloyd, as Prop Man (in 1921) but soon rose to the position of assistant director, making his fully-fledged directing debut in 1932 with a series of Zane Grey westerns, nearly all of which starred Randolph Scott. Hathaway moved up a bracket in 1934 with the making of the feature film *Come On, Marines*; in the same year he completed *The Witching Hour* and *Now and Forever* establishing himself as a competent feature director. He was always, in fact, highly professional and was to become regarded in the industry as a 'studio workhorse'; reliable, efficient and unlikely to cause any problems during production. He was awarded the honour of helming Paramount's first outdoor colour movie, *The Trail of the Lonesome Pine*, in 1936; having won his celluloid spurs in Westerns he was always at his best in the genre. In 1940 Darryl Zanuck persuaded Hathaway to join him at Fox and it was for this company that he worked almost exclusively for the next 20 years, his successes of the period including *Johnny Apollo, The Shepherd of the Hills* (his first film with his favourite star, John Wayne), *A Wing and a Prayer, Sundown* and *Nob Hill*. His *House on 92nd Street* in 1945 initiated a new kind of almost documentary, location-made movies, a style which he was to use later for *13 Rue Madeleine* and *Call Northside 777*. Other films of this period included *The Desert Fox, Garden of Evil, The Legend of the Lost, From Hell to Texas*, and

North to Alaska. In the 1960s Hathaway made two super-productions in *How the West Was Won* and *Circus World*, another of the many films he made with Wayne, who also starred in his *The Sons of Katie Elder* and, the film which brought Wayne his Oscar, *True Grit*, a marvellous movie. After this big success Hathaway made *Raid on Rommel* and *Shootout*, finishing his career with the uncharacteristic 1974 release *Hangup* (re-titled *Superdude*). During his long career Hathaway made more than 60 movies, some of which he also produced and for some of which he did not even get a credit – he was once reported as saying, 'My problem has always been a reluctance to personally promote myself', a claim confirmed by more than one movie he made anonymously.

Richard Haydn, who was found dead at his Californian home on 25 April 1985, at the age of 80, will always be remembered for his impression of Mr Carp, a Londoner whose hobby was the imitation of fish. Haydn's first job was as box-office manager at the old Daly's Theatre, subsequently appearing in numerous shows including Noel Coward's *This Year of Grace*. For a time he was the manager of a Jamaican banana plantation (a hurricane ended that); he then became a film make-up man and via this back to acting. He took his Mr. Carp to Broadway in 1939 in Coward's *Set to Music* and then went to Hollywood where he appeared in a long list of movies (and also directed three: *Miss Tatlock's Millions, Dear Wife* and *Mr Music*) including *Ball of Fire, Cluny Brown, The Emperor Waltz, The Merry Widow, Please Don't Eat the Daisies, Mutiny on the Bounty* and *Clarence the Cross-Eyed Lion*.

Louis Hayward, the romantic screen hero whose peak of popularity was during the 1930s and 1940s, died after long incapacitation from lung cancer at the age of 75, in Palm Springs, on 21 February 1985. Born in South Africa, educated in France and England, Hayward began his professional career acting small parts in a British touring theatrical company. Thereafter he switched to running a night club, but soon returned to the London stage, in a production of *Dracula*. He subsequently appeared in a number of plays on both sides of the Atlantic (winning a New York critics' award in 1934). He

Louis Hayward.

made his screen debut in a British studio in 1932, in *Self-Made Lady*, making one or two more movie appearances in British films before his Hollywood debut in *The Flame Within* in 1935. Some of his subsequent roles were in *The Man in the Iron Mask* (playing dual characters), *The Saint in New York* (as the Saint), *Anthony Adverse*, *My Son My Son*, *The Return of Monte Cristo* (again playing the Duke), *The Son of Dr Jekyll*. After serving for three years with the US Marines during the war (and winning a Bronze Star for his efforts), Hayward's first post-war movie was Rene Clair's *And Then There Were None*, after which he appeared in Fritz Lang's *The House By the River*. A steady series of roles followed – somewhere around 40 in all. In the mid-50s Hayward starred in his own TV series (*The Lone Wolf*), as well as appearing in two others. His final screen appearance was in 1973's *Terror in the Wax Museum*. He married three times, his first wife being Ida Lupino.

Harold Hecht, actor, dancer, choreographer and, finally, film producer of renown, died at his Beverly Hills home, from cancer, on 26 May 1985, at the age of 77. Born in New York, Hecht started his professional life as a stage assistant at the age of 16, subsequently appearing in a number of New York drama productions and (as dancer) with the Metropolitan Opera and the Martha Graham group. Hecht went to Hollywood in the late 1930s as a dance director, but suddenly switched to the literary agency business. It was after his

war service that, with Burt Lancaster as partner, he began his long series of outstanding movies. As Norma Productions they made a whole series of outstanding movies including *Marty* (which won a Best Film Oscar), *Cat Ballou*, *Separate Tables*, *Bird Man of Alcatraz*, *The Way West* and *Sweet Smell of Success*, most of which won various prizes around the world. Up to his death Hecht was continuing to work on various projected movies including a sequel to *The Crimson Pirate* to be made in Yugoslavia at some time in 1985. It is significant that in their obituary notice *Variety* credited much of Hecht's success to 'picking good writers' (Odets, Chayefsky, Waldo Salt, etc.) and 'reliably good directors' (Carol Reed, John Frankenheimer, Robert Wise, etc.).

Ian Hendry died, aged 53, from a heart attack on Christmas Eve 1984. Born in Ipswich, he began his acting career with the usual seasons of repertory and touring companies, apart from which he soon began to find plenty of TV work. In the early 1960s he appeared in *Children of the Damned*, *In the Nick*, *Live Now Pay Later* and a number of other movies. Toward the end of that period he began to get more important roles in films such as *The Hill*, *Repulsion*, *Casino Royale* and *The Sandwich Man*. His career peaked in 1971 with the British Academy Best Supporting Actor award for his performance in *Get Carter*. After this came roles in *The McKenzie Break*, *Tales from the Crypt*, *Assassin*, *The Passenger*, *Damien – Omen*

Ian Hendry.

II, *The Bitch* and his last film, in 1979, *McVicar*. His second marriage to star Janet Munro ended with her death in a car crash in 1972. Ian Hendry's particular forte was playing shady characters, bright-faced super-salesman types and others who live by their wits. Without great star potential he was an actor who was always worth watching, whatever the quality of his role or the film in which he appeared.

William Keighley died in New York on 24 June 1984, aged 94. He was a stage actor who turned to film direction and was responsible for such screen classics as *G-Men*, *The Green Pastures* and *Each Dawn I Die* (three of some 30 films to his credit). After studying in Paris, Keighley joined, as actor, a Shakespearean company in Britain and later toured the United States with the same company, during which *Variety* listed him as taking 32 parts in 13 plays. He made his New York acting bow in 1915 and some years later appeared with John Barrymore in a production of *Richard III*, also appearing with Ethel Barrymore in Paris in her *Romeo and Juliet*. Always a highly cultured man with wide literary interests, he remained in France to study literature and drama for a couple of years before returning to America to direct several Charles Hopkins productions. After further play direction in London, Keighley directed the Broadway production of *Penny Arcade* – which, re-titled *Sinner's Holiday*, gave the two stars Joan Blondell and James Cagney their first film chance, just as the play had given them their Broadway debut. Keighly got his first chance at solo film direction in 1933 with *Easy to Love*, which marked the start of a hectic period of direction for Warner Bros. In quick succession Keighley turned out *Journal of a Crime*, *Babbitt*, *Bullets or Ballots*, *The Prince and the Pauper*, *The Bride Came C.O.D.*, *The Valley of the Giants*, *Brother Rat*, *Yes, My Darling Daughter*, and *The Man Who Came to Dinner*. Between 1942 and '45 Keighley served with the motion picture unit of the US Army and after the war continued to direct a flow of movies such as *Honeymoon*, *Rocky Mountain* and *The Master of Ballantrae*. The last was made in 1953 and after it Keighley and his wife (former actress Genevieve Tobin, whom he had married in 1928) moved to Paris but returned to New York in

1972 with a collection of valuable paintings and many thousands of photographs they had taken while touring Europe. A director of France's Musée Carnavalet and a voluntary worker for New York's Metropolitan Museum, it was revealed when he died that Keighley had left some 70,000 of his photographs to the latter.

Jennifer (Kapoor) Kendal died, aged 50, from cancer in a London hospital on 6 September 1984 a week before the premiere of her last film, *The Home and the World*, in London. A member of a British theatrical family which toured India for many years with productions from the classical repertoire, including Shakespeare (shown in fictional guise in the marvellously successful Merchant-Ivory film *Shakespeare Wallah*), Jennifer married her Indian co-star of *Bombay Talkie*, Shashi Kapoor, and again appeared with him in 1983's outstanding *Heat and Dust*, in which she gave a performance of Oscar-winning proportion. She did, however, win one premier award, the *Evening Standard's* prize for best actress, for her performance in *36 Chowringhee Lane*. In addition to her film and stage work she was founder, with her husband, of the Prithvi Theatre in Bombay, where they presented classical and contemporary plays. Miss Kendal was a superbly polished performer of great range; every one of her screen roles, including her last, small one in *The Home and the World*, was a marvellous example of character acting. A personal judgement is that she was a far greater actress than many who appeared to outshine her on the screen.

Jennifer Kendal.

Norman Krasna, Oscar-holding (for his 1943 screenplay of *Princess O'Rourke*, which he also directed) director - screenwriter - playwright - producer, died suddenly and unexpectedly at his Los Angeles home on 1 November 1984 at the age of 74. Born and educated in New York, Krasna was a film and drama critic and columnist before writing his first play *Louder, Please*, which had a short run on Broadway. Turning to film scripting, he had amassed a considerable number of credits before he was 24 and was known as something of a boy wonder in Hollywood. Though he wrote, directed and produced many different kinds of films his particular forte was always light comedy – especially comedies built around the mistaken identity theme – and he was responsible for some of Hollywood's most delightfully entertaining productions during the 1930s and 1940s. Some of his best-known films include *Hands Across the Table, Bachelor Mother, Mr and Mrs Smith, The Devil and Miss Jones, The Flame of New Orleans, It Started with Eve, Indiscreet, Let's Make Love* and *Sunday in New York*. His last film was a remake of his earlier success *It Started With Eve*, retitled *I'd Rather be Rich*, released in 1964.

Peter (Sidney Ernest Aylen) Lawford, who passed away in a Los Angeles hospital on Christmas Eve 1984 after a heart attack (he had been admitted with kidney and liver ailments), was aged 61. Born in London, the only son of Lieutenant General Sir Sidney Lawford (who, incidentally, in his time accepted a number of bit parts in movies for the fun of it), Peter first appeared on the screen when he was 8 years old in *Poor Old Bill*. A few years later he played an English boy in MGM's *Lord Jeff*. After a stint as cinema usher he won a small role in *Mrs Miniver* and, through the great success of the movie, was offered a contract by MGM. Thereafter he was kept pretty busy during the 1940s with such films as *A Yank at Eton, The White Cliffs of Dover, Mrs Parkington, The Picture of Dorian Gray* and *Son of Lassie*. Post-war he appeared in a number of musicals, among them *Easter Parade* and *Good News*. After a short period away he returned to the studios in 1959 to make *Never So Few*, followed by *Exodus*, and *Oceans 11* in 1960, *Sergeants Three*, and *Advise and Consent*

Peter Lawford.

in 1962. In 1960 he formed his own company, Chrislaw Productions to make both TV and theatrical films, among the latter, *Johnny Cool* and *Billie*, and he personally co-produced *Salt and Pepper* and *One More Time*. In the 1960s his films included *The Longest Day*, and *The Oscar and Skidoo*. In recent years he had been less active but did appear in *That's Entertainment* in 1974, and a few other productions. His final screen appearance was in *Where is Parsival?* Specializing in light comedy and roles which called for an impeccable English accent, Lawford married John Kennedy's sister Patricia in 1954 (he was divorced in 1966). In 1971 he was married for a second time, to Patricia Season. Peter Lawford's most successful period was during the 1940s and 1950s. A leading member of the so-called 'Rat Pack' along with Sinatra and his pals, he was a hard liver and drinker and just a few months before his death he underwent treatment at the Betty Ford clinic.

Joseph Losey, expatriate director who left his native America in 1951 when he became involved in the McCarthy trials and was blacklisted by all the US studios after refusing to say whether or not he had ever been a communist, died in London on 22 June 1984, at the age of 75, almost immediately after completing his final film, *Steaming*. Born in Wisconsin, when a play he had written for a local theatre won an award he decided to pursue to a theatrical career, becoming first a drama critic, then stage manager of a number of London and New York productions. He made his acting debut in 1933 in *Little Ol' Boy*. After a number of similar small roles Losey set off on a series of East European tours, during which he attended Eisenstein's film production classes in Moscow. He returned to the American stage but in 1938 began a series of successful educational and other documentary movies which continued until the outbreak of war, when he toured the country with shows for the factory workers. After the end of the war (for a time he served with the US Army Signal Corps), he made his directing debut in 1948 in the fictional feature film *The Boy with the Green Hair* which he followed with a quartet of first-rate thrillers: *The Lawless*, *The Prowler*, a re-make of Fritz Lang's *M*, and *The Big Night*. Still blacklisted in the US, he continued stage and screen work in Britain, often using pseudonyms, his films at this time including *Time Without Pity*, *Blind Date*, *The Criminal* and *Eva*, leading up to his first really big commercial success, *The Servant*, starring Dirk Bogarde and written by Harold Pinter. This sent him back, for the premiere, to his native land, for the first time in eleven years. His next films enjoyed varying fortunes, including the strip cartoon feature *Modesty Blaise*, the Cannes prize-winning *Accident*, the flop *Boom* and the fascinating – and I happen to think outstandingly brilliant – *Figures in a Landscape*. Then came *The Secret Ceremony* and – another outstanding achievement, acknowledged by the premier prize at the 1971 Cannes Film Festival – *The Go-Between*. Losey went to Mexico to make *The Assassination of Trotsky*, to Norway to make Ibsen's *A Doll's House*, back to England to make *The Romantic Englishwoman* (from a Tom Stoppard script) and then across to France to make the brilliant *Mr Klein*, *Les Routes du Sud* (a flop) He also made one of the most original opera films ever screened, *Don Giovanni*. The films that Losey managed to get into production were almost certainly outnumbered by those he worked on but failed to get financial backing for, such as a projected star-laden version of Marcel Proust's great work *A la Recherche du temps perdu* (which got as far as a published screenplay by Harold Pinter), a new version of *Camille*, and

Track 39, which fell through at the last moment. Losey's greatest regret was that he was never given the chance to make a film with some political comment in his own country.

James Mason died, aged 75, at his home in Switzerland on 27 July 1984 from a major heart attack within a few days of Richard Burton. These two great British movie stars and fine actors had little in common beyond their beautiful voices and outstanding acting ability. In contrast to the hard-drinking, hard-living Welshman whose private life constantly made headlines, Yorkshire-born Mason was by nature retiring, even shy, and suspicious of publicity, jealously guarding his private life from public scrutiny. Mason, a Huddersfield wool-mill owner's son, went to Marlborough and Cambridge, where he gained a degree in architecture (few people beyond his closest friends knew what a considerable artist and biting cartoonist he was). Finding work difficult to come by in the worst period of the Depression, and having acted in some school dramatics,

James Mason in *The Shooting Party*.

Mason wrote off to a *Stage* advertisement and, somewhat to his surprise, won a role with a touring drama company. After this ended he spent a couple of years learning the actor's trade with a number of provincial repertory companies and then made his West End debut in 1933 in *Gallows Glorious*. Subsequently he became a member of the Old Vic company (appearing in *The Queen of Scots*) and then the famous Dublin Gate Theatre Company. His screen debut was made in 1934 in *Late Extra*. (He had been replaced after three days' work the previous year on Korda's *The Return of Don Juan*.) After this he was kept filming consistently, largely in a series of the old British 'quota quickies' but also in some superior productions such as *Fire Over England* (1937). In 1939 he made, with co-star and writer Pamela Kellino (one of the Ostrer family) and her cameraman husband Roy, *I Met a Murderer* which, although not a box-office success, was always one of Mason's (and my own) favourites – incidentally the cost of the production was something below £10,000! While furthering his stage career, Mason continued to appear in movies, including *Hatter's*

Castle, The Night Has Eyes and Thunder Rock. Then, with his dark and brooding – and brutal – Marquis de Rohan in The Man in Grey, he became Britain's favourite man-you-love-to-hate. After major performances in The Seventh Veil (1945) and The Wicked Lady (the following year), in which he played the handsome highwayman, Mason headed the British cinema's list of money-making stars and became the highest paid actor in the business that side of the Atlantic. Following his outstanding and critically acclaimed performance in Carol Reed's Odd Man Out (one of his own favourite performances) in 1946 he was lured to Hollywood, although his debut there was held up for a couple of years by legal tangles (during which he starred on Broadway with Pamela, now his wife, in the short-running Bathsheba). His American films include Madame Bovary (as Flaubert), Pandora and the Flying Dutchman, The Desert Fox (as Rommel, a role repeated in the subsequent film about the German Field Marshal, The Desert Rats) and two films by Max Ophuls (a director he greatly admired), Caught and The Reckless Moment. With his wife Pamela as writer and co-star he made Lady Possessed in 1952 and in the following year the Mankiewicz adaptation of Julius Caesar (another director he admired). Thereafter it was seldom that he was not working somewhere in the world even if the standard of the films he appeared in – always with some personal distinction – varied. The best included The Man Between, 20,000 Leagues under the Sea (as Captain Nemo) and George Cukor's remake of A Star is Born, in which he gave one of his greatest performances and for which he received an Oscar nomination (quite unfairly, he was never awarded an actual Oscar although he earned one many times over). Other films included Lolita, The Pumpkin Eater, Georgy Girl, The Deadly Affair, the remake of Mayerling (in the old Charles Boyer part) and Age of Consent, which he produced with Michael Powell in Australia with Australian actress Clarissa Kaye as co-star, whom Mason married two years later, having been divorced from Pamela in 1964. He won another supporting actor Oscar nomination with his brilliant performance in The Verdict in 1984 and completed his role in The Shooting Party not long before his death. In all, Mason appeared in

well over a hundred films; he directed only one, the half-hour feature The Child in 1954 in which he appeared with wife Pamela and daughter Portland. More recently he had been doing quite a lot of TV work, notably in Dr Fischer of Geneva. Apart from his wife he leaves two children by his first wife, Portland and son Alexander. As a personal footnote I have known and greatly admired Mason since I first met him early on in his acting career.

Mary Miles Minter, the silent screen star, died, having lived in retirement since 1922, aged 83, after a heart attack at her Santa Monica home on 4 August 1984. Once selected by Zukor to replace Mary Pickford and second in popularity only to the 'World's Sweetheart' at the beginning of the 1920s, Miss Minter made her stage debut when she was six years old. After becoming one of America's best-loved child stars she began her short film career when she was ten, in a 1912 film called The Nurse. In the following decade she made some 50 movies, playing the innocent little heroine, but of that total it is sad to think that the prints of not more than two exist today. Among the titles are: Anne of Green Gables, The Cowboy and the Lady, and The Trail of the Lonesome Pine. Miss Minter's career came abruptly to a halt in 1922, when director Desmond Taylor was found murdered (a mystery which remains

Mary Miles Minter.

unsolved to this day) and both Mary and her mother became involved in the investigation that followed. At that time when Hollywood was still reeling under the public's outraged reaction to the Fatty Arbuckle case, no one would chance using Miss Minter again, and she was forced into retirement at the age of 20!

Ivan Montagu, who died at his home in Watford, England, on 5 November 1984 at the age of 80, was a director-screenwriter who at one time or another worked for such divergent bodies as the British Government and the Communist Party, of which he was a life-long member. The disowned – because of his politics – son of Baron Swaythling, Montagu worked with both Hitchcock and Eisenstein. During his career he had been film distributor, importer, exhibitor and editor; also trade union organizer, film critic and the writer of several books on film theory. He will be best recalled, however, for his Ministry of Information shorts and for the co-scripting of Scott of the Antarctic.

Chic Murray, who died in his sleep in Edinburgh at the age of 63 on 29 January 1985, was best known as a music hall comedian. In recent years he had moved across to straight stage roles, TV and film character parts, including Casino Royale and Gregory's Girl. His final appearance was on New Year's Eve 1984, in a special, seasonal TV production.

Clarence Nash, Donald Duck's quackery voice in the Walt Disney cartoons for half a century, died on 20 February 1985, from blood cancer, in Burbank, California, at the age of 80. Nash began his theatrical career young, as an animal imitator in vaudeville. He moved to Hollywood in 1930, where he soon won an audition with Disney, who hired him in 1933. The rest is movie cartoon history. When the Donald Duck films were shown abroad the little duck – thanks to Nash's ability to learn languages phonetically – spoke in French, German, Spanish, Portuguese and even in Japanese and Chinese. Nash was the voice of a bullfrog in Bambi, a dog in 101 Dalmatians and Jiminy Cricket; on occasion he was the voice of Mickey himself. The last time he gave voice to Donald was in Mickey's Christmas Carol in 1983.

Pascale Ogier, 24-year-old daughter of film star Bulle Ogier and one of the most promising and talented of France's up-and-coming screen actresses, died in her sleep from heart failure at a friend's home in Paris on 26 October 1984. Just a few months previously she had scored her first big success in Eric Rohmer's *Full Moon in Paris (Les Nuits de la Pleine Lune)*, a performance which won her the best actress award at the 1984 Venice Film Festival. While still a student, Miss Ogier appeared in Rohmer's *Perceval* and later won roles in James Ivory's *Quartet*, Bolognini's *La Dame aux Camélias*, Jacques Rivette's *Le Pont du Nord* (in which her mother also appeared and for which she also had a co-scripting credit), Aline Isserman's *Le Destin de Juliet*, Jacques Monnet's *Signes Exterieurs de Richesse* and a British telefilm, *Ghost Dance*, which appeared in the cinemas in 1983. Her last film was Jacques Richard's *Ave Maria*. To give an idea of her versatility, she had the art direction credit for Rohmer's *Les Nuits de la Pleine Lune* as well as playing the star role.

Sam Peckinpah, who died in a Californian hospital, after several heart attacks, on 28 December 1984, aged 59, earned the reputation of being the screen's foremost exponent of violence, seen in such movies as *Straw Dogs*, *The Wild Bunch* and *Bring Me the Head of Alfredo Garcia*. Always a controversial figure, renowned for his rows with producers and feuding with his bosses (he was fired just four days after taking *The Cincinnati Kid* into the studio), he had been idle for four years before he made his last film *The Osterman Weekend*, in 1982–3. Coming from a family who had trekked west in a wagon train, most of his movies had western backgrounds and he defended their bloody violence by saying he wanted to smash through the myth of the Old West and present it as it was. Ironically, his least violent and best western, *The Ballad of Cable Hogue* released in 1970 was something of a flop. Educated at a Military Academy and serving with the US Marine Corps in China in World War II, he turned to stage direction when he was demobbed, acting and directing for several years before making his first movie in 1957, when he was signed up by Don Siegel to hold the post of dialogue director. After much TV work (*Gunsmoke*, *Pony Express*, *The Rifleman*, etc.) he made his screen directing debut with a low-budget feature, *The Deadly Companions*, in 1961 and the following year he completed a similarly modest but critically acclaimed movie, *Ride the High Country*, only to go on to make the expensive flop *Major Dundee*. In 1969 he returned to direction with *The Wild Bunch*, followed in 1970 by *The Ballad of Cable Hogue* and *Straw Dogs* in 1971. Then came *Junior Bonner*, *The Getaway*, *Pat Garrett and Billy the Kid*, *Bring Me the Head of Alfredo Garcia*, *The Killer Elite*, the war film *Cross of Iron* in 1977 and the indifferent *Convoy* in 1978. Peckinpah had a considerable talent but did not always use it wisely; however, without any question some of his productions such as *The Wild Bunch* are in their own way classic movies.

Walter Pidgeon (born Walter Davis Pidgeon), one of the strongest and most naturally dignified leading men that the movies have ever had, died at the age of 87 on 25 September 1984 in a Santa Monica hospital after a series of strokes. 'Pidge', as he was known to his friends, had been near death some seven years previously, when he was operated on for blood clots on the

Walter Pidgeon.

brain. With more than a hundred films to his name in a career that spanned half a century, Pidgeon had his greatest screen successes in the 1940s with such movies as *Mrs Miniver*, *Madame Curie* (for both of which he won Oscar nominations), *Mrs Parkington* and *The Miniver Story*. He volunteered for the Canadian Army during World War I (he was born in New Brunswick) a serious accident while training led to 17 months in hospital and subsequent discharge. In the early 1920s he was working in a bank but in 1924 made his theatrical debut in Shaw's *You Never Can Tell*. After small roles in silent movies his screen career really took off with the advent of the talkies, though at that time he was generally cast in singing roles. But Ford's *How Green Was My Valley* in 1941 established him firmly as a star and he went on to make a string of movies including *White Cargo*, *Blossoms in the Dust*, *Dream Wife*, *The Last Time I Saw Paris* and *Executive Suite*. He made a return to the theatre in 1956, but after appearing in many TV films and series, he accepted the role of the submarine commander in the 1961 feature film *Voyage to the Bottom of the Sea*. Then followed *Advise and Consent*, *Warning Shot* and quite a number of Italian productions. His final screen appearance was in Mae West's final film *Sextette*. In 1966 he returned to Broadway in a revival of *Dinner at 8* after which he seldom worked. Like several others who have died recently, he was one of the major ornaments of Hollywood's so-called golden age, a *real* Star.

Michael Redgrave died in a Buckinghamshire nursing home on 21 March 1985 at the age of 77 after suffering for several years the increasingly debilitating effects of Parkinson's disease. Born in Bristol and educated at Clifton College and Cambridge, it was only in 1934, after an initial career as a public school headmaster, that Redgrave switched to acting for a living, making his professional debut at the Liverpool repertory theatre in that year. Subsequently he became a star at the Old Vic in London, but he gave up his career in order to join the Royal Navy in 1941, only to be medically discharged the following year. A distinguished career in the theatres of London and New York followed. Redgrave's film career began in 1936 with a role in Hitch-

A young Michael Redgrave in *Fame is the Spur*.

cock's *The Secret Agent*; two years later he made a big hit in another Hitchcock thriller classic, *The Lady Vanishes*. There followed more than 50 feature films and starring roles including those in *The Dam Busters, The Stars Look Down, Kipps, Thunder Rock, Dead of Night, The Captive Heart, Fame is the Spur* and *The Browning Version*. In the 1956 film of Orwell's *1984* he played the role that Richard Burton was to end his screen career by playing in the more recent version. He also appeared in *The Quiet American, Time Without Pity, The Innocents, The Loneliness of the Long Distance Runner, The Heroes of Telemark, The Battle of Britain, Oh! What a Lovely War,* and the remake of *Goodbye Mr Chips*. His final appearance on screen was in Joseph Losey's *The Go-Between* in 1971. During those years he also made the occasional TV appearance. In spite of his fine work in such media Sir Michael was first and last, both by choice and skill, a stage actor and his distinguished work in the theatre included producing, directing

and writing as well as acting. He also has several books to his credit including the fiction volume *The Mountebank's Tale*. His was a theatrical dynasty: wife Rachel Kempson, daughters Lynn and the controversial Vanessa as well as son Corin have all had successful stage and film careers.

Flora Robson, one of Britain's most distinguished actresses, with a legion of outstanding, strong performances on both stage, screen and television to her credit died, at the age of 82, at Brighton's Royal Sussex Hospital on 7 July 1984, having been admitted a week previously with an undisclosed illness. Born Flora McKenzie Robson in 1902, she graduated from RADA with a bronze medal and made her stage debut in a minor role in London at the age of 19, subsequently appearing in provincial repertory productions for the next two years. Miss Robson then suddenly decided she would not pursue a theatrical career and took a job as a social worker (though retaining an interest in acting by directing a number of amateur productions). It was not until five years later, in 1929, that she returned to the professional stage, joining the Cambridge Festival Theatre for

several productions. A year later she was back on the London stage and during the 1930s appeared in a score of West End productions. In 1931 she had made her screen debut in *A Gentleman of Paris* and *Dance Pretty Lady*, the beginning of a whole string of outstanding film performances, notably in *Catherine the Great* (as the Empress Elizabeth), *Fire Over England* (as Queen Elizabeth I), *Wuthering Heights* and *Poison Pen*. It was the Brontë film which took her to Hollywood and she stayed on there to make a number of movies including *We Are Not Alone, The Sea Hawk* (again as Queen Elizabeth) and *Saratoga Trunk*. She also appeared in a number of Broadway stage productions which, while earning her critical praise, seldom had decent runs. She returned to Britain in 1944 to appear in a production of *Thérèse Raquin* and was from then on kept busy on both sides of the Atlantic, making her final appearance on Broadway in 1950 in *Black Chiffon*, which she took to New York after its British success. During this period she appeared in numerous films, notably *Caesar and Cleopatra, Black Narcissus*, the 1954 *Romeo and Juliet* (as the Nurse), *No Time for Tears, Farewell Again*, the unfinished *I, Claudius, Murder Most Foul, Those Magnificent Men in Their Flying Machines, The Beast in the Cellar, Alice in Wonderland* (which was never shown in the cinema but cropped up on TV years later) and her final movie, a 1981 release, *Clash of the Titans* (her final stage role was in a

Flora Robson.

Windsor Theatre production of *The Importance of Being Earnest* in 1975). She also appeared in a number of television productions.

Leonard Rossiter died of a heart attack during a performance of a revival of *Loot* at London's Lyric Theatre on 5 October 1984, at the age of 57. Although his biggest successes were on television he appeared in more than a score of movies during his career including *Billy Liar, This Sporting Life, Oliver!, 2001, Barry Lyndon,* two of the *Pink Panther* films, and – his last – *Water,* released after his death. Another successful Liverpudlian, Rossiter began his show business career at Preston Repertory in 1954, reaching London's West End four years later in *Free as Air.* In 1969 (he made his New York Broadway debut in 1963) he won the Variety Club's Best Actor of the Year award for his work in *The Resistible Rise of Arturo Ui.* But it was in his two TV series, *Rising Damp* and *The Fall and Rise of Reginald Perrin,* that he scored his widest and greatest success,

Leonard Rossiter in *Britannia Hospital.*

and it will be for these that he will best and most popularly be remembered. His unique facial expressions and special voice tone, along with a fine sense of comic timing, made him the outstanding comedian that he was.

François Truffaut, who died on 21 October 1984, in the American Hospital in Paris, as the result of a brain operation for cancer the previous autumn, was only 52. One of the more outstanding and certainly most influential of modern French moviemakers, Truffaut was a highly respected critic of film before he actually turned to *making* movies. His unhappy childhood provided the basis for several of his films, starting with *The 400 Blows (Les Quatre Cents Coups).* His venture into running his own cinema when he was 16 led, through mismanagement, to a spell in a reformatory, from which he was released thanks to the efforts of France's most famous film critic, André Bazin, who was later to aid Truffaut considerably in his passion for films. After a stormy military service in 1951–2 (which ended with him being sent to prison), Truffaut began to write the flow of controversial and caustic critic-

ism which led to the so called 'Auteur Theory' and the birth of the 'New Wave'. His first film was a short, *Une Visite,* made in 1954, to be followed four years later by a half-hour effort called *Les Mistrons.* After *The 400 Blows* in 1959 came another success, *Shoot the Piano Player* a year later, followed by what many critics consider his best film and certainly a classic of the cinema, *Jules et Jim,* shown in 1961. Then came *Soft Skin* and his only English-language production *Fahrenheit 451.* Then came *The Bride Wore Black, Mississippi Mermaid, Two English Girls* and his Oscar-winning *Day for Night,* the definitive film about filmmaking and film-makers. Other successes include *The Story of Adèle H, Small Change, The Man Who Loved Women, The Green Room, Love on the Run, The Last Metro* and *Vivement Dimanche!* His last film was *The Woman Next Door.* Having first appeared as an actor in his own film *The Wild Child,* Truffaut in the late 1970s accepted Spielberg's offer to play the French scientist in *Close Encounters of the Third Kind.* A deeply sensitive and literary director, Truffaut showed in all his films a delicacy of touch and a nice sense of subtlety and humour allied to a carefully restrained ability to convey the deepest human emotions. A fan of the slick American movie, his enthusiasm and respect for Alfred Hitchcock and his other idol, Renoir, was reflected again and again in his films. The author of several books, including an important one on Hitchcock, Truffaut, through his company Les Films du Carosse, produced or collaborated on the scripts of a number of films other than his own, including those of Godard, Rivette and Rohmer. Every Truffaut film from first to last, if inevitably ·of varying quality, was a cinematic gem and his name must be included in any lists of the all-time great moviemakers.

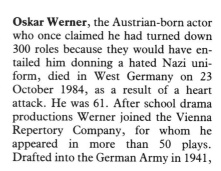

Oskar Werner, the Austrian-born actor who once claimed he had turned down 300 roles because they would have entailed him donning a hated Nazi uniform, died in West Germany on 23 October 1984, as a result of a heart attack. He was 61. After school drama productions Werner joined the Vienna Repertory Company, for whom he appeared in more than 50 plays. Drafted into the German Army in 1941,

Oskar Werner.

he somehow managed to continue appearing at Vienna's Burgtheater until it was closed down on Goebbels's orders in 1944. Theoretically a conscientious objector, Werner was thrown out of the German Officers' School and spent the rest of the war as a deserter (after a period in hospital as a result of being injured in an American bombing raid) hiding out in the woods. Post-war he enjoyed a successful theatrical career before gaining screen recognition in the 1950s. Apart from his highly successful casting in the classic *Jules et Jim*, he appeared in films such as *Ship of Fools* (which earned him an Oscar nomination), *Fahrenheit 451*, *The Spy Who Came in from the Cold* and *Voyage of the Damned*, which, shown in 1976, appears to have been his last movie, though he continued to appear on the stage and in one-man shows until alcoholism resulted in his becoming virtually a recluse during his final years.

Estelle Winwood (real name Goodwin) was still acting in movies up to the late 1970s (for instance, in *Murder by Death* in 1976) and even after that continued to make appearances on TV, right up to her 100th birthday. She died, after a year's hospitalization, on 20 June 1984 at the age of 101. Born in 1883 in London, and educated in Ealing, a graduate of the Lyric Stage Academy, she made her stage debut in Manches-

ter in a production of *School for Scandal* and appeared in the West End the following year when the play was transferred. Touring Liverpool repertory and London productions kept her busy until she crossed the Atlantic in 1916 to appear on Broadway and she stayed in America until 1931, when she returned for more British theatrical productions and, in 1933, her screen debut in *The House of Trent*. Four years later she appeared in *Quality Street*, after which she concentrated on theatrical work until the 1950s, when she began a long series of character performances, all of which added some extra special delight to the films in which she appeared, often in fey, eccentric roles. Her screen credits include *The Glass Slipper* in 1955, *This Happy Feeling*, three years later, *Alive and Kicking* (a 1959 British movie), *The Misfits* (1961), *Camelot* in 1967 and *The Producers* the following year. After considerable commuting across the Atlantic, Miss Winwood settled in her San Fernando Valley home in later life. She achieved her longlevity despite the 60 or so cigarettes a day she invariably smoked and an honest liking for a few drinks. Below 5 feet in height

Estelle Winwood.

she was, apparently, quite a character off-stage and off-screen, with a penchant for lively conversation.

Other Deaths During the Year:

Lina Montes died on 2 October 1984, aged 60, in Mexico City. Born in Cuba, she moved to Mexico in 1936 and after appearing in the local production of the *Folies Bergère* made her first movie – of a total of more than 50 – in 1943 *Cristobel Colon*. Her best performance was said to be in *The Lady of the Camelias*.

Joan Young died on 10 October 1984, aged 81, in London. She appeared initially in Music Hall but subsequently did radio, TV and straight plays. Her films include *The Lamp Still Burns*, *The Small Voice* and *The Fallen Idol*.

Jeanne Cagney Morrison – James Cagney's sister – who died on 7 December 1984, aged 65, from cancer, made her stage debut when she was only 7. Though primarily a stage actress she appeared in some dozen films (including several with her brother), among them *Golden Gloves*, *Yankee Doodle Dandy*, *The Time of Your Life*, *Man of a Thousand Faces* and *A Lion is in the Streets*.

The Ten Most Promising Faces of 1985

COMPILED BY JAMES CAMERON-WILSON

John Candy. A plum pudding of an actor who, with his role in *Splash*, finally sank his talons into film stardom. A television name since 1976 when he appeared in the satirical revue *SCTV* (on American television), Toronto native Candy went on to appear briefly in the films *It Seemed Like a Good Idea at the Time*, with Anthony Newley, *The Silent Partner*, *1941*, *Lost and Found*, *The Blues Brothers*, *Heavy Metal* (voice only), *Stripes*, *It Came from Hollywood*, *National Lampoon's Vacation* and *Strange Brew*. He nailed down his first lead in *Going Beserk*, a failure (which did not reach Britain), and then played Tom Hanks' fast-living brother in *Splash*. The success of this film secured Candy a starring role opposite Richard

John Candy.

Pryor in *Brewster's Millions* and another lead in *Volunteers*, with Tom Hanks. The upcoming *Summer Rental*, a comedy from Carl Reiner, is his most prestigious vehicle to date, and ensures a big career ahead for this talented Canadian. He is next due to co-star with Steve Martin in the western spoof *The Three Amigos*. Candy has also won two Emmy awards for his writing on SCTV.

Glenn Close.

Glenn Close has managed to lasso an Oscar nomination for Best Supporting Actress three years running (for *The World According to Garp*, *The Big Chill* and *The Natural*), but this year becomes a star in her own right. A fine actress, with a facial resemblance to Meryl Streep, Ms Close is fast becoming Hollywood's strongest new female star. She has three films awaiting release in the UK, *The Stone Boy*, *Maxie* and *Jagged Edge*, and is tipped

for the leading role in the film version of Tom Stoppard's highly acclaimed play *The Real Thing*.

Charles Dance is the sort of clean-cut British leading man who would make an ideal successor to Roger Moore as James Bond. In fact, Dance made his film debut in 007's *For Your Eyes Only* – before winning acclaim as Guy Perron in TV's sweeping success story *The Jewel in the Crown*. Since then, Dance has starred in two productions for television, *The Secret Servant* and *Rainy Day Women*, and won the male lead in the film version of David Hare's hit play *Plenty*. Playing a stuffy, straight-laced civil servant, he is well supported in the last-named by Meryl Streep, John Gielgud and Sting.

Charles Dance.

Emilio Estevez. When Ramon Estevez, alias Martin Sheen, was hailed the 'James Dean of the 'seventies', he could have little suspected that his own son would be christened the 'James Dean of the 'eighties'. But so it was. The 23-year-old Emilio made his film debut in Walt Disney's *Tex*, and went on to win much acclaim in Francis Coppola's *The Outsiders*. Since then he has starred in the cult *Repo Man* and the very successful *The Breakfast Club*. His next two movies, *St Elmo's Fire* and *That Was Then, This Is Now* (which he optioned from the S.E. Hinton novel), should cement his fame. For the record, Emilio also had a role in the omnibus film *Nightmares* and appeared in the TV movies *In the Custody of Strangers*, starring his father, and *Seventeen Going Nowhere*.

Emilio Estevez.

Lucy Gutteridge is an appealing, soulful-eyed English actress whose talent had been monopolized by television (*Love in a Cold Climate, Tales of the Unexpected, Nicholas Nickleby*, etc) until she was chosen for the female lead in *Top Secret!* In fact, she had made her film debut six years earlier in *The Greek Tycoon* (a walk-on) and in two London International Film School productions,

Lucy Gutteridge.

Mr Thames and *Bride of Christ*. When she won a Golden Globe nomination for Best Actress in TV's *Little Gloria . . . Happy at Last*, her career took off on an international scale, and she has since been seen in the films *Merlin and the Sword, A Christmas Carol, Hitler's SS: Portrait of Evil* and *The Trouble with Spies*. She will next star in *Fire in Eden*, with Andrew Stevens.

Kelly le Brock in *The Woman in Red* made the sort of debut that publicists dream of. It was her first film, and her first appearance in that film is how myths are created. In a flimsy red dress and high-heels the actress strutted on to the screen and over an underground air vent. Her skirt blew up over her waist and her leading man – Gene Wilder – fell in love. She *was* gorgeous. And she

Kelly le Brock.

was swooped upon by the media. Born in New York, Kelly came to London at the age of three and stayed until she was 18. She then went back to New York to model, and met her future husband Victor Drai, producer of *The Woman in Red*. She will next be seen in John Hughes' *Weird Science*, and she tells me she would like to concentrate on comedy.

John Malkovich.

John Malkovich for my money was the best new actor to emerge in 1985. Not only did he have good parts in two of the year's biggest successes, but he displayed a rare versatility in both roles. In *The Killing Fields* he was the extrovert, hard-drinking, dope-smoking photographer Al Rockoff, and in *Places in the Heart* he was the simple, proud, blind Mr Will. For the latter role he chalked up an Oscar nomination. He will next be seen as the male lead in Peter Yates' *Eleni* – with Kate Nelligan in the title role.

Kelly McGillis won a role in *Reuben, Reuben* straight out of Juilliard drama school. Tom Conti received an Oscar nomination for his role in this film, and his performance was matched tooth and nail by Miss McGillis. She followed up this role with the female lead in *Witness*, playing an Amish mother in love with a twentieth-century cop (Harrison Ford). The film was a blockbuster hit and secured her another female lead, in the *Chinatown* sequel, *Two Jakes*, with Jack Nicholson. She will also star opposite Tom Cruise in *Top Gun*.

Kelly McGillis.

Joanna Pacula.
Prince.

Joanna Pacula received an 'introducing' credit for *Gorky Park*, although she had already starred in ten Polish films, a Rumanian feature and a six-hour mini-series, *Green Love*. However, *Gorky Park* introduced her to Western audiences and hers was an impressive English-speaking debut. Since then, Joanna has top-billed Lewis Gilbert's *Not Quite Jerusalem* and will next be seen as *The Tigress*, opposite Keith Carradine.

Prince was an overnight sensation in his first film *Purple Rain*. Cutting a striking figure in a shiny purple suit astride an outsized motorbike, the rock singer captured the hearts of teenage girls the world over and took to celluloid like a duck to water. The megahit singles *When Doves Cry* and *Purple Rain* also ensured that his film was a box office smash.

Promises, Promises . . .

Six editions ago of *Film Review* I inaugurated a chapter on the year's most promising newcomers. I felt it only fair that if there was to be an *in memoriam* section there should also be a 'births column'. And as the preceding pages show this chapter is still going strong.

But for the time being I thought it would be interesting to look back at what had happened to my first, original top-ten newcomers – of 1980. I should however, point out that it is by no means easy to choose these names, as one virtually has to *guess* who will be important over the coming year.

My first tip for stardom in 1981 was Bo Derek, who has proved to be as true as my word. Her production of *Tarzan the Ape Man* (she produced, her husband John Derek directed) was an awesome box-office smash and ensured the stunner a permanent place in the media front line. However, not many people turned up to witness her following opus, *Bolero*, which none the less generated enough publicity to set Bo's legend in concrete. She is now working on a sexed-up version of the Adam and Eve story.

Paul Dooley fared less well, and failed to fulfil the promise he exhibited in *A Perfect Couple* and *Rich Kids*, when I likened him to Walter Matthau. None the less, he has turned in some sterling supporting performances. His most recent films include *Health, Paternity, Endangered Species, Kiss Me Goodbye, Strange Brew, Going Berserk* and *Big Trouble*. The man is at least keeping busy.

After the double glory in 1980 of *Yanks* and *The Europeans*, Lisa Eichhorn met with a series of career disasters. She was signed up for the female lead opposite Gene Hackman in *All Night Long*, but due to 'personality' differences – so the story goes – was excused from her contract (desperate for a leading lady at the eleventh hour, the film's director, John-Claude Tramont, called on an old friend to fill the part – Barbra Streisand). Next, Ms Eichhorn was signed up for a role in *Enigma*, opposite Martin Sheen, but this time Nature intervened: she had to renege on her contract when she discovered she was pregnant. She has, however, done some films: a television movie, *The Wall*, with Tom Conti; *Wildrose*; and two productions for the BBC, *The Weather in the Streets* and *East Lynne*. She will next be seen in *Clay Pigeons*, with Tom Skerritt.

Frederic Forrest was no luckier. After his remarkable performance as 'Chef' in Francis Coppola's *Apocalypse Now*, he was signed up by Coppola to star in two big-budget films, *Hammet* and *One from the Heart*. Both were mammoth turkeys, cost millions to get off the ground and were years in production. Between them, they hardly pulled in $2 million (*One from the Heart* alone cost $21 million). Since then Forrest has appeared briefly in *Valley Girl*, starred opposite Ann-Margret in *Who Will Love My Children?* and was much liked in *The Stone Boy*, even though the film was little seen.

After her Oscar-nominated role as Woody Allen's 17-year-old love interest in *Manhattan*, Mariel Hemingway has gone from strength to strength. Her films have been few, but she has chosen them carefully. In *Personal Best* she was top-billed as a lesbian pentathlete and won excellent reviews, though nothing like as glowing as those for *Star 80*. In the latter film she played the doomed *Playboy* centrefold, glamour girl and

actress Dorothy Stratten. Inexplicably, her performance failed to secure even a nomination for an Oscar. Since then, Mariel has appeared in two more movies, *Creator*, with Peter O'Toole, and *The Mean Season*, with Kurt Russell.

The Rose and *Divine Madness* established Bette Midler as a celluloid superstar, but her next film, *Jinxed*, alarmingly lived up to its title. There were squabbles on the set with the director Don Siegel and leading man Ken Wahl, and it showed on the screen. The film remains unreleased in the UK. Bette will next be seen in *Down and Out in Beverly Hills* with Nick Nolte and Richard Dreyfuss.

Ricky Schroder had one more success following his triumphant debut in *The Champ*, as the generous, warmhearted *Little Lord Fauntleroy*. Previously filmed with Mary Pickford(!) in the title role, the picture featured Ricky at his adorable best and Alec Guinness likewise at the top of his form as the little earl's cantankerous uncle. Afterwards, Ricky was honoured with his own TV show in the States, but plans to star in a remake of *Peter Pan* (with Guinness as Captain Hook) fell through.

After *The Deer Hunter*, John Savage starred in a number of important features, including *Hair, The Onion Field* and *Inside Moves*. Lately, though, the quality of his films (*The Long Ride, The Amateur, Coming Out of the Ice, Maria's Lovers*) has somewhat diminished, but it is an indication of his star power that he can still command billing over the likes of Willie Nelson, Robert Mitchum and Rod Steiger.

Like Mariel Hemingway, Sigourney Weaver has proved extraordinarily selective in her choice of roles. After her success in *Alien* there was an inordinate gap before the actress accepted another film. Then she landed the female lead in Peter Yates' superior thriller *Eyewitness* (*The Janitor* in America). Next, she starred opposite Mel Gibson in Peter Weir's lauded *The Year of Living Dangerously*, and did a successful comedy with Chevy Chase, *Deal of the Century*. But none of these

augured the triumph of her next picture, the mega-grossing *Ghostbusters*. As the possessed Dana Barrett on the run from Bill Murray and a cityful of ghosts, she displayed an engaging comedy skill and a seductive tomb-side manner. She will next be seen in *Half Moon Street*, set in London.

Robin Williams started his film career with a disaster and emerged as one of the cinema's most interesting new superstars. Robert Altman's *Popeye* was a truly awful film, but Williams was remarkable as the mumblin', stumblin' cartoon sailor. His next film was no less odd, but a lot more serious and a good deal funnier besides. Based on John Irving's best-selling novel, *The World According to Garp* was a delightfully eccentric and well-made dramatic comedy. After this, Williams made a dud, *The Survivors* (unreleased in the UK), with Walter Matthau, and then starred in a very engaging, very funny social comedy, *Moscow on the Hudson*. The actor played a Russian saxophonist who defects while shopping at Bloomingdale's in New York, and delivered his most versatile, sensitive performance to date. He will next be seen in the small-town football drama *The Best of Times* with Kurt Russell, and in Ivan Reitman's Caribbean farce, *Club Paradise*, with Peter O'Toole.

So, Bo Derek, Mariel Hemingway, Bette Midler, Sigourney Weaver and Robin Williams have all emerged as very big names indeed, while the careers of Paul Dooley, Lisa Eichhorn and Frederic Forrest have met with some turbulence. That leaves Ricky Schroder and John Savage, who are still in demand but are lacking that 'special' film which could launch them into the celluloid stratosphere. For the record, my runners-up in 1980 have also done pretty well for themselves and, in some cases, considerably better than the showcased personalities. They include: Beverly D'Angelo, Irene Cara, Tom Hulce, Diane Lane, Kristy McNichol, Bill Murray, Dennis Quaid, Mary Steenburgen, Christopher Walken and Treat Williams.

Roll on 1986.

The Continental Film

Voted the best foreign film of the year by the Film Section of the British Critics' Circle, and deservedly highly lauded elsewhere, *Sunday in the Country – Un Dimanche à la Campagne*, released by Artificial Eye, was another artistic success for Bertrand Tavernier, adding to his already impressive succession of outstanding productions since his initial impact with the marvellous *Clockmaker of St. Paul* in 1974. Undramatic, but a constant joy to watch, *Sunday in the Country*, an adaptation of a novel by Pierre Bost, was a quiet and delicate film relating the minor events which took place on a mellow Sunday afternoon at the country home of an octogenarian artist (played by Louis Ducreux – seen here dancing with his visiting actress daughter from Paris, Sabine Azema). A film to savour, treasure and recall with gratitude for its overall superb craftsmanship.

Jane Birkin, one of the two young actresses (the other was played by Charlie Chaplin's daughter Geraldine) who accept an invitation from a somewhat pompous playwright to spend a weekend at his country château, during which time they appear in the first production of his latest play. But the girls find it all rather different from what they had anticipated. In this Cannon/Gala importation of Jacques Rivette's *Love on the Ground – L'Amour par Terre* the writer/ director explored again the territory of the contrast between Life and Theatre which he has previously used more than once in the past, notably in the far superior *Céline et Julie Vont en Bateau*. Sharing this scene with Miss Birkin is Laszlo Czabo, who injected a vein of delightfully dry humour into the movie.

Without a single spoken word but with great visual charm and considerable imagination, Ettore Scola in his Columbia/Warner/EMI release of the French/Italian/Algerian co-production *The Ball – Le Bal* reproduced on the screen the big Paris stage success of the title originally produced by the Théâtre du Campagnol. Set against the background of a typical, ageless Parisian dance hall the film reflected some of the main French historical events that occurred between 1936 and 1983. Even by the time it opened in Britain the film had already earned a number of national and international honours.

Sadly, Eric Rohmer's latest addition to his *Comèdies et Proverbes* series of movies, *Full Moon in Paris – Les Nuits de la Pleine Lune* (an Artificial Eye release), was not only notable for its writer/director's usual literacy and general artistic polish but also for the fact that it marked the final screen performance of Pascale Ogier (the 24-year-old daughter of screen star Bulle Ogier), who died from a heart attack just a few days before the film's British premiere. An occasional screenwriter, the versatile Miss Ogier (shown here with Fabrice Luchini, playing her friend and would-be lover) doubled as star and art director for Rohmer's film.

Looking tantalizingly lovely and wholly feminine, Isabelle Adjani played – quite magnificently – a girl who dedicates her life to carrying out a lethal vengeance on the three men who brutally raped her mother (one of whom – which? – must be her father) but, when eventually learning the truth about what happened, is shocked into inertia while her loving husband guns down two quite innocent men. In Jean Becker's highly dramatic movie *One Deadly Summer – L'Été Meurtrier* (released by Cannon Films) Alain Souchon, right, played the husband.

A scene from one of the weirdest and certainly most surrealistic movies to be shown recently, BFI's *Three Crowns of the Sailor – Les Trois Coronnes du Matelot*, which told an extraordinary tale about a tar who comes upon a student horribly murdering his tutor. He subsequently regales the young man with stories of his convoluted and magical adventures in the ports and brothels of South America, at the end of which the student kills him, too, only for the *matelot* to immediately come back to life to carry on a new existence!

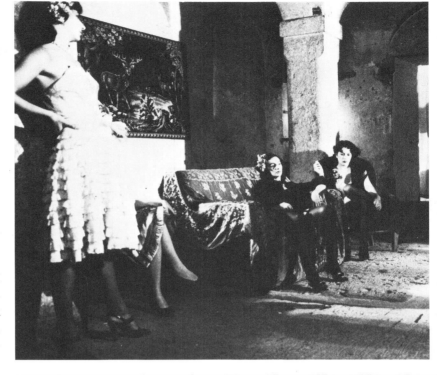

A scene from ICA's *The Last Battle – Le Dernier Combat*, which marked the screen debut of young scenarist-director Luc Bresson, who with style and imagination told a strange story set in some future time, after some unexplained catastrophe, when in a ravaged and ruined city (Paris, maybe?) a source of pure water is the ultimate base of power. A blend of wry humour, violence and science fiction, it was all whipped across at a commendably fast pace.

Fanny Ardant and Vittorio Gassmann in Flemish-born André Delvaux's French-Belgian co-production *Benvenuta* (An Artificial Eye import) which related a complicated and certainly never easy-to-follow story (typical of the film's ambiguity, one scene showed an authoress and her fictional heroine appearing at the same time in the same street) about a scriptwriter trying to ascertain how closely this authoress of a once scandalous novel, which he intends to make into a movie, is related to her heroine.

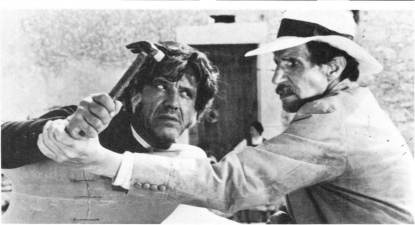

Scenes from four of the five segments which went to make up the Taviani Brothers' (co-writers and directors Paolo and Vittorio) outstandingly brilliant Cannon/Gala release *Chaos – Kaos*. 1. The resourceful and obstinate villagers in *Requiem*, who fight against the local landowning Baron for the right to take over some land in order to create a new and more convenient cemetery. 2. Maria Modugno as the bride in *Moon Sickness – Mal di Luna*, who quickly discovers that her husband goes dangerously off his head at the advent of each full moon and turns to a handsome young villager (Massimo Bonetti) for her comfort and defence – and, almost, more! 3. Omero Antonutti as author Luigi Pirandello (whose writings provide the material for all the episodes), who returns to his recently deceased mother's (Regina Bianchi) house in *Conversing with Mother – Colloquio con la Madre* and talks to her spirit about the past and, in particular, some of the events in it which he has long attempted – but so far always failed – to put into a story. 4. Franco Franchi as the 'best jar-repairer in all Sicily', who in *The Jar – La Giara* amusingly teaches the local feudal landowner and giant jar-collector Ciccio Ingrassia a lesson in guile. These various and highly diverse short films added up to a magnificently entertaining cinematic whole.

Claimed to be Brazil's most popular actress, Sonia Braga played opposite Italy's star Marcello Mastroianni in the South American-made UIP release *Gabriela*, in which she played the role of a fascinating young siren who enthrals bar-owner Mastroianni so completely that although he divorces her at one point for infidelity, he eventually welcomes her back under his roof . . . and into his bed.

Herbert Grönemeyer as the composer Robert Schumann and Nastassja Kinski as Clara Wieck in Blue Dolphin's West German production *Spring Symphony – Frühlingssinfonie*, a pleasant biographical musical relating the details of the great love affair between the two which began with the joyous triumph of Felix Mendelssohn's conducting the first performance of Schumann's last symphony and ended sadly with the composer's death in an insane asylum at the early age of 46.

Gudrun Landgrebe in the title role (shown with Mathieu Carrière) in Cannon's West German import *A Woman in Flames*. She gave a most impressive performance as an apparently normal middle-class housewife who without warning walks out on her husband, home and comfortable bourgeois existence to take up the career of a high-class prostitute, living with a male prostitute who, when, in turn, she is about to walk out on him, pours a bottle of spirits over her and literally lights her up.

A strange, intriguingly original film from Holland, Paul Verhoeven's *The Fourth Man – De Vierde Man* was about a homosexual writer, Jeroen Krabbé, who while on a lecture tour to augment his slender income is lured into the bed of one of the prettier members of his audience, subsequently discovering that the woman's boyfriend is the young man after whom he has been lusting; finding, too, through nightmares and premonitions, that the woman is, literally, a man killer . . . It all added up to a macabre mix of sex, the occult and bloody, violent death.

Mikhail Ulyanov as the Russian business executive in Contemporary's Soviet importation *Private Life – Chastnaya Zhizn*. Having resigned from his job in his late fifties when a company merger excludes him from the directorship he feels he has earned, he begins after a period of gloomy existence to realize what he has missed during his years as a workaholic, so much so that when urgently requested to return to his business career he is hesitant. Ulyanov is seen here with Iya Savvina, who plays the wife whom he also 'discovers' afresh in this beautifully played movie.

A long, three-part movie based on the general problem of deprived South Americans attempting to sneak across the border into the promised land of the United States and becoming illegal immigrants, *The North – El Norte* was more particularly the story of a Guatemalian brother and sister who after terror and hardship achieve the breakthrough and find a better life in California – until tragedy strikes. In this early scene the sister (Zaide Silvia Gutierrez, left) tries to comfort her mother and her brother (David Villalpando) as he shoulders his father's coffin at the funeral which marks the beginning of the pair's odyssey.

Victor Banerjee and Swatilekha Chatterji as the husband and wife in Satyajit Ray's beautifully crafted *The Home and the World – Ghare-Baire* (released by Artificial Eye). A long and leisurely-paced domestic drama, the film told the story of a human triangle against the larger background of the 1908 riots in India which were sparked off by the then British Governor General, Lord Curzon, with his divisive policies, setting the more liberal-minded local Indian rulers some harsh problems as they tried to care equally for their Moslem and Hindu subjects.

Charles Aznavour and Magali Noel in the French/Jewish farce *What Makes David Run? – Qu'est-ce qui Fait Courir David?*, about a young Jewish film director with a flawed personality who is continually trying to escape reality by running away from it and laughing off every serious situation he meets as he tries to get his next film on the move – which he eventually achieves, something which many might think is a totally undeserved victory.

Completing his trilogy of films that began with *Mon Oncle d'Amérique* and continued with *La Vie est Roman*, Alan Resnais's Cannon/Gala release *Love Unto Death – L'Amour à Mort* was again concerned with the eternal problems of life, love and death as seen from the philosophical and theological viewpoint. It was typical of the director's bleakly intellectual but woefully wilful approach: for instance, the method he adopts here of irritatingly breaking up the flow of action in the story about the love affair of a young Catholic girl (Sabine Azema – seen with her Protestant friends Fanny Ardant and André Dussollier) and an older Jewish archaeologist (Pierre Arditi) with something akin to a series of blackouts.

Another of France's foremost directors, Claude Lelouch, wrote, directed and produced the Cannon/Gala release *Edith and Marcel – Edith et Marcel*, the story of 'Little Paris Sparrow' Edith Piaf – marvellously brought to life by actress Evelyne Bouix (though given Miss Piaf's own inimitable and heart-breaking voice for the songs), who, incidentally, added to her success by also playing a fictional character in the movie and being completely unrecognizable when doing it.

The family – grandmother (superbly played by Marthe Nadeau), husband (Pierre Curzi), mother (Michèle Magny), son (Eric Beauséjour) and daughter (Claudia Aubin) – whose domestic adventures were followed in detailed fashion by writer/director Jean Pierre Lefevre in the Cinegate release of the French-Canadian production *Wild Flowers – Les Fleurs Sauvage*, a pleasant enough movie which meandered mightily however – though never less than interestingly – as it dealt with the difficulties of the uncommunicative if loving relationship between the old man and his more free-thinking daughter.

Filmed on more than 40 occasions with varying degrees of fidelity to the original story of *Dr Jekyll and Mr Hyde*, surely no version would have sent author Robert Louis Stevenson spinning more furiously in his grave than Walerian Borowczyk's New Realm release *Dr Jekyll*. This concentrated on such unpleasant aspects of the struggle between good and evil, which Stevenson suggested goes on in all men, as male and female rape. Typical was Borowczyk's switching the original story's steaming phial which magically alters the pleasant 'Dr' to the foul 'Mr' to a whole bath of viscous fluid in which the changeling convulsively flounders as he changes from one thing to another.

One could understand and sympathize with English husband Frank Finlay's obsession with the physical charms of his Italian wife Stefania Sandrelli, explored with such relish and in such detail by the camera's leering eye in the Enterprise release of *The Key*, which was set in Venice just prior to the start of World War II.

The two main characters, played by Michal Bat-Adam (who also co-wrote the screenplay and directed the film) and Brigitte Catillon, in Cinegate's French/Israeli production *Moments*, made back in 1979 but only reaching Britain in 1984. This was the story of two women who meet on a train bound for Tel-Aviv and quickly develop a passionate relationship, parting at journey's end only to meet again five years later (both women in the interim having married) when they find it difficult to recover the former magic of their friendship.

Happy days in Percy Adlon's *The Swing – Die Schaukel* with Anja Jaenicke, Lena Stolze, Joachim Bernhard and Susanne Herlet romping through the flower-strewn mountain meadows in true *Sound of Music* mood. This delightful Artificial Eye, West German movie was a real family piece, with a plethora of atmosphere as it followed the domestic adventures of a Munich Royal horticulturist professor, his French musician wife and their progeny of three daughters and a son.

One cannot help but wonder what Shakespeare would have made of the Mainline release *A Midsummer Night's Dream – Sueno de Noche de Verano*, an adaptation to the screen of the Lindsay Kemp Company's campy stage production of the Bard's play, concentrating on the visual aspects of the piece and introducing ambiguous sexuality and nude rompings at the cost of the dialogue. Nicely illustrative of the proceedings is this scene with Oberon (Michael Matou) and Puck (Lindsay Kemp in person).

A real celluloid mammoth, Edgar Reitz's *Heimat – Homeland* took well over five years to prepare, shoot and complete and some 15½ hours to run through the projector. Indeed, so long was the finished article that importers Artificial Eye had to break it up into sections, each a feature film in itself, which they showed on consecutive days. Partly autobiographical, partly fictional, the gargantuan motion picture was the story of a German village and the villagers between 1919 and 1982, and implicit within this was the story of Germany during that period of history. A remarkable achievement in every sense and a fascinating experience for any moviegoer with the right amount of stamina. (Shown, Gabriele Blum and Gudrun Landgrebe.)

One of the rare Danish films to reach the British cinemas, Artificial Eye's *Ladies on the Rocks – Koks i Kulissen*, was about two rather jolly and certainly liberated young women and the eyebrow-raising show they conceive and take on the road. Rude enough in its coarse comic sex content to cause one of the women's husbands to use it as grounds for divorce, it appears to please the rural audiences as the duo journey through a wintry landscape on their succession of one-night stands in village halls and the like. Marvellous performances by Helle Ryslinge and Anne Marie Helger outweighed any reservations one might have had about the film's content.

From a Russian director working in France, Georgian Otar Yosseliani's *Favourites of the Moon – Les Favoris de la Lune* (Artificial Eye) was, deservedly, a great critical success because it was a wholly personal, endlessly inventive off-beat comedy which in style and content owed quite a bit to such classical moviemakers as Clair and Tati, though it was finally wholly Yosseliani as it managed to remain superbly logical as it whirled madly along showing us how we all waste time in so many ways. Here the French detective Duphour-Paquet, played by Hans Peter Cloos, wastes some of that time threatening the large and frightened lady.

Few films during the year divided critical opinion more than Francesco Rosi's French/Italian neo-realistic screen version of the familiar Bizet opera *Carmen* (a Virgin release). Written opinion could hardly have differed more, but in the end those writers who found it something like superb screen opera just about made the majority. However, there was not much carping about the actual quality of the singing, including the exciting star Julia Migenes Johnson as Carmen.

The most delightful, winning and wonderfully contrived dragon in cinematic history was one of the main characters in Warner's release of the German production *The Never Ending Story*, which author and director Wolfgang Petersen (with the aid of Herman Weigel) brilliantly adapted to cinema. And you might just recognize our own inimitable Patricia Hayes in the inset scene.

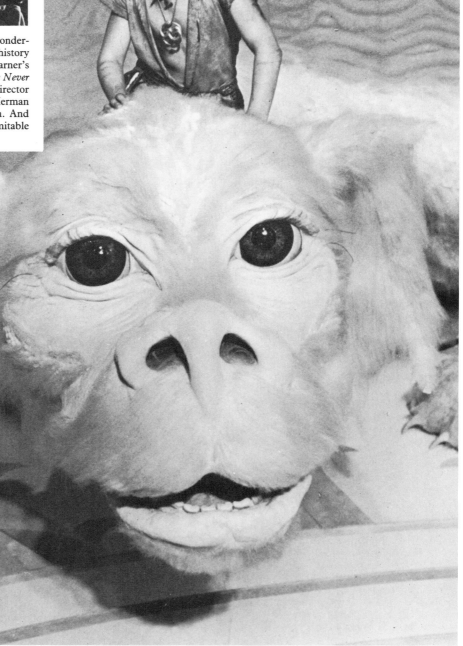

The 'girls' take a bath in Cannon/Gala's Hungarian production *A Very Moral Night*, the story of life in a small-town brothel at the turn of the century where everyone acts with impeccable taste and decorum, even to the extent of the madame closing up shop when the innocent out-of-town mother of one of her favourite clients turns up unexpectedly and is given a slap-up dinner to celebrate the occasion. A very moral night, indeed – and a very charming movie.

Mother Brigitte Fossey and small daughter Camille Raymond enjoy a romp on the sands in Mainline's *The Future of Emily*, a story about a popular film star who dreams of settling down to a life of domesticity while her mother – who looks after the child when she is away filming – secretly and bitterly envies her the life she leads. It was a Franco-German production which relied heavily on the dialogue and almost Ibsenish mood and atmosphere.

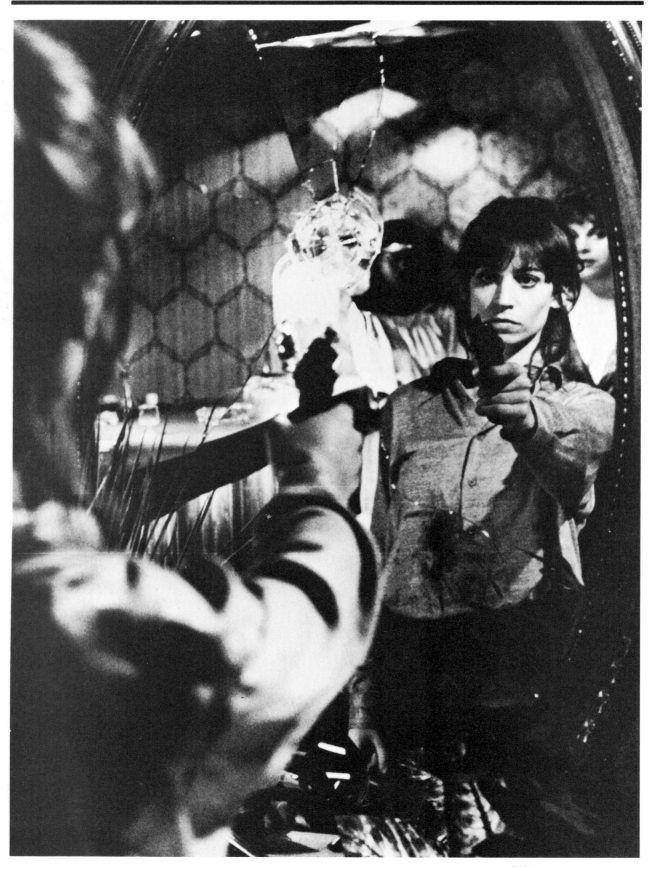

How the mirror came to be broken in Thorn EMI's *Broken Mirrors – Gerbroken Spiegels* (left), a Dutch import about life in an Amsterdam brothel, made with commendable realism and non-exploitation of the subject. Written and directed by Marleen Gorris, it was a worthy winner of the Best Dutch Film award of 1982.

A new comedy star, to British audiences, anyway, Coluche played with immense success one of the two long-established and close pals who are almost split apart permanently when a pretty little tart arrives on the scene – a winter ski resort in the French alps where both men work – in the Gala-Cannon release *My Best Friend's Girl*. And as the girl who does not mind in which of the two beds she sleeps, there was a surprisingly and delightfully out-of-character performance by Isabelle Huppert. The loose moral tone of this essentially French comedy-farce did nothing to quell its consistent chuckly progress.

Winner of two prestigious 1985 French Academy ('César') Awards – for Best Actor (Delon) and Best Original Screenplay (Blier), Bertrand Blier's Artificial Eye release *Our Story – Notre Histoire* (*Separate Rooms* in America) failed to gain an official place at the Cannes Film Festival, to the apparent annoyance of star/producer Alain Delon. But hovering as it does between dream and reality, always confusingly ambiguous, this story of a love affair between a nymphomaniac (Nathalie Baye) and the beer-soaked, depressed dreamer (Alain Delon), though stylishly presented and well acted, hardly seems worthy of major overall honours, even if likely because of its originality to gain them at other festivals around Europe.

Awards and Festivals

The Louis Deluc Prize, Paris, December 1984

This award went to Richard Dembo's chess world drama *La Diagonale du Fou – Fool's Gambit*, which was also awarded the French National Cinema Academy's 1984 Grand Prix.

The British Academy of Film and Television Arts Awards for 1984

Best Film: *The Killing Fields*, directed by Roland Joffé [the film also won the Best Screenplay Adaptation (Bruce Robinson), Best Cinematography (Chris Menges), Best Production Design (Roy Walker), Best Editing (Jim Clark) and Best Sound (Ian Fuller, Clive Winter and Bill Rowe) awards.]

Best Actress: Maggie Smith, in *A Private Function*.

Best Actor: Dr Haing S. Ngor, in *The Killing Fields* (he also won the Best Newcomer award).

Best Supporting Actress: Liz Smith, in *A Private Function*.

Best Supporting Actor: Denholm Elliott, in *A Private Function*.

Best Original Screenplay: Woody Allen, for his *Broadway Danny Rose*.

Best Foreign Language Film: *Carmen*, by Carlos Sauro.

Best Direction: Wim Wenders, for *Paris, Texas*.

French Academy César Awards, announced 5 March 1985

Best French Film: *Les Repoux*, by Claude Zidi (Zidi also received the Best Director award).

Best Foreign Film: Milos Forman's *Amadeus*.

Best Actor: Alain Delon, in *Notre Histoire*.

Best Actress: Sabine Azema, in *Un Dimanche à la Campagne*.

Best Supporting Actor: Richard Bohringer, in *L'Addition*.

Best Supporting Actress: Caroline Cellier, in *L'Année des Méduses*.

Best First Feature: *La Diagonale du Fou*, by Richard Dembo.

Best Original Screenplay: *Notre Histoire*, by Bertrand Blier.

Special 'Career' Césars to directors Christian-Jacques and Frank Capra, producers Alain Poiré and Christine Gouze-Renal and actress Danielle Darrieux.

The American Academy of Motion Picture Arts and Sciences Awards 1985, announced 25 March 1985

Best Film: *Amadeus*.

Best Direction: Milos Forman, for *Amadeus*.

Best Actor: F. Murray Abraham, in *Amadeus*.

Best Actress: Sally Field, in *Places in the Heart*.

Best Supporting Actor: Dr Haing S. Ngor, in *The Killing Fields*.

Best Supporting Actress: Dame Peggy Ashcroft, in *A Passage to India*.

Best Original Screenplay: Robert Benton, for *Places in the Heart*.

Best Screenplay Adaptation: Peter Shaffer, for *Amadeus*.

Best Cinematography: Chris Menges, for *The Killing Fields*.

Best Editing: Jim Clark, for *The Killing Fields*.

Best Foreign Language Film: *Dangerous Moves – La Diagonale du Fou*, an Arthur Cohn Swiss production.

Best Original Score: Maurice Jarre, for *A Passage to India*.

Best Art Direction: Karel Cerny, for *Amadeus*.

Best Shorts: Animated, *Charade* produced by Jon Minnis; Live Action, *Up* produced by Mike Hoover.

Best Documentaries: Feature, Robert Epstein and Richard Schmiechen's *The Times of Harvey Milk*; Short, Marjorie Hunt and Paul Wagner's *The Stone Carvers*.

The Jean Hersholt Humanitarian Award to David L. Wolper.

Honorary Award to James Stewart for 50 years of meaningful performances, high ideals, on and off the screen, with the respect and affection of his colleagues.

The Italian David Di Donatello Awards presented in Rome, June 1984

Best Film (shared): *And the Ship Sails On* by Federico Fellini and Ettore Scola's *Le Bal*.

Best Actor: Giancarlo Giannini, in *Picone*.

Best Actress: Lina Sastri, in *Picone*.

Best Supporting Actor: Carlo Giuffre, in *I Am Happy*.

Best Supporting Actress: Elena Fabrizi, in *Soap and Water*.

Best Director: Ettore Scola, for *Le Bal*.

Best Screenplay: Fellini and Tonino Guerra for their script for *And the Ship Sails On*.

Best Foreign Film (film, direction and screenplay): *Fanny and Alexander*, by Ingmar Bergman.

The Berlin Film Festival Awards, February 1985

Golden Bear First Prize: shared between *Wetherby* directed by David Hare (Great Britain) and *The Woman and the Stranger* directed by Rainer Simon (East Germany).

Silver Bear – Special Jury Prize: *Flowers of Reverie* by Laszlo Lugossy (Hungary).

Best Director: Robert Benton for *Places in the Heart* (USA).

Best Actor: Fernando Fernan Gomez, in Jaime de Arminian's *Stico* (Spain).

Best Actress: Jo Kennedy in Ian Pringle's *Wrong World* (Australia).

The 'Year's Outstanding Achievement' prize to Tolomush Okeyev for his art direction in *The Descendant of the Snow Leopard* (USSR).

'Outstanding Imagination' award to Tage Danielsson for his *Ronya, The Robber's Daughter* (Sweden/Norway).

International Critics' Prize: *The Tokyo Trial* (Japan); also honoured *Secret Honour* (USA) and *The Man Marked for Death* (Brazil).

Shorts prizes – Golden Bear: *From the Reports of Security Guards* by Helke Sander (West Germany). Silver Bear: *Paradise* by Ishu Patel (Canada).

The British Critics' Circle Awards, November 1984

Best Film: *Paris, Texas* Wim Wenders (USA).

Best Direction: Neil Jordan, for *The Company of Wolves* (Great Britain).

Best Screenplay: Philip Kaufman, for *The Right Stuff*.

Best Actor: (shared) Harry Dean Stanton, in *Paris, Texas*, and Albert Finney, in *Under the Volcano*.

Best Foreign Language Film: Bertrand Tavernier's *A Sunday in the Country* (France).

The Chicago Festival Awards, November 1984

Golden Hugo for best film: Mrinal Sen's *The Ruins* (India).

Silver Hugo: (shared) Lars Von Trier, for *The Element of Crime* (Denmark) and Anja Breien, for *Paper Bird* (Norway).

Bronze Hugo: Marta Meszaros, for *Diary for My Children* (Hungary).

Best First Feature: Monto Armendariz, for *Tasio* (Spain).

Best Actor: shared between Frank Ramirez in *A Man of Principle* (Colombia) and Michael Gwisdek in *No Time for Tears* (West Germany).

Best Actress: Louise Marleau, in *La Femme de L'Hotel* (Canada).

Special Jury Prize to George Stevens Jr's *George Stevens: A Filmmaker's Journey* (USA).

The London *Standard* Film Awards for 1984

Best Film: *1984*.

Best Actor: John Hurt for *Champions*, *The Hit* and *1984*.

Best Actress: Helen Mirren, for *Cal*.

The Peter Sellers Award for Comedy: Denholm Elliott, for *Trading Places*.

Best Screenplay: Bernard MacLaverty, for *Cal*.

Most Promising Newcomer: Tim Roth, for *The Hit*.

Best Technical Achievement: John Alcott, for *Greystoke*.

The Nyon Swiss Documentary Festival Awards, October 1984

Golden Sesterce: *The Times of Harvey Milk* (USA)

Silver Sesterces: *Truden Izbor – Difficult Choice* (Bulgaria), *En Cherchant Emile – Looking for Emile* (France) and *Les Tribulations de Saint Antoine* (Belgium).

Special Jury Prize: *2084: Video Clip Pour Reflexion Syndicale et Pour le Plaisir* (France).

The Australian Film Institute Awards, Melbourne, October 1984

Best Film: *Annie's Coming Out*, by Gil Brealey.

Best Direction: Paul Cox, for *My First Wife*.

Best Actor: John Hargreaves, in *My First Wife*.

Best Actress: Angela Punch McGregor, in *Annie's Coming Out*.

Best Supporting Players: Steve Bisley and Anna Jemison, in *Silver City*.

Best Original Screenplay: Paul Cox and Bob Ellis, for *My First Wife*.

The Venice Film Festival Awards, September 1984

Golden Lion for Best Film: *The Year of the Peaceful Sun – Rok Spokjnego Slon'ca*, directed by Krzysztof Zanussi (Poland/West Germany/USA).

Special Jury Prize: *Favourites of the Moon – Les Favoris de la Lune*, directed by Otar Ioseliani (France).

Best Female Performance: Pascale Ogier, in *Les Nuits de la Pleine Lune*, directed by Eric Rohmer (France).

Best Male Performance: Naseeruddin Shah in *The Crossing – Paar*, directed by Goutam Ghost (India).

Silver Lion Award for Best First Film: Micheline Lanctot, for *Sonatine* (Canada).

Special Award for Technical Merit: Pupi Avati, for *We Three – Noi Tre* (Italy).

The Montreal, Canadian Film Festival, August 1984

Grand Prix des Amériques: *El Norte*, directed by Gregory Nava (USA).

Best Actor: John Shea, in *Windy City* (USA).

Best Actress: Dorottya Udvarof, in *Oh, Bloody Life* (Hungary).

Special Jury Prizes: *La Femme Publique*, by Andrzej Zulawski (France) and *Khandar*, by Mrinal Sen (India).

Special Jury Award to Katharine Hepburn for her work in *The Ultimate Solution of Grace Quigley* and for her exceptional achievement in Cinema.

Jury Award for Best Screenplay: Dusan Kovacevic, for his *The Balkan Spy* (Yugoslavia).

The Locarno, International Film Festival, August 1984

Golden Leopard: *Stranger Than Paradise*, directed by Jim Jarmusch (USA).

Silver Leopard: *Le Rio de Chine – The King of China*, directed by Fabrice Cazeneuve (France).

Bronze Leopard: *Donauwalzer*, directed by Xavier Schwarzenberger (Austria).

Bronze Leopards (The Ernesto Artaria Prize): (shared) *Nunca Fomos Tao Felices – Never Were We So Happy*, by Murillo Salles (Brazil) and *Oeszy Almanach – Autumn Almanac*, by Bela Tarr (Hungary).

The Avoriaz Fantasy Film Festival Awards, France, January 1985

Best Film: James Cameron's *The Terminator* (USA).

Special Jury Prize: (shared) Neil Jordan's *The Company of Wolves* (Great Britain) and James Dearden's *The Cold Room* (Great Britain).

Best Acting Performance: Heather Langenkamp, in Wes Craven's *A Nightmare on Elm Street* (USA).

Critics' Prize: *A Nightmare on Elm Street* (USA).

The Karlovy Vary Festival Awards, July 1984

Grand Prize: *Leo Tolstoy*, by Sergei Gerasimov (USSR).

Main Prize: (shared) *Strikebound*, by Richard Lowenstein (Australia), *Strange Love*, by Lothar Warneke (East Germany) and *Runners*, by Charles Sturridge (Great Britain).

Special Prize: (shared) *The Doom of the Lonely Farm Berghof*, by Jiri Svoboda (Czechoslovakia) and *El Milusos*, by Roberto G. Rivera (Mexico).

Special Jury Prize: Sidney Lumet, for *Daniel* (USA).

Best Actress: (shared) Susu Pecoraro in *Camilla* (Argentina) and Marie Colbin in *The Bachmeier Case* (West Germany).

Best Actor: (shared) Augustin Gonzales in *Bicycles Are for Summer* (Spain) and Om Puri, for *Half Truth* (India).

The Zagreb International Animated Film Festival Winners, presented in Zagreb, June 1984.

Grand Prix for Best Feature Film: Osamu Tezuka's *Jumping* (Japan).

Best Shorts: less than 5 minutes, Pierre Veilleux's *Mushrooms* (Canada); 5–12 minutes, Aleksandre Tararski's *The Dark Side of the Moon* (USSR); 12–30 minutes, Stanislav Sokolov's *Black and White Movie* (USSR).

Best Educational Film: Csaba Varga's *Augusta Makes Herself Beautiful* (Hungary).

Best Children's Film: Eduard Nazarov's *The Adventures of an Ant* (USSR).

Best First Film: Zvonko Coh's *Kiss Me, Soft Rubber* (Yugoslavia).

Special Awards to: David Anderson for *Dreamland Express* (Great Britain) and *Snipe-Clam Grapple* (China).

The Paris International Science-Fiction Festival, December 1984

Golden Unicorn – First Prize: *Death Warmed Up*, directed David Blyth (New Zealand).

Special Jury Prize: *Warriors from the Wind* (Japan).

Best Actor: Peter Weller, for *Of Unknown Origin* (Canada) and *Buckaroo Banzai* (USA).

Best Actress: Frances McDormand, for *Blood Simple* (USA); the film which won the Critics' Award.

The Cannes Film Festival Awards, May 1985

Golden Palm for Best Film: *Father's on a Business Trip*, directed by Emir Kusturica (Yugoslavia).

Special Grand Jury Prize: *Birdy*, directed by Alan Parker (USA), 'for originality and spirit of research'.

Jury Prize: *Colonel Redl*, directed by Istvan Szabo (Hungary–West Germany–Austria).

Best Director: André Techine, for *Rendezvous* (France).

Best Actor: William Hurt in *Kiss of the Spider Woman* (Brazil/USA).

Best Actress: shared between Norma Aleandro in *Official Version* (Argentina) and Cher in *Mask* (USA).

Best Short Film: *Marriage – Jenitba*, directed by Slav Bakalov and Rouman Petkov (Bulgaria).

Best Artistic Contribution: *Mishima*; for John Bailey's cinematography, Eiko Ishioka's production design and Philip Glass's musical score.

Special Award for 'Career Achievement': James Stewart.

The International Festival of Comedy Films, Vevey, Switzerland, August 1984

Golden Vevey Cane for Best Comedy Feature: *Der Sprinter*, directed by Christoph Boell.

Golden Vevey Cane for Best Male Comedy Performance: Tom Conti, in *Reuben, Reuben* (USA).

Special Jury Prize: *Teddy Bear Prends L'Oscar Et Tais-Toi*, by Rolf Lyssy.

The Canadian Animation Festival, Toronto, August 1984

Grand Prix: *Chips*, by Jerzy Kucia (Poland).

Best Short longer than 5 mins: *Spotting a Cow*, by Paul Driessen (Holland).

Best Short shorter than 5 mins: *Gravity*, by Ferenc Rofusz (Hungary).

Best First Film: *Charade*, by Jon Minnis (Canada).

Best Children's Film: *Doctor de Soto* by Michael Sporn (USA).

The Taormina Festival Awards, July 1984

Gold Charybdis: *The Princes*, by Tony Gatlif (France).

Silver Charybdis: *Mountain on the Other Side of the Moon*, by Lenart Hjulstrom (Sweden).

Bronze Charybdis: *Constance*, by Bruce Morrison (New Zealand).

Special Mention to *The Almeria Affair*, by Pedro Costa Muste (Spain).

Golden Polyphemus for best acting: Gunilla Nyross and Thommy Berggren in *The Mountain on the Other Side of the Moon*.

Silver Polyphemus: Ida Di Benedetto, in *Der Schlaf der Vernunft* (West Germany).

Bronze Polyphemus: Tara MacGowran, in *Secret Places* (Great Britain).

Sitges Film Festival, Sitges, Spain, October 1984

Best Film: *The Company of Wolves* (Great Britain).

Best Director: Carl Schenkel, for *Out of Order – Abwärts* (Germany).

Best Actor: Joe Morton, for *The Brother from Another Planet* (USA).

Best Actress: Amy Madigan for *Streets of Fire* (USA).

Best Screenplay: John Sayles, for *The Brother from Another Planet* (USA).

Valencia Film Festival, Valencia, Spain, October 1984

Golden Palm for Best film: Mohammed Malass's *Dreams of the City – Les Rêves de la Ville* (Syria).

Silver Palm: Petro Almodovar's *What Have I Done to Deserve This? – ¿Que he hecho yo para merecer esto?* (Spain).*

Bronze Palm: Rajko Grlic's *In the Clutches of Life – U Raijma Zivota* (Yugoslavia).

*This film also won the International Critics' Award.

A Survey of the Australian Year

JAMES CAMERON-WILSON

The cinema Down Under was down but not out. As reported in this annual a year ago, Australian celluloid is smarting at the pocket. In 1983 its box-office successes, besides *Phar Lap*, were unexceptional, the highest earners – *We of the Never Never*, *The Year of Living Dangerously*, *Careful, He Might Hear You* and *Hostage* – barely pulling in two million Australian dollars between them. In 1984 the news was worse. There was not a single indigenous hit: at least, not one Australian

Tom Burlinson in *Phar Lap*.

film accrued more than 500,000 dollars gross. And when you think that *The Man from Snowy River* knocked up over eight *million* – in 1982 – you can appreciate the problem. The big earners last year were a predictable crop from America, namely *Indiana Jones*, *Police Academy*, *Terms of Endearment* and *Ghostbusters*.

The enormous talent kicked up by earlier Australian successes continued to pour overseas. Peter Weir, the Steven Spielberg of Down Under, followed in the footsteps of Gillian Armstrong, Bruce Beresford and Fred Schepisi, and finally left for America. Undoubtedly the Antipodes' favourite movie brat, Weir was responsible for some of the country's biggest triumphs, namely *Gallipoli*, *Picnic at Hanging Rock*, *The Year of Living Dangerously*, *The Last Wave* and *The Cars That Ate Paris*. His debut American film, *Witness*, explored his pet theme of the clash of opposing cultures – in this case an Amish community adhering to a seventeenth-century lifestyle *vis-à-vis* the violence of contemporary America. As is characteristic with Weir the film was breathtaking to look at (Pennsylvanian wheatfields caught in an autumnal glow) and was photographed by the Australian John Seale. In addition to being an artistic triumph, *Witness* was an affecting character study, an effective thriller and, at the time of writing, was the biggest money-making picture in America of 1985.

Another defector was Simon Wincer, who fled to America in the wake of his top-grossing horse operetta, *Phar Lap*. Previously known for *Snapshot* and *Harlequin*, the director hit the big time when he made *Phar Lap* and served as executive producer on *The Man from Snowy River*. Wincer's first non-Australian film is called *D.A.R.Y.L.* and has been described as a contemporary action adventure about a very special little boy. On paper it looks like a cross between *Kramer vs Kramer*, *The Sugarland Express* and *Starman*. *D.A.R.Y.L.* was filmed partly in Florida and partly at Pinewood studios, in England.

Razorback, one of the few Australian features to reach Britain in the last eighteen months, displayed a rare directorial style, and it was only a matter of time before its creator, Russell Mulcahy, was to be snatched away from his native roots. Mulcahy, too, has been

Eric Roberts (above), and Rebecca Smart in
The Coca-Cola Kid. Tina Arhondis (below)
in *Annie's Coming Out*.

filming in Britain, namely *Highlander*, starring Sean Connery and Christopher Lambert of *Greystoke* fame; a fantasy spanning four centuries and shot in Scotland, London and New York.

Following his success with *Psycho II*, Richard Franklin (also *Patrick* and *Road Games*) likewise moved to Britain, to start work on *Link*, a contemporary thriller with Elisabeth Shue and Terence Stamp, shooting in Scotland and at Shepperton studios. Meanwhile, Fred Schepisi left the failure of *Iceman* behind him, and crossed the Atlantic to take up directorial chores on *Plenty*, the new Meryl Streep film. George Miller, too, had a flightless vehicle on his hands, the lacklustre *The Aviator* (with Christopher Reeve), and returned to Australia to hedge his bets with *Mad Max: Beyond Thunderdome* which, if nothing else does, should inject new life into the Australian box-office.

The aforementioned Gillian Armstrong and Bruce Beresford, who had both been working on long-term, big-budget productions – *Mrs Soffel* and *King David*, respectively – saw their bids for American respectability crumble under the weight of public indifference.

Meanwhile, the Australian cinema itself was relying heavily on the importation of American names. James Coburn traversed the Pacific to topline the Philippe Mora drama *The Leonski Incident*, Eric Roberts starred as *The Coca-Cola Kid*, Matt Dillon was *The Rebel*, Gregory Harrison was chased by the *Razorback*, Tina Turner partnered Mel Gibson in *Mad Max III* and Ron Leibman guested in *Phar Lap*. Further Down Under still, Jodie Foster and John Lithgow were *Mesmerized* in New Zealand.

The Australian films which did surface in Britain were none the less impressive, albeit uncommercial. The best, in this reviewer's opinion, was *Annie's Coming Out*, a searing indictment on the neglect of the handicapped at a Melbourne institute for spastic children. To all outward appearances the film looked a depressing prospect, but in reality was both uplifting and thought-provoking. Angela Punch McGregor was once again superlative as the therapist who initiates a crusade to save the bright but misunderstood Annie O'Farrell from her grim surroundings. Based on a true story, the film was further blessed by a remarkable performance from Tina Arhondis – a spastic but beautiful child – as Annie, and an intelligent screenplay by John Patterson and Chris Borthwick that avoided sentimentality. Gil Brealey directed.

Next best was Dusan Makavejev's *The Coca-Cola Kid*, a surprising and witty comedy about an eccentric American salesman (Eric Roberts) who meets his match in a series of equally eccentric Australians. The Kid's aim is to sell Coke to the natives, but is thwarted by the local soda pop king, the imposing McDowell (Bill Kerr). Reminiscent of

John Hargreaves in *My First Wife*.

Bill Forsyth's *Local Hero* and *Comfort and Joy*, *The Coca-Cola Kid* was an Ealingesque comedy with a thick black edge, and one of the most unpredictable films of the year.

Lonely Hearts was another gem from Paul Cox, the director who brought us *Man of Flowers*, and once again starred Norman Kaye. Kaye plays a 49-year-old piano tuner who, when his mother dies, finds himself alone for the first time in his life. When he visits a dating service he is partnered by Patricia Curnow (Wendy Hughes), a shy 30-year-old bank clerk. And so evolves a tenuous, touching relationship that eschews every cliché in the book. It is a simple, wry and unusual film, with a gentle humour and a little sadness, and

was ably served by its two leads.

Careful, He Might Hear You won all the major Australian Awards in 1983 (eight of them), including those for Best Film, Best Actress (Wendy Hughes) and Best Director (Carl Schultz), but was not released in Britain until 1985. Concentrating on the rivalry between two aunts fighting for the possession of their 6-year-old nephew, the film was too melodramatic for its own good, but it had some powerful moments and a good script.

Phar Lap may have been the out-and-out box-office champ in Australia (again, in 1983), but it aroused little interest in Britain, and vanished almost everywhere after about three weeks.

At the time of writing this, *Razor-*

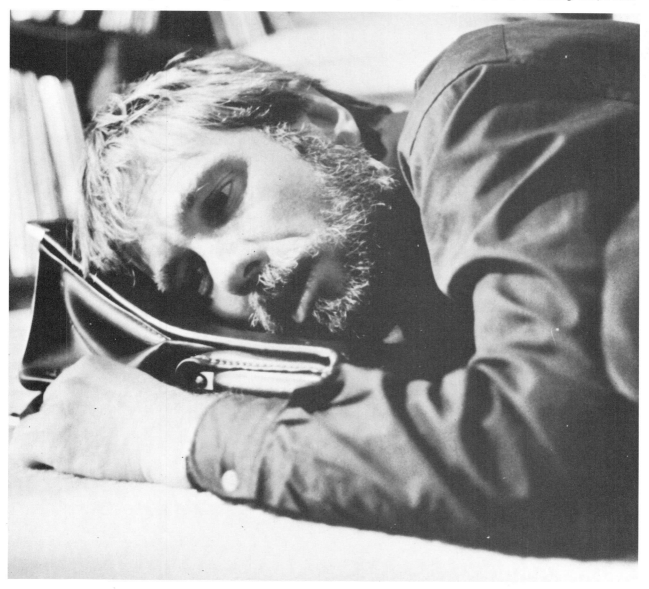

Nicholas Gledhill in *Careful He Might Hear You.*

back and *My First Wife* had still to be released, but were picked up for exhibition by EMI and Artificial Eye respectively. *Razorback* was a classy, ostentatiously directed thriller about a killer hog in the Outback, and was buttressed by two good performances from Chris Haywood and David Argue as a couple of whacky degenerates. Gregory Harrison, though, as the clean-cut American-in-peril was predictably uninspiring.

My First Wife was something else.

Directed by the aforementioned Paul Cox, surely now the best Australian film-maker still working Down Under, the film showcased a *tour-de-force* of acting from John Hargreaves and Wendy Hughes as a married couple coming apart at the seams. A film of genuine passion, it showered emotional sparks like confetti, and revealed Cox as the Antipodes' answer to Ingmar Bergman.

With *Fast Talking*, a well-meaning high school drama from Ken Cameron (*Monkey Grip*), and *BMX Bandits*, a stunt comedy aimed at the family market, the number of Australian features

released in Britain was considerably up from last year, although their success at the box-office was down. But the future does look rosier.

Stockbrokers and merchant bankers appear to be only too willing to plunge their fortunes into the native film industry. And if you look at the tax advantages, it is hardly surprising. Investors can look forward to a guaranteed return, via a presale or distribution advance, of upward of forty per cent of their outlay. Any nondeductible items in the budget will be picked up by the production company or a government body, entitling the financiers to their full 133 per cent tax write-off. And, with the presence of an underwriter (which will ensure the project is fully financed), they can expect an immediate tax break.

So optimistic was Alan Beasley, associate director of the merchant bank B.T. Australia, that he predicted by the middle of the summer (of 1985) there would be funds of 155 million Australian dollars available for film and TV investment. In short, there are few better tax incentives for Australian investors, that is, government-sanctioned ploys for minimizing tax.

And the films in the pipeline look commercially promising.

The third *Mad Max*, with the popular Mel Gibson repeating his leather-clad incarnation, must be a box-office certainty – especially with Tina Turner competing for the limelight. And there is the film version of Colleen (*The Thorn Birds*) McCullough's best-selling novel, *An Indecent Obsession*. With the excellent and ever-present Wendy Hughes starring as Honour Langtry, this, too, looks like a predestined success. And then there is *Burke and Wills*. Based on the ill-fated expedition into the Australian interior by the explorers (and national heroes) Robert Burke and William Wills, the film is directed by Graeme Clifford (an Australian editor who helmed his first feature, *Frances*, in America) and stars Jack Thompson and Nigel Havers in the title roles. Also in production is a promising-looking film called *The Umbrella Woman*, an erotic thriller starring Rachel Ward, Bryan Brown and Sam Neill; while Ms Ward already has an Australian drama, *Fortress*, in the bag. An exciting harvest of films, indeed.

Perhaps 1984 will prove to have been merely the calm before the storm.

Film Books of the Year

IVAN BUTLER

The number of books received this year has fallen slightly, but still represents a respectable output. Once again horror and science fiction films are well served; the demand – and supply – seem unlimited. The flood of popular biographies continues: often they are very good, but it is sometimes frustrating to see the same old star names reappearing time after time whereas those whose names appear in slightly smaller lights – but whose careers may be just as interesting – are ignored. British Film Year has brought out at least one welcome reprint (George Perry's updated *The Great British Picture Show*) and one or two good new studies of cinema in Britain.

Following last year's procedure, here is a purely personal choice of titles, in alphabetical order, which seem particularly interesting, entertaining, or useful for research:

The British Film Collection, Patricia Warren
Chaplin, David Robinson
Dietrich, Alexander Walker
Glenda Jackson, Ian Woodward
Hollywood Faction – Reality and Myth in the Movies, Bruce Crowther
Horror and Science Fiction Films, Vols. II and III, Donald C. Willis
Jacques Tati – Frame by Frame, James Harding
The Macmillan Dictionary of Films and Filmmakers, Vols. I and II, Ed: Christopher Lyon and Susan Doll
Ken Russell's Films, Ken Hanke
Science Fiction, Phil Hardy
The Story of Cinema, Vol.II
Travels in Greeneland, Quentin Falk.

And special mention for a pleasant nostalgic trip through the 'thirties and 'forties, *Seats in All Parts*, Leslie Halliwell.

The Age of the Dream Palace, Jeffrey Richards, Routledge & Kegan Paul, £19.95
Another in the very interesting 'Cinema and Society' series, this deals with the British film in the great age of the super-cinemas of the 1930s. It is a period which has often been neglected or unwarrantably despised by film historians but, as the author points out: 'a decade which produced such high quality work as Alfred Hitchcock's thrillers, the polished musicals of Jessie Matthews and Korda's historical and imperial epics cannot be written off so lightly'. The films are studied against the social background of their period, there is a long section on censorship, together with consideration of the class structure. Mr Richards, as in his other books in the series, is a lively, stimulating and eminently 'readable' writer.

The book is somewhat highly priced, but, as a specialized subject, it is essential reading for anyone interested in films not only as entertainment but as important reflections of the social climate of their time.

American Film Now, James Monaco, Tantivy Press, £14.95
This is an updated version of a book which appeared originally in 1979 and was highly recommended in *Film Review 1980–81*. It now contains additional chapters to cover the Eighties to date, together with minor revisions of the original text. An engrossing study of present day Hollywood from many aspects, it now appears in a handsomer format than previously, excellently illustrated and with such additional attractions as 10 excellent filmographies of famous contemporary directors such as Coppola, Scorsese, Altman and Spielberg. The book is a rather late arrival, and in order to insert it into the present *Film Review* this account has had to be briefer than the book deserves. The high recommendation of the first edition is emphatically repeated for the updated version.

Astaire, The Man and The Dancer, Bob Thomas, Weidenfeld & Nicolson, £9.95
In this handsome and very well illustrated book the reliable Mr Thomas has produced an excellent biography and critical appraisal, incorporating many personal comments by Astaire himself throughout the text. The early stage years of Fred and sister Adele, in particular, are covered in welcome detail, and there are full lists of theatre and television appearances in addition to musical and dramatic films. Much has already been written about Astaire but there is certainly room for so eminently readable and informative a study as this.

Barbara Stanwyck, Al DiOrio, W.H. Allen, £10.95
This is a sound, sympathetic biography of one of the brightest lights of the great Hollywood period. Her long wait for full recognition from the Academy establishment (four Oscar nominations and – at last – in 1982 a special Honorary Award); her marriages to Frank Fay and Robert Taylor (both ending in trouble); her triumphant return after nine years to work in television's *Thorn Birds* in her mid-seventies; her relationships with colleagues and friends; her supreme professionalism and generosity as an actress – are all set out in this very readable and enjoyable book. Illustrations, filmography but, alas, no index.

Bardot, Glenys Roberts, Sidgwick & Jackson, £9.95
There have been Bardot picture books aplenty, but few which deal with her life in detail, and this full-scale biography, issued to coincide with her 50th birthday, is all the more welcome on account of its generally high quality. Though much concerned with 'personal revelations' – love affairs, scandals (genuine or publicity-contrived) and masculine influences generally – it also presents a vivid picture of the Star and her Period, it is well written and researched, and pays due attention to her films. Whether the true secret of her 'impact on the world' is revealed may be open to question, but this very readable book should appeal to anyone interested in what might be termed charismatic cinema. It has plenty of illustrations, a good index but a somewhat skeletal filmography.

The Big Book of British Films, Robin Cross, Sidgwick & Jackson, £7.95
In this large glossy paperback the author recounts, in considerable detail, the history of the British cinema from 1939 to 1970. His intention in discussing the many films covered is evidently to arouse a gentle nostalgia

rather than put forward any fresh critical evaluation, and in this he may be accounted successful. Much useful detail of the business side of the industry is also included. The style is mainly informal, with the occasional unfortunate lapse into the 'flip' and the facetious, and a somewhat casual dismissal of some films which deserve better. The 300 stills – a generous amount – are of variable quality, but many are refreshingly unfamiliar.

(Note: Joyce Carey's railway buffet attendant in *Brief Encounter* was undoubtedly 'refained', but certainly not an 'old trollop'.)

The British Film Collection 1896–1984, Patricia Warren, Elm Tree Books, £15.00

And a vast collection it is : nearly 250 large pages filled with stills, portraits, production photographs, many of them rare, running well into a total of four figures. Each chapter is preceded by a concise but lucid section on business and studio history. In the photographic sections Mrs Warren has sensibly given plenty of space to many lesser-known films, dealing fairly briefly (though adequately) with others which are fully covered elsewhere.

Inevitably, in a collection which includes lobby cards and old stills which must have seen much wear, the quality of reproduction is occasionally variable, but on the whole it is very good. Captions are informative and well placed. This is a suitably celebratory volume for British Film Year: the approach is in the main light-hearted and genial, and firmly repudiates the denigration sometimes unjustifiably directed against the British cinema in past years. There is a useful bibliography, and two full indexes of names and film titles.

British Sound Films, David Quinlan, Batsford, £20.

As a companion to his excellent comprehensive guides to Directors and Stars, David Quinlan has assembled an equally detailed reference book on British cinema during the Studio Years 1928–1959. Titles are arranged alphabetically by decades, each film (over 3,000 in all) being given technical credits, cast, and brief appraisal, and each decade a fuller account of one chosen film and star. Many stills are included, rather small (except in the special sections) but adequate for reference purposes. Finally there is a title list of important 'shorts'. This is a useful, easily handled addition to the steadily increasing library on the cinema of Britain.

(Note: the leading stills on the opening pages of *The Twenties* and *The Thirties* (not the captions) have unfortunately been transposed.)

Burt Lancaster, Robert Windeler, W.H. Allen, £9.95

This is a good popular biography, tracing the career and various interests of the star concisely yet adequately. All the films are fully covered; in particular there is an interesting account of what is arguably Lancaster's best and most subtle performance, in the much underrated *The Swimmer*. Three generous sections of illustrations, a good index and a filmography.

Chaplin – His Life and Art, David Robinson, Collins, £15

Definitive is an over-used word which should be applied only sparingly but this massive study surely merits it. Over 600 pages of enjoyably readable text are followed by over 100 of superb reference sections. The latter include a chronology (35 pages), details of theatrical tours, a really full filmography, and a Who's Who of associates and others. There are five generous sections of illustrations, many of them rare, a family tree and even a map of London relative to Chaplin's youth.

The author concentrates on the Art rather than the Life, but there is perfectly adequate coverage of the latter also (after all, the two are obviously closely intertwined), while the detailed descriptions of Chaplin at work – gathered from access to many hitherto private papers and other sources – are wholly engrossing. This will surely remain the standard work of Chaplin for a very long time to come – a monumental memoriam.

Dietrich, Alexander Walker, Thames & Hudson, £12.95

Following his studies of Garbo and Crawford, Alexander Walker presents in this sumptuous volume the most attractive of a noteworthy trio. It is a warm but honest portrait, a perceptive critical reassessment and a lively career story, full of fascinating side glances such as von Sternberg's method of using Dietrich to make male actors, whom he detested, look small. Indeed, the comparatively brief account of the director is almost as revealing as that of his Trilby herself. The important films are dealt with thoroughly: the pages on the tensions and traumas during the making of *The Blue Angel* are engrossing, arousing vivid memories of the overpowering impact of this film on at least one young and possibly (by today's standards) impressionable enthusiast even when seeing it at a Trade Show on a cold morning in a huge half empty Northern cinema over fifty years ago.

The many illustrations, which include a delightful 'non-Marlene' one of von Sternberg on the marvellous *Shanghai Express* train set (the film neatly described by the author as *Grand Hotel* on wheels) are superb. Of particular interest are the early ones of the sometimes – but not always – recognizable Dietrich of the pre-Sternberg days.

Elstree – The British Hollywood, Patricia Warren, Elm Tree Books, £9.95

As Mrs Warren rightly points out, Elstree has been strangely neglected in comparison with other film studios in the matter of historical records and she makes welcome amends in this lively and informative survey, threading her way with ease through the sometimes tortuous passages of the cinema industry, and covering dozens of films concisely but adequately. The lavish illustrations are a major asset, including not only stills and production photographs but entertaining cartoons from *Punch* and other side issues, all excellently reproduced. A list of films 1927–1982, a bibliography and good index round off an enjoyable and attractive book – and a useful addition to British cinema history.

Everybody's Man – Jimmy Stewart, Jhan Robbins, Robson Books, £8.95.
Kirk Douglas, Michael Munn, Robson Books, £8.95

The publishers continue their useful series of modest-scale popular biographies with two brief but elegantly produced volumes. If, in the case of Stewart, the pages seem on occasion positively to glow with warmth this is surely understandable when dealing with someone so universally well regarded. This book is particularly commendable for its excellent filmography, and an arrangement of subheadings which makes reference easy. Both biographies, however, should appeal to admirers of their respective subjects.

Fantastic Cinema, Peter Nicholls, Ebury Press, £9.95 hardback/£5.95 paperback

The fantasy/horror/sci-fi trinity must be the most fully covered of all film *genres*. The attractions of this particular illustrated survey include ample coverage, generally handsome appearance, ease of reference and plenty of well reproduced black-and-white and colour stills – even if some of them, particularly from the earlier years, are rather too familiar. The text covers some 400 films with well written critical commentaries, and this number is increased to 700 in a useful annotated Chronology. The field is wide, including among all the more familiar movies, such titles as *The Elephant Man*, *The Seventh Seal*, *Britannia Hospital* (incorrectly indexed), *The Red Shoes* and even a version of Wagner's *Parsifal*. It also embraces examples of both rubbish and pornography, the author in one place apologizing for including a still from a video nasty. (One wonders why, if such an apology is considered necessary, the still is included at all?)

Fassbinder, Film Maker, Ronald Hayman, Weidenfeld & Nicolson, £10.95 hardback/£5.95 paperback

Rainer Werner Fassbinder's films may not be – in fact decidedly are not – to everyone's taste but there is no doubt that he was a figure of some significance in the cinema of his time. This biography helps to explore the roots of his somewhat grubby and self-indulgent – but undoubtedly powerful – output, in his tormented and lonely early life. Apparently deliberately seeking the cult of the ugly, often rather too obviously anxious to shock, he nevertheless left a handful of fairly memorable films, very much tied to their period, and this well documented and illustrated study does much to explain how they came to be created.

Fifty Years of Serial Thrills, Roy Kinnard, Scarecrow Press (dist. Bailey Bros. & Swinfen), £18.00
A first-class handbook for everyone interested in one of the liveliest and most entertaining aspects of the popular cinema of bygone years. Grouped by studio, every motion picture serial released in the USA between 1912 and 1956 is covered. The more important productions of each company are given historical and critical treatment, all the rest are entered in special indexes which provide details of date, director, number of episodes and full cast. In addition, the chapter on Universal contains a potted history of their best-known horror films, and included in that on independent serials is a summary of Bela Lugosi's career. There are interviews with Buster *(Flash Gordon)* Crabbe and Jean Rogers, numerous rare stills and a good title index.

Filmed Books and Plays, 1928–1983, A.G.S. Enser, Gower, £22.50
This massive and excellent reference work is a combined, updated and revised version of books previously published in 1968–75 and 1982. In some 700 pages it contains three immense indexes: (1) Film Titles (including date, production company, and publisher of the original book), (2) Author Index (with original title and film title) and (3) Title Changes, from original to film, which make it possible to check quickly and easily the details of any one of the thousands of films covered. These are mainly of British or American origin, and include television as well as cinema productions. The lay-out is attractive and admirably clear. The work of an experienced librarian, it is an essential addition to the library of any discerning film book collector.

Film Making in 1930s Britain, Rachael Low, George Allen & Unwin, £12.95
The 'thirties volume of Rachael Low's mammoth history of British cinema has been a long time a-coming, but it has been worth waiting for. It follows the same course as the earlier volumes – a history of an industry rather than a critical appraisal, as she makes clear in her introduction; but space is given also to many pertinent comments on individual films, and the often complicated convolutions of financial and other activities are lucidly and readably presented. One bonus is a fine 130–page list of films with credits,

another is a collection of over fifty splendid stills and production photographs, often rare, and reproduced with crystal clarity. The index is rather a let-down, with far too many entries being mere masses of page numbers.

French Cinema, Roy Armes, Secker & Warburg, £12.95 hardback/£6.95 paperback
An admirably compact yet comprehensive history by a writer who has long studied the subject. By skilful compression, this book of some 280 pages is not only an excellent introduction to more detailed reading, but also a satisfying survey for anyone wanting the whole history of French cinema presented in a comparatively brief form. Sixty good stills, a full bibliography and index round off a book useful for both quick reference or sustained study, a worthy companion to the same author's *Critical History of British Cinema* (see *Film Review 1979–80*).

Glamorous Musicals, see under **The Movie Stars Story**

Glenda Jackson, Ian Woodward, Weidenfeld & Nicolson, £10.95
This first full-length account of Glenda Jackson's life and career is a brave and readable exploration of a fascinating and complex personality. Mr Woodward pulls few punches, either in attack or defence, painting an interesting picture of a resolute, courageous – and at times ruthless – determination to succeed by a notably uncompromising and adventurous actress who, by a combination of will-power, intelligence and imagination became one of the leading figures of contemporary theatre and film. Well illustrated, and with good reference sections of filmography, theatre and television appearances, awards and honours.

The Great Book of Movie Villains, Jan Stacey and Ryder Syvertsen, Columbus Books, £9.95
The authors follow up their highly entertaining *Great Book of Movie Monsters* (see *Film Review 1984–5*) with a similar volume on villains – characters, not impersonators. Here are the descriptions, occupations, evil powers, current status, etc. of (among very many) Alex, of *A Clockwork Orange* fame, Fu Manchu, Dr Strangelove, Ming the Merciless, the Godfather, Caligari, Marie Antoinette – even Joan Crawford. Maybe the human villains do not provide quite so much scope for way-out humour as did the monsters, but even so this is an entertaining and often witty collection. Well illustrated and triple-indexed.

The Great British Picture Show, George Perry, Pavilion/Michael Joseph, £12.95
This is a revised and updated version of the history originally published in 1974, with

two new chapters, an extra section of illustrations and a foreword by David Puttnam. The useful 60-page Biographical Guide has also been slightly enlarged. The main text is more or less unaltered, and remains a lively and stimulating survey, threading its way easily through the maze of company amalgamations and general business intricacies (see *Film Review 1975–6*), with pithy and perceptive comments on hundreds of films. A pity, though, that the inconsistent spelling of Sidney Gilliat's and Werner Krauss's surnames has been permitted to remain!

Great Movie Actresses, Philip Strick, Orbis Publishing, £12.50
Gorgeous seems the only adequate word for this glittering collection culled from a Japanese movie magazine, *Star*, and embellished with witty and informative commentaries by the film critic and historian Philip Strick. From the silent days to the 1970s, in a dining-table rather than a coffee-table volume, literally hundreds of photographs shine from the pages; and whereas numerous portrait galleries of glamour have been published, this has the added attraction of a large number of stills – many of them refreshingly unfamiliar, and all excellently reproduced. These are mainly of American actresses, but Britain, France, Germany, Italy and Sweden are also represented. The adjective 'Great' is used generously, to ensure the presence of the slightly less than super-famous, and additional sections include Pin-up Parade, New Faces, Pick of the Tops and an admirable index.

Recommended both for reminiscent browsing and straightforward reference.

Hollywood Colour Portraits, John Kobal, Aurum Press, £6.95
This is a paperback reissue of a portrait gallery originally reviewed in the *Film Review 1982–3*; there is no loss of brilliance in the seventy or so photographs of the stars of the Golden Age, a tribute to the photographers as much as to their subjects. One may view with a certain scepticism the flawless beauty (male and female) displayed – almost too flawless, as the technical skill of the 'toucher-up' removes personality as well as wrinkles. In this respect Pal (as 'Lassie') comes off best. Certainly the unfortunate Lizabeth Scott comes off worst, sandwiched between Burt Lancaster and Kirk Douglas in an absurd double-page spread which reduces her to a couple of squinting eyes, half a nose and fiercely meeting eyebrows. All in all, however, a lavish conglomeration of luscious pin-ups, male, female and canine.

Hollywood Faction – Reality and Myth in the Movies, Bruce Crowther, Columbus Books, £12.95
The importance of this comparatively short book is disproportionate to its size. In only just over 200 compact pages the author

examines the treatment of history in the Hollywood film and how it is distorted and misrepresented. Very many people (probably all of us to some extent) have our views of past events – ancient and modern – coloured by what we see on the cinema and television screens. Mr Crowther, in his lucid and very lively study, has surprises for all of us. The period he covers is wide: from 1492 to 1984, and, in films, from *Birth of a Nation* to the television blockbuster *The Day After*. He is by no means entirely condemnatory and points to many instances of accurate commentary or re-creation. His engrossing account – complete with illustrations, bibliography and good index – should be required reading for anyone anxious to avoid being hoodwinked while still appreciating and enjoying the compulsively convincing art of the film and television media.

The Hollywood Reporter – Star Profiles,
see under **The Movie Stars Story**

Horror and Science Fiction Films II,
Donald C. Willis, Scarecrow Press (dist. Bailey Bros. & Swinfen), £34.20
Horror and Science Fiction Films – a Checklist, Volume I, was published in 1972; this is both a sequel and a supplement, a further 470 pages, making over 1,000 in all, crammed with titles, credits, technical details, casts, and in many cases brief critical and often caustic comments. In addition, this new book contains many additional facts and remarks on films (indicated by an asterisk) which appeared in Volume I. Taken together, they must represent the fullest checklist available – literally thousands of titles. As a reference work it is invaluable, a horror-sci-fi fan's Bible, covering up to 1981.

In order to save space over 100 abbreviations are used. The researcher would be well advised to put in a little preliminary study of these before setting to work, to avoid puzzling over such cryptic contractions as SpVisFx (fairly simple), to TVFFSB or HKFFest (slightly more difficult). Still, it all adds to the entertainment.

PS: Volume III of the above arrived as these pages were ready to go to press. It brings the Checklist up to 1983, with many retrospective entries and numerous lists as in Volume II.

Independent Feature Film Production,
Gregory Goodell, Columbus Books, £7.95
Subtitled 'A Complete Guide from Concept to Distribution' and written in simple language for the layman as well as the professional, this is an essential handbook for anyone interested in exactly how a feature film comes into being. Budgeting, production, casting, editing, sound, marketing, etc. – it is all here, clearly set out with many useful tables and plans. Who, in the

seemingly endless list of technical credits, is the Key Grip, and what does he do? What about the Gaffer – and his Best Boy? The answers are in these pages. Just a glance at any of these lucidly set out pages should be enough to hook the glancer into making sure of possessing the rest of the information contained in the book.

International Film Guide 1985, Ed. Peter Cowie, Tantivy, £6.95
The 22nd edition maintains its high standard, with a world survey of film production, in which every country is given a commentary, selected criticisms and cast list, stills and useful information. All the usual features are included – Festivals, Awards, Books and Bookshops, Animation, etc., together with a valuable new series of 'in depth' studies of particular aspects, starting in this issue with a dossier of 20 pages on French cinema of the past ten years compiled by the associate editor, Derek Elley. There is also an interesting 30-page insert on the history of the Shell Film Unit to celebrate its 50th year.

Jack Lemmon, Michael Freedland, Weidenfeld & Nicholson, £8.95
A good, workmanlike brief biography, dealing very fully with the films and public career – most of the chapter headings are, in fact, film titles. No filmography, but an adequate index and a good section of illustrations.

Jack Nicholson, David Downing, Comet, £5.95
A nicely produced paperback edition of a lively biography which also provides a wider and often wittily caustic commentary on the general American filmic scene of recent years. Mr Downing is apt to be careless over the spelling of names ('Paulene' Kael throughout) and his style is sometimes slipshod, but on the whole this is a perceptive and entertaining portrait.

Jacques Tati – Frame by Frame, James Harding, Secker & Warburg, £12.95
This is a totally enchanting book, a biography and detailed examination of Tati's five masterpieces, with briefer accounts of the minor works – how it makes one yearn to see the 25-minute *Cours du Soir*, made as a sort of relief during the onerous production of *Playtime*! In his introduction Mr Harding states, 'I have tried to avoid writing what Dr Johnson would have derided as a "honeysuckle life", but the truth is that Tati was an extraordinarily nice man', and indeed that fact shines through almost every page. Against his stubbornness (often necessary), his sometimes exhausting search for perfection, his occasional moodiness (fully understandable in view of his troubles after the commercial failure of *Playtime*) and his rough treatment of at least one well-meaning

professional, must be set his charm, his courtesy to all manner and class of people, his total lack of arrogance, his healthy scorn for the pompous analysts who grub through his films hunting solemnly for hidden meanings which are not there – and above all his genius and skill, which put millions of happy filmgoers in his debt.

The author's descriptions of the films (far too vivid to be dismissed as mere synopses) are superb memory-joggers. Best of all would be regular Tati seasons on the screen; failing that, this delightful book is a very satisfying substitute. Well illustrated, and with an excellent index.

James Dean, David Dalton and Ron Cayen, Sidgwick & Jackson, £12.95
One of the less explicable manifestations of star hysteria – complete with foolish mystery-making after his death – the image of James Dean has its undoubted niche in popular cinema history, and this richly produced book with its lavish, well-reproduced photographs will certainly help to preserve it – though, asking a keen young filmgoer recently what she thought of James Dean, I was surprised at her reply, 'Who was *he*?'. In Elia Kazan's words, quoted in the book, 'He was very twisted, almost like a cripple or spastic of some kind . . . He even walked like a crab, as if cringing all the time . . . He was never more than a limited actor, a highly neurotic young man. But he had a lot of talent and he worked like hell.'

The text takes second place to the illustrations, but it is adequate, and there is a useful potted chronology. It is interesting to note that in the advertising of his last film (posthumously released) he received only third billing (*vide p.143*).

James Stewart, Allen Eyles, W.H. Allen, £9.95
As one of the great Golden Age figures, James Stewart has been strangely neglected by biographers, but Allen Eyles redresses the balance here handsomely. With a subject whose private life has been, in the main, happily uneventful, he has been able to concentrate almost wholly on the films themselves, and the result is an enjoyable journey down memory lane, illuminated by apt criticism and evaluation. In his introductory chapter he gives a very acceptable reason – in this particular case – for the generally annoying habit of referring to the actors in a film by their own names rather than those of the characters they portray.

The filmography is superb, and there are some pleasant photographs. A book so carefully documented surely deserves an index.

Joan Collins, Robert Levine, Weidenfeld & Nicolson, £7.95
A brief, featherweight popular biography (with birthdate – see review of *Past Imperfect*), easy reading and well illustrated; uncensored – and unindexed.

Judi Dench, Gerald Jacobs, Weidenfeld & Nicolson, £9.95

Judi Dench's career to date has centred more on the theatre (and later, television) than the cinema, but just one of her few films, the remarkable and haunting *Four in the Morning* – for which she received the British Film Academy Award – would justify the inclusion of this authorized biography in these columns; particularly as it is one of the most enjoyable and entertaining of the year. The author's subtitle is 'A Great Deal of Laughter', quoting the director Trevor Nunn on Judi, and it is difficult to think of a more apt description. The book is a success story but also a record of inevitable occasional setbacks and resolute determination to overcome them: it is full of good – sometimes hilarious – theatre anecdotes.

A good list of stage performances is provided, but nothing on films or television in the reference section.

Julie Christie, Michael Feeney Callan, W.H. Allen, £10.95

An attractively produced and very well illustrated biography, with good accounts of all the star's main films – *Darling, Far from the Madding Crowd, The Go-Between, Don't Look Now, Petulia, Dr Zhivago*, etc. The author makes considerable use of criticisms from contemporary publications, always a useful record of how things looked at the time. Also covered are Julie Christie's extra-cinematic activities in connection with nuclear weapons, Greenham Common, Animal Liberation, the Vegetarian Society, etc., concerning which the *Daily Mirror* commented that she was becoming 'even more boringly committed than Jane Fonda'. Written in a brisk, lively style, with good filmography and index.

Katharine Hepburn – A Celebration, Sheridan Morley, Pavilion/Michael Joseph, £12.95

Katharine Hepburn's 75th birthday is suitably celebrated in a splendidly illustrated portrait (joining Cary Grant, Alec Guinness and John Gielgud in this attractive series). The author provides an informative, affectionate but always honest text, and the photographs (many of them rarely, if ever, published before) are a worthy collection to perpetuate memories of the career (so far!) of one of the small company of really great screen actresses. There is a very good illustrated filmography and even more useful (because less easy to come by) lists of TV and stage performances.

Ken Russell's Films, Ken Hanke, Scarecrow (dist. Bailey Bros. & Swinfen), £39.00

This is important as the first full, in-depth study – 450 pages. Russell's films are not everyone's choice, varying wildly from the brilliantly original and sensitive to the brashly self-indulgent and grotesque. But there is no doubt of his influence on the art of film-making even if, as the author states, it may be years before this can be fully assessed. In the space available it is not possible to do justice to this detailed, careful, well balanced survey, but it can be warmly recommended to all students of Russell's work. Copious notes end each chapter, and there is a splendid filmography, which also lists all the television productions.

(Note: It is surely stretching things a bit to say that Benjamin Britten's 'Sea Interlude' from *Peter Grimes* is actually 'enhanced' by being dragged from its context to serve the director's purpose in a film on Coleridge!)

Kirk Douglas – A Biography, Michael Munn – see under **Everybody's Man**

Laurence Olivier, Melvyn Bragg, Hutchinson, £12.50

Deriving this handsome and lavishly illustrated book from his memorable television interview with Olivier, and basing it on a sort of skeletal biography, the author has produced an enthralling and at times very moving tribute. His attempt to explore and analyse the *fons et origo* of the great performances with which one of the most exciting and versatile actors of the century has thrilled millions may not be totally revealing, but it is without doubt the most illuminating of all essays on its subject. It is, indeed, a book to be treasured, packed with superb photographs, written with authority and a disarming modesty and – particularly if taken in conjunction with Olivier's autobiography – a vivid and valuable memoir.

Macmillan Dictionary of Films and Filmmakers – *Vol. 1 (Films), Vol. 2 (Directors)*, Ed. Christopher Lyon and Susan Doll, Macmillan, £27.50 per vol.

These are the first two in a massive 4-volume reference work, with volumes 3 and 4, covering actors and actresses, writers and production artists, to be published in due course. Contributions are from an international panel of film historians, critics and researchers.

In Volume 1 some 700 films have been selected mainly for their technical, cultural, historical and generic significance. Each is given full cast lists and credits, a lengthy critical article and (particularly valuable because of its rarity) a very detailed list of relevant publications. In Volume 2 about 500 directors receive similar treatment, with comprehensive lists of titles (the films of Mack Sennett, for instance, fill six large columns), biographical/critical article and a list of publications both 'on' and 'by'.

Though these magnificently detailed books may be aimed chiefly at the student, historian and general writer on cinema (certainly no self-respecting library or university should be without them) they will assuredly be a source of information and enjoyment for anyone seriously interested in the art of the film, and a major addition to the reference shelf.

Meryl Streep, Diana Maychick, Robson Books, £8.95

Brief popular biography of the 'reluctant' star. Bland and fairly superficial, but with some interesting stories – such as her strained relationship with Dustin Hoffman during the making of *Kramer vs. Kramer*. Indexed, with two good sections of illustrations.

The Meryl Streep Story, Nick Smurthwaite, Columbus Books, £9.95

This is a handsomely produced and well written account of one of the fastest-moving careers in modern cinema: eleven films to date. The illustrations, many of them in colour and of coffee-table size, are excellent, there is a full filmography, and the text is illuminating and informative. The portrait that emerges is that of an intelligent and sensitive actress already showing a notable versatility – much more, in fact, an actress than a mere 'star'.

Movies of the Silent Years and **Movies of the Seventies**, Ed. Ann Lloyd, Orbis Publishing, £9.99 per vol.

With the publication of these two boundary volumes Orbis completes coverage of world cinema from earliest years almost to the present day. The format of the whole series is unusual and interesting – neither a straight chronological history nor a detailed analysis of a large number of films. Each volume consists of essays by a number of qualified writers on significant aspects of the decade, brief biographies (with *full* filmographies) of several notable film-makers or actors (not necessarily the most famous), and a synopsis and evaluation of about twenty films. The whole series is lavishly illustrated, and the quality, whether colour or black-and-white, is excellent.

(Note: In *The Silent Years* the lobby still from *The Temptress* features H.B. Warner, whose part was cut from the released print; and the still on p.183 is not of Buster Keaton's friendly cow 'Brown Eyes'; she does not appear until later in the film.)

The Moviegoers' Quiz Book, Ed. F. Maurice Speed, Columbus, £4.95 hardback

As a contributor, I refrain from commenting on the merits (or demerits) of the Questions and Answers themselves, but this is a very attractively produced and widely varied collection of 1001 posers, ranging from simple tyro-teasers to formidable buff-testers. It is divided into some forty sections such as Stars, *Film Noir*, Australian Cinema, Silent Era, Directors, Horror, Musicals, etc., concluding with Picture Posers which is well illustrated with stills and portraits. Its neat pocket-sized format makes it suitable either for increasing one's knowledge in private or for taking along to test one's friends at parties or other gatherings of film enthusiasts.

Mr Laurel and Mr Hardy, John McCabe, Robson Books, £4.95 paperback
It is good to see this attractive 'affectionate biography', first published in hardback by Robson some years ago, now made available again in paperback, for it is one of the most enjoyable books on the inimitable pair. It includes an interview with Hardy (1954) and full lists of both their separate and joint films. Only the illustrations are a disappointment, more smudgily reproduced than is acceptable today.

Natalie, Lana Wood, Columbus Books, £9.95
Described as 'A Memoir' by Natalie Wood's sister, this is – as might be expected – a warm-hearted tribute with the emphasis much more on personal than professional matters. Affairs abound (almost as much space being given to the authoress herself as to her subject), there is plenty of invented, or at least reconstructed dialogue, and though a claim of 'frankness' is justified the portrait is a sympathetic one. Comparatively little has yet been written about the star and, though a more comprehensive appraisal of her career may well appear one day, this easy-to-read, intimate and at times moving story (in the short account of her tragic death, for instance) may fill a gap until that time. Some attractive illustrations, but no index.

A Night at the Pictures, Ten Decades of British Films, Gilbert Adair/Nick Roddick, Columbus Books, £4.95 paperback
Described as the official book of the British Film Year, this glossy paperback is a neat potted history of cinema in Britain, divided into three main sections. The first, 'The British Tradition'; is a general survey of the period up to around the 1970s; the second, 'The British Revival', carries the story to the present day: somewhat confusingly, the page headings revert to the first section in the middle of the second. The final section is a concise chronology of notable films together with cinematic, social and political events. Finally, a number of critics make their best-of-all-time choices – in which, interestingly, the Revival wonder-twins, *Chariots of Fire* and *Gandhi*, are conspicuous by their absence. With a total of 144 pages, which include many excellent illustrations, 'information boxes' on selected film personalities, and nicely pointed cartoons by Alan Parker, everything is necessarily rather compressed, but (except for what might be considered an undue ideological bias in parts

of the first section) this is a very fair and balanced summary. A handsome and inexpensive book, particularly useful for reference purposes.
(Note: Mabel Poulton did *not* star with Ivor Novello in *The Rat* (1925) – Mae Marsh did!)

No Bells on Sunday, Rachel Roberts, Ed Alexander Walker, Pavilion/Michael Joseph, £9.95
After Rachel Roberts' tragic suicide a large number of notebooks were found, containing a mixture of journal, diary, and self-analysis of devastating frankness, but in confused chronology. Alexander Walker has performed an editorial miracle in arranging these into a more or less consecutive narrative interspersed with comments from numerous people who knew her – what he describes as a 'documentary biography'. It is a story of the disintegration of a vibrant and remarkable personality – often grim, but by no means wholly depressing, and always of riveting interest: the early marriage to Alan Dobie, the long tormented marriage to Rex Harrison and its aftermath, the loyalty of colleagues and friends and the many fine performances.

Now, Voyager, Ed. Jeanne Allen, University of Wisconsin Press (dist. Academic & University Publishers Group), £16.60 hardback/£6.60 paperback
Another in this excellent series of Warner Bros. film scripts, this time one of Bette Davis' most renowned performances in which she redeemed a not particularly memorable movie. Long historical, technical and critical introduction, complete script in readable and not too technical detail, notes, cast and credit lists, and twenty-three well-chosen frame enlargements. Twenty volumes are already available in the series – this is a welcome addition.

Olivia and Joan, Charles Higham, New English Library, £9.95
From the apparently inexhaustible mine of the Golden Era, Charles Higham digs a good, sound double biography of Olivia de Havilland and Joan Fontaine – sisters and lifelong rivals. He follows the two crisscrossing and occasionally interweaving threads of the sisters' careers with professional skill, paying due attention to famous personalities linked to one or other – and sometimes both – of the stars (Selznick, Hitchcock, John Huston, Hal Wallis, Errol Flynn, Howard Hughes) and to their respective films – *Gone With the Wind,* Olivia's highlight; and *Rebecca,* Joan's. There is also much about the notorious, often ruthless feuds and politics of the great Warner Studio. Good illustrations and index: a comparative double filmography might have provided an added interest.

Omni's Screen Flights – Screen Fantasies Ed. Danny Peary, Columbus Books, £8.50 paperback
Seeking to find a new angle from which to produce yet another book on science-fiction, this sturdily-made paperback is a collection of essays from notable writers on 'exploring the future' according to the films. Contributors include Isaac Asimov, Robert Bloch, Stanley Kramer, Philip Strick and Allen Eyles, and there are several interviews with well-known personalities, among them Roger Corman and Leonard Nimoy. The articles are widely varied in subject and style, and often caustically critical. There are a large number of black-and-white and coloured illustrations, and a vast checklist of titles.

Past Imperfect, Joan Collins, W.H. Allen, £10.95
A reprint, 'revised and updated', of the autobiography originally published in 1978 and reissued, no doubt, in the wake of the long-running television series *Dynasty*. The third descriptive word on the dust jacket, 'unexpurgated', may raise a few false hopes ('unexpurgated' from what?). It is a chatty, lightweight but lively and often amusing account of a determined and successful career in mainly forgettable films. marred only occasionally by remarks such as the foolishly coy statement about age – the writer's year of birth can be found in various reference books (which may, of course, be wrong) or calculated closely enough by a glance at the dates of the films in the chronology.

Planks of Reason, Barry Keith Grant, Scarecrow (dist. Bailey Bros. & Swinfen), £33.00
This fine, if slightly formidable work (a collection of some twenty essays on the Horror Film) is both essential and enjoyable reading for all those who take their horror seriously but not ponderously. A glance at one or two of the section headings will give some idea of the approach: 'The Aesthetics of Fright'; 'The Witch in Film – Myth and Reality'; 'The Lesbian Vampire'; '*King Kong*, Ape and Essence'; 'Biological Alchemy and the films of David Cronenberg'; 'Monster Movies, a Sexual Theory'. If some of these appear a little unnerving, do not be put off – there is much to entertain as well as stimulate in this collection, and the book, in Scarecrow's neat and attractive format, is well documented and indexed.

Raquel Welch, Peter Haining, W.H. Allen, £10.95
Raquel Welch has had to wait some time before receiving the sort of literary tribute given to stars such as Marilyn Monroe, Brigitte Bardot and Jean Harlow. In this first full biography, Peter Haining presents

an enthusiastic and lively portrait, complete with a large number of essential illustrations, including a colour quartet, which range from a Royal Film Performance presentation to Queen Elizabeth, to film stills and cheescake.

Science Fiction, Ed. Phil Hardy, Aurum Press, £17.95
Aurum have followed their award-winning *The Western* with an equally mammoth and magnificent volume in their Film Encyclopedia series. It follows much the same format, dealing year by year with every significant (and many insignificant) film from 1895 to 1983, the productions of each year being entered in alphabetical order. Every film is given synopsis, commentary, leading credits and technical data. Appendices include awards, Top Ten lists, etc., and the book is prefaced by a general survey. There are over 450 illustrations, including a fine colour section and the huge index refers to each film by year. The notoriously difficult problem of the dividing line between science fiction and horror has been neatly solved by including such films as *Frankenstein* and *Dr Jekyll and Mr Hyde*, with a note that these will also appear in a forthcoming Horror book. In other cases the field covered is wide, containing, for example, Hitchcock's *The Birds* and the 1937 *Charlie Chan at the Olympics*, which foresaw the 'robot plane'. A most handsome production, essential for every sci-fi aficionado.

Screen World – 1984, John Willis, Muller, £12.50
This complete annual record of the American film year reaches its 35th issue with no lowering of its high standard: stills and portraits (1,000, we are assured), massive cast lists, obituary and biographical sections, awards, a very lengthy list of foreign films and an enormous index. This year's 'dedicatee' is Joan Bennett. All embracing and indispensable in its field.

Seats in All Parts, Leslie Halliwell, Granada, £9.95
Mr Halliwell follows up his enjoyable personal selection of favourites ('Halliwell's Hundred') with an equally enjoyable fragment of autobiography suitably subtitled 'Half a Lifetime at the Movies'. Unashamedly nostalgic, it describes his early days in Bolton, Lancs., through the 1930s and the start of his lifelong love affair with the movies from the age of four. His descriptions of cinema-going conditions in the town are fascinatingly detailed, even to the inclusion of a map of all the picturehouses available to the fortunate young fanatic in those years. Later we accompany him through his National Service, to Cambridge. For those of us old enough to remember, this is a delightfully vivid journey into a lost past; for those without that advantage it is, apart

from filmic matters, an informative picture of everyday life during the period.

The Shirley Temple Story, Lester David and Irene David, Robson Books, £8.95
A popular biography of the infant phenomenon which manages, on the whole, to avoid both fulsomeness and sentimentality is to be welcomed. The later life in politics is well covered, and Shirley Temple Black's courage when faced with the fact that she was suffering from cancer is movingly described. There is a useful filmography which includes details of her early appearances in short comedies.

Splatter Movies, John McCarty, Columbus Books, £7.95
The term was invented by George A. Romero (*Night of the Living Dead*) to describe movies in which – despite the universally splattered gore – the intention is not so much to horrify as to 'astonish'. 'How on earth did they do it?' is the desired reaction as somebody's head is summarily removed in medium shot without a camera cut. 'Mindless, plotless violence' is certainly not to everybody's taste ('I feel inclined to apologize to all decent Americans for sending them a work in such sickening bad taste,' remarked C. A. Lejeune of Hammer's *Curse of Frankenstein* – what would she say today?), but John McCarty's study, which includes a history of Hammer and a chapter on Peckinpah's *The Wild Bunch*, is well written, researched and illustrated. He traces convincingly the growth of the subgenre from the famous French Grand Guignol, in the milder British version of which – it may be noted – players of the eminence of Dame Sybil Thorndike and Sir Lewis Casson appeared with evident relish.

The Story of Cinema, Volume 2, David Shipman, Hodder & Stoughton, £17.95
The long-awaited second volume brings this history of world cinema to a massive conclusion (1280 pages in all) – massive in conception, in scope and in weight! It covers the subject from *Citizen Kane* to *Gandhi* and brings the total of films seen personally by the author to over 7,000. As in the previous volume (see *Film Review 1983–4*) clarity of presentation and ease of finding any particular title are ensured by general arrangement, by printing every title in bold type (with date) and also by an index which, though microscopic in type, is comprehensive in scope. With so huge a field many of the comments are necessarily brief but they are almost always illuminating and stimulating. Mr Shipman is often forthright and fearless in his opinions while modestly acknowledging in some cases the influence of friends (see, for instance, Hitchcock, Michael Powell and Lindsay Anderson and their films).

Every major film-producing country re-

ceives a fair share of space, and special sections are devoted to, for example, the MGM Musical, Buñuel and Ingmar Bergman. All in all, a remarkable undertaking, which should remain in constant use for many a year.

Sublime Marlene, Thierry de Navacelle, Sidgwick & Jackson, £6.95
Handsome glossy paperback of fine black-and-white photographs of Dietrich, and stills from her films, selected from the Kobal Collection. A comparatively brief but adequate text is divided into a section on her personal life; the Sternberg films, including *The Blue Angel*, which is treated individually; and the later career. Appendices include a list of songs and a somewhat skeletal filmography. The illustrations are excellently reproduced.

A Talent to Amuse, Sheridan Morley, Pavilion/Michael Joseph, £12.95
This excellent biography of Noel Coward makes a welcome reappearance in a handsome new volume, with a new Epilogue, updated Bibliography, and an Introduction which, among other matters, makes a brief reference to Coward's homosexuality – *verboten* in the first edition (1969) when he was still alive, for, as he stated, understandable reasons. The splendid Chronology, setting out his varied career in six parallel columns (Actor, Composer, Playwright, Director, Author, and notable revivals) has also been briefly completed to his death. There are many good illustrations and an exemplary index.

Travels in Greeneland – The Cinema of Graham Greene, Quentin Falk, Quartet Books, £14.95
'Graham Greene has been translated to the cinema more than any other novelist in this century' – thus the author opens his riveting and exhaustive study. Every film is covered, with the story of its inception and production, sharp and sometimes caustic comments from Greene himself, opinions of actors and others (in particular director Carol Reed) connected with its making. Of particular interest are fascinating details of the most famous productions: the Roman Catholic elements in *Brighton Rock*, the creation of Bobby Henrey's remarkable performance in *The Fallen Idol*, the changes and problems that occurred during the making of *Our Man in Havana* (for which Greene refused Hitchcock's offer of direction) and the Greene/Reed masterpiece, *The Third Man*.

An annotated filmography (including *Dr Fischer of Geneva*), a list of Unrealized Projects and a generous selection of excellent stills complete a definitive work of its kind.

Vivien Leigh, John Russell Taylor, Elm Tree Books, £9.95
An attractive picture history, accurately de-

scribed as a celebration of her beauty and talent. The troubles and traumata of her tragic manic-depressive affliction are not glossed over but, very rightly in such a book, the approach is one of warmth and appreciation of the pleasure she has given to so many from stage and screen. Though the number of films she made is not particularly large the memories she left are more vivid than in many longer-lasting careers. The manifold illustrations are excellent.

Walter Matthau, Allan Hunter, W.H. Allen, £9.95

It is surprising that a full-length biography of Walter Matthau has taken so long to appear – with almost 50 films to his credit, many of them very successful. Allan Hunter has repaired the omission handsomely in this well-written and entertaining study. The film coverage is thorough, embellished with such personal details as his friendly professional relationships with Jack Lemmon, Goldie Hawn and Glenda Jackson; and the slightly less friendly (and highly publicized) one with Barbra Streisand. Good filmography, lists of stage and television appearances, adequate index and some excellent illustrations.

War Movies, Jay Hyams, Columbus Books, £8.95

Mr Hyams has followed up his admirable book on the Western (see *Film Review 1984–5*) with a similar study of the war film, concentrating, except for a brief introductory chapter, on those from *All Quiet on the Western Front* (1930) to the latest television productions. With so much material to cover, individual films are perforce treated somewhat cursorily, but the author has the knack of conciseness, and the comments are often sharp as well as enlightening. The accent is heavily on the American product, and such notable British films as *San Demetrio, London, Went the Day Well?* and *Next of Kin* are absent. However, on the whole an excellent survey and very well illustrated.

White Heat Ed. Patrick McGilligan, University of Wisconsin Press (dist. Academic & University Publishers Group), £16.60 hardback/£6.60 paperback

Another in the excellent series of Warner Bros. film scrips, affording James Cagney's arguably greatest film the full treatment of a long analytical and historical introduction, full script with notes, credits and cast lists and frame-enlargement illustrations. The series is the best record of individual films available; it would be a boon to the student, historian or nostalgic filmgoer alike if the other great studios could follow suit.

Words and Images, Brian McFarlane, Secker & Warburg, £7.95

After an introductory chapter in which the author sets out the problems of adapting novels for films and discusses the theory that very often the less concern the film-maker shows over slavish fidelity to the original the better the result is likely to be, he analyses in depth several recent Australian productions, including *Picnic at Hanging Rock* (Peter Weir) and the same director's disappointing *The Year of Living Dangerously*. The arguments are put cogently and lucidly, and – with interest in the flowering Australian cinema being encouraged by recent British television screenings – this well-written and well-illustrated book should appeal to the student and to the ordinary viewer alike.

The Movie Stars Story, Ed. Robyn Karney, Octopus Books, £10.95

The Hollywood Reporter – Star Profiles Ed. Marc Wanamaker, Octopus Books, £9.95

Glamorous Musicals, Ronald Bergan, Octopus Books, £8.95

These three glossy volumes are noteworthy for the colourful excellence of their lavish illustrations. The first and largest, presented as a companion volume to the indispensable Octopus series of studio histories, consists of brief biographies of some 500 stars, from the Twenties to the Eighties – from Ben Turpin to Nastassja Kinski – each accompanied by at least one photograph, including a considerable number of full page pictures in colour. The arrangement is alphabetical in decades, and an attempt has been made to break away from the usual Who's Who format by placing each player in the period most significant to his or her career. Thus, for instance, John Gielgud appears as a star of the Eighties, Ronald Colman of the Twenties.

Star Profiles, more conventional in approach, gives slightly fuller coverage to 91 of the most famous stars. Much of the information contained in both these books can, of course, be found elsewhere, but is here set out in attractive and easily available form.

The third book, on the musicals from early to recent days, might best be described as a Celebration – a warmly nostalgic survey of various types of the *genre*, gorgeously (and sometimes garishly) illustrated, and glowing with glamour.

Index